The Illustrated Directory of

SPECIAL
FORCES

The Illustrated Directory of
SPECIAL FORCES

David Miller

MBI Publishing Company

A Salamander Book

This edition first published in 2002 by
MBI Publishing Company,
Galtier Plaza, Suite 200, 380 Jackson
Street, St. Paul, MN 55101-3885 USA

© Salamander Books Ltd., 2002

A member of **Chrysalis** Books plc

The information in this book is true and
complete to the best of our knowledge.
All recommendations are made without
any guarantee on the part of the author
or publisher, who also disclaim any
liability incurred in connection with the
use of this data or specific details.

We recognize that some words, model
names and designations, for example,
mentioned herein are the property of
the trademark holder. We use them for
identification purposes only. This is
not an official publication

MBI Publishing Company books are
also available at discounts in bulk
quantity for industrial or sales-
promotional use. For details write to
Special Sales Manager at Motorbooks
International Wholesalers &
Distributors,
Galtier Plaza, Suite 200, 380 Jackson
Street, St. Paul, MN 55101-3885 USA

Library of Congress Cataloging-in-
Publication Data Available

ISBN 0-7603-1419-5

The Editor

David Miller is a former officer in the
British armed forces, who spent his
service in England, the Falkland
Islands, Germany, Malaysia, the
Netherlands, Scotland, and
Singapore. He subsequently worked
as a freelance author and for three
years as a journalist for Jane's
Information Group, including as a
staffer on the authoritative
International Defense Review. He
was Editor of the two-volume Jane's
Major Warships, and has written
more than forty other works, many of
them related to modern weapons
and warfare.

Credits

Project Manager: Ray Bonds
Designers: Interprep Ltd
Picture Research: Mirco De Cet
Reproduction: Anorax Imaging Ltd
Printed and bound in Slovenia

Acknowledgments

The publishers wish to thank all the individuals and institutions who have supplied illustrations for this volume, including: the many armed forces organizations; manufacturers of weapons and equipment; E. Nevill and TRH Pictures; David Reynolds and The Defence Picture Library; and James Marchington (for photos of combat knives).

Contents

Introduction

"Special forces" give rise to somewhat ambivalent feelings in others. On one side there is an aura of military glamor about the deeds of warriors who carry out short, sharp raids deep inside enemy territory, wreak havoc and then return to base to prepare for yet another foray. It is the stuff from which legend springs. These warriors – usually members of "special units" – are greatly admired by some, but are viewed somewhat skeptically by others, who question whether their activities justify the resources of manpower, money and specialized equipment devoted to them. Thus, when such special forces are successful, they are praised, but when they are not, then there is no shortage of people only too willing to condemn them. But, it cannot be disguised that, particularly in democracies, there is an inherent distrust of such "special" operations and those associated with them.

Various terms are used to describe these forces, including commando, elite, paratrooper, irregular, guerrilla, or simply – and perhaps more embracing – special forces. Whatever the choice of designation, however, these forces have always had an important role to play in their nations' defense forces, and their historical legacy is particularly rich.

Modern special forces have their origins in World War II and among the most famous is the British Special Air Service (SAS), which was raised in 1941 to carry out reconnaissances and attacks deep in the rear of the German/Italian forces in the Sahara desert. In fact, it was one of several such forces with similar missions – others included the Long-Range Desert Group and the romantically named Popski's Private Army – but they all were disbanded with the end of the war in North Africa. The SAS continued to operate in Italy and France, but was disbanded in 1945, as no further need for such an organization was foreseen in "peacetime." Without a war, it was argued, there was no mission and the critics, particularly those elsewhere in the regular forces, were only too happy to see them disappear.

By the 1950s, however, there was an epidemic of "wars of national liberation" and some World War II special forces such as the SAS were re-formed, while a few new units were raised. But, over the past 50 years various types of conflict have led to violent changes of government in many countries. Some of them, like the Vietnam War, were on a large scale, although the need to avoid global conflict in the overall setting of the Cold War, resulted in strong pressures to localize their impact. Once the Cold War had ended, however, and, in particular, with the demise of the Soviet Union and the emergence of the United States as the only, albeit sometimes reluctant, Superpower, such constraints have been lifted and conflicts continue unabated, some of them traditional in nature, others, such as the attack of 11 September 2001, of a completely novel nature.

Some observers argue that World War III has already started and that instead of military operations on the traditional, well-understood pattern, this new conflict is characterized by brush-fire conflicts, assassinations, terrorist bombings, attacks on civilian targets, coups, revolutions, and civil strife. There is no clean and easy way to categorize these crises and the types of conflict they represent. However, it is clear that terrorism, what is known as "low intensity conflict" and special operations need to be considered together.

There are literally hundreds of special and elite formations in existence—some number dozens, others several thousand members. Many, despite the sensitive nature of their missions, are relatively easy to identify, explain, and describe in a reasonable degree of detail; the French Foreign Legion, for example, and the British Special Air Service. In some cases, the mission of an elite force is strictly military in character – like the U.S. Army Rangers, and their operation in Grenada in 1983. In other cases, the mission is strictly counter-terrorist, such as that of the German GSG 9 and the French GIGN.

There is no agreed definition of elite forces beyond the fact that, generally speaking, they have quite different missions from those of conventional forces. Also, these units are constantly being formed, disbanded, and realigned to meet individual circumstances. One vital consideration is that of security, as the great majority of these forces are, for excellent and well-understood reasons, reluctant to discuss their mission, organization, tactics and equipment, and the British SAS, for example, was very embarrassed when their most famous operation, the Iranian Embassy Siege in 1980, was played out in front of the world's TV cameras.

This book is divided into three main sections, which describe, respectively, the special and elite forces, some of the major operations in which they have been involved, and a selection of their weapons. However, it must be appreciated that this coverage cannot be comprehensive: some elite units are so secret that even their very existence is totally unknown to the general public, while a number of operations, even by publicly identified units, remain highly classified. Similarly, some weapons and techniques are secret in order that an elite unit can achieve tactical surprise over its opponents.

Nor can it be forgotten that special forces have a firm place in conventional war, as was demonstrated by SAS participation in the Falklands War and of many special forces, including Delta and the SAS, in the Gulf War.

In such conflicts, special forces' ability to conduct clandestine operations in the enemy's rear enables them to attack targets which cannot be reached by any other means, and to exert an influence out of all proportion to their actual numbers.

Elite forces involved in the counter-terrorist mission face a unique set of contradictions. Their successes dissuade their opponents from trying again, often leading to long periods without action, which has two consequences. First, it makes it harder to maintain the essential high degree of training and readiness, known colloquially as "the cutting edge." Secondly, protracted periods of apparent inactivity result in politicians and government financiers starting to question the large expenditure necessary, sometimes even resulting in cutbacks. It is then that the terrorists strike again, often using some totally new technique.

There is a high degree of lateral cooperation between special forces, ranging from exchanging information, through conducting joint exercises and the exchange of personnel, to actually taking part in each other's operations.

Finally, the great majority of special forces traditionally find their recruits from elsewhere in their country's armed forces. This ensures that their operators have experience of the armed forces as a whole and are a known quantity when they start the selection process. This can, however, lead to complaints from units that their best, brightest and most promising young men and women are being "poached" by elite units. Also, the rapid down-sizing of many military forces since the end of the Cold War means that the size of the manpower pool from which such volunteers can be found is also diminishing.

As this book shows, elite units have a very important task in modern society, their value lying not just in their capability in conventional warfare, but also in the clandestine world of counter-terrorism, where they must be ready to meet any threat at any time. In addition, while most counter-terrorist forces are confined to their national homelands, some others, like those of the USA, UK, France, and Israel, may be committed anywhere in the world. They face a daunting challenge.

The Forces

There are now well over one hundred autonomous "special forces" units around the world and this section describes most of them. There are undoubtedly more than appear in these pages, whose existence is known only in military circles, but these are carefully screened from public scrutiny. Indeed, there are probably even more, which are known only to a very carefully selected few, even within the armies, navies or air forces to which they belong.

Most of these special forces units belong to the national army, but in some countries both navies and air forces also operate their own special units. Other countries have formed special units specifically for the domestic counter-terrorist role and these are part of the police, or, in the case of the German GSG-9, the border police, while a few have formed special forces units within their para-military police forces, such as the GIGN and GIS, which are part of the French Gendarmerie and the Italian Carabinieri, respectively. One notable limitation on both police- and border police-based units is that, except in the most exceptional circumstances, their jurisdiction is limited to within their national borders, rendering their personnel potentially open to legal consequences if they kill or wound someone on foreign soil in the course of an operation. This is an issue which, despite the operation's success, became apparent with the GSG-9 action at Mogadishu and special forces units have since been formed within the German armed forces to undertake foreign deployments.

Sources of Manpower

Almost all military and police special forces recruit from volunteers from those already enlisted or conscripted, and then only after a specified minimum period of service, usually between one and three years. This ensures that such volunteers are already well-trained and used to military discipline, and that they will normally have had some operational experience. As the size of most military forces decreases this means that the special forces are recruiting from a diminishing manpower pool, but, even so, this method is still seen as preferable to direct recruiting from civil life.

The Israeli armed forces, however, have an altogether different problem, since they depend to a very large extent on three-year conscripts. But, as the great majority of special forces units have selection and training periods lasting well over a year, and in some cases up to 20 months, the men have little enough time with the operational forces. As a result, there is no option but to make initial selections as the men start their mandatory service and then to start their training immediately; as a result they do not have a even a minimal period of service with line units.

Inevitably, there are some special units which do not fit into any general pattern. The French Foreign Legion, for example, has a unique composition and military ethos, being an integral part of the French Army, but composed predominantly of foreigners of any nationality. The Gurkhas, on the other hand, are an integral part of the British Army, but are composed entirely of men from certain tribal groups in Nepal.

Special Cases

Some countries deserve special mention. Most countries are secretive to a greater or lesser extent about their special forces units, but two countries stand out. The first is North Korea, which is known to have a huge special forces organization, but it is certain that there are many more units than is public knowledge; indeed, the sheer numbers of men in such units brings into question the term "special". The second country is the People's Republic of China, and almost nothing is known about its special forces, although it is self-evident that they must exist. At the least these must include a counter-terrorist unit, responsible for dealing with hijacking and hostage-taking situations, but it is also highly probable that there are also special forces units similar in organization, training and missions to the Soviet Spetsnaz units of the Cold War era.

The Israeli special forces are given separate treatment in this book, because this country makes very wide use of such units. Many of these units tend to have a single mission, which is primarily due to the problems of a conscript army, where the vast majority of soldiers are only in full-time service for three years and there is simply insufficient time to train them for a wider range of tasks.

The Soviet Army's Spetsnaz units caused major alarm in western Europe during the 1980s when their high degree of training and large numbers were seen as a major threat. With the end of the Cold War these units have been drastically reduced in numbers but it is highly probable that the expertise is retained.

British special forces have established a high reputation for daring, initiative and success. These consist of the army's Special Air Service (SAS) and the Royal Marines' Special Boat Service (SBS), which are both controlled by the Director of Special Forces.

The United States currently has the largest special forces community, which is scattered around the Army, Navy, Air Force, Marine Corps and various federal and state police forces. Not surprisingly, in comparison to those of other countries, US special forces have huge budgets and their facilities are positively lavish, particularly where weapons, equipment and transportation are concerned.

Close Relationships

There is a close relationship between many special forces units, who realize that they face many common problems. For example, while each hostage-rescue situation will have its own unique characteristics, there will always be some common complexities and dangers, and it is clear that sharing knowledge and experience will be of mutual value. Thus, it is known that forces like the Australian, British and New Zealand SAS have a very close relationship with each other and each also has ties with the US Special Forces Operational Detachment - Delta. Similarly, the British Special Boat Service (SBS) and the US SEALs are close. There are also bilateral relationships between the larger units and most of the smaller special forces units, which is of particular value in the training field, as it enables the smaller units to gain access to facilities which they are not able to afford themselves. There have been several reports that relations between Israeli SF and some of their counterparts in Western Europe were cool in the 1980s and 1990s; it is not clear what caused this but it seems to have been overcome.

The Future

There can be no doubt that the great majority of countries will continue to maintain the units described in these pages. Indeed, as the terrorist attacks on 11 September 2001 show, the threat is steadily increasing rather than diminishing. This will call for units which are not necessarily larger, although most could benefit from an increase in strength, but which are more versatile and even better trained, because only then will they be able to outfight the terrorists, as well as to take a full part in warlike operations.

Argentina

Brigada Especial Operativa - Halcon

Argentina's principal anti-terrorist unit is the *Brigada Especial Operativa – Halcon* (= Special Operations Brigade – Falcon), which was formed in 1978 to provide security for the World Cup soccer championships. It is a police unit answering directly to the chief of police in the national capital, Buones Aires. Apart from counter-terrorist duties, it is also responsible for VIP protection.

Brigada Halcon has a strength of 75 men, who are organized into five 15-man teams. The teams are identically organized, each with eight troopers and seven specialists: communications – one; explosives – one; intelligence – one; negotiator – one; medical – one; and snipers – two. Training lasts for six months and includes such topics as marksmanship, explosive identification and disposal, observation and intelligence-gathering techniques, parachuting and vehicle handling.

The unit wears locally manufactured uniforms and protective gear. Weapons are mostly foreign and include the Glock 17 automatic pistol, and the Franchi SPAS 12 shotgun. The snipers use the Heckler & Koch G3 GS/1.

Grupo de Operaciones Especiales (GOE)

The *Grupo de Operaciones Especiales* (GOE = Special Operations Group) is a company-sized counter-terrorist unit of the Argentine Air Force. The majority of the volunteers come from the Air Force Police and the unit's primary mission is to deal with aircraft hijackings. GOE's origins lie in the air force parachute school which was formed in 1947, which led to a unit designated 13th Parachute Regiment, which was air force-manned but Army-controlled. Later the Army

Australia

As of mid-2002 Australian special forces comprised:
- Special Air Service Regiment (SASR), consisting of 1, 2, and 3 "Sabre" Squadrons, plus 152 (SASR) Signal Squadron.
- 1st Commando Regiment (1 Cdo Regt), consisting of 1 and 2 Commandos and 126 (Commando) Signal Squadron. These are reserve units, consisting of mainly reservists with a small regular cadre.
- 4th Royal Australian Regiment, Commando (4 RAR Cdo) (four companies), including an air platoon.
- Navy Clearance Diving Branch (two regular and one reserve clearance diver teams).
- In addition, each state and the capital territory (Canberra) has a counter-terrorist force, known variously as "special operations groups" or "emergency response teams."

Special Air Service Regiment

Australian troops played a significant role in the Malayan Emergency, the fight against the Communist insurgents, which lasted from 1949 to 1961. During that campaign the British re-formed their Special Air Service (it had been disbanded after World War II) for deep-jungle operations and the Australian Army used this as a model when it formed its own special forces unit, 1st Special Air Service Company, on July 1, 1957. With the termination of the Malayan campaign, however, the SAS Company was absorbed into the regular infantry (Royal Australian Regiment [RAR]), but separated again in 1964 and expanded to become the Special Air Service Regiment (SASR) with three "Sabre" squadrons. Sub-units of the SASR took part in Indonesia's *Konfrontasi* (=

formed, first, its own parachute unit, and subsequently its own special forces, as a result of which 13th Parachute regiment gradually contracted until today, where it is some 100 strong. All unit members are qualified HALO parachutists and specialize in anti- hijacking operations and LRRP missions.

Below: Policemen of Argentina's special forces' unit, Halcon.

Right: Australian SAS trooper using a Ram-Air parachute, which enables him to make a silent and precise landing.

confrontation) campaign in Borneo, Brunei, and Sarawak in the early 1960s, and then also took part, with other Australian troops, in the Vietnam War, between 1966 and 1971, where the unit won four Victoria Crosses.

Following disengagement from Vietnam one squadron of the SASR was disbanded, but a terrorist bomb attack on the Sydney Hilton on February 13, 1978 showed that Australia was not immune to such activities and on February 23 the SASR was formally designated the national counter-terrorist unit. To help meet the new tasks the third squadron was re-formed in 1982 and since then, while other elements of the Australian Defense Forces have been cut back, the SASR has remained virtually untouched. ►

The SASR has been at the forefront of all Australian international commitments. During the Gulf War one SASR squadron (110 men) deployed to Kuwait in February-May 1991 where it joined with 23 men from the New Zealand SAS to form the ANZAC SAS Squadron, which was part of a joint force with British and U.S. special forces. Another deployment was to Somalia, where a 10-man close-protection group from the SASR formed part of the 67-strong Australian Contingent. SASR troopers were in East Timor well in advance of the UN intervention force in 1999, carrying out clandestine reconnaissances to establish precisely what the situation was and just what military help would be needed. The SASR also sent a squadron (150 men) to Afghanistan in 2001, where one man was killed when his truck drove over a landmine. This squadron was subsequently rotated and replaced by a second squadron in March 2002.

SASR is approximately 550 strong, with its main base at Campbell Barracks, Swanbourne, Western Australia, and comprises a Regimental Headquarters (RHQ) and six squadrons. There are three "Sabre" squadrons, which operate a thee-year training/operational cycle, starting with a work-up year, during which volunteers are inducted and more experienced soldiers attend advanced courses. The second year sees the squadron training for overt commitments, including special operations in a conventional war, while in the third year it trains for clandestine tasks, and forms the counter-terrorist Tactical Assault Group (TAG) (see below). The system is, however, flexible and can be accelerated, as was clearly the case in 2002 when a second squadron relieved the first to deploy to Afghanistan. Base Squadron provides administrative and logistic support, while Operational Support Squadron is responsible for specialist training and trials of new techniques and equipment. The highly specialized communications needed are provided by 152 (SASR) signals Squadron.

In peace-time the SASR's main task is counter-terrorism, which was given special emphasis in the run-up to and during the 2000 Olympic Games, which were held in Sydney. Prime responsibility for counter- terrorism lies with the Tactical Assault Group (ie, the "Sabre" squadron in the third year of its operational cycle). The enemy could include assassins, bombers, hijackers, kidnappers, or snipers, although, as was shown by the attacks on the World Trade Center, New York, and elsewhere in September 2001, terrorists repeatedly show themselves capable of coming up with some totally new method of operation. Tasks to be performed against such targets could include the neutralization and/or capture of individuals or groups on the land or at sea; the neutralization of hostile aircraft or ships; the safe recovery of hostages; and

Below: All SF selection courses are rigorous, but few more so than for these aspiring members of Australia's SASR.

Right: Australian SASR trooper strikes a nonchalant pose atop a pinnacle in the aptly-named Stirling range.

evicting terrorists from buildings, installations, ships or aircraft which they may have captured. Such tasks could take place anywhere in continental Australia or overseas where an Australian interest is involved.

Counter-terrorism training includes Close Quarter Battle (CQB) tactics, explosive entry using frame or water charges, tubular assaults as in vehicles, buses, trains, aircraft and high rise structures, and room and building clearance operations. The Offshore Assault Team (OAT) is part of the TAG and is responsible for similar tasks, but at sea, where the terrorist incident could involve ships, or gas/oil platforms, of which there are appreciable numbers around the Australian coastline.

The SASR is trained in counter-insurgency operations which provides troopers with the skills necessary to recruit indigenous people in wartime such as the SASR did in Borneo to help them gather information about the enemy or to help them fight the enemy. The SASR has many Southeast Asians in its ranks, who are trained in Southeast Asian languages, customs and traditions.

In conventional war, most of the SASR's tasks will be in the enemy's rear areas, and would include reconnaissance and surveillance, as well as ambushes, sabotage, raids on important targets (eg, HQs, airfields, communications centers), and target designation for air strikes.

The SASR works and trains in close liaison with U.S., British, and New Zealand special forces. Since 1992 there has also been considerable, and politically more controversial, contact with the Indonesian special forces, Kopassus, which has included annual special forces' exercises in the other's country, although this did not prevent the SASR being involved in the East Timor operation.

SASR parade, working and field uniforms are the same as those of the Australian Army, but with a sand-colored beret, cap-badge and wings similar to those worn by the British SAS. Special uniforms (eg, black coveralls) are worn according to the tactical situation.

Equipment includes the whole range of normal Australian weapons and equipment, but with appropriate specialist equipment according to the role. For example, the normal rifle is either the M16A3 or the F88 Austeyr (locally manufactured version of the Steyr AUG), but could include Ta'as 7.62 Galil, H&K PSG-1, Parker Hale 82, Finnish Tikka Finlander .223, Mauser SP 66, or SR98 Accuracy International AW-F sniper rifles, or Beretta or Remington shotguns. For road transport specially modified Nissan Patrol 4-wheel drive vehicles are used, while most air insertions are done by helicopter, usually naval UH-60 Sea Hawks or CH-3 Sea Kings, or Army UH-60 Blackhawks or CH-47 Chinooks.

Austria

Gendarmerieeinsatzkommando Cobra

In the late 1960s and early 1970s there was a wave of terrorist incidents, particularly in Europe, with the small, neutral country of Austria being particularly badly affected. At that time Jewish refugees were being allowed to leave the Soviet Union but they were not permitted to travel direct to their ultimate destinations (usually, either Israel or the USA) and the great majority staged through Austria. This led to several Palestinian terrorist operations which resulted in the Austrian government ordering the formation in 1973 of *Gendarmeriekommando Bad Voslau* (Bad Voslau was the name of the unit's base). It was put on high alert during several crises, once when terrorists seized hostages but were allowed to leave, and on another occasion when the international terrorist, Carlos Sanchez, seized several OPEC oil ministers who were meeting in Vienna, but was paid a multi-million dollar ransom and given a safe passage out of the country.

The Israeli rescue mission at Entebbe and the assault by the German GSG 9 on the airliner at Mogadishu showed that determined action by well-trained and properly equipped men could overcome even the most fanatical terrorists.

This led to a restructuring of *Gendarmeriekommando Bad Voslau* in 1978 and the new unit was redesignated *Gendarmorieeinsatzkommando* (GEK) (= police commando unit) "Cobra." The GEK's first commander, Oberst Pechter, established close ties with other counter-terrorist units, including, among others, the Israeli Sayeret Mat'kal and the (then) West German GSG 9.

Weapons used include the Steyr 5.56 AUG assault rifle, the French-made Manuhrin MR-73 .357 Magnum police-special revolver and the Austrian Glock 17 automatic pistol. Unit snipers are armed with the Steyr 7.62 police rifles.

Jagdkommando

The Austrian Army's *Jagdkommando* (= reconnaissance commando) is approximately equivalent to the U.S. Army's Rangers. This elite unit is trained to operate by land and on Austria's lakes and rivers, and all men are required to be qualified parachutists.

Below: Men of Austria's Jagdkommando, the Austrian Army's elite, parachute-trained special forces unit.

Belgium

Escadron Special d'Intervention

Like many other European nations, Belgium was shocked by the terrorist attack during the 1972 Munich Olympic Games into forming its own counter-terrorist unit as part of the *Gendarmerie Royale*. At first this was given the cover-name "Diane" but although this was changed to *Escadron Special d'Intervention* (ESI) in 1974, the name "Diane" continues to be used unofficially. Belgium has a particular security problem, because it is the host to so many international bodies who have their permanent homes in the country, particularly in Brussels. These include the headquarters of both the European Community (EC) and of the North Atlantic Treaty Organization (NATO).

ESI's primary mission is counter-terrorist operations, but it is also used to fight organized crime (particularly where the criminals are armed) and anti-narcotics work. Volunteers for the ESI must undergo a two-weekselection process (failure rate is some 50 per cent), following which they atten a three-month course. ESI is one of an increasing number of counter-terrorist forces which recruit female operators, although, in this case, they are employed only in observation and clandestine roles. The ESI also has an airborne and an amphibious capability.

Weapons used include the Heckler & Koch MP5 submachine gun, Remington 12-gauge shotguns and the Finnish-made Sako TRG-21 7.62mm sniper rifle.

Para Commando Brigade

The Belgian Army's elite military unit is the Para-Commando Brigade. Separate parachute and commando units were formed by the Belgian government-in-exile in Britain during World War II, and continued in existence after the war. In 1952 they were amalgamated into the Para-Commando Regiment, which continued in existence until 1991 when, in the reorganization and realignment following the end of the Cold War, new units were added, enabling the regiment to be upgraded to the Para-Commando Brigade. The brigade, which has a peacetime strength of about 3,000, comprises:

* Infantry: 1st and 3rd Parachute Battalions and the 2nd Commando Battalion, each some 500 strong (despite the different titles all three are organized identically).
* Reconnaissance: 3rd Lancers Parachutists Battalion.
* Artillery: Para-Commando Field Artillery Battery, 35th Para-Commando Anti-Aircraft Artillery Battery.
* Support: Engineer, Logistics and Medical Companies.

The Para-Commando Brigade is part of Belgium's contribution to NATO's Immediate and Rapid Reaction Forces, but also takes part in national and United Nations missions.

All members of the brigade are volunteers.

After a thorough medical examination they must attend a five-month commando course. On graduation they are entitled to wear the commando badge. They then proceed on a one-month parachute course, which involves seven jumps, which must include at least one balloon jump, one night jump, one from a C-130 aircraft and one with full equipment. To remain current, every member of the brigade must carry out four jumps every year.

During World War II the Belgian Army raised an SAS Regiment, which was an integral part of the British SAS Brigade. The Belgian SAS was reduced to battalion size until the early 1950s, when it converted to a conventional parachute battalion. The present 1st Parachute Battalion is directly descended from this unit and wears the SAS Dagger as its cap-badge, but with the paratroopers' red beret.

Recent Belgian special forces commitments have included operational deployments in Belgian Congo in1964; Zaire/Congo in 1978, 1979 and 1997; Rwanda in 1990 and 1994; and Somalia 1993.

Belgian Navy

The Belgian Navy operates a small frogman section, which is believed to be about 30-men strong and similar in organization and training to the British SBS.

Below: Belgian ESI troopers practice one of the most difficult of all SF missions - releasing hostages from a hijacked bus.

Brazil

1 Batalhòo de Forcas Especials

The first Brazilian counter-terrorist group was formed in 1953 but the present CT unit, 1st Special Forces Battalion, was raised in 1983. In common with many other such units in other armies, *1 Batalhïo de Forcas Especials* (= 1st Special Forces Battalion) does not recruit civilians direct, but takes volunteers only from other units in the Army. The selection process is very severe and is followed by a 13-week training course.

The battalion's missions include conducting its own unconventional operations; providing support for Army regular or irregular units during unconventional operations; and training other units in unconventional warfare techniques. The unit is trained in jungle warfare, amphibious operations, mountain warfare, airborne, airmobile, HAHO/HALO operations, and long-range reconnaissance operations. Operational elements of the battalion comprise two special forces companies, one commando company, and one counter-terrorism company.

Armament is a mix of Brazilian and foreign weapons. Pistols include various models made by Beretta, as well as the Colt .45 and Imbel M-976. Rifles include Belgian FN FAL and Heckler & Koch G53, and U.S. M4 carbines, while the preferred SMG is the popular Heckler & Koch MP5. Shotguns are also carried, including models by Franchi, Remington, and Mossburg, while snipers use the H&k PSG-1. One unusual weapon is the Hydroar T1M1 flame thrower.

Grupo de Mergulhadores de Combate

Grupo De Mergulhadores De Combate (GRUMEC = combat divers group) was formed in 1970 after initial training by SEALs in the USA and the French *Nageur de Combate*. (It should be noted that the Portugese abbreviated title is GERR/MEC). The Brazilian unit is small – some 20 operators, trained in all aspects of combat diving, including infiltration, explosives, sabotage, and above- and below-water fighting. The men are trained in open, semi-closed and closed-circuit diving gear; parachuting (including high altitude free-fall); submersible vehicles; and entry to and exit from submerged submarines. The arduous training course last for six months. Possible missions are highly classified but are known to include recapture and recovery of hostages from maritime targets such as ships and oil-rigs. Weapons are basically similar to those used by U.S. Navy SEALs.

Other Brazilian special forces units include:

- *Comandos Anfybios* (COMANFI) (= amphibious commandos).
- *Comandos de Reconhecimento Terrestre* (RECONTER) (= land reconnaissance commandos).
- *Grupos de Operaces Especiais* (GOE) (= special operations groups).
- PARASAR (paratroops).

Left: Special forces' troopers of Brazil's 1 Batalhoo de Forces Especials undergoing training in operations in a built-up area.

Canada

Joint Task Force 2

The present-day Canadian special operations force is "Joint Task Force 2" (JTF 2), which was formed in April 1993 (as far as is known, there is no such unit as "Joint Task Force 1"). For most of the past 50 years Canadian military special operations were the prerogative of the "Special Service Force," with counter-terrorist operations being the responsibility of the Royal Canadian Mounted Police's (RCMP) Special Emergency Response Team (SERT).

During World War II there were two Canadian Army airborne units: 1st Canadian Parachute Battalion, raised at Camp Shiloh in the USA in 1942; and 2nd Parachute Battalion, formed later in Canada. Following the war the Canadian parachuting capability was reduced to cadre level until 1968, when it was expanded and the Canadian Airborne Regiment (CAR) was formed, which was intended to be a light, independent, all-arms unit for deployment in low-intensity operations in jungle, desert or arctic warfare conditions. The capability was later expanded yet again with the formation of the Special Service Force, whose "teeth" elements comprised an armored battalion, an infantry battalion, the CAR, plus artillery and engineer battalions, and communications and logistics support. It also included the Canadian SAS, which had been formed in 1946 as a company-sized unit, closely modeled on the British SAS.

The CAR was disbanded in the mid-1990s as a result of an enquiry into activities of some elements during its participation in the UN operation in Somalia, and its three component companies were dispersed to form airborne companies in three conventional infantry battalions.

Joint Task Force 2 is a counter-terrorist unit on the lines of U.S. Delta and British SAS, with whom it maintains close contact. JTF 2 operational sub-units are designated "bricks", a standard SAS term. Volunteers can normally come only from those already within the Canadian Forces (CF) although it is believed that members may also include people from other Canadian government

Below: A marker team of Canada's special forces Joint Task Force 2 awaits the arrival of a stick of parachutists.

Above: Canadian counter-terrorist special forces carrying the most commonly used of all SMGs, the excellent H&K MP5.

services eg, Canadian Security Intelligence Service (CSIS). Their tour length is normally 4-5 years. JTF 2 is approximately 300 strong and is commanded by a lieutenant-colonel.

Volunteer standards are not normally specified, but the Canadian Forces have made their requirements for JTF 2 public (CANFORGEN 078/97 Adm(per) 056 301330Z Jul 97). Volunteers must be in the ranks of: officers – captain only; soldiers – warrant officer, sergeant, master-corporal, corporal, private. The general qualifications are at least three years' service and members maybe re-engaged for a second three-year engagement; no known phobias (eg, fear of heights, water or enclosed spaces); a valid civilian driving licence; and a demonstrated wish and ability to learn a second language. A high standard of medical and physical fitness is required and the volunteer must demonstrate capability of: running 1.5 miles (2.5km) inside 11 minutes; 40 consecutive push-ups; five consecutive overhand grip, straight-arm pull-ups; 40 sit-ups in 60 seconds; 143lb (65kg) bench press.

With all these completed, the next hurdle is a preliminary screening by a qualified JTF recruiting team, followed by a three-week course in which levels of physical fitness, weapons handling, and confidence are improved. The volunteers then undergo a one week assessment of suitability for special forces, but officer applicants must also undergo an additional four-day assessment of their planning and leadership skills. If the volunteers pass all that they then start the five month training course.

Approximately 30 men of JTF 2 were sent to Bosnia to rescue 55 Canadian soldiers being held by the Serbs, although in the event they were not used. The unit was also placed on stand-by for a possible operation in Peru during the 1996 Japanese Embassy hostage crisis. The plan was that the Canadian authorities would provide an airliner to take the terrorists to Cuba, but that men of JTF 2 would be hidden aboard and would capture the terrorists prior to take-off. The operation proved unnecessary because the crisis was resolved when Peruvian special forces stormed the embassy.

Men of JTF 2 guard selected Canadian VIPs when traveling abroad and foreign VIPs in Canada. They have also deployed to Kosovo, Haiti, Rwanda and in mid-2002 were also deployed in Afghanistan.

Chile

Grupo de Operaciones Policiales Especiales
Grupo de Operaciones Policiales Especiales (GOPE = Group for Special Police Operations) was formed in 1980. Chilean personnel were originally trained by German and Israeli instructors and the unit is currently believed to be approximately 100 strong. Its principal task is to undertake military special forces/commando duties but it also has a commitment to support the UAT (see below) in counter-terrorist operations in government and diplomatic buildings.

Unidad Anti-Terroristes
Unidad Anti-Terroristes (UAT = anti-terrorist unit), also known as "Cobra,"

Denmark

Jaegerkorpset
Faced with a growing threat of international terrorism in the late 1950s, the Danish Army sent a number of officers to the U.S. Ranger School and on attachment to the British Special Air Service in 1960/61. These officers were then used to raise a new body, the *Jaegerkorpset* (= Ranger Corps), which was trained for counter-terrorist duties in support of the Danish police's *Aktions-Styrken* (= Action Force) and for long-range patrol and sabotage duties in conventional war.

The *Jaegerkorpset* is based at Aalborg in North Jutland, and works and trains closely with other special forces, particularly the British SAS. It also receives helicopter support from the British Royal Air Force and German Army, since the largest helicopter available from Danish sources is the Hughes MD-500.

Weapons known to be used include: pistols – SIG P-210 7.65mm "Neuhausen"; submachine gunes – H&K MP5 and MP53; rifles – H&K G41; sniper rifle – H&K PSG-1 7.62mm.

Froemandskorpset
The Royal Danish Navy's *Froemandskorpset* (= Frogman Corps) was created in 1957 as part of the naval diving school, but it was taken away in 1970 and made directly subordinate to naval headquarters. The unit's tasks include: beach reconnaissance; boarding

belongs to the National Police Force. It is approximately 120 strong and is divided into seven-man teams, each led by an officer. The unit is based just outside Santiago.

Military Special Forces

There are two known military special forces groups:

- *Buzos Tacticos del Ejercito* (Army SF commandos).
- *Buzos Tacticos de la Armada* (Navy SF commandos).

suspect ships; diving; underwater demolition; and ship underwater security. The unit was deployed during the Gulf War aboard ships of the Royal Danish Navy.

Below: An observation post manned by men of the Danish Jaegerkorpset (Ranger Corps).

Egypt

Task Force 777

Faced with credible threats from extremists such as the Abu Nidal Organization (which had split from the Palestine Liberation Organization in 1974), Egypt established Task Force 777 in 1977, with an initial strength of three officers, four NCOs, and 40 soldiers. They received an early baptism of fire in 1978 when Arab terrorists, claiming to represent the PLO, killed an Egyptian newspaper editor in Nicosia, Cyprus, on February 19, 1978, and then seized 30 hostages. Task Force 777 went into action and killed the terrorists but then, due to misunderstandings in which the Cypriots thought the Egyptians were actually reinforcements for the terrorists, an attack by Cypriot National Guard and police resulted in the deaths of 15 members of TF 777. The incident resulted in a major row between the governments, with the Egyptians accusing the Cypriots of a lack of cooperation recklessly and killing their troops, while the Cypriots accused the Egyptians of failing to inform them of the arrival of Task Force 777 and of blatantly disregarding their national sovereignty.

Unfortunately, even worse was to follow in a second operation in October 1985 in the aftermath of the hijacking of the Italian cruise liner, *Achille Lauro*, when Palestinians hijacked an Egyptair Boeing 737 airliner, Flight 648, and forced the pilot to land at Luqa in Malta. The Egyptian president promptly ordered the despatch of Task Force 777 and this time ensured that the Maltese authorities knew that it was on its way. The operation was botched, however, probably due to political pressure on the task force commander to effect a very rapid solution. Although TF 777 did not have a plan of the internal layout of the Boeing 737, even though it belonged to Egypt's own national airline, it was

Right: Egyptian special forces trooper with a locally-made sniper version of the AK-47M rifle.

decided to create a diversion by blowing a hole in the roof which would distract the terrorists' attention, thus enabling the main attack to go in through the doors. The explosives team got on to the roof without being detected by the terrorists. Unfortunately, they then added extra explosive to ensure success. In fairness, it has to be said that this is by no means the only occasion where this has been done. The result in this particular case, however, was tragic, since the blast was so violent that some 20 passengers in the rows immediately beneath were killed. Taking the explosion as their signal to attack, the main force moved in but the TF 777 men used high-explosive grenades and fired indiscriminately into the interior of the cabin, while some of the passengers who did actually get

out of the aircraft were then mistaken for fleeing terrorists by TF 777 snipers outside the aircraft and several were shot. The result of all these errors was that 57 hostages were killed, making it one of the most costly rescue operations ever undertaken.

Egyptian President Anwar Sadat had been assassinated during a military parade in October 1981 but despite that, and the failure of these two missions, it was clear that the Egyptian authorities were determined to take immediate and forceful action against terrorists; it should be noted that there has been no major airliner hijacking incident since. Nevertheless, Task Force 777 has been kept busy by Egypt's internal war against the "Brotherhood" in which they have undertaken numerous actions and lost several men.

Like all such units, Task Force 777 maintains a "rapid reaction force" at very short notice to move, with further elements at longer notice. The unit is supported by a number of dedicated Westland Commando troop-carrying helicopters at similar degrees of notice. Task Force 777 is known to have received training from U.S. Special Operations Forces (Delta and SEALs), as well as from European forces, including the British SAS, French GIGN, and the German GSG 9.

Left: Egyptian Boeing 737 on the ground in Malta after the assault by Task Force 777. Many died, but no more Egyptian aircraft have been hijacked.

France

France has traditionally created numerous elite groups within its armed forces and over the past 50 years the two leading groups have been the *Legion Étrangère* (Foreign Legion) and *les paras* (the "paratroops"). There are also a number of "marine" units, which despite their name are not amphibious troops as understood in American and British usage, but are elite units which were raised specifically for overseas land service in France's colonial territories. One example is *6er Régiment de Parachutistes d'Infanterie de Marine* (6th Parachute Regiment of the Marine Infantry).

Four reasons caused the French Armed Forces to be totally reorganized in the 1990s. First was the end of the Cold War and, second, the reorientation required to fit in with the concept of rapid deployment overseas in combination with NATO allies or the United Nations. Third, it was necessary to incorporate the lessons learnt from the Gulf War and the various campaigns in the Balkan. Finally there was the conversion from a large, predominantly conscript Army to a smaller, leaner and much more efficient all-regular force. (Conscription formally ended in November 2001 when the final batch of 23,000 men returned to civil life after six months' service). These sweeping changes had a major impact on many elements of the French forces, but rather less on the Foreign Legion, the Paras and the marine force.

Another change, set up after the Gulf War, was that all French special forces from the Army, Navy, Air Force and *Gendarmerie* have been placed under command of *Commandement des Operations Speciales* (C.O.S. = Special Operations Command), which is commanded by a major-general. The C.O.S., together with *Direction des Renseignements Militaires* (DRM = defense military intelligence agency), are controlled by the Chief of the Joint Chiefs of Staff. In December 2001 the French Ministry of Defense announced that C.O.S. had been allocated an additional $US 400million to enable it to expand from 2,000 men to approximately 2,800 (ie, the equivalent of an additional regiment).

The Army provides two special forces elements which are placed by C.O.S. under a subordinate headquarters designated *Groupement Special Autonome* (GSA = Special Autonomous Group). The GSA comprises two elements, the first of which is *Premier Régiment de Parachutistes d'Infanterie de Marine* (1erRPIMa), a unit which is similar in most respects to the British SAS. This is not surprising, since its traditions stem from the French SAS units raised in England during World War II. Missions include counter-terrorist operations in conjunction with GIGN and RAID (see below) and special operations in conventional war, similar to those conducted by the U.S. SOFD-Delta and the British SAS.

The second Army special force is *Detachment ALAT Operations Speciales* (DAOS = Army Aviation Special Operations Detachment), which is currently composed of two helicopter squadrons. One squadron flies Puma/Cougar transport helicopters, the other Gazelle gunships armed with 20mm cannon (to be replaced by Eurocopter Tiger gunships, in due course).

Naval special forces are designated *Groupement des Fusiliers-Marins Commandos* (GROUFUMACO = Naval Commando Group) which is composed of four assault commandos (= teams or companies), plus a special commando of *nageurs de combat* (= underwater swimmers). Their missions and tactical methodology are similar to those used by U.S. SEALs and British SBS, with whom they have frequent exchanges.

The *Gendarmerie Nationale* is a national paramilitary police force administered by the Ministry of Defense. This organization includes its own special forces, *Groupement Speciale d'Intervention de la Gendarmerie Nationale* (GSIGN = Special Action Group of the National Gendarmerie), which

Above: French SF wear the NBC outfits, respirators and black Nomex suits that have become the counter-terrorist uniform.

has three company-sized components:
- *Groupe d'Intervention de la Gendarmerie Nationale* (GIGN). With a strength of 87, the GIGN is commanded by a commandant (major).
- *Groupe de Securite du President de la Republique* (GSPR) which is responsible for the personal safety of the president.
- *Escadron Parachutiste d'Intervention de la Gendarmerie Nationale* (EPIGN).

Legion Étrangère

The Légion Étrangère (= Foreign Legion) forms a solid core of highly capable and extremely well-disciplined professional soldiers at the center of the French Army. The recent reductions in the size of the Army reduced it by 47 percent (200,000 to 136,000), but the Legion's share of the cut was only from 8,300 to 7,500 (10 percent), although Legion units withdrew from many of its overseas ▶

▶ bases. The Legion continues to attract recruits, and according to current statistics the national origins of its manpower can be roughly divided into: Eastern Europe – one-third; France itself – one-third; and the rest of the world (103 nations) – one-third.

The Legion is responsible for its own administration, including recruiting, recruit training, specialist training (eg, engineers, radio operators), NCO training, career management, and discharges. To achieve this, there are two regiments:

- *1er Régiment Étrangèr* (1RE) (1st Foreign Legion Regiment). Located at Caserne Vienot in Aubagne, 1RE is responsible for the administration of the whole Legion. It also runs the band and the museum, and administers the large training camp. Of even greater importance, 1RE is the senior regiment of the Legion and the custodian of the Legion's traditions and keeper of its relics. For the individual legionnaire, his service begins and ends at Aubagne.

- *4er Régiment Étrangèr* (4th Foreign Legion Regiment [4RE]). 4RE is based at Castelnaudary, where it is responsible for recruit and NCO training.

There have been numerous changes in the Legion in the past 10 years and the current operational units are:

- *1e Régiment Étranger de Cavalerie* (1e REC) (= 1st Foreign Cavalry Regiment). This is one of the two armored regiments in *6eme Division Legere Blindee* (= 6th Light Armored Division) and is stationed at Orange, France. It consists of three armored car squadrons and an APC-borne infantry company. It is one of the spearhead units for the French rapid deployment force.

- *1e Régiment Étranger de Génie* (1e REG) (= 1st Foreign Regiment of Combat Engineers). Located in Laudun, France. Was formerly *6eme Régiment Étrangèr de Genie* (6REG). 1REG maintains engineer detachments overseas

Above: Combat swimmers of the Detachment d'Intervention Operationaelle Subaquatique of the Legion's engineers.

and includes *Detachement d'Intervention Operationnelle Subaquatique* which is responsible for combat swimmer operations and underwater explosive ordnance disposal. It consists of five companies: three field engineer companies; a bridging company; and command/support company.

• *2e Régiment Étranger de Génie* (2e REG) (= 2nd Foreign Regiment of Combat Engineers). Located in the Marseille region of France.

• *2e Régiment Étranger d'Infanterie* (2e REI) (= 2nd Foreign Infantry Regiment). Located in Nimes, France, 2REI has had a very busy time since it was raised in 1841 and has served in virtually every one of France's colonial campaigns since then.

• *2e Régiment Étranger de Parachutistes* (2e REP) (= 2nd Foreign Parachute Regiment). 2REP is a rapid deployment airborne-commando regiment, stationed at Calvi on the island of Corsica. The regiment is divided into specialized companies, each of which is specially trained in a particular form of combat, although there is regular cross-training between companies. There are six companies: 1 Company – night combat, anti-tank, urban combat; 2 Company – mountain and arctic warfare; 3 ▶

Left: Legionnaire at range practice with his 5.56mm FA MAS, one of the best of modern assault rifles.

‣ Company – amphibious warfare, combat swimmers; 4 Company – demolition, sabotage, sniping, unconventional warfare; HQ Company – administration, communications, medical, maintenance, and supply; and reconnaissance and support company.

- *3e Régiment Étranger d'Infanterie* (3e REI) (= 3rd Foreign Infantry Regiment). 3REI is stationed at Kourou in French Guyana. It specializes in jungle warfare and consists of four companies, although it is normally reinforced by a fifth company from another Legion unit. 3REI is composed of two infantry companies, whose basic responsibility is that of the security of the French missile launching site, plus an air defense company and an administrative company.

- *13e Démi-Brigade de la Légion Étrangère* (13e DBLE) (= 13th Half-Brigade of the Foreign Legion). 13DBLE is stationed in the Republic of Djibouti on the "Horn of Africa," a location of major strategic importance. 13 DBLE consists of an armored car squadron; an infantry company; and a headquarters and support company, armed with mortars and anti-tank missiles (Milan), and a medical section. 13DBLE provided the men who deployed to Rwanda and Somalia.

- *Détachement de la Légion Étrangère de Mayotte* (DLEM) (= Foreign Legion Detachment of Mayotte). Located in Dzaoudzi on the island of Mayotte. The DLEM is responsible for the security of this island, one of the Comoros group of islands and an important staging post on the French route to the Pacific.
[Note that *5e Régiment Étranger* (5e RE = 5th Foreign Regiment), which performed security and labor duties on French islands in the Pacific, including the French nuclear site on Mururoa Atoll, was disbanded in June 2000.]

Legionnaires come from any country except, in theory, France itself. However, the Legion has always contained a large proportion of Frenchmen, who circumvent the regulations by claiming to be Belgians, Swiss or French Canadians. It used to be customary for a new recruit to be given an alias, the use of which was mandatory for three years, but this is no longer compulsory. On signing his "contract" the recruit starts a six-month probationary period and it is only at the end of this that he becomes a fully fledged legionnaire for the remaining five years of his contract. Training is extremely thorough and lasts for one year, being conducted at a camp at Bonifacio, on the southern tip of the island of Corsica. Great importance is placed on obedience and physical condition; nobody, it is claimed, goes through Legion training without soaking his socks in his own blood at least once. Forced marches are frequent and a high standard of marksmanship is required, with live firing taking place two days a week for 13 weeks.

Right: Legionnaires on patrol in a bleak, rock-strewn desert; the rear man is carrying a French 7.62mm sniping rifle.

Once the basic training has been completed selected legionnaires proceed to advanced training (for example, as a communicator or as an engineer) at one of the special schools in or near Castelnaudary. Potential non-commissioned officers must attend the corporal's course, which lasts for eight weeks and is considered to be one of the most demanding physically courses in any army. The successful corporal would then expect to attend a 14-week course prior to promotion to sergeant. ▶

▶   The Legion wears standard French Army uniform, but with several special items, the most famous of which are the greatly prized *kepi blanc* (= white hat), which is worn on parade, and the green beret used for daily and operational wear; the Legion's paratroops also wear the green beret and not the more traditional red beret. The *kepi blanc* is actually a standard French Army blue *kepi*, with a red top and gold badge, but with a white cloth cover, which is permanently removed on promotion to sous-officer. Special items of parade dress are the *kepi blanc*, green shoulder-boards with red tassels, a green tie, white belt over a blue sash, and white gauntlets. Officers also wear a green waistcoat. Members of the assault pioneer platoon also wear a white, hide apron, carry a ceremonial axe with a chromed blade, and are permitted to grow a beard.

Paratroops

The French paratroops have probably carried out more operational jumps than any other parachute corps in the world in the course of their campaigns in Indochina, Suez (1956) and Algeria, and others since in many parts of Africa. They were among the most effective units in the French campaign in Indochina and carried out some 156 operational drops, but were defeated in the battle of Dien Bien Phu in 1954-55.

Following the Indochina ceasefire and the French withdrawal in 1955, the paratroop units went to Algeria, arriving just as the war there started. In January 1957 10th Parachute Division took over the city of Algiers which was virtually in the hands of the FLN, and inside two months restored control. Their methods were seriously questioned, however, and there were many allegations of torture. To this day, an element of distrust of *les paras* remains; for example, the number of years an officer may serve with paratroop units is now strictly limited.

After the Algerian war the paratroops returned to France, but the French have maintained a strong parachute capability, and have regularly used these excellent troops overseas in pursuit of French diplomatic policies. Units of what is now 1lth Parachute Division have served in Zaire, Mauretania, Chad, and Lebanon, among other locations.

Below: French paras deploying from a Puma helicopter; the French were among the pioneers of such helicopter operations.

Above: French special forces trooper; note his face mask, personal radio and submachine gun with large silencer.

The approximately 14,000-man 1lth Parachute Division is based at Tarbes. At least one-third of the Division is abroad, either on training missions of one kind or another, or maintaining a visible presence in Africa or the Indian Ocean. It is part of the French rapid-intervention force, together with 9th Marine Light Infantry Division, 27th Alpine Division, 6th Light Armored Division, and 4th Airmobile Division. 1lth Parachute Division comprises two brigades, with seven battalion-sized parachute units, one of which (1erRPIMa) is under divisional control and has a para-commando/special forces role. The other six units are: 3, 6 and 8 RPIMa (equivalent to the former "colonial" paratroop units); 1 and 9 ▶

▶ RCP(*chasseurs* or light infantry); and 2 REP (the Legion parachute unit).

All French paratroops are volunteers and undergo the same sort of selection and training as other parachute forces. The standard of training is high and certain volunteers can go on to join one of the para-commando units (eg, 1erRPIMa).

For many years the French Army used the MAS 49/56 7.5mm rifle, but they have now re-equipped with the revolutionary short, light but effective 5.56mm FA MAS "bullpup" assault rifle, with the parachute units being among the first to receive it.

French paratroops wear standard French Army uniforms. Their parachute status is indicated by their red beret (except for Foreign Legion paras who wear a green beret). Para wings are large and in silver, and are worn on the right breast.

RAID

The acronym RAID stands for Reaction, Assistance, Intervention and Dissuasion, although the force is known throughout France as "The Black Panthers" from its all-black operational uniform. A very secretive unit, RAID was formed by the Police Nationale in 1985 to help combat the wave of terrorism and crime which seemed to be sweeping through France at that time. RAID's mission is to

Below: French special forces pass a seemingly unconcerned civilian jogger; note that each man has his own personal radio.

Above: GIGN on a training exercise. The man to the left of the door has thrown a stun grenade into the closet, while his comrade waits to shoot or arrest any dazed survivors.

"...lead the National Police in tactical combat against serious crime and terrorism." Its tasks are:

• To intervene in extreme criminal and terrorist attacks where hijacking and/or hostage taking is involved.

• To assist the police and other security agencies, when dealing with violent criminal and terrorist organizations.

• To assist other law enforcement agencies in security at major events of national and international importance.

• To protect both French VIPs and visiting foreign presidents and heads of state throughout their visits to France.

The unit comprises a very small command and administrative element, plus four 10-man operational sections, one 10-man specialist section, making a total of about 60. Naturally, most of its duties involve the capital city, so it is stationed on the outskirts of Paris. Volunteers must be 25-35 years old, physically very fit, and must have already had a minimum of five years' service in the police. It is reported that the pass rate at the selection test is about 2 percent. These selected undergo nine months of arduous training before they are operationally qualified. ▶

▶ Training for all includes about six hours of physical training daily, marksmanship, martial arts, surveillance, paramedic techniques, tactical operations including entry techniques and assaults on various targets; hostage rescue scenarios including negotiating; heliborne assaults, high-speed driving; basic parachuting skills and boatwork. Some operators are also sent on further courses to obtain further skills such as HALO/HAHO parachuting, and combat diving.

RAID's best known success to date was an incident in May 1993 when a lone man, probably more deranged than a terrorist, strapped 16 sticks of dynamite to his chest, entered a school and then held a teacher and 21 nursery children hostage. The stand-off lasted for two days until microphones, which had been placed by RAID, showed that the terrorist had fallen asleep. At this, the 15-man RAID team sprang into action. One group formed a human shield between where the terrorist was thought to be and the children, thus providing cover for the second group to start evacuating the children. Meanwhile the third group raced for the terrorist's position and when he came into view he was killed by three shots. The entire operation lasted 30 seconds and no hostage was harmed.

RAID is very well equipped. Most men carry the H&K MP5 SMG, but for longer range work the SIG SG551 5.56mm rifle is used. Operators are allowed to select their own handguns, and models used include the Matra-Manurhin MR-73 .357 revolver, or automatic pistols such as the Beretta 92FS, Glock 19 or one of the Sig-Sauer family. Operational dress comprises flame resistant coveralls, balaclavas, and gloves, all in black.

Groupe d'Intervention de la Gendarmerie Nationale

Groupe d'Intervention de la Gendarmerie Nationale (GIGN) was raised in 1974 and since then has probably carried out more operations than any other counter-terrorist unit, in the process of which it has lost five men killed and some 30-40 seriously wounded. GIGN was formed in 1974 and its maximum strength was laid down as "...no greater than 100" although it has never been above 90. The unit has traveled widely and is known to have been involved in operations in the Comoros, Djibouti, Lebanon, New Caledonia, and Sudan, but there have probably been more, of which details have yet to be made public. This world-wide commitment means that the operators must be capable of functioning in any environment from snow to jungle and desert, in both rural and urban settings and by sea as well as by land.

GIGN operators come exclusively from the ranks of the *Gendarmerie* and applicants must have at least five years' service and an exemplary record. Training lasts for ten months. The unit consists of a command and administrative section, a negotiating section, and four 15-man assault groups. It admits eight volunteers per year, who then have to undergo a one-year training course, before being admitted to the operational ranks. Weapons include handguns, usually the Manurhin MR73 0.357 Magnum revolver, Beretta 92F or one of the Sig-Sauer family, and a rifle – the H&K G3, FAMAS or SIG S551. The usual sniper rifle is the FRF1 with special sights, while for long-range sniping they have used the Barrett 0.50in although this has recently been replaced by the French 12.7mm Hecate II. For SMGs they use the H&K MP5 family. Remington 870, Benelli and Beretta shotguns are available for use if needed.

Above: GIGN operators. Note the silenced MP5 (left) and FR1 sniper rifle (right). Both wear night-vision goggles.

Germany

Grenzschutzgruppe 9

Following the Black September terrorist attack at the 1972 Munich Olympics, the West Germans created a totally new counter-terrorist group, but as part of the *Bundesgrenzschutz* (the Federal Border Police) rather than the Army or Police, and designated it *Grenzschutzgruppe 9* (GSG 9); it was declared operational on April 17 1973. This unit proved itself in dramatic and very public fashion in October 1977 at Mogadishu in Somalia when a team of 27 men carried out a six-minute assault on a hijacked Lufthansa airliner and released all 87 hostages.

There were few public incidents until 1993 when, on June 27, the unit was involved in overcoming Wolfgang Grams, a member of the Red Army Faction (RAF) at Bad Kleinen. Grams died, but there have been repeated allegations that he was shot by GSG 9 rather than committing suicide, as was decided by an official enquiry. Only two months after the Bad Kleinen incident a KLM Tunis-Amsterdam flight was hijacked by a single armed terrorist. His demand was for the release of Sheikh Omar Abdel Rahman, then being held in the United States in connection with the New York World Trade Center bombing. The airliner was diverted to Dusseldorf, where GSG 9 operators captured the hijacker without a shot being fired.

The unit was 180 strong at the time of Mogadishu and as a result of that operation it was decided to increase it to 300, but selection and recruiting difficulties kept the strength at about 160-200 for some time; in mid-2002 it was about 250 strong. Overall, GSG 9 consists of a headquarters; a communications and documentation sub-unit; an engineer sub-unit; a training sub-unit that can be used as another combat unit, if required; a helicopter flight of three helicopters and 11 pilots and mechanics; and a supply unit. The three operational sub-units are: GSG 9/1 (ca. 100 men), the counter-terrorist assault group; GSG 9/2 (ca. 100 men) specializes in maritime operations; GSG 9/3 (ca. 50 men) specializes in airborne missions.

Like many counter-terrorist units, GSG 9 uses various specially modified vehicles, including unmarked Mercedes limousines and Volkswagen mini-buses. The unit is also supported by the *Bundesgrenzschutz Grenzschutz-Fliegergruppe* (= Border Troops Border-Flying Group) which provides helicopters to transport GSG 9 operators on their missions.

All members of GSG 9 must be volunteers from the ranks of the Police or Border Police. Thus, any soldier who wishes to join must first leave the Army and join the Border Police. The training course is 22 weeks long and is directed at mind and body. The first 13 weeks are devoted to police duties, legal matters, weapons skills, and karate.

Training takes place in a variety of locations as befits a unit which does not necessarily know in advance where it will be committed. The second part of the course comprises a detailed examination of terrorist movements combined with a final development of individual skills, including new developments in the optics and communications industries. The students become acquainted with sharpshooter tools such as night vision devices, observation glasses and the like. Evasive driving techniques are also taught. Failure rate on the course is about 80 percent. There is a stronger emphasis on academic work than in most such counter-terrorist units.

A wide variety of weapons are used, but the basic weapon is the standard police sub-machine gun – the Heckler & Koch MP5 9mm. Other MP5s in the armory include the MP5SD (*Suppressed*) and the MP5K (*kurz* = short). Operators usually carry the Heckler & Koch 7.62mm G8 rifle, although there have been reports that GSG 9 is trialling the SIG SG 551-1P 5.56mm assault rifle. Sniper rifles include the Heckler & Koch PSG-1, Mauser SP86, and (despite ▶

Above: Troopers of Germany's famed GSG-9 descend from a balcony using an Ikar descender, during a training exercise.

▶ its age) the Mauser SP66, all of which are chambered for the NATO standard 7.62mm round. Personal handguns include the Ruger .357 Magnum revolver and the Glock 17 9mm. The men are allowed to select their own model pistol, a rare degree of choice in such units. Most unusual of the weapons is the H&K P9P 9mm P7 pistol which features a unique cocking device operated by gripping the gunframe – release it and the gun is totally safe!

GSG 9 members wear standard *Bundesgrenzschutz* uniform – a green battledress with a dark green beret. On operations the standard German paratrooper helmet is worn, together with a flak jacket where necessary. No special unit identification is worn, although the wearing of a parachute qualification badge by a policeman may be an indication of his role.

Kampfschwimmerkompanie

The *Kampfschwimmerkompanie* (KSK = Combat Diver Company) was raised in 1959 to meet a Cold War operational requirement for a specialized diver unit trained in modern underwater warfare. Initial training was done in France, but the unit then set up its own training center on the island of Sylt. The KSK became a fully operational, independent unit in 1964, but in 1991 it became part of the Mine Clearing Fleet. Among its Cold War operations were covert reconnaissance of harbors in East Germany; in war it would have been responsible for securing landing sites for NATO amphibious operations and attacking high priority shipping in enemy harbors. The mission has changed with the ending of the Cold War and members of the unit were deployed aboard German warships in the Persian Gulf for enforcing the UN embargo of Iraq. At the end of the Gulf War, they were among the divers of many navies who helped clear the many mines laid by Saddam Hussein's forces.

Kommando Spezialkräfte

The operational requirement for *Kommando Spezialkräfte* (KSK = special commando unit) originated following the Rwanda crisis in 1993 when some German officials had to be rescued by Belgian and French parachutists because Germany did not have any forces of its own trained to carry out such a task and at such a great distance from Germany's borders. The formation, organization

Below: A ball-mounting for a weapon; the distance between the mounting plates shows the thickness of the armored glass.

Above: GSG-9 trooper in a fire position. Note the silenced MP5, one of the most widely used special forces' weapons.

and initial training of the unit was carried out in close cooperation with and advice from similar units in France, the UK and the USA. The unit began its life by combining the commando companies which had, until then, formed the long-range reconnaissance units for the airborne brigades, together with the men from two of the three *Fernspähkompanie* (the third was disbanded) which had provided long-range reconnaissance for the three German Army corps. The unit formally came into existence on April 1, 1997, and a small detachment accompanied the German force in Kosovo in the late 1990s, but it did not reach its full strength of some 1,000 fully-trained men until 2000. KSK and GSG 9 do not duplicate each other: KSK is a military force responsible for special operations outside Germany; GSG 9 is a unit of the Border Guards (ie, a civil force) and is responsible for counter-terrorist operations inside Germany.

KSK is commanded by a one-star officer (brigadier-general) and consists of four commando companies, a long-range reconnaissance company, a headquarters/communications company, a logistic/administrative company, and ▶

▶ its own training center. Throughout the operational elements of the KSK, the organization is based on four-man teams (ie, the British SAS's "bricks"). Volunteers for KSK can come from any part of the German Army, must be already airborne qualified; maximum age on admission is 30 years for officers, 32 years for NCOs, and all must complete a minimum of six years with KSK following the completion of training.

Weapons known to be used by KSK include the Heckler & Koch G8 7.62mm and G36 5.56mm assault rifles, P8 9mm pistols, and MP5SD3 9mm SMGs. For sniping, the G22 Sniper Weapon System is used; it is the British Accuracy International Model AW chambered for .300in Winchester Magnum rounds, with a folding stock and German sights. If shotguns are carried they are Heckler & Koch Model 512 12-gauge weapons. The unit is also known to use Panzerfaust 3 and Milan anti-tank guided missiles against buildings. On operations, the men wear an all-black Nomex coverall, balaclava and black leather gloves, with a Kevlar helmet.

Right: German special forces with the G36K submachinegun version of the new Heckler & Koch weapon system.

Below: Members of the Kampfschwimmerkompanie, with G36 rifle (kneeling) and G36E with bipod (prone position).

India

As is to be expected in such a large and populous country, the armed forces of India are also large, with 1,100,000 in the Army, 55,000 in the Navy and 110,000 in the Air Force, and every one of them a volunteer. Since Independence in 1947 the Indian Army has seen a great deal of active service and aggressive confrontation, particularly against its traditional enemies, Pakistan and China. There are also numerous internal problems, ranging from the long-running dispute in Kashmir to numerous internal anti-guerrilla campaigns, many of them involving terrorist tactics. Finally, there has been a variety of other military commitments, including operations in Sri Lanka and the Maldives. It is not surprising, therefore, that the Indian armed forces should have given birth to a large number of special forces.

Para Commandos

There are three Parachute/Commando battalions, the first to be raised being the 9th Para Cdo Bn in 1966, followed by 10th Para Cdo Bn in 1967; the third, 1st Para Cdo Bn, was converted from 1st Parachute Battalion in the mid-1970s. Some years after being formed 9th Para Cdo Bn specialized in desert warfare and 10th Bn in mountain warfare, but 1 Para Cdo Bn has not specialized and remains as a strategic reserve. The primary mission of the Para Commandos battalions in wartime is to conduct covert operations in the enemy's rear areas in order to disrupt his operations and to attack enemy command-and-control and logistic facilities. In peacetime their mission is to serve as a highly capable and flexible, rapid-reaction force.

All the para commandos saw active service in the 1971 Indo-Pakistan war. 9th and 10th Para Commandos deployed to Sri Lanka in 1987-88 as part of the Indian government's aid to the beleaguered government in Colombo, where they conducted several heliborne assaults, albeit with varying degrees of success. 10 Para Cdo Bn also took part in the peace-keeping operation in the Maldive islands in November 1988. The para commandos have also taken part in numerous internal security operations including the 1984 attack on the Sikh Golden Temple, although they lost 17 killed and many wounded.

National Security Guards

The National Security Guards (NSG) were raised in 1985 and form one of the largest special forces groups in the world, with a current strength of some 7,000. It also unusual in that, whereas other countries have units which are either all military or all police, India's NSG is a mixture of the two. In overall terms it is divided into two elements: the Special Action Group (SAG); and the Special Rangers Group (SRG). The SAG, which is slightly the larger of the two and composed entirely of soldiers, is responsible for offensive action, while the SRG, whose task is to support the SAG, particularly by cordoning off the area of the intended action, is entirely composed of policemen. Men serve with the NSG for 3-5 years and are then rotated back to their parent unit. Like many other modern units they wear an all-black operational uniform, which has earned them the nickname of the "Black Cats."

The main tasks of the NSG include: counter-terrorist action, resolving hijacking operations in the air or the ground, rescuing hostages, explosive ordnance disposal (EOD), VIP protection, and anti-sabotage checks prior to VIP visits. The scale of SAG commitment to an incident depends upon the site, the number of terrorists, the surrounding situation, and so on. The SAG is committed in "hit teams," each of which is composed of five men: two two-man pairs, and a technical support specialist. Four "hit teams" make an "action team" which is commanded by a captain. The NSG can, however, deploy in much larger units and on at least one occasion has fielded an entire battalion.

Above: Indian Army paratroops prepare to emplane for an operational deployment; note the FN 7.62mm FAL rifle.

▶ Three occasions when the NSG is known to have deployed were twice against the Sikh Golden Temple in Amritsar in 1986 and 1988 when they deployed in considerable strength, and once in an aircraft hijacking incident at Amritsar in 1994 where a lone hijacker was successfully overcome. Like most special forces, the NSG maintains close links with similar organizations in other countries and some are known to have visited Israel for additional training.

Marine Commando Force

The Indian Navy's Marine Commando Force (MCF) was raised in 1987 as an elite force for special operations in a maritime environment, with tasks which include reconnaissance, raids, and counter-terrorist operations in coastal, beach, and riverine environments. Volunteers for the MCF undergo arduous physical tests over a period of a month following which they start on a nine-month training course. This is followed by posting to an operational unit on probation where they undergo further training, which, if they pass, ends with them being declared fully qualified some two years after starting. Strength of the MCF is believed to be well over 1,000 and these are divided into three groups, one with each naval command: West (Bombay); South (Cochin), and

East (Vizag). Each group includes a small platoon-sized Quick Reaction Section (QRS), responsible for the counter-terrorism commitment.

One of the unusual roles undertaken by elements of the MCF is harbor attack and ship sabotage, for which they are equipped with eleven two-man submarines capable of carrying explosive charges or magnetic anti-ship mines, and being delivered to the operational area by conventional, diesel-electric submarines. The MCF can also deploy using the Indian Navy's small force of landing-ships, landing-craft, and air-cushioned vehicles, as well as helicopters.

Special Protection Group
The Special Protection Group (SPG) is responsible for guarding VIPs, clearly a task not without its difficulties in a country which has lost two prime ministers by assassination: Indira Gandhi in 1984 and Rajiv Gandhi in 1991. The SPG numbers approximately 3,000, who come principally from the police.

Below: Special forces of India's National Security Guard on deployment outside the Golden Temple at Amritsar in 1988.

Israel

Development

Israeli Special Forces have established an international reputation for being among the most efficient, successful and ruthless in the world; they are also by far the most numerous and have followed a different organizational pattern from other special forces. They are certainly among the busiest special forces in the world, having carried out many operations over a period of seemingly endless conflict, which has lasted for many decades. Their successes, such as the release of the hostages at Entebbe airport (see "Operations" section) have achieved legendary status, but there have also been many other less spectacular successes as well as some failures, although these have not usually been so well reported.

There are three notable tendencies in the story of Israeli Special Forces. First, with only a few exceptions, SF units are manned predominantly by soldiers undergoing their mandatory service, which lasts for 36 months. Due to the highly specialized nature of their work, however, virtually all SF units have a 20-month training period, which means that individual soldiers are fully operational for only about 16 months. Second, the majority of SF units have been raised to perform a specific role or to cover a limited geographical area, which often means that when an incident occurs or a particular operation is being planned, teams from various units have to be brought together to give the necessary spread of expertise. In the past this has caused confusion due to differing operational methods, styles of command and, in a few cases, inflated egos, although such problems have now been largely overcome. Third, the hard selection process, the arduous training and the daring operations mean that it is in the nature of special forces units to have very high morale, which results in a feeling of superiority not only over more conventional military forces, but also over other SF units. In many ways this is thoroughly praiseworthy and can lead to men carrying on under difficulties which would have defeated others, but it can also, on occasions, lead to arrogance, disputes between units,

Below: Israeli special forces are among the most highly skilled and are certainly the most practiced in the world.

***Above: The contact between Israelis and Palestinians takes place on a
daily basis and each such contact could be fatal.***

political manoevering (especially by people wanting "their" unit to be selected
for a forthcoming operation), and frequently failure to share experiences and
expertise.

The situation today

On 28 September 2000 Ariel Sharon, once one of the most distinguished
generals in the IDF but now a politician, walked, with an escort of some 1,000
policemen, to the Haram al-Sharif, the esplanade on the Temple Mount, a
deliberately provocative act which led to rioting and then to what is now known
as the "Jerusalem *Intifada.*" This led in its turn to Sharon becoming Prime
Minister in 2001 and also to the rapid escalation of violence. In particular, there
was a marked increase in suicide bombings, which claimed an ever-increasing
number of Israeli civilian victims, including the assassination of the Israeli
Minister of Tourism and a suicide bombing in Natanyha where 20 Israelis
celebrating Passover were killedIn response, Sharon unleashed large-scale
attacks on a variety of targets in the Occupied Territories.

Little publicity has been given to the activities of the Special Forces in this
latest round of violence, but it is clear that they have been heavily involved. One
example is the extraordinary precision with which cars carrying individuals
wanted by the Israelis are "taken out" by helicopter-launched missiles, which
would be possible only with good intelligence and precise target marking.

Israeli Special Forces Units

The overall policy for contemporary Israeli Special Forces is laid down in a plan
which requires three types of unit. *Takeover Units* have the highest capability,
their primary mission being the safe rescue of hostages. There are currently ▶

▶ only three such units: *Sayeret Mat'kal*, *Shayetet 13* and *Unit Yamam*. Next come *Engagement Units*, which have hostage rescue as a secondary capability, and third come *Assisting Units* which support the Takeover and Engagement Units by providing a specific and specialized function, such as dog-handling, explosive ordnance disposal (EOD), observation or target marking.

Thus, when a military Takeover or Engagement Unit arrives in the operational area it meets the men of one or more Assisting Units, who have the necessary specializations for this particular mission. Such an arrangement is necessary since the vast majority of Israeli soldiers are on three-years' mandatory service and as they already have to undergo some 20 months' training, there is simply insufficient time to make them into multi-capable all-rounders. Nevertheless, this multi-unit requirement has caused problems in the past due to differences between the various units in command style and training standards, although these have now been reduced.

The various Israeli Special Forces units are described below, but it should be noted that much of their organizational and equipment details remain highly classified and there may still be some units whose existence is not publicly known. The units are listed in the order Army, Navy, Air Force, Police, Border Guards, and within those categories in the order of their unit's numerical designation (where known).

ARMY

Unit 217 (*Sayeret Duvdevan*)
This is a counter-terrorist unit which conducts raids in the Occupied Territories, the aim of which is to either kill or snatch Palestinians accused of terrorist acts against Israel. This differentiates it from most other Israeli SF units, whose role is to either gather intelligence or to conduct specific missions such as target marking. Thus, while the operators in Unit 217 study Arabic and learn disguises, the major emphasis is on combat skills.

Today, due to the Israeli incursions into Palestine-controlled areas, *Sayeret Duvdevan* is one of the busiest units in the whole of the IDF, conducting some

Below: Men of Sayeret Duvdevan pursue their enemy through the ruins of a Palestinian town; weapons are Colt Commandos.

Above: Naval commandos of Shayetet 13. These are among the most highly trained of all Israeli special forces.

200 operations per year, some of them in uniform and others in plain clothes. Frequently, several teams from the unit operate simultaneously in different areas. The unit has a reputation, even within Israel, for being "trigger happy" and preferring to kill rather than take prisoners, and this, combined with their very high mission rate has led to allegations that many of its soldiers end their three years' mandatory service with both physical and psychological problems and officers have been removed for allowing excessive force to be used.

In August 2000 the unit suffered three deaths in a "friendly fire" incident during an operation in the Occupied Territories. As a result of the inquiry which followed, the selection and training processes were considerably improved and ▶

► the training period was increased from 13 to 15 months, although this is still much shorter than that for other SF units, most of which have 20 months' training. *Sayeret Duvdevan* was also permanently allocated a team from Unit 869, the IDF's specialist observation unit.

Sayeret Duvdevan uses the standard CAR15 with 14.5 inch barrel, IMI Micro or Mini Uzi submachine guns and the SIG Sauer P226 automatic pistol. At least one P226 in each team is fitted with a suppressor, primarily to kill dogs, of which there are a large number in Palestinian areas. Sniper weapons include Mauser SR86, Mauser SP66 and the Israeli-developed Sirkis M36. *Sayeret Duvdevan* has a large vehicle fleet, most of them military types, but also including civilian vehicles which superficially appear to be Palestinian cars (complete with forged license plates and documents) but with internal modifications to suit their use by clandestine operators.

Sayeret Duvdevan's commanding officer was killed on February 15, 2002, when the wall of a house collapsed on him during an operation in a Palestinian village.

Unit 269 (*Sayeret Mat'kal*)

Sayeret Mat'kal (also known as General Staff Reconnaissance Unit 269) was raised in 1957, since when it has taken part in virtually every operation, whether inside or outside the country's borders. One of its most famous operations was the Entebbe rescue operation; *Mat'kal* was the lead unit and was supported by *Sayeret Tzanhanin* (see next entry).

Today, it is considered to be the leading unit in Israel's fight against terrorism and is tasked with the most risky intelligence-gathering operations, a function it has reportedly accomplished successfully on numerous occasions. It is the principal unit dedicated to hostage rescue missions within Israel and despite its all-round capabilities it is assisted in some operations by other Israeli units such as the elite *Sayeret Tzanhanin*, *Shayetet 13*, and also in the past by *Sayeret Golani*, which has since been disbanded. .

Unit 621 (*Sayeret Egoz*)

Sayeret Egoz (Unit 621) was raised in 1995 as a counter-terrorist unit for deployment on the Lebanon front under the orders of Northern Command. Since the need for the unit was urgent, trained manpower from existing Israeli Special Forces units was drafted in, including men from *Sayeret Mat'kal*, *Sayeret Tzanhanin*, and the Navy's *Shayetet 13*. In addition, the unit was given (and still retains) at least one combat dog team from *Sayeret Oket'z*.

In May 2000 the IDF withdrew from southern Lebanon leaving *Sayeret Egoz* without a *raison d'etre*, and for a time its future was uncertain. One possibility was that it might simply be disbanded. However, in view of the continuing conflict between Israel and the Palestinians, it would appear that it is more likely that the unit will be retained, but that its manpower and expertise will be redirected to another geographical area or to a different role. Training has recently been extended from 14 to 16 months. *Sayeret Egoz* use the standard CAR15, with the new heavy barrel, which enables it to fire the SS109/M855 ammunition. One unusual feature is that for a light machine gun the unit employs the Soviet-made RPD.

Unit 869

Unit 869, the IDF's primary VISINT (Visual Intelligence [ie, observation]) unit, is relatively unusual in the IDF in that it is not in itself an SF unit, but includes a number of SF sub-units. *Unit 869* is approximately battalion-sized and is composed of at least four companies, three of which cover the northern and southern fronts, and the Occupied Territories, respectively. These companies are relatively conventional in nature with a primarily static role, but the fourth company includes a number of small and highly specialized sub-units, some of which remain highly classified, and which have an SF role.

Above: Israeli special forces on an operation. Note the face masks, Colt Commando rifles and bandoliers with magazines.

This company, designated T'zasam (*T'zevet Siour Modiyin* = Reconnaissance Intelligence Teams), consists of a number of teams which are responsible for deploying deep into hostile territory on their intelligence-gathering missions, and thus need to have a high fighting capability. Such missions might require the team to remain to keep the target under direct observation, or to place remote sensors or cameras in position. Unit 869 also ▶

▶ provides twp observation teams which are permanently attached to and work as integral parts of *Sayeret Mak'tal* and *Sayeret Duvdevan*. These two teams are not part of the T'zasam company. (It should be noted that the Israeli Air Force Unit 5707 T'zasam (*qv*) is in no way related to the Army's Unit 869.)

Unit 5101 (*Shaldag*)

Unit 5101, commonly known as *Shaldag*, is primarily responsible for locating and laser designation of enemy positions, buildings and vehicles for attack by Israeli Air Force fighter bombers and Army AH-64 attack helicopters. They are particularly interested in high-value targets such as missile launchers. Because of its expertise in patrol work it is also sometimes used for more general reconnaissance missions, and can also take part in counter-terrorist operations.

The unit is approximately 50 strong and is divided into teams of about eight men each. Volunteers undergo a rigorous selection and training process, with particular emphasis on long distance marches, a high degree of proficiency in land navigation, and communications with ground-attack aircraft and attack helicopters. Weapons carried are M16 or M4A1 assault rifles with the M203 grenade launcher attached. When performing counter-terrorist/hostage rescue duties they carry the Sig-Sauer or Glock 9mm series pistols. Unit snipers use the Mauser SR 82/66 sniper rifle.

Unit 7142 (Unit *Oket'z*)

Unit 7142 is an independent dog-handling unit under the direct command of *Mak'tal* (IDF General Staff) and its dogs are primarily intended for counter-terrorist activities. The unit was formed in great secrecy in 1974, and it started with just 20 men, of which 11 were dog-handlers. Its role at that time was exclusively counter-terrorism and its dogs were trained to attack kidnappers and hostage takers, either directly or with explosives, and thus to save Israeli lives. The unit's existence first came to light in 1980, but its role does not seem to have been fully appreciated by the general public until the notorious and unsuccessful Operation Blue-and-Brown in 1988, when some of its dogs were used to carry explosives into caves occupied by terrorists.

The unit consists of five company-sized elements, each with a particular

Below: Unit Oket'z dog under training; these dogs have proved invaluable to the IDF in a variety of tactical roles.

Above: Unit Oket'z handler with his war dog; these animals are no longer used to carry explosives into enemy positions.

specialization, and with its handlers and dogs selected and trained accordingly. The Attack Company uses attack dogs, mainly either Belgian or German Shepherds, in counter-terrorist and hostage rescue applications. The Pursuit ▶

55

▶ Team is responsible for manhunts, for which it uses Belgian Shepherds and bloodhounds. The Weapons Company's role is to operate in support of special and conventional forces, using "sniffer" dogs to search for hidden weapons and explosives in houses, caves, cars, tracks, tunnels, etc. The Weapons Company uses mainly Belgian and German Shepherds, but Jack Russel terriers are also used. The largest single element in Unit 7192 (it is almost battalion sized) is the Explosives Company whose main role is to deploy dogs ahead of IDF convoys to detect hidden roadside explosives charges. Finally, Rescue Company is composed mainly of reservists and female personnel and takes part in civilian operations such as hunts for missing persons, and especially in natural disasters. It also deploys abroad to participate in international rescue missions. The Rescue Palga is located in the Sirkin AFB and use mainly German and Belgium Shepherds.

The great majority of the members of Unit 7142 use the standard range of special forces weapons, but the dog-handlers in the Attack Palga use the IDF sawn-off barrel version of the CAR-15, because not only will they find themselves in very close-quarter combat situations, but they will also have to handle a very large, aggressive dog in the process. They also carry a handgun, usually the Sig-Sauer P226.

Unit 7707 (*Lotar Eilat*)
Unit 7707 was formed specifically to conduct SF operations in and around Eilat. Situated at the head of the Gulf of Aqaba, Eilat is particularly vulnerable because of its distance from the main part of Israel, and the fact that it is the country's premier holiday resort, with a large number of high-value targets. Originally, the unit was formed as an engagement unit, hence a rapid deployment unit that can provide an initial response until a better equipped and a bigger size takeover unit will arrive and conduct the hostage rescue raid. In 1995, *Lotar Eilat's* status was raised to "takeover unit" placing it on a par with *Sayeret Mat'kal* and *Shayetet*. Training is very intense and concentrates on activities such as storming hotels, but if the operation was against a maritime target, such as a ship in the harbour, then *Lotar Eilat* would act as the engagement unit while *Shayetet 13* would serve as the takeover unit.

Sayeret Tzanhanin
This is a commando force which bears some similarities in role and capability to the United States Army's Rangers. It is capable of airborne operations, and conducted many long range patrols into Lebanon during the Israeli occupation of the southern part of that country. *Sayeret Tzanhanin's* most public mission was the raid on the Entebbe Airport in Uganda, during which its personnel assisted *Sayeret Mat'kal* by preventing soldiers of the Ugandan Army from threatening the success of the operation. *Tzanhanin's* men also placed the beacons necessary to guide the pilots of the Israeli C-130s during their take-off from the pitch-dark runways.

Sayeret Tzanhanin commandos are trained in the use of numerous weapons. Assault rifles such as the M16, AK-47, and Galil 5.56mm are familiar to its members; as are the FN-MAG and a IMI modified M14 sniper rifle. Grenades, mortars, LAW rockets, and RPGs are also part of their arsenal.

Unit *Alpinistim*
Unit *Alpinistim* is another SF unit raised to conduct a very specific task, in this case, the protection of the strategic electronic warfare (EW) station situated on Mount Hermon, and is one of the three all-reservist units. The Mount Hermon *massif* has three distinct peaks, each about 9,200ft high, and stretches for some 20 miles in a NW/SE direction astride the border between the Occupied Territories and Syria. One of the three peaks lies in Syria, but the other two are under Israeli control, and because they overlook southern Syria (Damascus is

only about 23 miles distant) they are covered with electronic warfare equipment. Because of their strategic importance and as they are barely 550yd from the border, these EW stations are very vulnerable and are protected by a strong permanent garrison. There is, however, a requirement for military operations on the mountain outside this defensive perimeter.

The higher reaches of the mountain are snow-covered for most of the year and this, coupled with altitude, rugged terrain and the strategic importance of the installations, requires a particular type of mountaineer/soldier, which is provided by reservists of Unit *Alpinistim*. The unit is trained in skiing, mountain warfare, snow combat maneuvers and survival, and open field combat under harsh winter conditions. It has a secondary mission of search and rescue in the mountains. Unit *Alpinistim* members are drawn mainly from former soldiers of the *Sayeret Golany*, but recent immigrants with mountaineering erxperience are also recruited.

The soldiers do only 45-60 reserve days per year and their training is spread over several years, each year having a different training focus. A major problem is that Israeli winters rarely provide good snow conditions, suitable for intense winter training, so the unit's personnel often travel to France and the U.S. at the state's expense, which, not surprisingly, makes service with the init very popular. The unit also runs an "Extreme Weather School" which provides courses for other IDF units requiring such training. However, the unit is not necessarily confined to Mount Hermon and can be deployed to other mountainous areas, if the threat requires it to do so. The unit uses standard IDF SF weapons and equipment, but with the addition of extreme weather equipment such as skis, white overclothes, cold weather inner clothing, etc.

Unit *Rotem*

The third of the all-reserve Special Forces units is Unit *Rotem* (named after its founder, Rotem Talor) which is responsible for long-range patrols along the Israel-Egypt border in the Sinai Desert, and for taking direct action, if tactically necessary. Its primary mission is thwarting Egyptian reconnaissance, but it can ▶

Below: Sayeret Tzanhanin, the Israeli equivalent to the U.S. Rangers, has a wider mission than most Israeli SF units.

▶ also be used to counter criminal activities, such as smuggling. The unit is primarily jeep-borne and has a high degree of expertise in desert navigation.

Force 100

Force 100 is the Special Emergency Response Team (SERT) composed of specially selected and trained members of the IDF's Military Police. Its mission is to quell disorder in Megiddo Military Prison, which currently holds some 800 terrorists. Some 80 of the most dangerous men are segregated in a high security building, but the remainder are accommodated in tents. This, together with the prison's proximity to a number of *kibbutzim*, makes for a sensitive security situation with the potential for disorder, escapes and hostage-taking situations. As a result the prison has a very high staffing level, a large guard force for the perimeter, and Force 100. Force 100 is some 25 strong. Its men are carefully selected and undergo an eight-month training course. They are armed with the standard Special Forces CAR15, plus an FN High Power 9mm handgun. They also carry full anti-gas equipment plus non-lethal riot control gear, and each man has his own hands-free communications equipment.

AIR FORCE

Unit 669

Unit 669 is responsible for Combat Search And Rescue (CSAR); ie, finding and rescuing Israeli Air Force aircrew who have been shot down in enemy territory. It is a basic assumption that such aircrew will be injured, so not only does every team include at least one doctor, but in addition all members of Unit 669 also receive extensive training as paramedics and in trauma treatment in addition to their normal SF military training. The unit is equipped with Bell 206 *Sayfaneet* (JetRanger), Agusta-Bell 212 *Anapha* helicopters as well as Sikorsky UH-60 *Na'mer* (Blackhawk) helicopters. All of these are equipped with hoists and are able to carry stretchers, as well as weapons such as rockets and machine guns, if required to do so. On warlike operations, two or more AH-64 *Peten* (Apache) are also attached to Unit 669. During peacetime the unit is organized into approximately six teams, each of four to five operators, but this changes to some four teams each of nine men. Weapons are the usual M16/M4A1 assault rifles with M203 grenade launcher attachment, while the medical officers carry 9mm Micro Uzi and/or Sig-Sauer and Glock 9mm pistols.

Unit 5707

Although long-range rockets had been used for some time against Israel, the problem became particularly acute during Israel's mid-1990s campaign in southern Lebanon, when terrorists took to launching such rockets from launchers sited in densely populated areas. Indiscriminate carpet bombing of such areas would have incurred heavy civilian casualties and attracted adverse publicity in the international media, so precision attacks were required, but these were possible only if there was very close reconnaissance and very exact information as to the location and description of the target and of any nearby civilians. Providing such information had been previously one of the tasks carried out by Unit 5101 (*Shaldag*), but a new unit was formed in 1996 specifically for this mission – Unit 5707. Further, since the operators would have visual contact with the target during the engagement, they would also be able to provide post-attack bomb damage assessment (BDA). Finally, in the event that the strike had been against a headquarters, then Unit 5707 operators would also search the target for documents or other intelligence material. Although formed to operate in the Lebanese theater, the unit has worked elsewhere and during 2002 operated in the Occupied Territories. The unit consists of some 50 men, with a headquarters and support element, and four teams, each consisting of some seven to eight men. They carry normal SF weapons, plus special radios and laser target markers.

Above: The mission of these men of Unit Alpinistim, is to defend the electronic warfare station atop Mount Hermon.

Sayeret Maglan

This is a very specialized anti-tank guided missile (ATGM) unit, with a secondary role using ground-based lasers to designate targets for Israeli Air Force (IAF) ground attack aircraft and attack helicopters. The need for such a unit was first appreciated in the early 1980s when it became apparent that potential enemies were re-equipping with very modern tanks clad with sophisticated armor to defeat existing anti-tank weapons. At the same time new ATGM technologies (eg, laser guidance and fire-and-forget systems) were becoming operational. It was therefore decided to form a specialized long-range anti-tank force armed with these latest ATGMs, and *Sayeret Maglan* came into existence in 1984.

Sayeret Maglan is an independent unit, coming under the direct orders of the General Staff (*Mat'kal*). All elements of *Sayeret Maglan* can be dropped by parachute and the unit's main wartime function is to provide strong and rapidly-deploying anti-tank defense for deep-penetration forces, both when on the move and when holding captured enemy strongholds. *Maglan* can also use its missiles to destroy important pinpoint targets, such as high-ranking officers' personal vehicles. *Sayeret Maglan* also has a role in counter-terrorist operations where the precise targeting of its guided missiles is used to eliminate specific terrorist vehicles and to engage gun positions in buildings. To perform these tasks, the unit comprises two elements: patrol teams which acquire the targets and guide the missiles, and the missile teams who carry the missiles and launch them. In general war *Sayeret Maglan* is not intended to attack large enemy formations, but rather to provide a rapidly deployable, strong and very effective defense or attack over a strictly limited period, until stronger and more conventional forces arrive.

All personnel for *Maglan* come from the *Tzanhanin* brigade and are fully parachute-qualified. In addition, all their equipment can be mounted on jeeps or be man-portable, and can be dropped by parachute. The units is armed with three Israeli-made ATGM systems: IAI Nimrod, Rafale Michol, and IMI MAPATS. ▶

▶ Parachute Brigade (Paratroops)

The IDF Parachute Brigade is an elite unit with a long history of daring and well-executed operations. The brigade, which is commanded by a colonel, is a regular element of the IDF and in addition to its parachute infantry battalions includes reconnaissance, engineering, signals and anti-tank companies.

NAVY

Unit *Yaltam*

The Israeli Navy's Underwater Missions Unit (*Yechida Lemesimot Tat-Memiyot = Yaltam*) has a number of missions, all of them defensive, including: Search And Rescue (SAR); disposal or neutralisation of sea-mines or other explosive devices; preemptive dives in Israeli harbors to prevent enemy underwater incursions by combat swimmers; and support to Unit *Yaban* (Israeli Navy Harbor Security Unit) in underwater inspections of foreign shipping to ensure no underwater mines are attached. The unit's home base is in Haifa, but detachments deploy to other naval bases, as required. Most of the volunteers for the unit come from men who have completed their three years' mandatory service in Unit *Yaban*, while others are former members of *Shayetet 13*. As all these newcomers are already trained combat divers, Unit Yaltam training tends to be shorter than in other SF units, and focusses on very deep diving and the use of specialized underwater equipment.

Shayetet 13

Shayetet 13 (S'13) is the Israeli Navy's elite commando unit, based at Atlit Naval Base. It is one of the oldest Israeli Special Forces units, but has had something of a checkered career, with some outstanding successes to its credit, but also with a number of disaster, as well. For some years in the 1960s the commanding officer set some extraordinarily high training standards which not only resulted in several deaths, but also ensured that the failure rate was so high that it seldom had enough qualified men in its ranks. In 1969 the unit was about 30 strong when it took part in the 1969 Green Island Raid where it lost three killed and ten badly wounded, as a result of which it was barely operational for several years. In the late 1960s the Navy's Unit 707 (not to be confused with today's Unit 707 which is an IDF training establishment), which was responsible for defensive underwater operations, began to undertake offensive operations, as well, duplicating the efforts of *Shayetet 13*. After some inter-unit rivalry Unit 707's operators were absorbed into *Shayetet 13* and 707 ceased to exist.

Shayetet 13 comprises a headquarters element, with the combat element divided into three companies (*palgot*), each company (*palga*) having a specialized role. *Raiding Company* is responsible for assassinations, incursions and counter-terrorist operations. *Underwater Company* is responsible for underwater missions such as beach surveys, submerged attacks on enemy ships and seaborne attacks on enemy harbours. *Above Water Company* is responsible for operating *Shayetet 13*'s fleet of boats and for cooperation with the Israeli Navy's warships and submarines. Their task is to either provide or arrange the sea transportation of Raids and Underwater teams safely to and from their targets, using either their own boats or naval ships. The Above Water Company resembles the U.S. Navy's SBU (special boat section) and the British Royal Marines Rigid Raider Squadron, except that in the Israeli case the boat unit is an integral part of the attack force and not a separate unit.

Unlike in many other Israeli Special Forces units which take men only for their 36-month mandatory service, volunteers for *Shayetet 13* must agree to serve at least 4$\frac{1}{2}$ years' ie, 18 months over and above the normal commitment. The training course lasts 20 months, which is the same as most other SF units, but it is considered among the very toughest, and there is a very high drop-out rate throughout the course due to accidents, most of them incurred during the diving phase. Unlike most other IDF SF units, *Shayetet 13* continues to carry out training with foreign forces with a similar role. The unit carries out dozens of operational missions every year, mainly against terrorist targets in southern Lebanon. Most of these missions involve the destruction of enemy boats and shore installations, or ambushes in coastal areas. Shayetet 13 uses the same range of weapons as other Israeli SF, but is alone in continuing to use the Soviet AK-47, whereas all the others use the CAR15.

POLICE

Unit 33 (Unit *Gideonim*)
This is a police undercover unit which was raised in 1994, largely as a result of orders from the Commissioner of Police Asaf Hefet'z, who had earlier been responsible for raising Unit *Yamam*. *Gideonim*'s primary mission when it was raised was to gather counter-terrorist intelligence in East Jerusalem, but its role gradually expanded so that today it has a full CT capability and operates in other Arab cities and villages both inside Israel's traiditional borders and in the Occupied Territories. Unit *Gideonim* is also used to fight hard-core crime.

Since 1998 *Gideonim*'s attention has been refocussed onto more tradtional police missions, more equvalent to SWAT teams in the USA. Some friction has been reported Between *Gideonim* and Yamam, since their operational tasks and geographical areas of reponisibility tend to overlap, a situation complicated by the fact that one reports to the Border Guards and the other to the Police. Principal weapons are the Colt Commando and CAR15, Mini Uzi and IMI 941 Jericho pistol. ▶

Below: Israel maintains a larger number of special forces units than any other country, each with its own specific mission.

▶ Unit *Yoav*

One of the soft targets regularly attacked by Islamic extremist suicide bombers are the buses of Israel's public transport system, particularly in the north of the country. As a result, the Police set up Unit *Yoav* in 1996 specifically to counter this threat at two levels, the first of which was by very obvious patrols of bus stations in full tactical gear, including vests and weapons, which are intended to deter terrorists from entering the perimeter as well as to provide an immediate tactical response if needed. Such overt measures include the use of bomb-sniffing dogs and mobile X-ray devices similar to those used in airports, to detect explosives and weapons. The second level was the use of covert patrols by *Yoav* operators dressed in civilian clothes, who deploy both inside he bus stations and in nearby streets, wearing plain clothes and armed only with concealed handguns. Their task is to detect terrorists before they enter the stations and to arrest them before they can do any harm, although they may also follow suspects as far as the buses. They do not normally act as escorts inside the buses. As with other engagement units, Unit *Yoav* is permitted to assault the objective only if the terrorists begin to execute the hostages, otherwise it must await the arrival of the Takeover unit (ie, Unit *Yamam*) which will then assume responsibility for resolving the situation.

Unit *Yagal*

Unit *Yagal* (*Yechidat Gvoul Lebanon* = Lebanon Border Unit) is a Police SF unit which was formed following the May 2000 Israeli withdrawal from southern Lebanon. Prior to that withdrawal the IDF had established a security zone in South Lebanon which was intended to prevent Lebanese civilians from approaching the border. Following the withdrawal anyone can approach the border. *Yagal*'s mission is to prevent terrorists infiltrating through the border fence and to prevent gun and drug smuggling. Most of the unit's operations consist of ambushes, which may last days or even weeks in adverse weather conditions. As such, the unit places a focus on camouflage and field craft. Weapons used are the standard Colt Commando and IMI Jericho 941 handgun.

BORDER GUARDS

Unit *Yamam*

Similarly to Germany's GSG 9, Unit *Yamam* is an integral part of the Israeli Border Guard (*Magav*), the name being the acronym for the unit's Hebrew name: *Yechida Mishtartit Meyuchedet* (= Special Police Unit). The unit is primarily responsible for civilian hostage rescue within Israel's borders, but from about the mid-1990s it has also been used for tasks such as arresting police suspects who have barricaded themselves in and in police raids against organized crime targets. It is also rumored that they are involved in VIP escort and in security at important national events. Despite its official role within Israel's borders, it is reported to have been involved in operations in the Occupied Territories and across Israel's northern border in Lebanon. Currently the unit conducts some 300 missions per year, split approximately 50:50 between civilian missions, such as criminal hostage rescues, VIP protection, security at major political and sporting events, and counter-terrorist operations in the Occupied Territories, for which it is tasked by *Shabach*. This results in a very high mission rate, probably between 20-30 per month.

Magav began to make plans for its own SF unit in the early 1970s but nothing substantial was done until after the Mahalot massacre in 1974 when *Magav* was instructed by the government to form a CT unit. This was to be a civilian unit, manned by men selected by the IDF, but under the organizational control of *Magav*, although it could also operate in support of the police. The unit began to form in February 1975 under its first CO, Asaf Hefet'z, an IDF SF officer who was later to become Commissioner of Police.

Above: Unit Yamam is the Border Guards special unit, equivalent in many ways to Germany's GSG-9.

Unit *Yamam* is about 200 strong and comprises a headquarters element, an intelligence section and a small team responsible for the development of new operational techniques and testing new equipment. These central elements apart, the bulk of the unit is divided into a number of sections, each consisting of five teams, each containing operators with a particular specialization, so that the section includes within its numbers all the elements needed for a successful operation: roping team, entry team, sniping team, dog team, EOD team (demolition and bomb disposal). Thus, whereas an IDF special forces operation needs to assemble elements from different specialist units, in *Yamam* they are all permanently part of the same unit, living, training and operating together.

Applicants for *Yamam* must be between 21 and 28 years of age and must have completed their three-year service in the IDF, but no previous police experience is required. Many of those successful in applying are former members of either *Sayeret Golany* and *Sayeret Duvdevan*. Training lasts 12 months and is carried out in *Magav*'s own training center, although some use is made of the facilities at the IDF Counter Terror Warfare School (Unit 707). The course is divided into an eight-month general CT training period at the end of which recruits are selected for their specializations and then concentrate for the remaining four months on that specialization. On graduation, individuals are posted to fill gaps in the sections. *Yamam* considers that it has several advantages over the IDF counter-terrorist units, first, because the men are more mature and spend much longer in the unit than the equivalent military units, and, second, because the units contains a far broader range of ages and experience.

Unit *Yamam* has its own funds which give it a certain degree of independence in selecting and purchasing weapons. The unit uses the standard Colt Commando assault rifle, but while other Israeli SF units use the Sig-Sauer P226, FN Browning High Power or IMI Jericho 949 pistols, *Yamam* uses the higher powered (and more expensive) Glock 17. *Yamam* snipers use the Mauser 86SR and the U.S. M24SWS, but also have stocks of the IMI Galil 7.62mm SWS (Galat'z), a weapon no longer used by any other SF unit. The SMG is the IMI Mini-Micro-Uzi SMG, but it is specially adapted to take Glock 17 magazines.

Italy

Gruppo D'intervento Speziale

Italy's primary counter-terrorist team, the 100-strong *Gruppo d'Intervento Speziale* (GIS = Special Operations Group) was raised in 1978 and is manned from volunteers from 1st Carabinieri Airborne Regiment, a unit of Italy's paramilitary police force, the Carabinieri. The GIS comes under the direction of the Ministry of the Interior and is one of the most experienced groups in any country, having been involved in numerous operations against the Red Brigade, the Mafia and, more recently, northern separatists. Among its recent actions was a rather unusual event in May 1997 when a group of northern separatists occupied the bell-tower in St. Mark's Square in Venice.

The selection process is rigorous and, as with any elite organization, starts with an exhaustive security check, which is followed by a stringent medical examination and an interview with a panel of GIS officers. More unusually, it also includes an interview with a psychiatrist. Successful applicants undergo a two-week selection board and the relatively few who pass that hurdle then attend a 10-month training course, which is very comprehensive and involves the best facilities available; for example, it is reported that the driving segment is done at Ferrari's justly famous racing track.

The GIS is approximately 100 men strong and is split into three operational sections and a number of sniper/reconnaissance teams. Each operational section is divided into four-man detachments (the traditional SAS "brick"). The sniper-reconnaissance teams each consist of three snipers, two armed with Mauser 86SRs and the third with a Heckler & Koch PSG-1.

GIS operators have a large choice of weapons for their counter-terrorist operations, including the widely used Heckler & Koch MP5A5, SD3 and KA4 submachine gun family. The group also uses Italian weapons such as the Beretta SC70/90 5.56mm assault rifle and the Beretta Model 92 SB 9mm automatic pistol. Some operators prefer revolvers, using such types as the Smith & Wesson Patrolman .38 caliber and .357 Magnum. Sniper rifles include

Below: Italian Navy COMSUBIN trooper immediately after landing on a roof from an AS-61 Agusta Sea King.

Above: COMSUBIN on a training range; like so many special forces they are armed with the Heckler & Koch MP5 SMG.

Below: A GIS command station; video feeds from individual snipers enable the commander to control their shooting.

▶ the Heckler & Koch PSG-1 and Mauser 86SR 7.62 rifle, to which the Accuracy International AWP Suppressed has recently been added. There is also a small number of Barret M82 .50in (12.7mm) caliber.

Commando Raggruppamento Subacqui e Incursori

Commando Raggruppamento Subacqui e Incursori (COMSUBIN = Naval Frogmen and Raiders Commando), informally known as "the *Incursori*", is the Italian Navy's special forces group and has a long and very distinguished history. The use of swimmers in combat is nothing new, having been part of warfare since ancient times, but the Italian Naval Assault Divisions were the pioneers of modern warfare of this type. The operations they carried out at Trieste and Pola in World War I, and at Gibraltar, Suda Bay, Malta and Alexandria in World War II were all extremely daring, very imaginative and inflicted heavy losses on their enemies. COMSUBIN is the heir to this legacy and its missions include clearing enemy-laid mines, explosives and underwater obstacles in Italian waters; conducting landings on friendly or foreign territory for reconnaissance purposes; clearing beaches of obstacles prior to amphibious landings; and carrying out commando raids against ships, dry-docks, and fuel storage areas.

Reports that COMSUBIN had also been given a counter-terrorist role were first made in 1978 and were confirmed the following year, when the unit was called out when a hijacked airliner from Beirut was brought to Rome. Subsequent counter-terrorist involvement has included COMSUBIN deployment aboard Italian vessels near Lebanon during the Achille Lauro incident, and more recent operations in Albania, the Lebanon, Persian Gulf, Rwanda, Somalia, and former Yugoslavia.

The 200-man strong COMSUBIN reports to the Navy Chief of Staff and is headquartered just outside La Spezia. The unit consists of two main elements. The *Gruppo Operativo Subacqui* (Raider Operations Group) has responsibility for offensive operations, while the Frogman Group provides Italian coastline

Below: COMSUBIN commando with the highly specialized H&K P11, 5-round, electrically-operated underwater pistol.

Right: GIS troopers conduct a simulated building assault using Land Rovers modified to their requirements. Some men are armed with the Beretta SC90 assault rifle, others with MP5 SMGs.

support. Volunteers for both units can come from anywhere in the Navy, but mainly from the crack San Marco marine battalion. All San Marco battalion personnel receive general commando training from the COMSUBIN, but they must leave the battalion when they volunteer for full-time service with it. Support is provided by a schools group, a research and study group, and a special naval group.

Currently, the all-volunteer *incursori* are required to complete a 10-month training course. Rigorous physical tests are a part of it and, in fact, are required every three months for everyone in the unit. The program includes ranger skills, parachuting, hand-to-hand combat, demolitions, and weapons training, in addition to Scuba (self-contained underwater breathing apparatus) and other swimming skills. Those who go on to be part of the Raiders Group get an additional 42 weeks of specialized training with emphasis on parachuting, mountain climbing and vigorous physical endurance tests. This phase is completed with a six-week command course. The COMSUBIN unit, not surprisingly, is rated very highly by those who have observed it. The *Incursori* use the same weapons as other Italian units in the main, with the Beretta 9mm Model 12 submachine gun a particular favorite because of its compactness.

San Marco Battalion

The Italian Navy Marine Corps special force as the elite San Marco Battalion, whose motto "Per Mare, Per Terram" (= by sea, by land) is the same as that of Britain's Royal Marines. This highly-trained unit has participated in several international peace-keeping missions, including the protection of Palestinians in Lebanon (1982) in which one marine was killed, in the Persian Gulf (1987 and 1991), in Somalia (1992) and in Albania (2000). The San Marco Battalion has its own operational and logistic structure that enables it to operate independently and the Italian Navy operates three well-designed amphibious transports – San Giorgio, San Marco, San Giusto – whose primary mission is to move the battalion. The San Marco also operates LVTP-7 amphibious personnel carriers and VCC-1 light tanks. Air transport ois provided by SH3D and AB212 of the naval air arm.

Jordan

Special Forces Brigade

A company of paratroops was formed in Jordan in 1963 and, having quickly proved its value, there then began a process of steady expansion until today, when the Special Forces Brigade consists of three para/commando battalions, plus supporting groups. Over the years these units have taken part in various Middle East wars and have also been heavily involved during peacetime in keeping control of their troubled country. They played a leading part in the operations to suppress and finally expel the Palestine Liberation Organization's commandos in 1970-71 and also retook the Intercontinental Hotel in Amman in 1976.

Such is the reputation of these Special Forces that in 1983 the U.S. military authorities suggested that it should be expanded to two brigade size and be used to help cope with the security problems in the Gulf. This proposal, while it recognized that Jordan's special forces were among the best in the Middle east, foundered on two points. First, the cost would have been some $US200million (in 1980 dollars) and it was unclear where the money would have come from, and, secondly, a divisional sized force of such highly-trained and well-equipped troops could also have been used against Israel. As a result the proposal was quietly dropped.

There is a particularly strong link between the Special Forces and King Abdullah II, who succeeded his father, King Hussein, in 1999. During the 1990s, Abdullah was first deputy commander and then commander of the Special Forces and in 1998 he personally led the successful storming of a cave where

hostages were being held, including the charge-de-affaires of the Iraqi Embassy in Amman.

The three commando-paratroop battalions are organized on standard Jordanian Army lines, with three companies, each of three platoons. Battalions are approximately 500 strong.

Members of the Jordanian Special Forces are hand-picked. They must be bedouins with personal tribal links to King Abdullah II, and possess a proven record of undoubted loyalty to the king. Their training is far-and-away the roughest and toughest in the army - both physically and professionally. They are trained in sabotage and guerrilla operations. In combat they take part in elite military operations, such as anti-terrorist deployments, recce patrols, road blocks and raids. They undertake missions which other elements of the army may be either unable or unwilling to take on. The three Special Forces battalions are equipped as light infantry, while land transport is based on the usual jeeps and trucks. Air mobility is proved by the Royal Jordanian Air Force. As with the rest of the army, the special forces' uniform shows a mixture of American and British influences. U.S.-style leaf-pattern camouflage suits are worn and most items of personal equipment are of U.S. origin. Parachute wings are worn on the left breast and the major visible mark is the maroon beret, but worn with the standard national cap-badge.

The Special Forces badge is a white bayonet surrounded by symbolic yellow wings and surmounted by a Hashemite crown; this is backed by a maroon shield and worn on the right upper sleeve.

Left: Nightime at an airport in Afghanistan as men of Jordanian SF arrive to establish a field hospital.

Below: The Jordanian SF Brigade has a very high reputation for efficiency and toughness

Korea (North)

The communist rulers of the Democratic Republic of Korea (North Korea) have two priorities: the survival of the leader and of the communist party he controls; and the conquest of South Korea. Other factors, such as the well-being or the prosperity of the people of North Korea, or the international reputation of their country, count for nothing. One facet of this is that the regime maintains one of the largest special forces organizations in the world, whose size is estimated to be between 50,000 and 100,000, the unusual width of the bracket reflecting the outside world's lack of knowledge about this most secretive regime. The special forces are believed to be organized into 22 brigades and 7 independent battalions, although it is quite possible that there are other clandestine organizations whose existence is totally unknown to the outside world.

The Ministry of the People's Armed Forces (= ministry of defense) includes three bodies involved in directing special forces operations: the General Staff Directorate (GSD), the Reconnaissance Bureau (RB) and the Training Unit Guidance Bureau (TUGB). The General Staff Directorate controls the efforts of 14 "sniper brigades," six of which are airborne, two amphibious and six conventional, each consisting of between five and ten battalions. These brigades could, in theory, fight as an entity, but it appears more likely that they would disperse for independent operations. The airborne and conventional brigades are approximately 3,500 strong, but the two amphibious brigades are somewhat stronger – approximately 5,000 men each – with one brigade on each coast. The Korean title of these units is translated into English as "sniper" but it seems highly improbable that every single man in these units is a fully qualified sniper in the Western sense of the word. Thus, "sniper" may simply be a cover name, intended to camouflage their real role, or may be a complete mistranslation, or it might more properly be translated as "sharpshooter" to indicate a higher than normal standard of marksmanship.

Between them, the Training Unit Guidance Bureau and the Reconnaissance Bureau are responsible for collecting strategic intelligence, which involves despatching and controlling both individual agents and small teams and the bureaux also control self-contained reconnaissance brigades, consisting of some 10 battalions each and supporting units.

At the operational and tactical levels the "special purpose" units are roughly equivalent to the "*Spetsnaz*" units of the former Soviet Army. In war, each forward corps would be supported by a "special purpose" brigade, with, in addition, one "special purpose" battalion allocated to each infantry division. These "special purpose" troops would be responsible for infiltrating enemy positions, and attacks on enemy command-control-and-communications and logistics facilities, target acquisition and other deep penetration tasks.

There are a number of naval special forces units, including those which operate submarines and landing craft in support of Reconnaissance Bureau operations. The North Korean Air Force supports special operations missions with transportation using its large fleet of some 250

Antonov An-2 (Colt) aircraft.

The North Korean soldier is a highly disciplined and well trained fighter. Indoctrinated against South Korea and its leadership since childhood, he is likely to be conscripted between the ages of 17 and 21, and will remain in service until the age of 27. Annual training is between March and August and consists of a month-long basic training program. Once assigned to his unit, the trainee goes through further basic unit, small unit and large-scale unit training exercises. Soldiers in the special warfare units get special emphasis on infiltration, intelligence gathering, sabotage, underwater demolition, hand-to-hand combat, night operations, surprise attack and political education. Specific indoctrination and information sessions on all aspects of communist ideology are carried out on a daily basis.

Equipment is flexible and varies considerably. Common to all are a dagger and/or bayonet; pistols, including the silenced versions of the 9mm Browning automatic and the Soviet Tokarev 7.62mm automatic; the AK-47 or M16 rifle; hand grenades and demolitions; rocket launchers, either the RPG-7 or the AT-3 Sagger; and 60mm mortars.

The light infantry, during training, are provided with the same standard uniforms as the infantry of the North Korean People's Army. However, during combat operations they can be attired in civilian clothing, South Korean Army uniforms (usually with incorrect ranks for the personnel wearing them), mottled camouflaged uniforms in summer, and an all-white over garment in winter.

Below: South Korean SF struggle to keep the Sang-O class submarine, containing six enemy, afloat in September 1996.

Korea (South)

The armed forces of the Democratic Republic of Korea (North) invaded the Republic of Korea (RoK – South Korea) on June 25, 1950. The resulting war dragged in the People's Republic of China on the northern side, and 16 nations, including the United States on the southern side. After a very bitter war an armistice (not a peace treaty) was signed on July 27, 1953, and an uneasy cessation of hostilities has continued since.

707th Special Missions Battalion
The ROK's dedicated counter-terrorist unit, 707th Special Missions Battalion, was not formed until hostage-taking at the Munich Olympic Games showed the need for such a unit. The unit was on stand-by throughout the Seoul Olympics in 1988, but its presence, possibly coupled and the known efficiency of RoK army and police units, ensured that they did not have to be used. The unit is about 200 strong and comprises a headquarters, support and specialist staff, and two companies, each consisting of four 14-man teams. Volunteers for the unit must come from elsewhere in the "Special Warfare" organization and undergo a rigorous selection and training procedure. Once in the unit, training is particularly tough and all men are trained as underwater swimmers.

707th Special Missions Battalion uses Korean weapons wherever possible, including the Daewoo 9mm pistol and Daewoo K1 and K2 assault rifles. However, foreign weapons, such as the Heckler & Koch MP5 sub-machine gun, are also used.

National Police Unit 868
In the lead-up to the 1988 Seoul Olympics ROK National Police Force formed a special counter-terrorist squad, designated Unit 868, intended for counter

Below: All members of South Korean SF must reach "black belt" standard in the traditional Tae-Kwon-Do martial art.

Right: South Korean SF, having come ashore from canoes, ascend a difficult cliff face. The lead soldier is armed with an Uzi SMG.

terrorist and hostage rescue missions. Strength is about 100, with the bulk organized into 12 seven-man teams.

Special Warfare Brigades

The ROK has seven special warfare brigades organized on the same lines as U.S. special forces groups, with whom there is a close working relationship. The battalions of these brigades are often used in the ranger role for the destruction of tactical targets. These ROK special forces units are capable of using either continuous guerrilla operations from bases within enemy territory, or carrying out single operations from bases within friendly territory. The usual allocation of the special forces is one battalion to each Army corps.

Following the usual physical and psychological tests, the volunteers undergo a hard training course which includes weapon handling skills to a very high standard and parachute training. All ROK special forces troops must also reach black belt standard in Tae-Kwon-Do or a similar martial art, and when not on operations some four to five hours a day are spent in practice of such arts. They are also trained in tough, realistic exercises for dangerous missions along the DMZ, such as clearing North Korean tunnels. They have also been used as pursuit units when North Korean raiders have infiltrated the South.

Normal uniform is a camouflage combat suit. The Special Forces distinguishing mark is a black beret with the SF badge in silver. Weapons and personal equipment are all of U.S. origin. Pocket patches are sometimes worn for each brigade: a lion on the special warfare patch; an eagle on the 3rd Brigade's; a dragon on the 5th's; a Pegasus on the 7th's; a winged cat on a parachute on the 9th's; a bat over a lightning bolt on the 11th's; and a panther on the 13th's.

Malaysia

Malaysian special forces have their beginnings in the Federation of Malaya Police, which raised the Police Field Force in the 1950s which played a major part in bringing the jungle war to a successful conclusion. Then, during the mid-1960s it was decided to form the "Special Service Group" with the early instructors being trained by the British Royal Marines. Malaysian special forces today consist of three elements: Grup Gerak Khas (GGK) – Army; *Pasukan Khas Laut* (Paskhal) – Navy; and *Pasukan Gerakan Khas* (PGK) – police.

Grup Gerak Khas
The *Grup Gerak Khas* (GGK = Special Service Group) consists of 11th, 21st and 22nd GGK Battalions and is the largest of the contemporary Malaysian special forces. Its mission is to two-fold, the first being to undertake operations in the enemy's rear in general war, by carrying out long-range patrols and ambushes, either on its own or in combination with guerrillas. Its second mission is to conduct unconventional warfare within the national territory. One of its greatest skills is in jungle warfare.

Pasukan Khas Laut
Pasukan Khas Laut (Paskhal = special naval unit) is the Royal Malaysian Navy's special force and was established in October 1980, as an off-shoot of the navy's Security Regiment which was responsible for the defense of harbor facilities and anchorages. Paskhal is a commando unit and is responsible for the defense

Mexico

Mexico's Force F, usually known as "the Zorros," is an all-volunteer unit of the Mexico City Police, which was formed in 1983 as a specialist unit to counter drug-related crime and armed gangsters, but has since also been tasked with counter-terrorist and hostage rescue missions. It is quite large, between 300-400 strong, and is divided into three special-to-task elements, responsible for explosive disposal, snipers and assault missions.

The Zorros unit consists of some 350 men divided into three sections: one

Netherlands

As with a number of colonial powers in Western Europe, the Netherlands found itself with a variety of problems in its colonies, notably in the Dutch East Indies (now Indonesia) in the post-war years, but these have now been resolved. Domestically, however, there are occasional problems arising from one or other of its immigrant communities, although mainstream Dutch life has seemed remarkably stable.

Royal Netherlands Marine Corps
The Royal Nehterlands Marine Corps has a long tradition of working closely with the British Royal Marines, and the *Amfibisch Verkennings Peloton* (= amphibious reconnaissance platoon) is similar in mission and structure to the British Special Boat Service (SBS). The Dutch unit is 25 strong and is divided into mission-oriented teams for boat-handling; underwater operations; and counter-terrorist operations. The unit is responsible for the security of Dutch passenger-carrying vessels and oil rigs in peacetime, and

of Malaysia's Exclusive Economic Zone (EEZ), which includes several islands in the Spratly group as well as Malaysia's coastal regions, which includes a large number of oil rigs (currently 31). One consequence of the latter mission is that the companies owning the rigs pay part of the costs of the unit, which has resulted in it having some excellent equipment. Paskhal is also involved in anti-piracy operations and is responsible for traditional maritime special forces missions, such as beach reconnaissance, attacking enemy shipping in harbours, and mine clearance.

Police
During the Emergency (1947-59) the Federation of Malaya Police maintained a number of para-military units as part of the "Police Field Force." Following independence this was redesignated the *Pasukan Polis Hutan* (PPH = police jungle unit). This consisted of several battalions, one of which was an elite unit, designated 69th Commando Battalion (although its popular nickname was "VAT 69" from the name of a respected brand of Scotch whisky).

The police also raised *Unit Tindakan Khas* (UTK) in the early 1970s which was a SWAT-type unit responsible for close-protection and operations against armed criminals. When the communist terrorists finally gave up in 1989 these police paramilitary forces had to reorientate themselves and in 1997 the jungle units (PPH) were redesignated *Pasukan Gerakan Am* (PGA) while VAT 69 and UTK were amalgamated into *Pasukan Gerakan Khas* (PGK).

---

s responsible for urban commando tasks, the second for EOD, and the third for snipers. The Zorros use a wide variety of weapons. The usual handgun is the Beretta 9mm, and other personal weapons are either Heckler & Koch MP5 SMG, or CAR-15/M16A2 and Heckler & Koch HKJ33 5.56mm assault rifles. Snipers use the venerable but still very effective Springfield M1903A4 0.30-06 sniper rifle, while Smith & Wesson 12-gauge shotguns are used for short-range work.

---

for intelligence gathering and sabotage missions in war; in many war scenarios it would come under the command and work as an integral part of the British SBS. A variety of weapons is used, including Glock and Browning pistols, Uzi and Heckler & Koch MP5 sub-machine guns, and the Steyr SSG sniping rifle.

It may seem a contradiction in terms that a country well-known for its flat, low-lying countryside should have a specialized mountain warfare unit, but the Dutch Marine Corps has a commitment to form part of a joint amphibious group with the British Royal Marines in general war, and the Netherlands has also accepted commitments in various peacekeeping forces, such as those in former Yugoslavia, all of which require mountaineering expertise. As a result the RNIMC formed a Mountain Leader Platoon in 1997 by consolidating all the existing qualified mountain leaders into one unit, which is similar in organisation, mission and skills to the British Royal Marines' Brigade Patrol Troop. ▶

▶ Bijzondere Bijstands Eenheid

The main Dutch counter-terrorist group is the *Bijzondere Bijstands Eenheid* (BBE = Special Support Unit) which is part of the Royal Dutch Marines' 1st Amphibious Combat Group, and is based at Doorn. The unit has two 33-man platoons, each organized into a small headquarters and four five-man teams. The unit includes the usual complement of specialists, such as snipers and explosives experts, but is also known to include psychologists, trained in communicating with terrorists, particularly in hostage-taking situations. Elements of the unit are on call at all times and are expected to reach any spot in the Netherlands within 90 minutes. The BBE is composed of volunteers from the Royal Dutch Marines who must complete the usual selection process, followed by a 48-week course.

In peacetime the BBE is part of the Dutch Amphibious Combat Group, but as soon as a terrorist incident occurs the BBE comes directly under the control of the Government Crisis Management team. The BBE has seen action on a number of occasions, including regaining control of a prison from armed Palestine terrorist prisoners (1977) and rescuing hostages from a train (also in 1977). Members of the BBE were in the Adriatic Sea ready to board vessels attempting to break the Serbian arms embargo in the early 1990s but were never used.

The BBE uses a variety of weapons, although it has a publicly declared policy of seeking to solve terrorist situations by non-violent means, wherever possible. Weapons used include the Colt Lawman .357 revolver or SIG-Sauer P-226 pistol, and the almost inevitable Heckler & Koch MP5 sub-machine gun. Snipers use either the Heckler & Koch G3 MSG or Steyr SSG.

Korps Commando Troepen

Korps Kommando Tropen (KCT = Commando Troops Corps), the Dutch Army's special forces regiment, is organized, selected trained and has missions similar to those of the British SAS. The KCT is currently undergoing a reorganisation at the completion of which it will comprise three special operations companies, a headquarters and support company, and a training company. The three "sabre" companies are designated 104th, 105th and 108th Special Operations

Right: The Royal Dutch Marines are one of the most efficient SF units in the NATO alliance.

Companies (SOC), of which 108 SOC has been an active regular unit since the early 1990s. SOCs 104 and 105, however, were in the reserves as *Waarnemings-en Verkennings Companien* (reconnaissance companies) until the recent reorganization brought them back into the regular order-of-battle. All three units are trained in conducting direct action, sabotage, and reconnaissance missions and their troops are skilled in airborne, airmobile, amphibious, arctic and mountain operations. Some troops have also undergone training in the use of powered hangliders. 108 SOC has seen action in Bosnia, apprehending war crimes suspects, and may also be active in Afghanistan.

Koninklijke Marechaussee
The *Koninklijke Marechaussee* (KMar = Royal Constabulary) maintains an elite ▶

▶ force, *Brigade Speciale Beveiliging-sopdrachten* (BSB = Special Protection Unit), which is responsible for providing bodyguards for Dutch VIPs and also acts as a SWAT team, as well as conducting covert intelligence operations.

The *Bijzondere Bijstand-seenheid Krijgsmacht* (BBEK = Armed Forces Special Assistance Unit) is the Military Police's SWAT team, which is responsible for dealing with attacks on Dutch military installations.

Civil Police
The national civil police force, *Regionale Politie*, maintains an elite, special intervention unit, the *Politie Bijzondere Bijstand-seenheid* (Police BBE = *Police Special Assistance Unit*). This is responsible for providing spe-cially trained marksmen and intervention teams though out the county.

Right: Dutch marines storm ashore from an LCA Mk 2; alongside are two canoes.

New Zealand

Special Air Service
The New Zealand Special Air Service Squadron was formed in 1954 to join the British and Rhodesian SAS in the anti-guerrilla campaign in Malaya (the "Emergency"). As in Rhodesia, the initial volunteers were taken straight from civilian life and 138 were accepted from a list of some 800. With 40 regular officers and NCOs, they were trained in New Zealand from June until November 1955 when the survivors were sent to Singapore to complete their parachute and jungle training. They soon deployed onto operations and spent 17 months out of the next two years in the jungle, killing 26 terrorists for the loss of just one of their own soldiers.

The squadron returned to New Zealand in November 1957 to be disbanded, but was resuscitated in August 1958. A troop of 30 men was sent to Korat in Thailand from May to September 1962 in support of SEATO. In 1963 the unit was redesignated 1st Ranger Squadron, New Zealand Special Air Service, and shortly afterwards the unit deployed to Borneo where it served, once again, along-side the British SAS. It also operated from time to time with Britain's SBS. 4 Troop NZSAS served in Vietnam from November 1968 to February 1971, where it served with the Australian SAS Squadron. The unit is now stationed near Auckland, New Zealand. It has five troops, a headquarters, and a separate small training establishment. Its task is to support New Zealand defense forces in their operations and, like the SAS in the United Kingdom, has a major commitment to counter-terrorist missions. The uniform is standard New Zealand Army, but with a sand-colored beret and cap-badge identical to those of the British Special Air Service.

Right: New Zealand SAS trooper at the moment his drogue parachute deploys. Although small, this unit is noted for its high efficiency and very tough training.

Poland

Grupa Reagowania Operacyjno Mobilnego

Grupa Reagowania Operacyjno Mobilnego (GROM), the Polish armed forces' counter-terrorist unit was formed in 1991 and consists of volunteers from *1 Pulk Komandosow Specalnego Przez-naczenia* (1 PSK = 1st Commando Regiment) and combat swimmers from 7th *Lujcyka* Naval Assault Division. The unit is estimated to have some 300 members, including women, the great majority of whom work in four-person teams. The operators are trained in counter-terrorist techniques, including hostage rescue, EOD and VIP protection. A number are trained as combat swimmers.

Despite their relatively recent appearance on the counter-terrorist scene, GROM participated in the USA's Operation Restore Democracy in Haiti in 1994, where one of their main roles was in VIP protection. It is also believed that approximately 50 members of GROM accompanied the Polish battalion to Bosnia. In one of their many successful operations, in June 1998 they successfully "snatched" a Bosnian national suspected of war crimes.

Weapons include Heckler & Koch MP5 sub-machine guns and the Polish-designed Tantal 5.45mm assault rifle. Sniper rifles are usually either the Mauser 86 or Heckler & Koch PSG.

Right: Polish GROM swimmers; note sea-horse badge.

Portugal

Grupo De Operacoes Especiais

Portugal took several years to absorb the lessons of the 1972 Munich Olympic Games disaster and did not start to form its *Grupo De Operacoes Especiais* (GOE) (= Special Operations Group) until 1979, with the unit becoming fully operational in 1983. It is a branch of the *Policia de Seguranca Publica* (Public Security Police) and was developed from an earlier unit, *Corpo de Intervençao* (Intervention Corps), which was then disbanded. The careful groundwork, most of it in close liaison with the British Special Air Service (SAS), paid off and the unit has established a fine reputation during its relatively short existence. It is believed that close ties with U.S. Delta and Germany's GSG 9 have been established, as well as with Israeli special forces.

The unit carries out recruiting at two-yearly intervals and personnel are all volunteers who must first undergo a rigorous two-week vetting and selection process before being allowed to start an intensive eight-month training course. This covers hostage-rescue techniques against targets such as aircraft, buildings, buses, and trains, as well as maritime assault and VIP protection. Current strength of the GOE is some 150, who are grouped into 25-man platoons. ▶

Right: Four RIBs of the Portuguese Marine Battalion; note sign "Fuzileiros" on bows.

▶   GOE's main tasks are counter-terrorist operations and personnel protection. The only known GOE operation was a hostage rescue attempt against a group of terrorists holed-up in the Turkish Embassy in Lisbon in 1983. This ended unsuccessfully because the terrorists blew themselves up, apparently by accident, before any assault could be made.

Weapons used include Heckler & Koch MP5 sub-machine guns and the same company's PSG-1 sniper rifle, although some Israeli weapons, such as the sniper version of the 7.62mm Galil, may also be used.

Destacamento De Accoes Especias

Destacamento de Accoes Especias (DAE = Detachment for Special Duties) is the elite reconnaissance unit of the Portuguese Marine Corps., which has also

Russian Federation

Spetsnaz

During the 1970s, when the Cold War was at its height, Western intelligence became aware of the existence of a new type of Soviet unit, known as "diversionary brigades." Today, although the Cold War is long since ended, such units are still part of the order-of-battle of the Russian Federation, although their missions have changed.

These troops, known as *Spetsialnoye nazranie* (*Spetsnaz* = special purpose troops) were raised as the troops of the *Glavnoe razvedyvatel'noe upravlenie* (GRU = main intelligence directorate [of the General Staff]) and in the 1980s numbered some 30,000. These were deployed: one *Spetsnaz* company per Army; one *Spetsnaz* regiment in each of the three "theaters of operations"; one Naval *Spetsnaz* brigade in each of the four Soviet Fleets; and an independent *Spetsnaz* brigade in most military districts of the USSR. There were also special *Spetsnaz* intelligence units, one to each Front and Fleet, for a total of 20.

A *Spetsnaz* company was 135 strong, normally operating in 15 independent teams, although they could also combine for specific missions. A *Spetsnaz* brigade was 1,000-1,300 strong and consisted of a headquarters, three or four battalions, a communications company, and supporting troops. It also included an anti-VIP company, composed of some 70-80 regular troops (ie, not conscripts) whose mission was to seek out, identify and kill enemy political and military leaders. A Naval *Spetsnaz* brigade had a headquarters, two to three battalions of combat swimmers, a parachute battalion, supporting units, and an anti-VIP company. It also had a group of midget submarines, designed to deliver combat swimmers to distant targets.

Some of the republics which broke away from the old Soviet Union either took over the *Spetsnaz* units within their borders or have converted parachute units to the *Spetsnaz* role. Within the Russian Federation *Spetsnaz* units are less well trained and equipped, at a lower strength, and at a lesser degree of readiness than during the 1970s and 1980s. Despite that, they continue to exist, although their numbers are not known for certain.

Naval *Spetsnaz* also continue to serve in the Northern, Baltic, Black Sea, and Pacific fleets. Most of these are subordinate to the Fleet commanders, but some are under the direct control of the Naval Commander-in-Chief in Moscow. Again, their manning levels are not known and it may be that, like other areas in the Russian armed forces, they are seriously under strength.

Although *Spetsnaz* units may be used for other purposes during peacetime, their primary role is to carry out strategic missions during the final days prior to war breaking out and in war itself. These wartime tasks would include: deep reconnaissance of strategic targets; the destruction of strategically important command-control-and-communications (C3) facilities; the destruction of been given responsibility for maritime counter-terrorist operations. It is a very small unit, currently comprising just two officers and eleven NCOs/marines, who are formed into three patrols of three men each plus a headquarters element, but there are plans to increase the total number to 28.

Two unusual pieces of equipment used by DAE are the Skua, an inflatable, outboard-powered assault boat which is designed to be deflated and hidden while an operation is in progress and then retlated for the exfiltration, and hang-gliders, which are used for operational insertions. DAE is one of the very few units to use either item.

DAE conducts regular training with other NATO special forces groups, such as the British Special Boat Service, German *Kampfschwimmerkompanie*, Dutch *Bijzondere Bijstands Eenheid* (BBE) and U.S. Navy SEALs.

Above: Russian airborne troops (note the blue beret) conduct unarmed combat training.

strategic weapons' delivery systems; demolition of important bridges and transportation routes; and the kidnaping or assassination of important military and political leaders. The aim would be to carry out such missions before the enemy could react and to add to the chaos and confusion as the enemy tried to place its troops on a war footing.

During the Soviet era, the existence of *Spetsnaz* was a closely guarded secret and individual troops were not allowed to admit membership, to the extent that army *Spetsnaz* wore standard airborne uniforms and insignia, while Naval *Spetsnaz* wore naval infantry uniforms and insignia. However, the Russian Federation now acknowledges the existence of *Spetsnaz* units and, as a result, special badges are worn, identifying such troops.

On operations the majority of Spetsnaz soldiers would carry a 5.45mm AKS- ▶

▶ 74 rifle and a 5.45mm PRI automatic pistol. All would also carry combat knives, which are specially designed for *Spetsnaz* troops. One such design is the NR-2, an ingenious device which in addition to the blade incorporates a short 7.62mm caliber barrel in the handle and is fired by clipping the scabbard and knife together to give some control. Quite when such a weapon would be used instead of a knife or a pistol is open to question. *Spetsnaz* troops are also trained in all types of foreign weapons.

Those joining *Spetsnaz* with no previous military experience must be given the normal recruit's basic training in discipline, marching, fieldcraft, weapon handling and range work. Once the recruit moves on to proper *Spetsnaz* training, however, the pressure intensifies:

- weapon handling, including the use of foreign weapons and marksmanship;
- physical fitness, with an emphasis on endurance and strength;
- tracking, patrolling, camouflage, and surveillance techniques, including survival in a variety of harsh environments;
- hand-to-hand combat, both unarmed and with knives (both hand-held and throwing), and assassination of designated targets;
- sabotage and demolitions;
- language training and prisoner interrogation;
- infiltration by air, including parachuting for fixed-wing aircraft, and exit from helicopters by parachute or ropes.

Naval *Spetsnaz* must, in addition, learn combat swimmer techniques, the use of underwater weapons, canoeing, arrival and exit over beaches, exit and entry to submerged submarines.

Other *Spetsnaz* Troops

During the 1970s and 1980s special operations troops became increasingly the vogue in various ministries of the (then) Soviet Union. Indeed, such was the large and disorganized nature and wastefulness of the Soviet system that similar bodies with similar missions were set up by different parts of the same ministry, particularly within the Committee for State Security (KGB) and the Ministry of Internal Affairs (MVD). These special troops went under the generic

Below: Russian Spetsnaz troops deplane from a Mil Mi-8 (Hip) armed helicopter in mountainous terrain.

Above: If war had broken out in Europe, Spetsnaz would have conducted urban operations, such as this, in Western cities.

title of *Spetsgruppe* and were paramilitary forces which received special training and indoctrination for a variety of missions. Many of these units served in a variety of roles in the war in Afghanistan but for most of them a defining moment seems to have been reached during the 1991 coup, when they were ▶

▶ forced to take sides, or at least to refuse to take action. After the coup had been defeated, President Yeltsin transferred most of them to his personal control but they have since been transferred yet again back to various ministries. Many of the groups have been involved in the recent conflicts in the Russian Federation, including Chech'nya.

Spetsgruppa "Al'fa" (= special group A) was set up by the KGB's Seventh Directorate in 1974 and appears to have been inspired by the British SAS and U.S. SFOD-D (Delta) as a counter-terrorist and hostage-rescue group. *Al'fa* is generally credited with being the unit that attacked the Presidential palace in Kabul, Afghanistan, on December 28 1980 and murdered President Hafizullah Amin and his family. *Al'fa* is now controlled by the FSB (*Federal'naia sluzhba bezopasnosti* = Federal Security Service) in general terms, equivalent to the USA's FBI. Current strength is estimated to be about 300, with the main group in Moscow and three smaller groups elsewhere in the federation.

Also raised by the KGB, but this time the First Chief Administration, was *Spetsgruppa Vympel* whose mission was to fullfil the KGB's wartime role of assassinations and kidnaping. After the collapse of the Soviet Union it was transferred to the MVD but is now with the FSB with a primary responsibility for a hostage rescue.

The Ministry of Internal Affairs also has at least two groups of special troops known as the *Omsn* (= black berets), which were originally raised to provide additional security and (if necessary) hostage rescue at the 1980 Moscow Olympics. Since then they have been used for counter-terrorist activities and defeating armed criminals, and are currently involved in campaigns against drug cultivation.

Symbolizing the disorganized nature of contemporary Russia is the GROM Security Company, which is a quasi-private organization working under exclusive contract to the Federal Government. GROM (the Russian word for "thunder" and with no relationship to the Polish group of the same name) is manned by former troops of the various KGB special forces and provides security for selected government personnel and buildings, as well as for trains and aircraft.

Naval Infantry

Russia's *morskaya pekhota* (= naval infantry) is graded as a "Guards" unit, and great emphasis is placed on the elite status this confers, which is reflected in its special uniform and accoutrements. Like many elite forces the Russian Naval Infantry has its own battlecry, "*Polundra*," which roughly means "Watch out below." As with the *Spteznaz* and other elements of the armed forces of the former Soviet Union, the Naval Infantry is now a shadow of its former self, but, nevertheless, it still exists.

The basic amphibious assault unit is the battalion group, and its likely composition was described in a Russian military journal as "A motorized infantry battalion detailed to operate as advanced detachment was reinforced with an artillery battery, an ATGM battery, AA, frogman and engineer platoons. It also included reconnaissance and obstacle-clearing parties, road-building teams, communications facilities, transport vehicles, and landing craft to perform transportation missions. The advanced detachment was to be supported by aviation, tactical airborne troops, support ships and minesweepers."

While some members of the Naval Infantry may be volunteers, most are conscripts, although, as befits its elite status as a "Guards" unit, it is allocated high quality men. Units and individuals are highly trained in amphibious operations and land warfare, and, like all marines, must also know something about life on board ship as well.

Physical training for the Black Beret is emphasized during routine unit training. Forty percent of the training program is devoted to wrestling, drill with the bayonet, and the techniques of knife attack. The training is identical for both officer and enlisted man. Marines are also required to undergo training in the Military Sports Complex and master the set of skills offered there, such as horizontal bar work; sprint in uniform; a cross country rush; a swim in uniform with assault rifle; and a longer version of the cross country rush.

In the platoon the officer, NCOs and most marines are armed with the AKM assault rifle, while the APC driver has the AKMS folding-stock version. Each squad also has an RPK machine gun and an anti-tank rocket launcher. Sniper teams are armed with the highly effective SVD 7.72mm Dragunov sniper rifle.

The uniform of the Naval Infantry is a combination of Army and Navy items, with a few unique embellishments of their own. Combat dress consists of black fatigues, with a "bush" type blouse and calf-length black leather boots. A black leather belt is also worn, with the appropriate fleet badge on the buckle. A horizontally striped blue and white T-shirt is standard with all forms of dress. The usual range of metal award brooches is worn, with all officers and men wearing the "Guards" badge. A round cloth badge with an embroidered anchor is worn on the left sleeve just above the elbow.

Various items of headgear are worn. In assault operations a black steel helmet is worn with a large five-pointed red star on the front, and a stenciled anchor inside a broken anchor on the left. On other occasions a soft black beret is worn with a small anchor badge above the left ear; the main badge is a large enameled naval badge for officers and a small red star for NCOs and marines.

The Naval Infantry would be of limited value without special-role shipping, and a whole range of purpose-built craft was developed during the Soviet era. Largest of these was the Ivan Rogov-class of 14,000-ton Landing Platform Dock (LPD), each of which was capable of carrying a complete battalion group with all its vehicles and supporting arms, but none of these remain in service. Some smaller Ropucha-class and Alligator-class Landing Ship Tanks (LST), both of some 4,500 tons displacement remain, together with a number of smaller vessels and air-cushion landing craft. ▶

Below: Combat swimmers from a Naval Infantry unit lead the way ashore in an amphibious landing exercise.

South Africa

Special Forces Brigade

Following the introduction of majority rule in 1994, the Republic of South Africa has become the major strategic power and the most powerful military force in sub-Saharan Africa. During the same period, the military forces have undergone a remarkable transformation as the former government and African National Congress (ANC) forces have fused into the new South African Defense Force (SADF). As in other areas, the SADF has not ditched the experiences of its predecessors, but rather to build on them and as a result the history of the previous South African units is relevant to today's Special Forces Brigade.

South Africa's first official special forces unit, 1 Reconnaissance Commando (1 Recce), was formed in October 1972, followed by 4 Recce (which was responsible for maritime operations) and 5 Recce in 1975. With three regiments in being, the special forces were now given their own headquarters and the direction of their activities was transferred from the Army to HQ Defense Force. The title of the headquarters was changed to "Reconnaissance Directorate" in 1991 and then only two years later, the entire organisation was redesignated 45 Parachute Brigade, and then in 1996 it a

Spain

For many years following its Civil War Spain held itself apart from the rest of Western Europe, but following the accession of King Juan Carlos and the restoration of democracy it has become increasingly integrated. Its primary defense commitment is to NATO, but it also has to deal with internal strife involving the long-running Basque separatist movement, which has frequently employed terrorists tactics, and also has a national commitment to the defense of its last two remaining enclaves on the North African coast at Ceuta and Melilla.

The Spanish armed forces and police maintain a number of special forces. Some of these are either earmarked or assigned to the *Fuerza de Accion Rapide* (FAR = rapid action force), which is part of NATO's Allied Rapid Reaction Corps (ARRC). Such special operation forces include the army's *Brigada Paracaidista* (BRIPAC = parachute brigade) and the Navy's *Unidad Especial de Buceadores de Combate* (UEBC = SEALs), but here two specific organizations will be covered: the Spanish Legion and the Garda Civil's *Unidad Especial de Intervencion* (UEI).

Spanish Legion

In contrast to the better-known French Foreign Legion, the Spanish Legion consists almost entirely (90 percent) of native Spaniards. Following the Moroccan War (1920-27), the Legion continued to guard Spain's remaining African possessions. These included two small enclaves – Melilla and Ceuta – in northern Morocco, where Spanish Legion units are still based today. Ultimately, the decolonization process played itself out, armed conflict erupted with the Algerian-backed Polisario Front, and by 1981 the last of the Legion's monuments commemorating African battles was dismantled. In recent years the Legion has been involved in operations in Bosnia, Croatia, Angola, Nicaragua, Haiti, El Salvador, and Guatemala.

The Spanish Legion is approximately 7,000 strong and is made up of *tercios*

Right: Looking down on a Spanish UEI trooper as he uses his MP5 to engage a target while suspended on his rope.

changed yet again, this time to the present organisation under the title "Special Forces Brigade" with the units designated "Special Forces Regiments." Today's SF Brigade consists of two active SF Regiments and a Maintenance Unit.

After meeting stringent preliminary requirements applicants must pass a selection test and stringent physical requirements. The volunteer must then pass the parachute course and Special Forces orientation course, before then being deemed ready to undergo the actual selection process, which is reputed to be among the toughest in the world. Only when all this has been passed does the volunteer start the proper training course, which includes segments on: bushcraft, which includes tracking and survival, obstacle crossing, and water orientation; plus military skills such as fighting in both rural and urban settings, sniping, ground/air cooperation, and demolitions. In addition, the volunteer will learn military free-fall parachuting using HALO/HAHO techniques, plus rappelling and fast-roping from helicopters. Finally, maritime training includes boat handling, underwater demolitions, swimming, diving, beach reconnaissance, and navigation.

▶ (regiments), each of which is named after a person famous in Spanish history. These are made up of four *banderas* (battalions), each of a number of companies, depending on the unit's role. In addition, Legion headquarters, stationed at Almeria, is responsible for the selection, training and administration of the Legion, but also provides the operational staff for *Brigada de la Legion Alfonso XIII*, which is committed to the FAR. This brigade would comprise VII, VIII and X Banderas, supported by artillery, logistics, and communications elements.

The permanent elements of the Legion are:

- *1st Tercio Gran Capitan* is stationed in the Spanish enclave of Melilla on the north African coast and consists of *I Bandera Legionaria Mecanizada* (1st Legion Mechanized Battalion), *II Bandera Legionaria Motorizada* (2nd Legion Motorized Battalion), each of three rifle companies, a headquarters company and a service support company. There is also an anti-tank company armed with MILAN missiles. Its primary mission is the defense of Melilla.
- *2nd Tercio Duque de Alba* is stationed at the second Spanish enclave of Ceuta. It is organized the same as 1st Tercio, with one mechanized battalion (V Bandera) and one motorized battalion and an anti-tank company.
- *3rd Tercio Juan de Austria* is stationed at Fuerteventura in the distant Canary Islands. It consists of VII and VIII Banderas and is earmarked for the FAR, although it would obviously take some time for it to return to the mainland prior to an operational redeployment.
- *4th Tercio Alejandro Farnesio*, which is assigned to the FAR, is stationed at Ronda, Malaga, and is composed of two banderas, one of which, X Bandera, is a parachute-assault unit. The second unit, XIX Bandera, has the additional title of *Bandera de Operaciones Especiales* (BOEL = special operations

Above right: Spanish legionnaire crawls through an assault course whilst under live fire from instructors.

Right: A smart, confident legionnaire guards the barrack gate; the Spanish Legion has an idiosyncratic but effective ethos.

Below: Spanish legionnaires machinegun team; the weapon is a Spanish-built version of the German 7.62mm MG3.

▶ battalion) and has amphibious, mountain, parachute and long-range patrolling capabilities.

The Spanish Legion uses basic infantry weapons, which include the 7.62 CETME Model 68 rifle, the 9mm Star Z-70B submachine gun, and the 60.7mm ECIA mortar. The Legion also has M41 and AMX-13 light tanks, and AML-90 light armored cars, as well as a number of American eight-ton trucks, British Land Rovers, and Nissan 4x4 field cars.

Enlisting in the Legion is an easy and relatively straightforward process. A passport will work, or the applicant need only certify to the information he gives. To enroll, he need only go to a military or government building, police station or civil guard station at any port, airport or city within Spanish national territory or its islands. After a thorough briefing, the candidate is given the option to quit; however, after passing a medical examination and upon being accepted, he incurs a minimum obligation of three years a term he can expand to four or five years if desired. Training is short, intensive and strict. The Legion's objective is to instill basic military skills in as short a time as possible the usual training period is three months. It takes place at Ronda and includes drill, physical courses and familiarization with the traditions and disciplines of the Legion. Discipline is harsh and based on fear. Offenders are liable to find themselves in prison (not a desirable thing since prisoners sleep on concrete slabs and can be beaten at whim by the guards), or the recipient of a rain of blows to the head for poor shooting at a standard target. All things being relative, however, this punishment is mild compared to earlier times when, under some circumstances and for certain offenses, the legionnaire could be shot.

Much time is devoted in the field to the route march. Long distances are covered over rough terrain – either in light order or with heavy pack, depending

upon the individual commander. The typical legionnaire, however, is heavily dependent upon his officers for such basic things as navigation, tactics and first aid in the field. His training in advanced weaponry and modern forms of warfare is negligible, something that may change with the anticipated modernization of the Army. To become an officer, it is first necessary to become a Spanish citizen. The highest rank to which one can be promoted as a legionnaire is that of major.

Green is the traditional color of the Legion's uniform. The caps are specially designed and have a small red tassle. Short sleeve blouses are worn, which are open at the collar. Breeches are like jodhpurs, and legionnaires wear gauntleted gloves and white-lined capes with a fur collar and hood for cold nights. Webbing straps and belts are used instead of the leather versions found in the rest of the Spanish Army.

Unidad Especial de Intervencion

The *Unidad Especial de Intervencion* (UEI = Special Intervention Unit) was formed in February 1982 and is the elite unit of the *Guarda Civil* and is the country's premier counter-terrorist unit. It is responsible for countering any foreign terrorists who may commit crimes on Spanish territory, but also has a major domestic commitment in the continuing war against the Basque separatist movement, ETA. Although its strength is secret it is believed to be in the region of 50 men, all volunteers from the *Guarda Civil* who have passed stringent selection tests.

The troops wear normal *Guarda Civil* uniforms, except when on operations, when they will usually wear the black Nomex coveralls adopted by most counter-terrorist squads. Weapons are the usual mixture of Uzis, plus Heckler & Koch and Mauser sniper rifles.

Left: Members of the Grupo Especiale para los Operaciones (GEO), Spain's leading counterterrorist unit, which is manned by some 70 carefully selected volunteers from the national police force.

Sweden

Two major factors effect the special forces scene in Sweden, the first being the country's long-standing policy of "active neutrality," which continues despite the end of the Cold War. This means that the country has strong and well-equipped armed forces, whose overall strategy is one of homeland defence; there is no question of Swedish forces deploying abroad. The second factor is that international terrorism takes no account of eithe

national boundaries or neutrality, which means that the Swedish people are as vulnerable to terrorist attack as are those of any other country in the ▶ world.

Below: Sweden has a very long coastline, for whose defense special forces are trained and special equipment procured.

▶ **Försvarsmaktens Särskilda Skyddsgrupp**

Försvarsmaktens Särskilda Skyddsgrupp (SSG - Special Protection Group formed in the early 1990s, is very unusual in that it is composed entirely c officers taken from the Navy, Army or Air Force. Virtually nothing is know about the size or organization of the SSG, except that it is a joint service uni responsible directly to the Chief of Defense Staff. Its mission is to provid bodyguards for the most senior officers in the Swedish Armed Forces, t undertake hostage rescue operations and to undertake short-term protection c critical buildings for specific purposes (eg, a high-level conference). Applicant have completed several years service as commissioned officers and must hav already undergone Ranger training. Once accepted, they undergo training i parachuting, diving, amphibious operations, advanced marksmanship, and clos protection (bodyguard) duties. They are then required to undertake furthe individual training in specializations such as combat diving, sniping, explosives communications, or combat medicine.

Fallskarmsjagarna

The Army's *Fällskärmsjägarna* (= Airborne Rangers) are trained to undertak reconnaissance and direct action missions deep in the enemy's rear areas. The operate in five-man teams and are trained to be capable of operating for up 30 days without outside help or support. The training course is 15 months lon for soldiers with an additional 2.5 months for NCOs. The men are trained undertake operations in any all types of Scandinavian environment fror mountains and snow, to coastal. They carry standard Swedish army weapon: including the Swedish Ak-5 assault rifle and the Ak-5b sniper version, and Ks M/90 light machine gun.

Militärpolisjägarna

Militärpolisjägarna (= Military Police Rangers) were formed in the late 1990s undertake counter-terrorist operations either inside or in the vicinity of Swedis Army installations.

Marines

The Swedish Marine Corps provides onc amphibious brigade composed of 1: and 4th *Amfibieregementen* (Amf 1/ Amf 4 – amphibious regiments). Togethe they in wartime form the 1st Amphibian Brigade) (Amphibian Regiments which are trained to conduct amphibious operations along the country's lor Baltic coastline. Their primary missions are to conduct amphibious operation and to repel enemy amphibious assaults.

Kustjägarna

The *Kustjägarna* (KJ = Coastal Rangers) are trained for operations along the lor and vulnerable Baltic coastline and in particular among the many offshor islands in the Swedish archipelago. The force also includes assault divers conduct underwater reconnaissance missions. There are two Coastal Rang companies in every amphibious battalion. The KJ makes extensive use of th very effective Combat Boat 90 which was specifically designed for suc operations, but can also use kayaks or helicopters. In addition, the KJ a trained to attack enemy ships and to sabotage enemy installations. The weapons are primarily those used by the rest of the Swedish armed forces.

Attackdykarna (A-dyk = Attack Divers) are the Royal Swedish Navy's eli combat swimmer unit and is similar in mission and training to U.S. Navy SEAL and the British SBS. They are trained to attack enemy shipping; conduct beac reconnaissance and hydrographic surveys; and to carry out small-sca amphibious raids and sabotage operations. Volunteers for the A-dyk a recruited from the ranks of the Navy's elite Coastal Ranger units.

Bassäk (= Naval Counter SOF Company) is the Swedish Navy's count

SOF unit. It is company sized and is tasked with protecting Swedish naval installations from attack by hostile forces. The unit conducts security and reconnaissance patrols using specially trained dog teams, small boats, and in some situations combat divers.

Flygbasjägarna

The *Flygbasjägarna* (FBJ = Air Force Rangers) were formed in the early 1980s with the primary mission of guarding the dispersed sites used by Swedish military aircraft in time of war. On receipt of a threat warning these aircraft immediately fly to specially prepared "mini-bases" which use widened roads or runways and which obviously require ground protection. This is provided by the FBJ, which is organised into Ranger-trained, platoon size units assisted by combat dogs.

Ordningspolisens Nationella Insatsstyrka

Sweden's *Ordningspolisens Nationella Insatsstyrka* (ONI = National Police Counter-Terrorist Unit) is manned by serving policemen, normally those already serving with the Stockholm (the Swedish capital) SWAT teams. ONI has 48 members divided into five groups: two Assault Groups; one Intelligence/Liaison Group; one Sniper Support Group and one Command/Control Group. ONI is based in Stockholm and comes under control of the Prime Minister, and who must personally give authorisation if it is proposed to use armed force against terrorists. ONI's tactical training is similar to other counter-terrorist teams and most of the unit's training concerns urban hostage rescue, with particular emphasis on trying to achieve a peaceful outcome through negotiation. Weapons include Sig-Sauer P226 automatic pistols, various models of the Heckler & Koch MP5 SMG and the PSG 90 7.62mm sniper rifle.

Below: Swedish special forces disembark from a Stridsbat-90H fast landing craft. The cabin is aft and troops pass under the bridge and up steps to exit over the bow, as shown here.

Thailand

Army

Since the early 1980s the Royal Thai Army has had a special forces/counter terrorist unit, with the somewhat obscure designation of 4th Battalion of the 1st Infantry Regiment. This unit's primary mission is VIP protection. The unit is some 140 strong and is commanded by a lieutenant-colonel.

Navy SEALs

In 1956 the Royal Thai Navy formed a combat diver unit in 1956, whose tasks were virtually identical with those of a U.S. Navy Underwater demolition Team (UDT). Nine years later, the capability was expanded and a new SEAL element was established in addition to the UDT team. The SEAL team is responsible for intelligence and reconnaissance missions, together with maritime counter terrorist missions, while the UDTs is responsible for underwater demolition and obstacle clearance operations in support of Thai Marine Corps' amphibious operations. Selection for both teams is rigorous and training lasts for six months, ending with a basic airborne course.

SEAL teams have been involved in several incidents on the Cambodian border, and have also carried out anti-piracy operations in the Gulf of Thailand.

Turkey

Turkey has large armed forces to face up to a number of major threats, including shared borders with Armenia, Azerbajan, Bulgaria, Georgia, Greece, Iran and Syria, none of them comfortable neighbors. Particular problems are the continuing activities of Kurdish separatists in the east and confrontation with Greece on the island of Cyprus as well as in the Mediterranean and Aegean seas. Turkey's armed forces are well over 500,000 strong and it is not surprising that these should include a large number of special forces.

There have been few occasions when Turkish special forces have become visible to the general public. One was the arrest of Kurdish dissident, Abdullah Occalan, in Kenya and his extradition to Turkey in February 1999, when he was seen to be escorted by armed men wearing black balaclavas. The other occasion is the recent announcement that some 90 men of the Turkish special forces are operating in Afghanistan. In neither the Occalan arrest nor the Afghanistan operation has the identity of the specific Turkish unit been disclosed.

Army

The Turkish Army operates at least one counter-terrorist special force battalion some 150 strong. It is highly secretive, but can be assumed to have similar characteristics and capabilities to British SAS and U.S. Delta. There are also three commando brigades (note that these are Army and not Navy units):
- 1st Commando Brigade, whose mission is described as Su Alti Savunma (SAS = underwater defense). This unit is normally based in Kayseri, but has recently operated in Southeast Anatolia against separatist terrorists.
- 2nd Commando Brigade, whose mission is described as Su Alti Taaruz (SAT = underwater attack) is based at Bolu.
- 3rd Commando Brigade is responsible for conventional amphibious operations, including infiltration from the sea, intelligence gathering, and sabotage. It is based at Foca and Izmir and its wartime missions could include operations against island targets – eg, in the Aegean and Mediterranean.

he SEALs currently consist of some 150 men, who are divided into two teams, ach of four platoons. Weapons are almost exclusively of U.S. origin, except for leckler & Koch MP5 series SMGs.

Marine Reconnaissance Battalion

A Marine Corps amphibious reconnaissance company was raised in 1965 and his unit deployed a small group to Laos in 1972. In 1978 the company was xpanded into its present battalion size. The battalion comprises three econnaissance companies (one amphibious, two land-based), plus a counter-errorist platoon and a war dog platoon. Volunteers for the battalion come from erving marines, who, having been selected, then undergo a three month ourse. They must also qualify as parachutists.

Royal Thai Air Force Commando Company

his 100 man unit, part of the Royal Thai Air Force's Special Combat Operations quadron, has been in existence since the late 1970s. They are based near Don Muang Airport and provide anti-hijacking capabilities. They have three assault latoons, each divided into two smaller sections.

Right: Turkish amphibious troops come ashore in a rubber dinghy. Turkey has a very long coastline facing the Black, Aegean and Mediterranean seas, the latter two being potential areas of conflict.

Navy

he Turkish Navy has an Amphibious Marine Brigade whose primary mission is nfiltration and sabotage/intelligence gathering behind enemy lines, with ossible wartime targets including airfields and communications centers. The rigade is based in Foca/Izmir.

Air Force

here are no known air force special forces units, but a number of Turkish air orce helicopters, including UH-60 Blackhawks and AS-90 Cougars, are fitted for CSAR (Combat Search And Rescue) missions and are also used for covert nsertion and extraction.

Ozel Jandarma Komando Bolugu

Ozel Jandarma Komando Bolugu (OJKB) is a police special forces unit, whose missions include counterterrorist operations and hostage rescue, as well as high-threat criminal actions. Volunteers for the unit receive extensive training at he Jandarma (police) training establishment at Foca and also from the Army. he unit comprises three companies, one assigned to each of the country's hree regions, but they can also be tasked direct from Police Headquarters in Ankara.

United Kingdom

Gurkhas

The bonds which link the legendary Gurkhas from the hills of the Himalaya kingdom of Nepal with the British Army are slightly difficult to understand, bu their strength is self-evident. When the British were expanding their Empire India in the early 19th Century, they fought two short wars against the Gurkha the first in 1813, the second in 1816. Both resulted in very hard-won Britis victories, but both sides also gained considerable mutual respect for eac other's martial qualities, which resulted in three battalions of Gurkhas beir raised for service in the British Indian Army. Gurkhas have served the Britis Crown ever since, with the original three battalions expanding and changir titles over the years, but for most of the time there have been ten regimen (each with varying numbers of battalions). The biggest change of all came 1947 when the British left India and it was agreed to split the regiments ar their assets between the newly independent Indian Army and the British Arm As a result, the 1st, 4th, 5th, 8th and 9th Gurkha Rifles went to the Indian Arm (where they still serve), while the balance, the 2nd, 6th, 7th, and 10th Gurkh Rifles, transferred to the British Army.

These British Gurkhas served throughout the Malayan Emergency (194 1959) as 17th Gurkha Infantry Division and then in the Brunei Revolt and th Indonesian "Confrontation" campaign in North Borneo. Following the Britis withdrawal from Malaysia the main Gurkha base was moved to Hong Kon where Gurkha battalions provided most of the garrison; there was also or

Below: Although the Gurkhas come from the mountains of Nepal, these hardy soldiers have made the jungle their own.

bove: Gurkha paratrooper of 2nd Battalion, The Parachute Regiment on atrol in Afghanistan in 2001.

urkha battalion in Brunei and another in the UK. This organization lasted until e British withdrawal from Hong Kong in 1997 and it was in anticipation of this at the Gurkhas were again reduced in strength, this time to some 3,700 men. this reorganization a new "large" regiment – the Royal Gurkha Rifles – was rmed, with the 2nd and 6th Gurkha Rifles amalgamating to form 1st Battalion oyal Gurkha Rifles (1RGR), while 7th and 10th Gurkha Rifles amalgamated to rm 2nd Battalion Royal Gurkha Rifles (2RGR).

This organization has remained unchanged and is still in force today. All ▶

▶ British Gurkha administrative elements are now in the UK and the tw
battalions of the Royal Gurkha Rifles alternate between a new purpose-bu
barracks in Folkestone, Kent, and the Sultanate of Brunei, although both alway
have at least part (sometimes the whole) of the unit away from base c
peacekeeping duties. There are also independent demonstration companies .
the Royal Military Academy Sandhurst and the Infantry Training Center
Wales, and reinforcement companies are also provided from time to time
bolster the strength of British infantry battalions. The Gurkha Engineer
Queen's Gurkha Signals and Gurkha Transport Regiment are also now based
the UK, all consisting of two squadrons.

Over recent years Gurkha units have served in the Falklands campaign, th
Gulf War, East Timor, Sierra Leone, Kosovo and Bosnia. There will doubtless b
many more campaigns for these eager warriors to take part in.

1 and 2 RGR are organized as standard British Army infantry battalions, bu
with some minor amendments to comply with regimental custom and traditio
The infantry battalions have very few British officers, the great majority bein
Queen's Gurkha Officers who have worked their way up through the ranks
Warrant Officer before being commissioned. The most senior is the Gurkh
Major, a figure of immense prestige, who is the Commanding Officer's advis
on all Gurkha matters.

Selection and Training

Gurkhas are recruited from the hill tribesmen in the Himalayan kingdom
Nepal. They are signed up at the age of 17 by itinerant gallah-wallahs (form
Gurkhas soldiers) who receive a bounty for each successful sign-up) and ser
a minimum commitment of 15 years, with recruit intakes arriving in the UK
January of every year to begin training. Instead of being called by nam
Gurkhas are referred to by serial numbers – the last two digits of this numb
becoming their "nicknames." Gurkha tribal names are left behind for the ne
life. The secret of their training and fortitude is a concept called kaida, whic
translates into a system of order, ritual, and loyalty to officers and each oth
that is unquestioned. As might be expected, boot camp is rigorous an
transforms the Gurkha recruit in nine months from an often illiterate an
barefoot mountain tribesman into a solid member of one of the world's mo
unusual – and ferocious – fighting forces.

Uniform and Weapons

Gurkhas wear their own variations of British Army uniform. Combat kit
standard camouflage pattern smock and trousers, with green canvas webbin
except, of course, for the addition of the famous kukri weapon. Parade unifor
is rifle-green in temperate climates and white in the tropics, with black, pater
leather waist belts for soldiers and cross-belts for officers. Buttons and badge
are black. Soldiers wear a black pill-box hat on parade or the Gurkha slouch-ha
and a green beret in other forms of dress.

The kukri is the subject of many myths. The knives come in various size
but the dog-legged shape is constant. The rear edge is thick and blunt, makir
the knife quite heavy, but the cutting-edge is razor sharp. The kukri is in no wa
a throwing knife, but it is quite excellent for hand-to-hand fighting and is th
Gurkhas' preferred close-combat weapon. It is therefore always carried in w
and there are many stories of its use against Germans, Japanese, and Malaya
Communists, to mention but a few of the Gurkhas' more recent enemies, whi
simple fear of its imminent use has caused many an enemy to surrender.

The Gurkhas' Future

It would be idle to deny that these Gurkha regiments are a legacy of Britain
Imperial past, but it would be a very sad day were the ties to be severe
between these legendary soldiers and the British Crown they have served s

Above: British Gurkha troops rapelling from a U.S. Army UH-1 during training at Fort Lewis in Washington State, USA.

well. Nowhere is the depth of this unique relationship more clearly described than in (of all places) the introduction to a Nepali language dictionary compiled by Sir Ralph Turner some 90 years ago: "As I write these last words, my thoughts return to you who were my comrades, the stubborn and indomitable peasants of Nepal. Once more I hear the laughter with which you greeted every hardship. Once more I see you in your bivouacs or about your fires, on forced march or in the trenches, now shivering with wet and cold, now scorched by a pitiless and burning sun. Uncomplaining, you endure hunger and thirst and wounds, and at last your unwavering lines disappear into the smoke and wrath ▶

▶ of battle. Bravest of the brave, most generous of the generous, never had a country more faithful friends than you." Or, in the less flowery words of a recent Gurkha commander, "They are just bloody good soldiers."

The Parachute Regiment

The very name of The Parachute Regiment (the "Paras") has come to signify both a type of soldiering and a certain "style" S dramatic, forceful and with panache, Paratroops would, it seems, always need to be fighting against heavy odds and either succeed brilliantly or suffer glorious defeats: the one performance that is never allowed is an indifferent one. It was Winston Churchill who demanded that a slightly reluctant War Office establish a corps of parachutists on the German model, and after a somewhat hesitant start the first unit was formed in late 1940. During the remainder of the war "the paras established a splendid reputation, with their greatest achievement being the Battle of Arnhem in 1944.

There was a major reduction in parachute troops in the immediate postwar years, and again in the 1960s and 1970s. 16th Parachute Brigade existed in Aldershot from 1949 to 1977 when it was redesignated 6th Field Force in one of the British Army's endless series of reorganizations, and although three regular and one territorial battalions remained, only one regular battalion was

Above right: British paratrooper and RPG-7-armed Afghan mount a joint security guard in Kabul, Afghanistan.

Right: Despite the tactical setting, these British paratroopers still wear their red berets, symbol of their famous unit.

Below: Falklands, 1982; men of 2 Para on a cold, cloudy morning, with their 7.62mm GPMG ready for instant action.

Below right: British paratroops are always among the first to be called into action whenever a new crisis occurs.

▶ actually organized and equipped for the parachute role. On January 1, 1982, 6th Field Force became 5 Infantry Brigade and included among its units 2nd and 3rd Battalions The Parachute Regiment, and when the Falklands War broke out in 1982, these two battalions were attached to 3 Commando Brigade and sent south with the Marines. In the Falklands these two units added to their already formidable reputation, and at Goose Green 550 men of 2 Para took on 1,400 Argentines and defeated them utterly, even though their commanding officer, Lt. Col. "H" Jones, died in the battle. In the finest Para tradition he died at the head of his men, personally leading an attack against a machine gun position that was holding up the entire attack. He was posthumously awarded the Victoria Cross.

In December 1982 the (then) British Secretary of State for Defence, Michael Heseltine, went to Aldershot to announce in person that 5 Infantry Brigade was to be redesignated 5 Airborne Brigade forthwith. The long-awaited British Strategic Defence Review was published in July 1998 and, as expected, The Parachute Regiment featured, although the effects of the Review on it were much less significant than had been feared in some quarters. The Review stated that "we can no longer identify circumstances in which Britain would need to undertake parachute operations at greater than battalion-group level. Maintaining a smaller battalion-level capability, which confers important operataional flexibility, and modernizing the role of the remainder of The Parachute Regiment to take advantage of their unique skills and ethos, have been central to the Review." As a result, a new 24 Airmobile Brigade was created, but the title has since been changed yet again, this time to 16 Air Assault Brigade.

Organization

There are currently three battalions of The Parachute Regiment in the British Regular Army (1, 2 and 3 Para), and a further battalion in the Territorial Army (4 Para). One of the regular battalions is part of 16 Air Assault Brigade, where it forms the Airborne Battle Group (ABBG), and is required to be ready to undertake operations anywhere in the world and at very short notice. A parachute battalion is organized similarly to a standard infantry battalion, with three rifle companies and a support company. However, it has a far lighter scale of transport. Because the battalion depends on the physical fitness and fighting efficiency of the men, more emphasis is placed upon selection and effective training.

Selection and Training

All officers and men must volunteer for The Parachute Regiment. Prospective recruits undergo thorough mental, educational, and psychometric tests – and then only the most educationally and mentally alert are selected as candidates for the Regiment. The extremely arduous training course of 23 weeks is similar in many ways to that for Royal Marine Commandos. The first eight weeks follow the lines of what is laid down for recruits for the Army as a whole: drill, weapons training, everything on the double, plenty of exercise, and map reading. Then, in the 12th week comes the dreaded "P Company" week, in which members are selected for further training and about 80 percent of the recruits who have gone this far will pass. Following completion of training, the men, who pride themselves on being the "Spearhead of the Army" and on their ability to fight in any terrain and climate, will join their battalions. Only 30 percent of those who started the course will have gained their "wings."

Weapons and Equipment

When there was an independent parachute force (16 Parachute Brigade) there was sufficient demand for it to be economical to produce special equipment for paratroop units. When the commitment was reduced in the past few years to just one battalion in the parachute role, with virtually no back-up from

Above: British troops on patrol in Afghanistan, the first time their army had been in the country for some 80 years.

arachute-trained and -equipped supporting arms and services, such special quipment virtually disappeared. Thus, UK parachute units currently use tandard British Army weapons and equipment, such as the 5.56mm L70A1 ndividual Weapon, an excellent weapon using the "bull-pup" design. This rifle neat, compact and well-balanced and has proved very popular in service. bviously, The Parachute Regiment is also able to take full advantage of ▶

▶ advanced weaponry and equipment as it enters service with the British Army.

Uniforms
The British paratroops' red beret has been adopted around the world and has given rise to their nicknames of "The Red Devils" and "The Red Berets." (History has it that Major-General Browning and another general were arguing over the color of a beret for the paratroops and, unable to agree, they turned to the nearest soldier to ask his views. "Red, sir," came the instant answer.) The red beret can be worn only by members of The Parachute Regiment (throughout their service) and by members of other corps who are parachute qualified, but only when on service with a parachute unit. The sleeve badge is a winged Pegasus.

Royal Marines Special Boat Service
To a large extent, the whole of the 7, 000 Royal Marines is an elite force in itself; every Marine would certainly claim it so. However, within the Royal Marines there are a number of smaller and more select groups of which the best known and most highly trained is the Special Boat Service (SBS), the Royal Marines equivalent to the British Army's Special Air Service (SAS). This unit has its roots in the special units raised in World War II for raiding and reconnaissance on the shores of the European mainland. Despite many cutbacks and amalgamations, however, the techniques evolved so painfully in war were preserved in peace and the Amphibious School of the Royal Marines at Eastney (now at Poole in Dorset) included a "Small Raids Wing," which was later redesignated the "Special Boat Company" then the "Special Boat Squadron," but it is known as the "Special Boat Service."

Headquarters Special Boat Service, which controls the activities of the Special Boat Squadrons, itself comes under the control of the joint-Service Director Special Forces Group, whose headquarters are in London. When deployed, SBS sections can come under the operational command of Commando units, but can also act autonomously on special tasks, but all these activities and organization are always secret. The mission of the SBS can roughly be equated with that of the *Spetsnaz* in the Russian Federation and the SEALs in the U.S. Navy. They are responsible for coastal sabotage operations and ground, surface, or underwater reconnaissance of potential landing beaches and enemy coastal facilities. They also have particular responsibility for security of Britain's off-shore oil and gas rigs. The headquarters is now located

Left: Combat swimmers of Britain's elite SBS emerge from the hatch of a submarine during training. The ability to deliver such men on to a hostile shore is invaluable and was used several times during the 1982 Falklands War.

Above: Men of the British Special Boat Service (SBS) in a Klepper lightweight, collapsible, two-man canoe.

at Whale Island in Portsmouth, Hampshire. The SBS is organized into three squadrons. C Squadron consists of swimmer-canoeists, S Squadron is responsible for handling small boats, mini-submarines and swimmer delivery vehicles, while M Squadron is the maritime counter-terrorist unit and includes "Black Troop."

The SBS has seen action in Oman, Borneo, the Falklands War, the Gulf War, former Yugoslavia and recently in Afghanistan. In the Falklands War, the SBS were early ashore on South Georgia, having flown from the UK in a C-130 and then parachuted to a submarine in the South Atlantic. The submarine took them close inshore and they then completed their long journey in inflatable Gemini boats. The SBS is also rumored to have put patrols ashore on the Argentine mainland, landing from the conventional submarine, HMS *Onyx*, although this has never been confirmed. The SBS and SAS operated on the Falkland Islands 12 days before the amphibious landings, and the SBS reconnoitered the actual landing sites at San Carlos Bay. They welcomed the first landing-craft to reach the shore, and also silenced the Argentinian outpost on Fanning Head, overlooking the landings.

The way in which the SBS fits in with the much larger SAS organization is a matter for speculation, particularly as the SAS is known to have a Boat Troop, with similar equipment and capabilities to the SBS. One suggested demarcation between the two is that the SBS is responsible for operations from the high-water mark to a line 12 miles (19km) inland, beyond which is an SAS responsibility. This does not explain, however, why SBS patrols were operating in Afghanistan in late 2001/early 2002. Nevertheless, there is no known friction between the two units, and it must therefore be assumed that the responsibilities are not a problem in practice.

Selection and Training

Recruitment to the SBS is from volunteers who have already had two years' ▶

▶ service in the Royal Marine Commandos. All such officer and Marine volunteers undergo the usual physical and psychological tests, followed by a two-week selection test, which is reputed to "weed-out" approximately 90 percent of the applicants. Those who pass then go on a one-year training course in reconnaissance, demolitions, communications, diving, and use of the Klepper canoe or Gemini craft. One of many tests requires two-man teams to paddle a canoe 30 miles in the open sea, and in another they mast carry their canoe 10 miles cross-country. On completion they are awarded the much coveted "Swimmer Canoeist Grade 3" badge and then proceed on a four-week parachute course. Only then are they posted to an operational Special Boat Section. SBS officers and Marines are not compelled to leave the SBS after a set period, but like some other special forces they are usually forced to leave if they wish to obtain promotion past a certain rank.

One of the most famous former members of the SBS is Lord Ashdown, who as "Paddy" Ashdown went into politics and became the leader of the Liberal Democrat Party in the British Parliament. Unlike the six Israelis former special forces men, however, he never became Prime Minister.

Uniforms
The SBS wear standard Royal Marine uniform and the Commando green beret. The only indication in parade and barrack dress that a man belongs to the SBS is the wearing of Royal Marine parachuting wings on the right shoulder and of the "Swimmer Canoeist" badge on the right forearm. The latter has a crown above the letters "SC" flanked by laurel leaves. In parade dress both badges are embroidered in gold on a black backing. Officers of the SBS wear the wings, but not the "SC" badge (even though they are qualified to wear it by having passed the course).

Weapons and Equipment
The SBS operates in four-man "half sections" and their men are usually armed with the U.S. MI6A2 Armalite rifle and M203 grenade launchers, although a special silenced version of the Heckler & Koch MP5 is also used. Included in the patrol's equipment are plastic explosives, laser designators, and burst-transmission radios.

SBS reconnaissance patrols travel light and have three-layered kits (escape-and-evasion, belt, and pack). Very little is known about the escape-and-evasion kit, which presumably has survival devices and equipment hidden in clothing and other equipment, A handgun, knife, fishing line, water bottles, snares, and a food pouch are in the belt kit. The pack kit contains some extra food, dry clothing and a waterproof poncho.

Boats used by the SBS include paddle-boards (akin to surfboards), specially produced Klepper Mark 13 collapsible boats, and the somewhat larger Gemini boats, inflatables powered by 40bhp outboard motors. The SBS can also be transported by "Rigid Raider" boats, a militarized version of the glassfiber "Dory" fishing-boat, powered by outboards of up to 140bhp, operated by the specialists of the Royal Marines' Rigid Raider Squadron, with the capacity to carry ten personnel. There is also the "Kestrel," a three-man collapsible, which is small enough to be attached to the leg of a parachutist; powered by a 9.5hp motor, which is dropped separately, the Kestrel is inflated by carbon dioxide. Largest of the SBS's boats are a small number of very fast, covert operations boats (LCP), built by Halmatic, Havant, and designed by the Italian racing-boat designer, Fabio Buzzi. They are capable of some 45-50kt or of moving extremely quietly at very low speed. Few details have been revealed, but photographs suggest a crew of two and up to eight passengers.

Special Air Service
The SAS was formed early in World War II during the British "Desert

Above: Combat swimmer of the British SAS approaches a simulated target using special devices to climb the thin rope.

Campaign" in North Africa, with the appropriate motto "Who Dares Wins" at a time when many "special" units were being raised. Known originally as "L Detachment," the unit grew to 390 men in 1942 and was redesignated lst Special Air Service Regiment (1SAS). After various reorganizations and a period of further growth, the SAS operated in Sicily and Italy, and also raised an SAS Brigade in Scotland in January 1944, which consist of two British regiments (1 and 2SAS), two French regiments (3 and 4SAS), a Belgian ▶

▶ squadron (later 5SAS), and a signal squadron.

At the end of the war in Europe the British Army rushed to divest itself of "private armies," the SAS among them, and it appeared that it had washed its hands of the "SAS concept" forever. It takes more than that to keep a good idea down, however, and within months it was decided that there would be a future role for SAS-type activities. This led to the conversion of a Territorial Army (TA) unit, "The Artists' Rifles," into 21st Special Air Service Regiment (21SAS) (Artists) (Volunteers), the number 21 being obtained (so it is said) by combining and reversing the numbers of the two British wartime SAS regiments (1 and 2SAS)!

Meanwhile the British were fighting the Malayan "Emergency" (1948-60) on the far side of the world, where again a need for a clandestine, deep penetration force was required. This gave rise to the "Malayan Scouts (Special Air Service)" which started as a single company but quickly built up to regimental size. In 1952, the Malayan Scouts were redesignated 22nd Special Air Service Regiment (22SAS), thus marking the official return of the SAS to the British Army's regular army's order of battle. The SAS carried out a series of very successful operations in Malaya, following which they moved to the UK where, after a short period in Malvern, they settled down in Sterling Lines, Hereford.

By now the regiment had been reduced to an HQ and two "sabre" squadrons, but the Far East soon beckoned again and men deployed to northern Borneo to take part in the "Confrontation Campaign" against Indonesian infiltrators. The first SAS squadron arrived there in January 1963 and their success led to more demands for the SAS's services and the third squadron was re-formed in mid-1963. All three were involved in campaigns in Borneo and Aden during 1964-66 in a period known in the regiment as the "happy time." By 1967, these two wars were over and the SAS had a short period of consolidation and retraining.

In 1969 the situation in Northern Ireland exploded and the SAS began a long acquaintanceship with the Province. Simultaneously, renewed problems in both Malaya and the Oman led to a return there, and the SAS remained in the latter

Below: SAS troopers on the roof of the Iranian Embassy in London moments before they launched their successful attack.

*Above: SAS trooper in Borneo in the 1960s, during the "Confrontation"
campaign inspired by President Soekarno.*

country for many years. In August 1983 it was disclosed that the SAS was
training a similar unit for the Sultan of Oman's "Special Force."

The anti-guerrilla campaigns of the 1950s, 1960s, and early 1970s were
succeeded by a new role in which the SAS quickly built up an unrivaled
expertise – counter-terrorist actions. Spurred on by operations in Northern
Ireland against the Irish Republican Army (IRA) and Irish National Liberation
Army (INLA), the SAS has developed techniques which are copied
throughout the Western world. This has led to the SAS not only being
consulted by overseas governments and special forces, but also in being
directly involved, sometimes as participants but more often as observers or
advisers, in many "foreign" operations. Thus, in October 1977, two SAS
men were with the West German GSG 9 unit at the attack to recapture a
hijacked German airliner at Mogadishu, and SAS members were also
present at the earlier Dutch operation against the Moluccan terrorists who
had taken over a trainload of hostages.

The most famous of all UK episodes was the London Iranian Embassy
siege of May 1980 when the SAS had perforce to conduct the operation in front
of the world's TV cameras. In strict compliance with English law, the
Metropolitan Police conducted the operation until the terrorists murdered one
of the hostages and threw his body out on the street. The police then requested
the SAS to take over, and the troops stormed in, using special weapons and
tactics. The hostages were rescued, four of five terrorists killed, and not a
single SAS man was lost. This spectacular success, while a godsend for the
hero-hungry world media, gave the SAS far more publicity than it liked and it has
since made conscious efforts to disappear once again into obscurity.

By 1982 the SAS seemed to be settled in a counter-terrorist role when the
Falklands War broke out with Argentina. 22SAS was immediately involved,
being given the opportunity to remind the world that they are first and foremost ▶

▶ professional soldiers, trained for war. They spearheaded the return to South Georgia island, although the first reconnaissance landing in helicopters had to be aborted in truly appalling weather. The second landing was by inflatable boats and most men got ashore. One boat, however, broke down and the soldiers refused to compromise the operation by calling for help on the radio and were blown rapidly eastwards and were later rescued by helicopter. Meanwhile, at Grytviken, the squadron headquarters and one troop of D Squadron took advantage of the crippling of the Argentine submarine ARA *Santa Fe* to rush in and overwhelm the garrison, and South Georgia was quickly back under British control.

The first SAS soldiers were ashore on East Falklands by May 1 and remained there, close to the enemy and in foul weather, for some thirty days. They provided vital intelligence on troop movements and deployments, and also targeted enemy aircraft and naval gunfire support. On May 14 the SAS raided Pebble Island and blew up 11 Argentine aircraft; they also reportedly operated on the mainland of Argentina itself, although this has never been confirmed officially. Their final role in the Falklands was to carry out a noisy and valuable diversionary attack on the eastern end of Wireless Ridge on the day before the Argentine surrender.

SAS teams were also inserted into Iraq during the 1991 Gulf War, their primary missions being to seek out and destroy Scud missile launchers, to report on Iraqi military movements from road-watch patrols behind enemy lines, and to locate, report on, and destroy Iraqi communications systems. Also during the 1990s, it is reported that SAS teams operated behind Serb lines in Bosnia, providing intelligence reports and calling down air strikes on Serb armor, artillery, and anti-aircraft positions.

As these examples make clear, the principal SAS mission is one of special operations – sabotage, raids, intelligence gathering, etc. – in denied areas. Contrary to popular belief, the counter-terrorist mission in the UK is not the sole province of the SAS; it provides assault and rescue forces when facilities have been seized in the UK proper and operates covertly against the Irish Republican Army (IRA). A secondary SAS mission is to organize and train friendly resistance forces, as well as to provide specialized security assistance training to friendly nations.

Organization

The present organization includes three regiments of approximately 600 to 700 men each. One regiment (22SAS) is all-regular, while the other two – 21SAS (Artists Rifles) and 23SAS – belong to the Territorial Army. There is a regular signal squadron with 22SAS and another (63 (SAS) Signal Squadron) with the TA. These units are controlled by Director Special Forces (DSF), a brigadier whose headquarters are in London.

Each SAS regiment is composed of four squadrons, each having around four 16-man troops that work, operationally, in patrols of four, which the SAS refer to as "bricks.". Some variations in size exist, of course, to accommodate special requirements for elements such as the Mountain Troop and Boat Troop.

There is a very close relationship between 22SAS and the Territorial regiments. 21SAS (Artists) is based in London, with four outstations, and 23SAS is based in Birmingham, with outstations in Manchester, Leeds Newcastle, Dundee, and Glasgow. Both Territorial regiments have a strong cadre of regulars, who ensure that professional standards are maintained, and who pass on the benefits of recent operational experience.

22 SAS has been based at Sterling Lines, Hereford for forty years, but it was announced in the 1997 Defence White Paper that the entire unit will move to a new, purpose-built base at Credenhill, a former RAF station, which is only a short distance away.

Selection and Training

No officer or soldier enlists directly into the regular regiment (22SAS). Instead, volunteers come from the other regiments and corps of the British Army, which sometimes leads to the accusation that the regiment is "poaching" some of the best and most enterprising young officers and soldiers. All volunteers for the SAS must first pass the selection course, which is based on the regimental depot at Credenhill. The tests take place in the Brecon area of Wales and consist of a series of tasks designed to find out whether the individual has the qualities of mental resilience, physical stamina, self-discipline, initiative, independence, and spiritual toughness which the Regiment has found necessary for its missions.

The process starts with ten days of fitness and map-reading training in groups of twenty to bring everyone up to the same basic standards. Typical of such training, SAS members are not allowed to write down map references or to fold maps in a way that will reveal the area they are concerned with. This is followed by ten days of solitary cross-country marching, culminating in a 40-mile (64km) march in 20 hours carrying a 55lb (25kg) Bergen rucksack. They must also demonstrate an aptitude for languages, since they will be expected to learn at least two. Those who have not either voluntarily or compulsorily withdrawn now undertake fourteen weeks' continuation training which includes a parachute course and combat survival training. At the end of this phase the survivors are presented with their coveted sand-coloured beret and SAS badge, and are at long last members of the SAS, although the training ▶

Below: SAS troopers during the 1992 Gulf War on a "Scud-busting" mission against the forces of Saddam Hussein.

▶ continues with specialist courses in signaling, languages, field medicine, demolition, shooting, free-fall parachuting, and other military skills. Even after a soldier becomes a fully fledged member of the Regiment, there can be periods of high-intensity training for roles such as counter-revolutionary warfare commandos.

Unlike in the earlier years, the emphasis during today's SAS selection and training is on encouraging men to get through the tests and course, but without relaxing the high standards, Nevertheless, the pass-rate is only about 20 percent, although it must be appreciated that only rarely is there any reason for any of the other 80 percent to feel ashamed; the fact is that the SAS are, of necessity, looking for an extremely special combination of talents which is possessed by or can be developed in only a few people.

Once fully in the Regiment, the normal tour of duty of some three to five years is followed by return to the parent regiment or corps. This ensures that the Regiment does not become too introspective and also serves to spread around the rest of the Army that curious blend of ideas and training which constitute the SAS.

Weapons and Equipment
In the past the SAS used standard British Army small arms but now it regularly uses a wide variety of weapons, foreign as well as British. In addition, the SAS specializes in training and using virtually any type of foreign weapon, either to take advantage of some particular attribute, or to blend in with the local "scenery." Special "stun" grenades have been developed for SAS use in which the blast effect has been maximized at the expense of damage potential.

Since 1984 the SAS have used two Italian-built Agusta 109 helicopters captured from the Argentinians during the Falklands War. The aircraft, operated by the Army Air Corps, carry up to seven troops and are equipped for many roles. The SAS have incorporated "high-tech" into their arsenal of tricks: thermal imagers to verify the presence of personnel in buildings, satellite communications systems, infrared night equipment, and a host of surveillance, target acquisition, and sensory devices.

Uniforms
The SAS wear standard British Army uniforms on operations, though they do not wear insignia of rank, with only the customary "regimental" items permitted under British practice. The three basic distinguishing marks of the SAS are the sand-colored beret, the capbadge (a winged dagger with the motto "Who Dares Wins") and SAS-wings worn on the right shoulder. In parade dress (No. 2 Dress) buttons, officers' Sam Browne belt, gloves, and shoes are all black. Combat dress is standard British Army pattern with either the sand-colored beret or the peaked camouflage hat with no badge. With this latter hat on there is nothing about a soldier's uniform to show that he is a member of the SAS. One small idiosyncracy of SAS uniform is that in "pullover order" (the popular dress worn in barracks) the rank chevrons of NCO are worn on the shoulder straps, not on the right sleeve.

A unique combat uniform is available for use on anti-terrorist operations. This is an all-black outfit, with a black flak-vest, belt, and boots. The standard issue respirator (made of black rubber) and gray anti-flash hood complete the outfit. Every item of this dress is worn for strictly practical reasons, but the effect is awe-inspiring.

Liaison and Cooperation
The SAS was one of the first counter-terrorist units to appreciate that terrorism is a global problem and that to deal with it effectively the special forces of democratic countries must cooperate and learn from each other. As a result they have actively promoted exchanges of personnel and ideas, and mutual

Right: A scene during the Falklands War as SAS men exit a British Army Scout helicopter at Bluff Cove.

discussions on training. Indeed, unlike some special forces, the SAS has never become arrogant and considered that it knows everything there is to know about their business; thus they are always ready to learn methods of dealing with new threats, or of new methods of dealing with old threats..

Police

It is a legal requirement in the UK that the first line of defense in any counter-terrorist activity is the police and that the armed forces, such as the SAS, are brought in only when the police no longer have the manpower, resources or expertise to deal with the situation. British police forces are organized on a regional basis, but the Metropolitan Police Service, which is responsible for policing Greater London, also has a leadership role in many activities across England and Wales.

The British police in general have had to deal with sporadic outbreaks of Irish terrorism for some 150 years; indeed, the Special Branch was originally formed specifically to provide intelligence on Irish dissident activities on the mainland. However, serious crime that was politically-motivated but unrelated to Ireland began to increase in the late 1960s , with the activities of such groups as the Angry Brigade beginning to cause such problems that the Metropolitan Police formed the "Bomb Squad" in 1970. But, although it started as an organization to deal with unexploded devices its responsibilities grew so rapidly that in 1976 its name was changed to "Ant-Terrorism Branch." (Its formal designation in the Metropolitan Police is "SO13" (SO = special operations). The activities of the branch can be gauged by the fact that between its establishment in 1970 and 1997 (the last known benchmark) the Bomb Squad/Anti-Terrorist Branch was involved in dealing with 1,312 bombings and 58 shootings.

The main responsibility of this elite organisation is to investigate all acts of terrorism within the Metropolitan Police area including economic terrorism, politically motivated crimes, and cases of kidnap and extortion with possible political implications. In addition, the Association of Chief Police Officers (ACPO) (the body upon which all Chief Constables sit) has made the Commander of the Anti-Terrorist Branch responsible for coordinating the investigation of acts of terrorism across the United Kingdom as a whole. Thus, the Anti-Terrorist Branch (SO13) is now a very large organization and among its many resources are D11, which provides highly trained marksmen and other armed specialists. Another section, the Counter-Terrorist Search Wing advises generally on all aspects of specialist searches, with responsibility for the policy, training and licensing of search trained officers within the Metropolitan Police Service.

The growing number of incidents involving explosives and guns in the UK have forced many regional police forces to form their own armed squads, which are the equivalent of U.S. SWAT teams. The personnel for all of these are volunteers, and their selection and training are rigorous.

United States

United States Special Operations Command (USSOCOM) Overview

USSOCOM is the fifth service branch of the U.S. Department of Defense, with its HQ at MacDill Air Force Base, Florida, where it is commanded by a four- star flag/general officer. The establishment of this unified command was mandated by Congress in 1987 to correct serious deficiencies in the United States' ability to conduct special operations, and it consists of three major elements, U.S. Army Special Operations Command (USASOC), U.S. Naval Special Operations Command (NAVSPECWARCOM); and U.S. Air Force Special Operations Command (AFSOC), but it should be noted that no Marine Corps units are integral parts of USSOCOM.

Army

U.S. Army Special Operations Command (Fort Bragg, NC) (For reasons of space only major units are listed; training, logistic and maintenance units have been omitted.) comprises four major combat elements. Special Forces Command (Airborne) (Fort Bragg) consists of five active force special forces airborne groups (1, 3, 5, 7, 10 SFG) and two National Guard groups (19, 20 SFG (NG)). There is also a Civil Affairs and Psyops Command (Airborne) comprising three Psyops Groups and four Civil Affairs Commands. Finally, there are two regimental-size combat units which report direct to SOCOM: 75th Ranger Regiment (Airborne) and 160th Special Operations Aviation Regiment (Airborne).

Below: U.S. Special Forces were originally raised in order to use guerrilla tactics against conventional forces, but are now trained to fight any type of enemy in any terrain.

Above: Lead scout of a Special Forces patrol group.

Below: Unarmed combat; an essential skill for Special Forces.

119

▶ Navy

The U. S. Naval Special Operations Command located at San Diego, California comprises two groups. Naval Special Warfare Group ONE (NAVSPECWARGRU 1) includes: Naval Special Warfare Units One and Three (NSWU-1/-3); SEAL Delivery Vehicle Team One (SDVT-1), and SEAL Teams One, Three, Five and Seven (ST-1/-3/-5/-7). NAVSPECWARGRU-2 comprises NSWU-2/-4/-10 and SEAL Teams Two, Four and Eight (ST-2/-4/-8); Special Boat Squadron One (SBS-1) with four Coastal Patrol Boats (PC), and SBS-2 with nine PCs.

Air Force

Air Force Special Operations Command (Hurlburt Field) comprises 16th Special Operations Wing (also at Hurlburt Field), two overseas groups and an Air Reserve component.

SOCOM Assets

SOCOM has its own centrally controlled assets which include the Special Operations Plans and Policy (SOOP) Center, Special Operations Intelligence and Information Operations (SOIO) Center, and the Special Operations Command Support (SOCS) Center. There are also central bodies responsible for acquisition and logistics, and requirements and resources. The Joint Special Operation Command (JSOC) is responsible for studying and developing special operations requirements, tactics and techniques, to ensure interoperability and equipment standardization, and to conduct special operations training.

KEY COMBAT UNITS - ARMY
The 75th Ranger Regiment (Airborne)

The 75th Ranger Regiment's primary missions are to seize airfields and to conduct raids, which will include movement to contact, ambush, reconnaissance, airborne

Below: 1/75th Rangers board an Air Force C-141 as they set out on Operation Just Cause in October 1989.

Above: Men of 2/75th Rangers receiving their awards following their return from Operation Urgent Fury in 1983.

and air assaults, and hasty defense all of them in any region of the world. In addition, Rangers may also be called upon to perform missions in support of general-purpose forces. Headquarters 75th Ranger Regiment is located at Fort Benning, Georgia, and the regiment is composed of three Ranger ▶

Below: Instructors take great pleasure in devising ever more challenging obstacles, such as this ladder at Fort Bragg.

▶ battalions: 1st Battalion (1/75), based at Hunter Army Airfield, Georgia; 2/75 at For Lewis, Washington; and 3/75 at Fort Benning, Georgia. There are also three training battalions: 4th Ranger Training Battalion at Fort Benning, Georgia; 5th at Dahlonega Georgia; and 6th at Elgin Air Force Base, Florida.

The 75th's three 580-strong Ranger Battalions are identically organized into a headquarters, three rifle companies (each of 152 men) , and a headquarters company. Each battalion is required to be capable of infiltrating and exfiltrating by land, sea, and air; conducting direct-action operations; carrying out raids recovery of personnel and special equipment; and conducting conventional o special light-infantry operations. On every day of the year one Ranger Battalion is at Ready Reaction Force 1 (RRF1) status, which rotates between battalions at approximately 13-week intervals. Being on RRF 1 requires the battalion to be airborne en route to the operational theater within 18 hours of the order "go" In addition, at periods of heightened tension, battalion headquarters plus one company can be placed at nine hours notice to move.

Standard weapon systems carried by each battalion are:
- 84mm Ranger Anti-Armor Weapons (RAAW) system – 16
- 60mm mortars – 6
- M240G machine guns – 27
- M249 Squad Automatic Weapons (SAW) – 54
- Mk 19 grenade launcher – 12
- M2HB .50cal machine gun – 12
- Javelin – 9
- 50 cal Barrett Sniper System – 6

Each Ranger Battalion also operates twelve Ranger Special Operation Vehicles for its airfield seizure mission. These are modified Land Rovers, each carrying a six/seven-man crew and mounting an M240G machine gun and either a Mk19 Grenade Launcher or an M2HB .50 cal machine gun and an anti-armor weapon. These are not assault vehicles but are intended to provide a highly mobile capability. Each Battalion also possesses ten 250cc motorcycles.

It is important to appreciate the limitations of Ranger battalions. They have a limited anti-armor capability and apart from their six 60mm mortars they lac

Below: Rangers employ the "buddy system" to help each other prepare for a parachute jump.

Above: U.S. Army Rangers; the soldier in front carries a Colt Commando, the one in rear is in full sniper outfit.

organic indirect fire support; similarly, their only air defense capability is the Stinger system. Further, Ranger units are light infantry and thus have no organic combat support or combat service support, own very few vehicles and when they deploy they do so with only five days of supplies. Thus, they require support from other units and require early relief, particularly in airfield seizure missions. ▶

123

▶ Special Forces Group (Airborne)

Each Special Forces Group (Airborne) comprises a Group Headquarters, three 383-strong, Special Forces Battalions (SF Bn), Support Company (176 strong) and HQ Company (HHC) (89 strong). The tasks of the group are to:

- Conduct operations in remote and denied areas for extended periods of time with little internal or external support.
- Develop, organize, equip, train, and advise or direct indigenous military and paramilitary forces.
- Plan and conduct unilateral SF operations.

Above: Members of U.S. Army 10th Special Forces Group Airborne practice hand-to-hand combat.

Below: Completing the action started above, the opponent is disarmed (see pistol in instructor's hand) and disabled.

bove: Special Forces must be capable of deploying rapidly by land, sea
r air to conduct missions anywhere in the world.

Perform other SF operations as directed by the NCA or unified commander.

Special Forces Groups are trained to infiltrate by air (parachute, onventional landing in fixed/rotary wing aircraft, rappel and fast rope), sea urface ships and submarines) and by land, in all weathers and under any onditions.

st Special Forces Operational Detachment - Delta

ne Army SOF unit about which very little is published and whose existence is ot officially acknowledged by the U.S. government or USSOCOM is 1st pecial Forces Operational Detachment - Delta (1SFOD-Delta) usually known mply as "Delta." It was formed by Colonel Charles (Charlie) Beckwith, U.S. rmy, who as a major had carried out an attachment to the British Special Air ervice (SAS) in 1962-63, and then returned determined to raise a similar body the United States. He had to overcome considerable resistance in a very ▶

▶ conservative chain-of-command, but the unit was officially formed on 1 November 1977, its credo, as laid down by Charlie Beckwith, being "surprise, speed, success."

The unit's title sometimes causes misunderstandings. 1SFOD-D was a totally new unit and had nothing to do with the "Delta Project (Detachment B-52)" set up by Army Special Forces in Vietnam in the mid-1960s (and which was, at one time, commanded by Charlie Beckwith) which was a totally different organization and concept. The reason for the name of the new unit was, in fact, quite simple. At that time there were three Special Forces Operational Detachments, designated Alpha (commanded by a captain), Bravo (commanded by a major) and Charlie (commanded by a lieutenant-colonel) and it seemed a natural progression, Beckwith suggested, that the new should be designated Delta and commanded by a full colonel (himself).

Delta is based at Fort Bragg in a large and well-protected area known as "The Stockade." Not surprisingly, Delta at least in its early years reflected SAS organizational patterns, with a headquarters and three operational squadrons each composed of two or more troops, each of four-man squads (equivalent to the SAS "bricks"). There is also a support squadron, a communications squadron and a covert troop. The main aviation support comes from 160 SOAR (see below) but Delta also has its own aviation troop which uses helicopters with civilian color schemes and registrations, similar to the British SAS with its two ex-Argentine Agusta A-109s. Delta is manned by volunteers who come from anywhere in the Army, although in practice most come from Special

Forces' units and Rangers.

Delta has undertaken a host of operational deployments, some of which have appeared in the Press and some of which have been learnt about by other means; there have also doubtless been deployments which remain totally classified to this day. Some of the operations have been unsuccessful, but in most the aim has been achieved. Among known deployments have been:

- Operation Eagle Claw (24-25 April 1980), the attempted rescue of the U.S. hostages in the embassy grounds in Teheran.
- Air Garuda Boeing 737 (March 1981). A single four-man squad killed four highjackers at Bangkok airport, successfully releasing the hostages.
- Brigadier-General Dozier rescue (January 1982). Dozier was taken hostage by Red Brigade terrorists. A Delta team deployed to Italy, but the Italians carried out the successful rescue.
- Operation Urgent Fury (25 October 1983). Delta and SEAL teams took part in the U.S. invasion of Grenada.
- Olympic Games, Los Angeles (1984). Delta played a major role in the security arrangements, for which Colonel Beckwith, by then retired, was the security consultant.

TWA Flight 847 hijack (June 1985). The aircraft was hijacked to Algiers where two U.S. passengers were murdered. A Delta detachment was sent to ▶

Below: Sea Stallion helicopters prepare to takeoff from USS Nimitz *for the Iranian Embassy rescue mission.*

▶ Europe but the Algerian government refused permission for them to take action.

- *Achille Lauro* incident (October 1985). Again a Delta team went to Europe but was not employed.
- Atlanta City prison riots (1987). Delta deployed to help quell the riot, but prisoners surrendered before they arrived.
- Operation Just Cause (1989). Delta and SEAL Team Six took part in the invasion of Panama, where their prime task was to apprehend General Noriega.
- Operation Desert Storm (1990-1). Delta deployed to Iraq, where it worked alongside British, Australian, and New Zealand SAS units in seeking out and either destroying or calling down fire on Scud missile launchers.
- "Branch Davidian" siege, Waco, Texas (1993). Delta teams were deployed to assist the FBI and other civil agencies in breaking the siege at the sect' headquarters. Delta's role was somewhat controversial, although as far as i known it was not actually used.
- Operation Restore Hope (1993). Delta was deployed to Somalia where i became embroiled in the unsuccessful attempts to arrest "General" Aidid.
- Operation Uphold Democracy, Haiti, (1994). Delta took part in the peacekeeping operation.
- Atalanta Olympic Games (1996). Delta was again on stand-by to deal with terrorist incidents at the games.
- Bosnia (1996-). It is believed that Delta teams (possibly accompanied by SEAL Team Six) have deployed to Bosnia on several occasions. One possible mission is the arrest of the war criminal, Radovan Karadizc, although, in th event, this has not been achieved.
- Afghanistan (2001-). Delta teams are known to have deployed to Afghanistan

The 160th Special Operations Aviation Regiment (Airborne)

The 160th Special Operations Aviation Regiment (Airborne) (160 SOAR(A)) flies specially modified versions of the OH-6 Little Bird light observation helicopter MH-60 Blackhawk utility helicopter, and MH-47 Chinook medium-lift helicopters. The unit dates back to the early 1980s, when, in the aftermath of Operation Eagle Claw, the failed mission to rescue the Teheran embassy hostages, the Army decided to form its own dedicated aviation unit for special operations. This was officially formed on 16 October 1981 as 160th Aviation Battalion, and in view of its focus on night operations it adopted the nickname "The Night Stalkers." On 16 May, 1990 the unit was considerably expanded and reorganized, redesignated to its current name, and assigned to USSOCOM. 160 SOAR(A) is based at Fort Campbell, Kentucky, and is composed of four active-duty battalions and one forward-deployed company:

- Three battalions are based at Fort Campbell: 1/160 AH-6, MH-6, MH-60K and MH-60L DAP; 2/160 MH-47E; and 4/160, which is responsible for "black" (covert) missions.
- The remaining battalion, 3/160, is based at Hunter Army Airfield, Savannah Georgia, and flies the MH-60L and MH-47D.
- Detachment D/160, based at Ft. Kobbe, Panama, where it operates five MH-60Ls.
     The tasks performed by 160 SOAR include:
- Clandestine insertion, extraction, and resupply of Special Operations Force (SOF).
- Aviation support for special forces' missions, including armed escort reconnaissance, surveillance, and electronic warfare.
- Command, control and communications (C^3) for SOF.
- General support aviation during peacetime and contingency operations.
     Members and aircraft of 160 SOAR have seen action in support of U.S. forces all over the world and have been deployed in such high-profile

undertakings as Operations Urgent Fury, Just Cause and Desert Shield/Desert Storm. In one relatively unusual but very successful mission in April 1996, 3/160 took part in Operation Assured Response, which involved the evacuation of U.S. citizens from strife-torn Liberia. For the battalion this involved stripping down four MH-47 Chinooks, loading them into C-5 Galaxy aircraft which were then flown to Africa, and then unloading and reassembling them. They were actually in the air on their first mission In Africa within seventy-two hours of receiving the initial order to deploy from their base in Georgia a most remarkable achievement. These four helicopters then flew solidly for ten days during which, in conjunction with five USAF MH-53Js, they lifted more than ▶

Below: An MH-47 Chinook of 160th Special Operations Aviation Regiment (160 SOAR).

▶ 2,500 U.S. citizens to safety.

Not surprisingly, 160 SOAR's activities are not without risk and severa aircraft and their crews have been lost. Two MH-60L Blackhawks were sho down over Mogadishu, Somalia, in 1993, with the loss of three pilots, while fourth was captured and used as a hostage. In the same operation, two othe MH-60s were heavily damaged, but succeeded in limping back to their base where they crash-landed. In a totally separate incident in April 1996, an MH 47E Chinook suffered an electrical failure and crashed with the loss of five lives

KEY COMBAT UNITS – NAVY
SEAL Teams
The SEALs take their title from the environments in which they operate Sea, Ai

And Land – and are, by doctrine and in practice, maritime special forces. They operate mainly in 16-man platoons from sea-based platforms, either surface ships or craft, or submarines and submersibles. Their stealth and clandestine methods of operation allow them to conduct multiple missions that larger forces cannot accomplish undetected. SEALs operate either independently or integrate with carrier battle groups, amphibious ready groups and joint Special Operations Forces. Forward-based and forward-deployed SEALs, Special Boat Units and SEAL delivery teams can be operational anywhere in the world withing seventy-two hours of being given the order, and with 50 percent of the ▶

Below: A SEAL Delivery Vehicle, with the pilot at the controls and a SEAL returning from a mission.

▶ world's population and industrial facilities located within one mile of an ocean or navigable river they can find targets with relative ease.

SEAL Delivery Vehicle Teams (SDVT)
SDVTs are specially trained SEALs and support personnel who operate and maintain SDVs and dry deck shelters (DDS). SDVs and DDS are described in the "Weapons" section of this book and in combination with their submarine "mother ships" these provide the most clandestine maritime delivery and extraction facilities in the world.

Special Boat Squadrons (SBS) and Units (SBU)
SBS and SBU are composed of specially selected and trained naval personnel who are responsible for operating and maintaining a variety of special operations ships and craft, such as rigid inflatable boats (RIBs) and patrol coastal ships (PCs). These conduct coastal and riverine interdiction and support naval and joint special operations worldwide. They provide the Navy's only riverine capability. (Despite the similarity of the titles, U.S. Navy SBS and British Royal Marine SBS have different functions.)

SEAL Team Six
As with the other U.S. armed forces in the aftermath of Operation Eagle Claw the Navy conducted a review of its counter-terrorist and special operations capabilities and training. In the Navy's case, this resulted in the formation of SEAL Team Six in October 1980 as a specialist naval counter-terrorist unit and it became operational in April 1981. The new unit was given the cover name of Naval Special Warfare Development Group (NAVSPECWARDEVGRU), which seems to imply a training and/or development role, but it is quite clear that it is an operational unit and its proper title is SEAL Team Six, which will be used here. The unit is based at Dam Neck, Virginia, and is organized into troops, with combined strength of some 200-300, which specialize in different roles together with support elements (communications, medical, transportation, etc) which probably account for another 200-300, or so.

SEAL Team has been involved in numerous special operations, particular

Below: After fast-roping from an AFSOC MH-53 Pave Low, SEALs cover each other during a search-and-seize exercise.

Above: Marines and a CH-46, a helicopter that is considerably older than both its aircrew and passengers.

Below: SEALs take care and help each other as they prepare to deploy from a U.S. Navy carrier.

involving submarines, only some of which have reached public notice. Among these are the extraction of deposed, legal rulers (Scoones in Grenada, and Aristide in Haiti) and the capture of General Noriega in Panama.

The unit is known to have close relations with a number of foreign units, particularly the British SAS and Italian COMSUBIN.

KEY COMBAT UNITS – AIR FORCE
16th Special Operations Wing

16 SOW is the oldest of the Air Force's special operations units and is located at Hurlburt Field, Florida. Its mission is to organize, train and equip Air Force ▶

▶ Special Operations Forces for global employment, with the primary focus on unconventional warfare, especially counterinsurgency and psychological activities in operations other than general war.

16 SOW operates nearly 100 aircraft and includes seven Special Operations Squadrons (SOS), all of which are based at Hurlburt Field, except for 9 SOS which is located at nearby Eglin Air Force base. The flying squadrons are: 4 SOS (AC-130U Spectre); 8 SOS (MC-130E Combat Talon I); 9 SOS (MC-130P Combat Shadow); 15 SOS (MC-130H Combat Talon II); 16 SOS (AC-130H Spectre); 20 SOS (MH-53J Pave Low III); and 55 SOS (MH-60G Pave Hawk). In addition, 6 SOS is responsible for providing U.S. military expertise to foreign governments in support of their internal defense and development efforts.

352nd Special Operations Group

The Air Force's special forces component in Europe is 352nd Special Operations Group, based at RAF Mildenhall, in the United Kingdom. This has four special operations squadrons: 7 SOS (MC-130H Combat Talon II); 21 SOS (MH-53J Pave Low III); 67 SOS

Below: AFSOC combat controllers establish drop zones, landing zones, and other ground services.

Above: Air Force Special Tactics Squadron members perform a breathtaking high altitude - low opening (HALO) jump.

(MC-130P Combat Shadow), and the 321 Special Tactics Squadron. The latter is responsible for pararesceuemen and combat controllers to establish drop zones, landing zones, air traffic control and combat search and rescue. The squadron also has combat weathermen to provide weather support for Air Force and Army special operations.

353rd Special Operations Group
The Pacific component is 353rd Special Operations Group, has its headquarters at Kadena Air Base, Japan and consists of three flying squadrons: 1 SOS (MC-130H Combat Talon II) and 17 SOS (MC-130P Combat Shadow) are both based at Kadena, while 31 SOS (MH-53J Pave Low) is based at O-san AFB in Korea.

Reserve Units
AFSOC also includes several reserve components. 919 Special Operations Wing is based at Duke Field in Florida and consists of two squadrons, 5 SOS (MC-130P) and 711 SOS (MC-130E). The 193 Special Operations Wing at Harrisburg International Airport, Pennsylvania, flies EC-130E Commando Solo. ▶

▶ U.S. MARINE CORPS

The Marine Corps is not part of SOCOM, but no review of America's special forces would be complete without reference to the Corps in general and to some of its units in particular. When USSOCOM was set up in the late 1980s, the Marine Corps elected to remain separate, although it instituted an aggressive special operations capability training program to optimize the inherent abilities of its Marine Expeditionary Units (MEU). This resulted in the formation of forward-deployed MEU(SOC)s to conduct selected maritime special operations as the Marine Corps "first-on-the scene" force. Normally embarked aboard three or four ships of an Amphibious Ready Group (ARG), a MEU(SOC) unit is task-organized and consists of: a command element, a reduced infantry battalion as the ground combat element, a reinforced helicopter squadron as the aviation element, and a combat service support element, designated the MEU Service Support Group.

MEU(SOC) Capabilities

The MEU(SOC)'s maritime special operations capabilities are based upon its expeditionary and amphibious nature, and are primarily an enhancement of the traditional capabilities of the Marine forces afloat. These capabilities do not transform MEU(SOC)s into dedicated special operations forces or national counter-terrorist forces, but, rather, they make them far more useful forward-deployed forces in a wider range of contingency and response situations.

The primary objective of the MEU(SOC) program is to provide the National Command Authority (NCA) and geographical combatant commanders with an effective means of dealing with the uncertainties of future threats, by providing forward-deployed units which offer a variety of rapid-reaction, sea- based, crisis-response options, in either a conventional amphibious role, or in execution of selected maritime special operations.

Task organized from MEU(SOC) assets is a Maritime Special Purposes Force (MSPF) which provides a special operations capable force that can be quickly tailored to accomplish a specific mission and employed either as a complement to conventional naval operations or in the execution of a selected maritime special operations mission of its own. Particular emphasis is placed on operations requiring precision skills that normally are not resident in traditional amphibious raid companies. Command and control of the MSPF remains with

Above: U.S. Marines are among the toughest and most flexible soldiers in the world, as their operations in Afghanistan have shown.

Left: The Maritime Special Purposes Force (MSPF) is formed for specifric missions from within the assets of the MEU(SOC).

the MEU(SOC) commander. The MSPF is not designed to duplicate existing SOF capabilities and is not capable of operating independently of its parent MEU. The MSPF task organization can be enhanced by the addition of ARG elements such as the Assault Craft Unit detachment, equipped with LCACs or the Naval Special Warfare Task Unit (NSWTU) detachment attached to the ARG.

The MSPF is specially trained and equipped to conduct direct action missions using close-quarters battle (CQB) skills. The capabilities of the MSPF include: ▶

- Reconnaissance and surveillance.
- Specialized demolitions.
- Seizure/recovery of offshore energy facilities.
- Seizure/recovery of designated personnel or materiel.
- Visit, board, search and seizure operations.
- Tactical recovery of aircraft and personnel.

The MEU(SOC) is task trained to operate with special forces as mission requirements dictate. This interoperability may be in the role of a supporting force or as the supported force, as directed by the Chairman, Joint Chiefs of Staff. The Naval Special Warfare Task Unit (NSWTU) consisting of SEALs and SBU personnel, embarked aboard amphibious shipping may be employed in a supporting/supported role with the MSPF or other elements of the MEU(SOC). Effective operational and tactical interoperability between the MEU(SOC) and the embarked NSWTU, across the spectrum of MEU(SOC) operations, is essential. Prior to deployment the MEU(SOC) will be required to demonstrate interoperability with the NSWTU.

USMC Reconnaissance

Reconnaissance groups are elite teams within the USMC. There are two

Below: U.S. Marine and the art of jungle survival. Bamboo can provide food, water, container, carrying pole or spear.

Above: At the opposite extreme, arctic survival involves different techniques but the same qualities of determination.

varieties: Recon and Force Recon. Recon operates in a strictly reconnaissance role, while Force Recon's missions are analogous to the U.S. Navy's SEALs ▶

139

▶ (albeit they are not under USSOCOM's command). Within the 1998 reorganization of Marine reconnaissance elements, there are Recon battalions and Force Recon companies. The Recon Battalions work in support of the division gathering intelligence out to approximately 10 miles (16km) past the forward edge of the battle area (FEBA), while the Force Recon companies gather all intelligence past that limit, a more demanding task for which they receive more elaborate training.

USMC Fleet Anti-Terrorist Security Team (FAST)

Another elite Marine Corps unit, and one about which very little is published, is the Fleet Anti-Terrorist Security Team (FAST), which was formed in 1987 in response to the world-wide increase in threats to the U.S. armed forces and government facilities. Their prime mission is to provide additional, highly trained protection over short periods, when the threat is beyond the capabilities of the usual security forces. Following the principle that "prevention is better than

Below: "Mission accomplished" as U.S. Marines stand outside the U.S. Embassy in Kuwait City in February 1991.

Above: Marines undergoing weapon training aboard a carrier; constant training ensures that they are ready for anything.

ture" FAST companies are also responsible for carrying out threat assessments, for helping security officers to prepare proper security plans, and for improving individual standards in a security force (for example, of surveillance and marksmanship).

FAST companies are some 300 strong and can be deployed very rapidly when the need arises. Following the bombing of U.S. troops in Saudi Arabia on 25 June 1996, in which 19 people were killed and some 500 wounded, FAST Marines from Norfolk, Virginia were actually on site within ten hours of the explosions. They then provided not only additional security by deploying their own Marines, but also carried out security assessments which, in many instances, found the existing arrangements wanting.

FAST units have deployed with U.S. forces on numerous operations, including: the Gulf War; Liberia (Operation Sharp Edge); Panama (Operations Just Cause and Promote Liberty); Haiti (Operation Safe Return); Cuban refugee evacuation (Operation Safe Passage); and the United Nations withdrawal from Somalia.

Major Operations

The examples that follow illustrate the extent of the threat spectrum whic[ ] has increasingly given rise to the need for special forces, and also the globa[ ] reach and operational flexibility that must be possessed by the "big league[ ] special operations players, such as those of the United States, the Unite[ ] Kingdom, France, Germany and Israel. The history of the past fifty years ha[ ] shown that these armed threats can appear from anywhere, from any directior[ ] at any time, and frequently with little, if any, notice. There is some evidence o[ ] occasional contact and cooperation between some of the terrorist movements[ ] but while there is no evidence whatsoever of a "grand plan" the various terroris[ ] groups have shown a constant talent for discovering new ways to attack th[ ] governments and the societies that they oppose. As a result, the police an[ ] military special forces must not only maintain the capability to deal with repeat[ ] or minor variations of previously encountered threats, but must also have th[ ] flexibility to deal with totally new and unexpected ones.

Hostage Rescue Operations

One common theme running through many incidents is the taking and holdin[ ] of hostages, with innocent bystanders being used to provide the terrorists wit[ ] political and emotional leverage and, above all, with exposure in the national an[ ] international media for their cause. There seems to be an almost infinite variet[ ] in the way hostage-taking is done. One method used by terrorists many time[ ] from the 1960s through the 1990s was hijacking airliners, when the crew wou[ ] be forced by threats to the safety of themselves and their passengers to fly t[ ] an airfield where the terrorists would then seek to negotiate their freedom an[ ] the achievement of some political purpose in return for the safe release of th[ ] hostages. For the counter-terrorist forces the first priority in such a situation [ ] always to get the airliner onto the ground and only then to start negotiatin[ ] although it was quickly learnt that negotiations could be allowed to continu[ ] only as long as the hostages remained safe; as soon as one was killed an attac[ ] had to become inevitable. The first two operations to be described here, th[ ] Israeli rescue at Entebbe in 1976 and, the German rescue at Mogadishu [ ] 1977, show how determined special forces can successfully conduct suc[ ] operations, even at a considerable distance from the security forces' hom[ ] country. Once it became clear that counter-terrorist forces would react rapid[ ] and ruthlessly, the number of hijackings fell off, although they still happen fro[ ] time to time.

Airliners are an obvious target for hijacking since they and the[ ] passengers are so vulnerable when airborne and then, even when th[ ] aircraft is on the ground, the pasengers and crew can be kept under contr[ ] by a very small number of terrorists. Ships, railroad trains and buses are n[ ] such obvious targets, but all have been used by terrorists, and each of the[ ] poses quite distinct challenges to the special forces trying to deal wit[ ] them. As the threat to airliners began to be contained in the 1970[ ] terrorists found new targets. Thus, in 1976 and again in 1977, Sou[ ] Molluccan terrorists hijacked trains in the Netherlands (Example 3) which [ ] till then had seemed unlikely targets, but the second siege lasted thre[ ] weeks and ended in the deaths of six terrorists and two hostages. Sin[ ] then, however, no further trains have been targeted.

In 1961 Portuguese dissidents hijacked the liner *Santa Maria* ar[ ] eventually surrendered in Brazil without intervention by special forces. Th[ ] hijacking of the Italian liner, *Achille Lauro*, in 1985 was much more serio[ ] and involved not only the cold-blooded murder of an elderly man in [ ] wheelchair, but also brought a serious confrontation between Italy and th[ ] United States.

Another type of hostage rescue situation occurs when the terrorists take a building, sometimes readily accessible as in the Iranian Embassy siege in London but on other occasions very remote and difficult to reach, as was the case with the U.S. Embassy in Teheran.

The great majority of these special forces' hostage rescue operations known to the public are of spectacular events which take place in the full glare of publicity, such as the rescues at Entebbe and Mogadishu, but many others are hidden from public view, even to this day. It had, however, been generally understood that while most such terrorists were prepared to die, if necessary, they nevertheless preferred to live. The end of the 1990s and the early 2000s, however, have seen the rise of a new and sinister phenomenon, which is the appearance of terrorists who actually intend to die, as, for example, in the suicide bombers in Israel and the Israeli-occupied West Bank, and the terrorists who took control of the airplanes that were hijacked on September 11, 2001, and then crashed into the World Trade Center in New York and the Pentagon in Washington. In such cases there is very little scope for a special operations reaction, unless they are already aboard every single airliner, which is clearly impracticable.

Humanitarian Operations

A totally different type of special forces mission arises in the curious area of modern military operations which is loosely labeled "humanitarian aid." This involves assistance of limited scope and duration to supplement or complement the efforts of host-nation civil authorities or agencies to relieve or reduce the results of natural or man-made disasters. Such assistance can take a wide variety of forms, ranging from mine clearance, through the provision of transport and the distribution of food and other supplies, to training (or retraining) local security forces.

During 1997, U.S. Special Operations Forces deployed to 144 countries around the world, and had an average of 4,760 personnel deployed in any one week throughout the year – some 10 percent of the total USSOCOM manpower. Some of the humanitarian aid tasks they performed could have been done by civil agencies, but the military are frequently the only organization with the resources, skills, transportation and manpower, and the responsive communications and command systems necessary to undertake such missions.

It sometimes transpires, however, that despite excellent intentions and agreed short-term objectives at the start, the mission becomes protracted and the situation deteriorates into a military firefight. Thus it was in Somalia, where the United States and a number of partners deployed in order to ensure the distribution of United Nations humanitarian supplies and ended up involved in the Battle of Mogadishu.

Conventional Warfare

The media tend to seize upon the dramatic special forces operations, such as those involving hostage rescues, which occur in what is, somewhat euphemistically, known as "peacetime." What special forces are really preparing for, however, is their military role in conventional and general war, when they can use their special techniques and knowledge to further the campaign.

Thus, the American Special Operations Forces took part in the landings on Grenada and Panama, while the British Parachute Regiment played a major role in the Falklands War. Perhaps nothing, however, shows the various special forces in a better light than their cooperation in the coalition force during Operation Desert Storm.

Rescue at Entebbe (1976)

At 0900 hours June 27 1976, Air France flight AF 139 left Tel Aviv airport e
route for Paris with 254 passengers and crew aboard. The A300 Airbus aircra
staged through Athens and it was on the second leg of its flight when, at 121
hours, it was sky-jacked by a combination of Palestinian and Baader-Meinh
terrorists led by a German called Wilfried Boese. The pilot succeeded
pressing the "hijack button" as he turned for Benghazi, where, after a 6-ho
delay, the plane was refueled; it then flew on to the terrorists' destination
Entebbe, Uganda, which was under the erratic rule of "Field Marshal" Idi Am
Dada.

Amin purported to maintain an apparently neutral posture, but covertly h
supported the terrorists in their demands that unless 53 Palestinians or oth
terrorist prisoners held in a number of countries were released the hostage
aboard the Air France flight would be shot at 1200 hours on July 1. Uganda
troops were deployed to Entebbe airport, supposedly to "keep the peace," b
they in fact assisted in guarding the hostages. Amin even visited the hostage
and, after he had left, the Israelis and Jews of other nationalities we
segregated, although the Air France aircrew insisted on joining them.

On the morning of July 1, the Israeli government, playing for tim
announced that it was willing to consider the release of Palestinian prisoner
The hijackers, increasingly confident of eventual success. responded k
extending their deadline by three days. They also released all the non-Jewis
hostages, who were flown to Paris, where they were debriefed by French an
Israeli intelligence.

From the beginning, the Israeli planners had many problems. The fir
clearly was shortage of time to set up any form of rescue operation before th
terrorists killed any of their hostages. The second was to find out just where th
hostages were being held and under what conditions. Third, there was th
problem of getting a rescue force to Entebbe and back. Fourth, there was th
problem of what to do with the non-Jewish hostages.

Fortunately, the problems resolved themselves one after another. T
Kenya government agreed to the use of Nairobi airport, and a coup in Sud
resulted in the closure of that country's air control radars. Intelligence (
Entebbe airport and the local situation began to be processed, aide
considerably by the debriefing of the released non-Jewish hostages. This ease
the problem of consulting foreign governments. U.S. sources mae
information, including satellite photographs of Entebbe, available, and Fran
remained involved not only because it had been an Air France airliner that ha
been hijacked but because its courageous crew had insisted on staying with t
Jewish hostages.

The Rescue

Lieutenant-General Mordecai Gur, Israeli chief-of staff, considered that a raid
the airport was feasible, and at 0730 hours on July 3 Prime Minister Rak
reviewed all the facts and then gave the political go-ahead for the operatic
Later that morning a full-scale dress rehearsal was held in northern Isra
Drawn from the 35th Parachute Brigade and the Golani Infantry Brigade, t
100-plus force, commanded by Brigadier-General Dan Shomron, aged 4
performed well in an attack on a dummy layout manned by Israeli troops, a
all seemed to augur well for the real thing, which was scheduled for the ne
day. The dress rehearsal lasted just 55 minutes from the time the resc
aircraft landed to the time it took off again (the actual rescue was to take ju
53). The primary weapons selected for the raid reportedly were the MAC-
and Galil assault rifles, the latter equipped with night sights. The force to ent
the airport terminal and rescue the hostages was to be led by Lieutena

Colonel Jonathan Netanyahu, known throughout the Israeli Army as "Yoni."

At 1600 hours that afternoon (July 3), two hours after the full Israeli government cabinet had been made aware of the "go" decision, four Israeli C-130 Hercules took off for the long flight to Entebbe. The route took them down the middle of the Red Sea at high altitude in the hope that Saudi Arabian radars would treat them as unscheduled civil flights. There was, in fact, no reaction, so they were able to turn and fly down the Sudan-Ethiopia border and into Uganda.

Two Boeing 707s were also involved, leaving two hours after the slower C-30s. One was a flying command post fitted with special communications gear; it caught up with the four C-130s near Entebbe and remained in the area ▶

Below: Entebbe airport as it was at the time of the Israeli raid, with the hostages being held in the old terminal building.

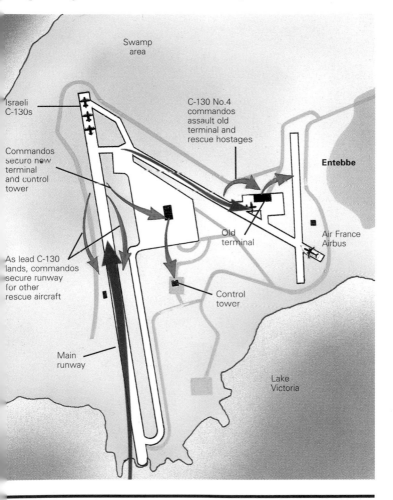

▶ throughout the operation with Major-Generals Benny Peled and Yekutiel Adam aboard. The other 707, fitted out as an emergency hospital, went straight to Nairobi, arriving just before midnight; it then waited, its medical staff ready for any wounded from the operation just across the border in Uganda.

The four C-130s arrived at Entebbe without incident and landed at precisely 0001 hours. The first aircraft landed close to the control tower, disgorging its paratroops in a Mercedes car and three Land Rovers while still moving. The men charged into the tower and succeeded in preventing the controllers from switching off the landing lights; even so, emergency lights were deployed, just in case. These were not needed and the second and third aircraft taxied up to the terminal where the hostages were being held and discharged their paratroops straight into action. The fourth C-130 joined the first near the control tower.

The main Israeli squad brushed aside the ineffective resistance from the Ugandan Army guards and charged into the terminal building. The second group destroyed Ugandan Air Force MiG fighters to prevent pursuit when the raiders took off again and also as a noisy and obvious diversion.

The third group went to the perimeter to cover the approach road, since it was known that the Ugandan Army had a number of Soviet-built T-54 tanks and Czech OT-64 armored personnel carriers some 20 miles (32km) away in the capital, Kampala. Had this force appeared, it could have had a major effect since the Israelis had no heavy weapons. The fourth group was made up of 33 doctors who, being Israelis, were also well-trained soldiers and brought down ▶

Below: The scene at the old terminal building; extreme speed and ruthless determination were essential to Israeli success.

▶ covering fire from the area of the C-130s.

With Shomron in control in the tower and satisfied that the first phase ha[s] been successful, it was now "Yoni" Netanyahu's turn to lead the crucial assau[lt] on the terminal building to rescue the hostages. The terrorist leader, Boes[e] behaved with surprising indecision, first aiming at the hostages and the[n] changing his mind, going outside, loosing off a few rounds at the Israelis a[nd] then heading back for the lounge; as he returned he was shot and killed. H[is] fellow German, Gabrielle Tiedemann, was also killed outside the building.

The Israeli soldiers rushed into the lounge where the hostages were bei[ng] held, shouting at everyone to get down on the floor; in the confusion, three [of] the hostages were hit by stray bullets, an almost inevitable consequence [of] such a situation. While some of the soldiers rushed upstairs to kill the tw[o] terrorists remaining there, the hostages were shepherded out to the waiting [C-] 130s. At this point "Yoni" Netanyahu emerged from the terminal to supervise th[e] loading and was killed by one shot from a Ugandan solider in a nearby buildin[g,] a sad loss.

At 0045 hours the defensive outposts were called in as the first C-1[30] roared off into the night with its load of rescued hostages on their way [to] Nairobi, with the fourth and last leaving at 0054.

Apart from the loss of Colonel Netanyahu, three Israeli rescuers we[re] wounded. Three hostages were killed in the rescue, while a fourth, Mrs Do[ra] Bloch, who had been taken off to a local hospital earlier, was murdered by th[e] Ugandans in revenge for the raid. On the other side, in addition to the terrorist[s] there were 20 Ugandans killed and more than 100 wounded.

The whole operation was a brilliant success, mounted on short notice an[d]

*Right: Chief-of-staff,
General Gur, briefs the
press on the return of the
commando from Entebbe.*

...n a most unexpected direction.
...confirmed the Israeli rep-
...tation for quick and deter-
...ined "ad hoc" action, con-
...ucted with great dedication
...nd skill. The Ugandans could
...ot be described as substantial

...oes, but the terrorists had obviously been trained for their task. Interestingly, it later
...ecame known that Colonel Ulrich Wegener of Germany's GSG 9 was with the
...sraelis on the operation, possibly because of the known presence of the two
...ermans with the terrorists.

The first rescue attempt of its type – unless one considers the U.S. raid on
...on Tay Prison in Vietnam, which the Israelis reportedly used as a model – the
...ntebbe rescue caught the terrorists and Ugandans completely off guard.
...ollowing Entebbe, all terrorists have to take into account the possibility that a
...escue mission could be carried out in hostile territory over great distances. ▶

*Below: C-130 carrying the rescued hostages taxis in at Lod airport, on its
...riumphant return from Entebbe.*

Above: The scene at Lod airport as Israelis celebrate one of the most daring hostage rescue operations ever undertaken.

Mogadishu Rescue (1977)

On October 13, 1977, a Lufthansa 737 airliner en route from Palma in the Balearic Islands to Germany was hijacked by terrorists over the French Mediterranean coast. On board the aircraft were five aircrew (two pilots, three stewardesses), 86 passengers, and four terrorists, two of them women. The hijackers' leader called himself "Captain Mahmoud," and was subsequently identified as a notorious international terrorist, Zohair Youssef Akache. He ordered the aircraft captain to fly to Fiucimino airport in Rome, where the airliner was refueled.

From Rome, the airliner set off eastwards and landed at Larnaca in Cyprus at 2038. Here, "Mahmoud" demanded that the aircraft be refueled again, or he would blow it up, the first of many threats to use explosives. After refueling, the airliner took off and overflew various Middle East countries. Permission to land at Beirut was denied and the runways were blocked, so it was taken on to Bahrein in the Persian Gulf where the same thing happened. It was flown on to Dubai, where, despite being refused permission to land, the crew were forced to do so for lack of fuel.

At one point at Dubai the airliner lost power and the temperature inside rose to over 120°F (49°C); many of the passengers, some of them quite elderly, became very distressed. While here, the crew managed surreptitiously to signal that there were four hijackers.

Then on Sunday, October 16, the airliner suddenly took off, only 40 minutes

Below: German GSG-9 operators, accompanied by two British SAS men assault the hijacked Boeing 737 at Mogadishu.

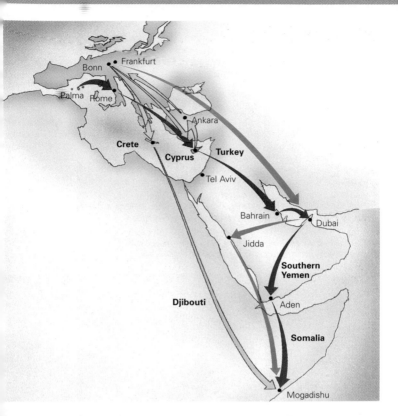

Above: The Lufthansa jet, en route from Las Palma to Germany, was hijacked over France and ended up in Somalia.

before the first deadline for blowing it up. It was refused permission to land in Oman and arrived over Aden airport with sufficient fuel for another 10 minutes' flying. Despite warnings from air traffic control, the aircraft was brought down safely on the taxi track.

Pilot Executed

By now conditions inside the aircraft were very bad, and "Mahmoud" was acting in an increasingly unpredictable and unstable manner. Jürgen Schumann, the pilot, was allowed to leave the airliner to check the under-carriage, and disappeared for a few minutes. When he returned he was taken to the first-class cabin and made to kneel on the floor; "Mahmoud" then shot him in the head, killing him instantly, directly as a result of Schumann's earlier, successful effort to feed information about the terrorists to authorities.

The next morning the co-pilot, Jürgen Vietor, took off and flew the airliner to Mogadishu, the capital of Somalia. There, German government spokesmen contacted the hijackers and said that they were prepared to release 11 terrorists held in jail and fly them to Mogadishu; "Mahmoud" postponed his deadline to 0145 hours the next morning (October 18).

The Rescue

A 30-strong contigent from GSG 9 was in the air within hours of the hijacking ▶

▶ and arrived in Cyprus just as the Boeing 737 was taking off. Following a brief discussion with the Cypriot police, the GSG 9 team took off in their aircraft again and returned, via Ankara, to Frankfurt. Meanwhile, a second aircraft containing Hans-Jürgen Wischenewski, West German Minister of State, psychologist Wolfgang Salewski, and another 30-strong group from GSG 9, led by their commander Ulrich Wegener, had left West Germany and gone to Dubai. From there they went to Mogadishu, where they were given permission to land.

In Mogadishu, Wischenewski took over discussions with the hijackers. As the 1600 hours deadline approached and it was clear that "Mahmoud" would in all probability carry out his threat to blow up the aircraft, the German minister said that the 11 prisoners would be released. "Mahmoud" gave them until 0245 hours the following morning to produce the 11 at Mogadishu. At 2000 hours the first group of GSG 9 who had gone to Cyprus and then returned to Germany

Right: Sole terrorist survivor, Suhaila Sayeh, is carried away. She now lives in Norway, resisting extradition to Germany.

Below: Lufthansa Flight LH 747 on the runway at Mogadishu; inside are five aircrew, 86 passengers and four terrorists.

▶ arrived in Mogadishu and the rescue briefings began.

At 0205 hours, just 40 minues before the deadline, Somali troops lit a diversionary fire ahead of the aircraft. Two hijackers went to the cockpit to assess its significance, whereupon the tower contacted them by radio and started to discuss the conditions of the exchange. They said it would commence in the near future, when the aircraft arrived from Germany with the released prisoners on board.

At 0207 precisely the emergency doors over the aircraft wings were blown open and members of the rescue party tossed in some "stun grenades." The men of GSG 9, with two British SAS men lent by the British government, had reached the aircraft and climbed onto the wings completely undetected; the hijackers (and the hostages) were taken by surprise.

The men of GSG 9 rushed into the aircraft shouting to the hostages to keep down on the floor, and opened fire on the hijackers. "Mahmoud" was fatally wounded in the first few seconds, but managed to throw two hand-grenades

Below: Welcoming VIPs disperse following the return of the GSG-9 and the rescued hostages; note man with rifle, center.

Above: GSG-9 men run past the welcoming crowd; success at Mogadishu relegated the Munich fiasco to a distant memory.

efore he died; fortunately, their effects were cushioned because they rolled eneath seats. One of the women terrorists died also and the second man was ⁄ounded inside the aircraft but died outside it a few minutes later. The second ⁄oman, Suhaila Sayeh, was wounded but did not die. Meanwhile, the assengers were herded off the aircraft through the doors and emergency ⁄xits; three hostages had been wounded, but none was killed.

The operation ended at 0212 hours and was entirely successful. GSG 9 had ⁊roved itself and the men received a well-merited heroes' welcome when they ⁊turned to Germany.

Mogadishu was, at the very least, a tribute to the intensive physical and ⁊ental training undertaken by the GSG 9, as well as to that unit's attention to ⁊chnological back-up, examples being the special rubber-coated-alloy assault ⁊dders used, and the stun grenades. At its best, it formed a new standard for ⁊scue operations in that no hostages were killed during the assault – unlike at ⁊jibouti and Entebbe which, though outstandingly successful in their own right, ⁊d resulted in at least one hostage death.

Moluccan Train Incident (1977)

Throughout the Netherlands in the 1970s, repeated terrorist incidents by Sout
Moluccans grabbed headlines. The incidents were used by the terrorists t
press demands that the Dutch government support independence for the
homeland - the Moluccan Islands, now a part of Indonesia, but formerly a Dutc
colonial possession. (They were at one time known as the Spice Islands.) The
radicals spearheading the terrorist activity were generally the Dutch-bor
children of Moluccan immigrants, and had begun forming guerrilla squads in th
late 1960s and accumulating arsenals of weapons.

Violence included the killing of a policeman in 1973 when South Moluccan
seized the Indonesian embassy in The Hague; the following year, Sout
Moluccans stormed and damaged The Hague Palace itself; and in 1976, the
killed three hostages during a train hijacking.

But on May 23, 1977, two groups of South Moluccan terrorists launche
their most spectacular attack yet in the opening phase of what was to becom
a three-week drama. The groups simultaneously hijacked a Dutch train an
occupied an elementary school in a northern part of the Netherlands,

The raid began when two terrorists pulled an emergency cord to sto
Express Train 747 as it traveled between Assen and Groningen. Five maske
gunmen rushed aboard, herding 49 hostages into the first-class compartments

Minutes later and a few miles away, seven terrorists invaded an elementar
school, forcing 110 hostages into the main classroom. Of the 110 hostages, 10

*Below: Dutch troops stand beside their blue-painted armored personnel
carriers (APCs), awaiting the call to action.*

Above: The setting of the spectacular South Moluccan operation in the north-east corner of the Netherlands.

were released unharmed a few days later after a virus struck the children.

In addition to demanding assistance in their independence efforts, the Moluccans insisted that they, as well as 21 other South Moluccans jailed for various assaults (including the planned kidnapping of Queen Juliana), be allowed to leave the country. Dutch officials handling the situation steadfastly refused to meet the terrorist demands, but continued to negotiate with them. There was a reluctance to use force, despite the previous train seizure only 18 months earlier. However, the order for the June 10 rescue assault came only after negotiations dragged on for three weeks with no progress . . . and as the Dutch public grew increasingly impatient and bitter over the stalemate. What was to follow was later characterized, appropriately enough, as a switch from psychology to technology.

Execution

Even though the Dutch government was reluctant to use force, contingency plans had been put in place from the start. To break the dual siege, it was determined that a dual attack would be required. If either the train or the school were taken individually, the terrorists at the remaining location seemed certain to exact vengeance on the hostages in their custody.

Throughout the siege, the specially picked Royal Dutch Marines, and civilian and military police had been rehearsing assaults on an empty train at the nearby Gilze Rijin Air Force Base. Eight combat swimmers had approached the train by way of a canal that ran within 15 yards (5m) of the tracks and had put sensitive bugging devices in place. ▶

▶ Special radar that could detect the heat differences in hot and cold surface had also been put in place; this allowed the Marines to monitor the movement of the terrorists through the metal in their weapons. Other sophisticated device were used so that the Marines would know where the terrorists and hostage were likely to be should the "go" decision be made for the assault.

When it came, Marines wearing night-vision goggles approached the train and launched what was to be a 20-minute attack. Six F-104 Starfighter aircra immediately flew in criss-cross patterns just a few feet above the train, kickin in their afterburners in an attempt to distract the terrorists and encourage th hostages to keep their heads down. As the jets roared overhead, a force Marine and police sharpshooters raced across a 100-yard (30m) field and opene up with their weapons on areas of the train where the terrorists normally slep Shortly before 0500, the assault force blew the doors off with framing charge and went in with Uzis blazing.

Six of the nine terrorists were killed during the assault; two hostages wh had panicked and stood up as bullets blazed about were killed also. Seven othe hostages, two Dutch Marines, and one terrorist were wounded.

Simultaneously with the assault on the train, Marines assaulted the scho at Bovensmilde, rushing the building with armored personnel carriers from four sides, one of them bursting through a wall. The 10-minute attack met r resistance; four terrorists were captured (three were asleep in their underwea and the four hostages were rescued unharmed.

Assessment

The assault demonstrated that the Dutch would resort to force if necessa to counter terrorism. This was particularly important to the governmer since the belief had been prevalent among South Moluccans that forc would not be used, no matter how hard the Dutch were pushed. Perhap another salutory effect of the split-second, high-tech and successful attac was that it helped temper some of the derogatory remarks directed at lon haired Dutch troops by their more conventional colleagues from othe European nations.

Another point was eventually driven home: terrorism would not g unpunished in the courts either. Seven of the terrorists, aged 18 to 28, receive prison terms ranging from six to nine years, while another received a one-ye term for helping plan the dual seizure.

above: The siege broken, two South Moluccan terrorists sit in the doorway of a carriage, awaiting their fate.

below: A school was also occupied; here a rifle (left) pokes through a curtain of a room where 110 hostages are held.

Above: Terrorists struck the Netherlands again in 1978; here Dutch troops surround a building where 70 hostages are held.

Achille Lauro Incident (1985)

The saga of the *Achille Lauro* began when four Palestinian guerrillas, armed with Soviet-made machine guns and brandishing hand grenades, took 80 passengers and 340 crewmembers hostage aboard the Italian cruise liner in October 1985. They threatened to kill the passengers, beginning with the Americans, then moving on to Jews and British citizens, if their demands for the release of 50 Palestinians held in Israel were not met.

What followed were 51 hours of threats and violence. Walls and ceilings were sprayed with bullets. The terrorists pulled pins from grenades and tossed them in the air. Gasoline bombs were placed in various parts of the liner. Ultimately, the grisly scenario led to the execution of Leon Klinghoffer, a 69-year old handicapped American, murdered in his wheelchair.

As these events were unfolding, the *Achille Lauro* wandered along the north coast of Africa seeking haven. Ultimately, the cruise liner anchored off Port Said, Egypt, and the "seajackers" – after negotiations with Palestinian, Italian, and Egyptian officials – went ashore.

Americans, predictably, were demanding that the terrorists be brought to justice, and Egyptian President Hosni Mubarak announced they had already left Egypt allegedly under terms of an agreement struck before the murder of Klinghoffer was known. U.S. intelligence, however, indicated that the four hijackers were still in Egypt and that neither that country nor the PLO had quite figured out what to do with them. This delay provided the United States with an opportunity to shape a plan to help deal with the emerging situation.

Execution

The U.S. Navy aircraft carrier USS *Saratoga* was cruising off Albania and was called into action just two hours before the mission. The Italian government later to play a key role in dealing with the terrorists, was not notified until after the mission had begun,

The plan involved calling in the *Saratoga*'s aircraft to surprise the terrorists as they boarded an airliner to fly over the Mediterranean, and force the aircraft to land in Sicily. Intelligence sources had in fact confirmed that the hijackers were still in Egypt, but that they planned to fly to Algiers aboard an Egyptair Boeing

Below: Hijacking an ocean liner seemed an improbable scenario until it happened with the Italian **Achille Lauro.**

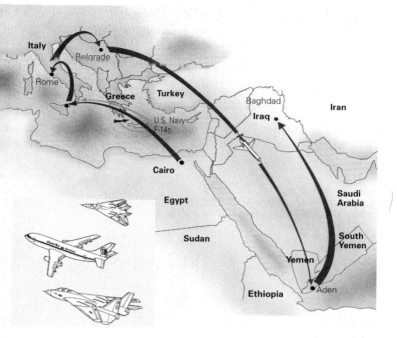

Above: The air chase as aircraft from carrier USS Saratoga force Egyptair Boeing 737 to land at Salerno airport.

737. Just 45 minutes after the 737 took off from Al Maza Air Base, northeast of Cairo, it was intercepted.

Awaiting it were E-2C Hawkeye radar aircraft, F-14 Tomcat fighters, and EA-6B Prowler electronic warfare aircraft. At first, the F-14s trailed the 737 with no ▶

Below: The Achille Lauro hijackers threatened to kill the American passengers, followed by the Jews and the British.

▶ lights on and with cockpits darkened. When they prepared to intercept, they turned on their lights and surrounded the airliner.

The Egyptair pilot desperately tried to radio Cairo for instructions, but his communications had been jammed by the EA-6B aircraft. The airline pilot, recognizing his position, eventually agreed to follow American orders.

The formation approached Sigonella Air Base, a NATO installation on Sicily's densely populated eastern coast. However, Italian air traffic controllers refused the 737 permission to enter their airspace. It was only after the Egyptian pilot declared an in-flight emergency that clearance was finally received.

One F-14 led the 737 into Sigonella while three others stayed in formation up to the traffic pattern. Following the lead F-14, the 737 taxied to an isolated corner of the base, where it was immediately surrounded by Italian carabinieri. Its passengers were taken into custody.

Not only were the four hijackers aboard, but also Abul Abbas, a high-ranking aide to PLO Chairman Yasir Arafat. Abbas was not only the suspected

Below: Her wanderings over, the Achille Lauro lies in harbor under armed guard; there have been no further sea hijackings.

mastermind behind the *Achille Lauro* incident, but the person who was instrumental in getting the terrorists off the liner when it finally docked in Egypt. Abbas later slipped out of Italy before he could be prosecuted. Because an American citizen was killed during the "seajacking," U.S. chagrin at the escape of Abbas was great, creating diplomatic difficulties between Italy and the United States.

Assessment

In the eyes of many observers, the operation demonstrated that high technology can indeed work well in a counter-terrorist situation. It was considered a triumph of electronics and communications carried out on short notice under cover of darkness and at high speeds.

To this day, a definitive account of all the high tech that went into the operation has not been made available. However, it worked and the United States clearly demonstrated that it had the resolve to back its threats to strike back at terrorists who attacked American citizens. What really counted was that terrorists who took the law into their own hands for whatever motive were ultimately brought before the bar of justice.

Above: One of the hijackers listens attentively as his case is heard in an Italian courtroom.

Iranian Embassy Siege (1980)

The siege of the Iranian Embassy in London in April-May 1980 caught the imagination of the world and brought the SAS into the limelight because the denouement took place before the gathered press photographers and TV. The eerie, black-clad figures, their efficiency, and the success and sheer drama of the event established for the SAS a public reputation and created an expectation of success which will endure for many years.

The Iranian Embassy at No. 16 Princes Gate, London, opposite Hyde Park, was taken over at 1130 hours Wednesday April 30 by six terrorists armed with three 9mm automatic pistols, one 0.38in revolver, two 9mm sub-machine guns and a number of Chinese-made hand grenades. There were six men directly involved: Oan, the leader (27 years old), and five others, all in their early twenties. They were all from Arabistan, an area of Iran some 400 miles (643km) from Teheran, which had long resisted the rule of the Aryan northerners. Most had supported Ayatollah Khomeini's takeover from the Shah, only to find him as ruthless a suppressor of minorities as his predecessor. The terrorists represented a group entitled the Democratic Revolutionary Movement for the Liberation of Arabistan (DRMLA), a Marxist-Leninist group based in Libya whose cause was regional autonomy (not independence) for Arabistan.

The occupants of the embassy at the time of the takeover numbered 26

Below: Black-clad SAS man, armed with a Heckler & Koch MP5, climbs over the balcony in front of the Iranian Embassy.

Surveillance devices lowered down chimneys to determine location of hostages and terrorists

SAS men abseil down the rear wall of the building, one becoming stuck and having to be cut free

SAS assault squads use stun grenades and shaped charges to gain entry and create shock. Fire and smoike must have added to the terrorists' panic

Based on an artist's impression which appeared in The Elite, issue No.1, published by Orbis Publishing Ltd.

Above: The five-storey, 50-room Iranian Embassy at Princess Gate, London, is a large and complex building.

four British and 25 Iranian men and women, three of whom escaped during the early minutes. The terrorists' demands were initially that 91 prisoners in Arabistan be released by the Iranian authorities. The deadline was set for 1200 hours Thursday May 1, and during that night the terrorists had the first of many contacts with the London police and the media.

One sick Iranian woman was released late on Wednesday night and a sick Englishman the following morning. The first deadline was postponed when the police transmitted a message from the terrorists to the press, and a second deadline (1400 hours) passed without a move from either side.

By Friday morning there had been numerous contacts between the terrorists and the police, some direct and some through intermediaries, but by now specific threats were being made against the lives of the hostages. Negotiations continued throughout Saturday and a major advance was achieved when the terrorists agreed to release two hostages in return for a broadcast on the radio of a statement of their aims. One hostage was released in the early evening and after the statement had been broadcast word for word another was released. The atmosphere in the embassy became almost euphoric, helped by a good meal sent in by the police. ▶

▶   Throughout Sunday the British government discussed the situation wit various Arab ambassadors, but no agreement could be reached on a possib role for them in reaching a resolution to the crisis. In the embassy the majo event in an anti-climactic day was the release of an Iranian hostage who ha become ill. On Monday the terrorists were noticeably more nervous and shouted discussion between two British hostages and the police at noon di little to ease the tension. At about 1330, Oan's patience apparently snapped an

Above: Two SAS troopers armed with 9mm pistols; unseen at their feet are rifles, tear-gas launchers and other weapons.

e shot Abbas Lavasani, one of the embassy staff, in the course of a telephone iscussion with the police. This was the turning point.

Any doubts about whether anyone had actually been killed were resolved just fter 1900 when the dead body was pushed through the front door of the embassy. ▶

► SAS soldiers had visited the scene on the first day of the siege, and thereafter they stood by in an Army barracks some two miles away. The police had obviously tried their best to identify just where the hostages and their captors were and what they were all doing; many highly classified surveillance devices were used. The SAS were therefore as ready as it was possible to be in the circumstances when, in accordance with British legal practice, the police formally asked the military to deal with the situation.

Rescue

plan was to use just 12 men in three teams of the customary four-man SAS groups; two teams were to take the rear, descending by rope from the roof, one team to reach the ground and the second the first-floor balcony. Both teams ▶

Below: Pictures that raced around the world, as the SAS stormed the Iranian Embassy; the attack lasted a few minutes.

▶ would then break in using either frame-charges or brute force. Team three w
to be at the front, crossing from a balcony at No. I5 Princes Gate to No. 16. On
inside all three teams were to rush to reach the hostages before they could
harmed.

Everything that could be done to heighten the impact of the attack w
done. The 12 SAS men were dressed from head to foot in black, even including
rubber anti-gas respirators, and looked extremely menacing. They would ga
entrance using 4ft x 2ft (1.2 x 0.6m) frame-charges, followed by stun grenad

Above: A hostage escaping; one SAS aim was to reach the hostages before they could be harmed by their captors.

"flashbangs"). Teargas would also be used. The combination of explosions, noise, smoke, speed of action, and the appearance of the men was intended to strike confusion and dread into the minds of the terrorists – and it succeeded brilliantly.

The SAS men had, naturally, pored over the plans of the 50-room building in ▶

175

▶ minute detail and had also spent many hours studying the photographs of the hostages. But, in the end – as every soldier knows – all the training and planning have to be translated into action.

At 1926 hours precisely the men of the rear attack force stepped over the edge of the roof and abseiled down. The first two went down each rope successfully, but one of the third pair became stuck, a hazard known to abseilers everywhere. In the front, SAS men appeared on the balcony of No. 15 and climbed over to the embassy, giving the world's press and the public an image which will last for years.

Simultaneously, police spoke to the terrorists on the telephone and distracted their attention at the critical moment the SAS burst in. Stun grenades exploded, lights went out, and all was noise and apparent confusion. Some parts of the embassy caught fire and the SAS man hanging on the rope at the rear was cut free and dropped onto a balcony – a risk preferable to that of being roasted alive.

The SAS men swept through the embassy. Two terrorists were quickly shot and killed. One started shooting the hostages in an upstairs room, but stopped after causing a few wounds. Within minutes five of the six gunmen were dead, with the sixth sheltering among the newly freed hostages. All survivors were rushed downstairs into the garden, where the remaining terrorist was identified and arrested.

The entire operation took eleven minutes from start to finish. While the SAS is the last organization in the world to seek out publicity, its well-heralded assault had at least two effects: first, it reinforced the message to potential terrorists that their activities could be dealt with in a severe, if effective, manner; and, secondly, it gave the British public a healthy shot of national pride.

Right: This was the first time that the SAS all-black combat uniform had been seen in public; it has since been copied by many other military and police anti-terrorist units around the world.

Operation Eagle Claw (1980,

On November 4, 1979, a group of Iranian "students" poured into the
Embassy compound in Teheran and seized 53 occupants. They were to ⌐
them hostage for 444 days.

From the earliest days of the crisis one of the options under consta⌐
review and development was a military rescue, although both diplomatic an⌐
military endeavors were constantly bedeviled by the continuing chaos in Iran
the uncertain, ever-changing intentions of the captors, and the vacillatin⌐
position of the Iranian leadership. An unchanging factor was the remoteness o⌐
Teheran from available U.S. bases. The plan that was eventually decided upor
centered on Colonel Charlie Beckwith and the elite Delta force, although i⌐
obviously involved many more resources both directly and indirectly. The overa⌐
codename was "Operation Eagle Claw," its helicopter element "Operatior
Evening Light." The plan was complicated mainly by the problems of time an⌐
space, and comprised some preliminary moves and a three-phase operation.

Preliminary Moves

In the preliminary moves Delta was to fly, via Germany and Egypt, to Masira⌐
airfield in Oman. There they would transfer to C-130s and, flying at very lov
level to avoid radar, cross the Gulf of Oman and southern Iran to land at Deser
One, a remote site in the Dasht-e-Karir Salt Desert, 265 nautical miles (490km
south east of Teheran. Meanwhile, eight U.S. Navy RH-53D helicopters, whic⌐
had been deployed some weeks earlier via Diego Garcia, would take off from
the carrier USS *Nimitz* and, flown (also at very low level) by U.S. Marine Corp⌐
crews, join up with the main party at Desert One.

Phase 1: Insertion

At Desert One the plan was for the six C-130s (three troop carriers; three t⌐
refuel the helicopters) to land and await the helicopters, which were schedule⌐
to arrive some 30 minutes later. Because Desert One was beside a road (judge⌐
to be little used), a 12-strong Road Watch Team was the first to deploy t⌐
intercept and detain any passing Iranians.

When they had refueled, the helicopters were to load the assault team an⌐

Leading RH-53Ds
fly into unexpected
"haboobs" – dust
storms

RH-53D No.6
aborts. Crew
picked up by
RH-53D No.8

Disaster at Desert One, as
RH-53D collides with C-130
tanker, after entire mission
had been aborted. Eight
servicemen are killed.
Remaining servicemen,
including Delta Force, flown
to Masirah airfield, Oman

RH-53D No.5
returns to
Nimitz,
aborting mission

*Above: The helicopter debacle; one had a
malfunction, another a rotor problem, the third
collided with a C-130 at Desert One.*

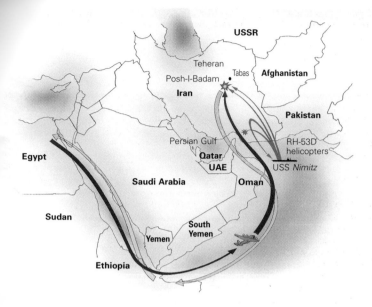

Above: The plan was for C-130s to fly to Desert One (red), meet RH-53s (green); after the disaster they returned (brown).

fly on towards Teheran, dropping off the men at a landing zone and then proceeding to their helicopter hide some 15 miles (24km) to the north. The assault group was to be met by two agents at the landing zone and guided by them to a remote wadi, some 5 miles (8km) away. Helicopters and men would then rest in their hides through the day.

Phase IIA: The Rescue

After last light one agent would take the 12 drivers/translators to collect six Mercedes trucks, while the other agent would take Colonel Beckwith on a route reconnaissance. At 2030 hours the complete unit would embus at the hide and drive to Teheran, the actual rescue operation starting between 2300 and 2400 hours. Having disposed of the guards and released the hostages, it was planned to call in the helicopters, either to the embassy compound if an LZ could be cleared (the "students" had erected poles to prevent a surprise landing) or, if this was impracticable, to a nearby football stadium. Once all the hostages were clear the assault party would be taken out by helicopter, the White Element being the last out.

▶ Phase II: Rescue at the Foreign Ministry

Concurrently with Phase IIA the 13-man special team would assault the Ministry, rescue the hostages there, and take them to an adjacent park they would all be picked up by a helicopter.

Phase III: Extraction

While the action was taking place in Teheran, a Ranger contingent would seize Manzarieh airfield, some 35 miles (56km) to the south, and several C-141 turbojet transports would fly in. Once everyone had been evacuated from Teheran to Manzarieh they would be flown out in the C-141s, the Rangers leaving last. All surviving helicopters would be abandoned at Manzarieh.

Contingency Plans

Various contingencies were foreseen and plans made accordingly; for example in the event that not enough helicopters were available to lift everyone out of Teheran in one lift. One critically important condition had been agreed throughout the planning, namely that there had to be an absolute minimum of six helicopters to fly out of Desert One, since planners expected at least one to fail during the mission.

Command and Control

Ground force commander Colonel Beckwith reported to Major-General James Vaught, the Commander Joint Task Force (COMJTF), who was at Wadi Kena airfield in Egypt; they were linked by portable satellite systems. General Vaught had a similar link back to Washington, DC, where General David Jones, then Chairman of the Joint Chiefs of Staff, was in session with President Jimmy Carter throughout the critical hours of the operation. In a last-minute change of plans, Air Force Colonel James Kyle was appointed commander at Desert One.

Execution

The C-141 airlift of the ground party went according to plan, as did the C-130 flights to Desert One. The first aircraft, carrying Colonels Beckwith and Kyle

Above: The RH-53D was large and impressive, but like all helicopters of the era, had mechanical weaknesses.

Left: The RH-53Ds had the longest range and greatest capacity of any U.S. Navy helicopter of its time.

Blue Element and the Road Watch Team, landed safely and the Road Watch Team deployed, immediately having to stop a bus containing 45 people who were detained under guard,

Minutes later two more vehicles appeared from the south; the first, a petrol tanker, was hit by an anti-tank rocket and burst into flames, but the driver escaped in the second vehicle which drove off at high speed. The first C-130 then took off, leaving those on the ground briefly on their own. The second C-130 then came in and unloaded and, after the remaining four C-130s had landed, took off again for Masirah. The four C-130s and the ground ▶

▶ party then waited for the helicopters and waited ....

The eight helicopters were, quite literally, the key to the operation. Th[e] taken off from USS *Nimitz* some 50 miles off the Iranian coast at 1905 (local), as scheduled, and headed north for Desert One. At about 2145 h helicopter No. 6 indicated an impending catastrophic blade failure, one of two really critical problems requiring an abort. The crew landed, confirmed [the] problem, removed sensitive documents and were then picked up by helicopt[er] No. 8 which then followed the others some minutes behind.

About one hour later the leading RH-53Ds ran into a very severe and totall[y] unexpected dust storm; all emerged from this, flew on for an hour and the[n] encountered a second and even worse dust storm. (What they encountere[d] was a *haboob*, a meteorological phenomenon in which gusts generated b[y] thunderstorms kick up masses of dust many miles away. In Iran, where th[e] dust is extremely fine, a *haboob* can linger in the air for hours.)

The helicopter force commander – Major Seiffert, USMC – had earlier los[t] his inertial navigation system and, entirely blinded, flew back out of the firs[t] dust storm and landed, accompanied by helicopter No. 2. Major Seiffert had [a] secure radio link to COMJTF, who told him that the weather at Desert One wa[s] clear; consequently, after some 20 minutes on the ground both aircraft took of[f] again and followed the others to Desert One.

Meanwhile, helicopter No. 5 suffered several problems, including the los[s] of its gyro, a burnout of its tactical navigation system, and a radar receive[r] failure. With no artificial horizon or heading, and with mountains ahead, the pilo[t] was compelled to abort, and barely made it back to the *Nimitz*, thus leaving si[x] helicopters to continue the mission.

The first helicopter (No. 3) cleared the dust storm some 30nm (56km) from Desert One and, using the burning Iranian petrol tanker as a beacon, lande[d] some 50 minutes late. The remaining aircraft straggled in over the next half-an hour, all coming from different directions (except Nos. 1 and 2, which wer[e] together). The crews were shaken by their experience, but the helicopters wer[e]

Below: On the flightdeck of USS **Nimitz***, the helicopters are readied for their part in Operation Eagle Claw.*

Above: Eight lives were lost at Desert One – five USAF, three Marines – all aircrew; this is the USAF memorial service.

quickly moved to their tanker C-130s, refueling began, and the assault party started to board their designated aircraft.

Colonel Beckwith was fretting on the ground, 90 minutes behind schedule, when he was informed that helicopter No. 2 had had a partial hydraulic failure during the flight; the pilot had continued on to Desert One in the hope of effecting repairs, but these proved impossible. The decision to call the whole thing off was quickly reached. There was no problem in aborting at this stage, even though the rescue team had never practised an abort order. The only minor complication was that helicopter No. 4, which had been on the ground longest, needed to top up with fuel before setting off to the

Nimitz. Only one C-130 had enough fuel left and to clear a space for No. 4 helicopter No. 3 took off and banked to the left, but, because of the height (5,000ft/l,525m) and its weight (42,000lb/19,050kg), it could not maintain the hover and banked right into the C-130.

The effect was instantaneous and disastrous: both aircraft exploded, debris flew around and ammunition began to cook off. Five USAF aircrewmen in the C-130 and three Marines in the RH-53D died, but 64 Delta men inside the C-130 escaped quickly from the aircraft and rescued the loadmaster. The decision was then made to abandon the remaining helicopters and the whole party returned to Masirah in the three C-130s.

In hindsight, it can always be said mission planners should have done more, that 10 helicopters should have been sent instead of eight, that much more should have been known about *haboob*s, and so on. But the Chief of Naval Operations, Adm. Thomas Hayward, summed it up rather cogently in an interview shortly after the attempted rescue. "There had to be some mistakes made," he conceded. But, in the end, the mission was affected at least as much by an incredible string of misfortunes.

The Battle for Mogadishu (199

Operation Restore Hope shows what happens when missions are unclear special forces are used in roles for which they were not intended. During 1980s and early 1990s, unending violence in Somalia led to increasi international frustration as aid was seen to be getting into the hands of gunme and failing to reach the starving Somali people who were regularly seen on TV This was hardly surprising as Mogadishu port was held hostage by some 1,000 young gunmen belonging to five separate armed groups, each of which charged aid authorities "protection money" and then stole from the very convoys the were being paid to guard.

In late 1992 international indignation peaked and outgoing U.S. Presiden Bush committed American troops to Somalia in what was planned to be a short sharp operation, to be completed before incoming President Clinton took office in January 1993. U.S. Marines carried out a tactical amphibious landing on the night of December 9 1992 – to be greeted by waiting pressmen equipped with cameras and floodlights.

The U.S. force quickly became bogged down as troops and the Press corps tried – and failed – to understand Somali politics. Military attention – encouraged by the Press – concentrated increasingly on one warlord: "General" Aidid. Then on June 5 1993, 24 Pakistani troops of the UN force were killed, resulting in UN Resolution 837 ordering the "arrest and detention for prosecution of those

Below: Pakistani corporal (left) tries to control an angry crowd; the Pakistan army suffered numerous casualties.

Above: Loudspeaker-equipped Marine Corps HMMWV in Mogadishu; but the gulf with the locals proved unbridgeable.

▶ responsible." In practical terms, that meant Aidid, but repeated atten~
capture him failed and matters got worse: Pakistani troops fired into a
(20 dead); U.S. gunships attacked suspected arms dumps; Italian soldiers
attacked (3 dead); U.S. helicopters attacked Aidid's command post (70 d~
and Somalis attacked pressmen (4 dead). Meanwhile, Aidid, despite an offe~
a US$25,000 reward for his capture, led a charmed existence.

The senior UN administrator, retired U.S. Admiral Howe, requested t~
despatch of U.S. Special Forces. The 400-man "Task Force Ranger," consisting ~
Rangers and Delta commandos, arrived, its mission to capture Aidid; in oth~
words, a man-hunt. Intelligence passed to Task Force Ranger was poor:
September they mistakenly arrested eight members of a UN-sponsore~
development program and later they "snatched" a Somali, thought to be Aidi~
Not only was he not Aidid, but he was also a well-known U.S. supporter. Then ~
September 23, a U.S. helicopter was shot down and its crew of three were kille~

Aidid's men carefully observed U.S. special forces tactics in these action~
and noted that raids always consisted of an assault by heliborne troops, ropi~
down in two parties: one (Delta) entering the house, the other (Ranger~
forming a cordon outside. Meanwhile, helicopters flew overhead, observi~
providing covering fire and summoning reinforcements. The Somali gunme~
then devised a plan which combined attacks against the helicopters and the u~
of overwhelming ground forces.

The Somalis were particularly adept at their specialized style of urb~
warfare. There were a few wide boulevards, but the greater part of Mogadis~
was a labyrinth of narrow, twisting alleys, lined on both sides by houses, ma~
with small, high-sided courtyards. The U.S. troops, used to wide open stree~
and grid patterns of their home towns found these most confusing a~
frequently got lost. They also found the complex clan structure, which rule~
Somali lives, impossible to comprehend, resulting in an enormous gulf betwe~
them and the Somalis; the Americans were totally mystified at the way of li~
and ingratitude of the Somali people, while the latter bitterly resented outsi~
interference in their affairs. On top of all this, Mogadishu was awash wi~

Below: Italian troops taking part in Operation Restore Hope; the former
colonial ruler's advice was often rejected.

Above: Heavily armed U.S. patrol in downtown Mogadishu; the good humor and smiles did not last long.

weapons and the Somali clans could mobilize thousands of armed men, women and children in a matter of minutes.

Then U.S. intelligence learnt of a top-level meeting to be held on October 3, 1993, in a second-floor room in a building known as the "Aidi house." They were told that Aidid would attend, so a "snatch" was set up, involving AH-1 and OH-6 gunships, UH-60 troop-carrying helicopters, Delta hit squad, Ranger cordon troops and a ground vehicle convoy. Command was exercised by a Delta colonel in a UH-60 command helicopter circling at some 3,000ft (1,000m), with a U.S. Navy P-3 Orion surveillance aircraft about 900ft (300m) above that.

The battle started with Cobra gunships firing TOW missiles into the Aidi house, where some 90 men had assembled, although not Aidid himself. Then 20 Delta men and Rangers roped down beside the smouldering building: the Delta force stormed inside, while Rangers set up the cordon. Inside, many Somalis were already dead. Some managed to escape, but U.S. troops captured 24.

The Somali militia mobilized and the U.S. troops were quickly brought under fire. One militiaman fired an RPG-7 missile at a low-flying UH-60, destroying the tail rotor, and the aircraft spun into a house then tumbled into an alleyway (Crash 1). Another helicopter arrived and its combat rescue troops roped to the ground, but while hovering it, too, was hit by an RPG and the pilot just managed to return to base.

The U.S. ground convoy of HMMWVs en route to the Aidi house took casualties from close-range fire, responding with rifles, machine guns and .50in cannon. Whenever the vehicles stopped (usually because they had taken a wrong turning) men jumped out to guard them and took yet more casualties. Despite this, the convoy reached the Aidi house and took the 24 prisoners on board, together with some wounded Delta and Rangers; men were packed ▶

187

► inside like sardines, the remainder had to walk.

The convoy was about to move off when new orders were rec[eived]. Instead of heading out of the city the convoy was to go to Crash 1, which [was] only three blocks distant, and rescue any survivors who could be reached [some] other way, while the remaining unwounded troops moved to the crash site [on] foot. Then news was received that a second UH-60 was down (Crash 2) a[nd] they were ordered to proceed there after rescuing the survivors at Crash 1.

Matters then got worse. In the foot party, cooperation between Ranger[s] and Delta became very strained, although, despite being under constant fire, they eventually reached the crash site and joined in a defensive battle. The vehicle convoy, however, repeatedly took wrong turnings and after 45 minutes ended up back where it had started – in front of the Aidi house. Since he had many wounded and virtually all vehicles were seriously damaged, the convoy commander refused to make another attempt to reach either helicopter crash site and he headed back to base.

Meanwhile, a second vehicle convoy (four HMMWVs; three 5-ton flatbed trucks) was hastily assembled at the base 2 miles (3km) down the beach to rescue the crew of the second downed UH-60. This convoy also came under heavy fire and was forced to turn round and take a different route, but that too was blocked. They then decided to go right around the city but en route they met the original convoy and the two commanders joined up to return to base.

andoning the rescue of the troops in the city.

By nightfall there were some 90-odd men in and around Crash Site 1, scattered between various buildings. A UH-60 had dropped some medical supplies and ammunition, but their situation was desperate. At this point it was decided to commit the UN Quick Reaction Force (QRF). The force that was cobbled together comprised some 300 men from U.S. 10th Mountain Division, with some Rangers and Delta men, desperately eager to rescue their comrades. Multinational contributions including four Pakistani tanks and 28 Malaysian armored personnel carriers, the latter painted UN white. The convoy rolled at 2320 and made its way slowly into the city, drawing heavy fire and encountering several roadblocks. However, part of the convoy eventually reached Crash 1, where it took some time to locate and load all the dead and wounded and then to reorganize for the journey out. This was finally achieved and the weary survivors of Delta and the Rangers reached the assembly temporary field hospital in a football stadium in the early hours of the morning.

U.S. losses were 18 dead, 73 wounded and one wounded helicopter pilot held prisoner. Somali losses were far greater: some 500 dead and 1,000 wounded, many of them women and children. This was not peace-keeping.

Below: The scene of devastation and carnage in Mogadishu after the terrible events of October 3, 1993.

Rescue in Grenada (1983)

Following the end of the Vietnam War, American forces tried to keep a low profile on the international scene. Two rescue operations were attempted in efforts to secure the release of the crew of the Mayaguez and the Iranian embassy hostages. U.S. troops also took part in various peacekeeping forces such as those in the Sinai and in Beirut. However, major use of force was eschewed for both international and domestic reasons.

But in October 1983 President Ronald Reagan, at the request of the six-member Organization of Eastern Caribbean States, sent troops to the island of Grenada "to restore peace, order and respect for human rights; to evacuate those who wish to leave; and to help the Grenadians re-establish governmental institutions." On October 19, Grenada's Prime Minister, Maurice Bishop, and several Cabinet members and labor leaders had been murdered by former military associates. A 16-man Revolutionary Military Council, headed by Army Chief General Hudson Austin and Deputy Prime Minister Bernard Coard, took power. The council imposed a 24-hour curfew, warning that violators would be shot on sight, and closed the Port Salines airfield.

U.S. Intelligence reported Soviet/Cuban backing for the revolutionary regime, with Cubans establishing new fortifications, arms caches and military communications on the island. President Reagan viewed Grenada as "a Soviet

Right: President Reagan ensured that Grenada, which lies just off the South American coast, would not become another Cuba.

Below: U.S. entry points (red arrows) and Port Salines airfield, the major U.S. objective, being built by Cuban engineers.

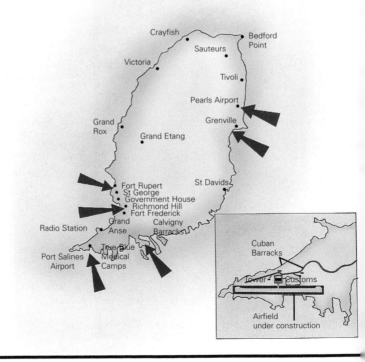

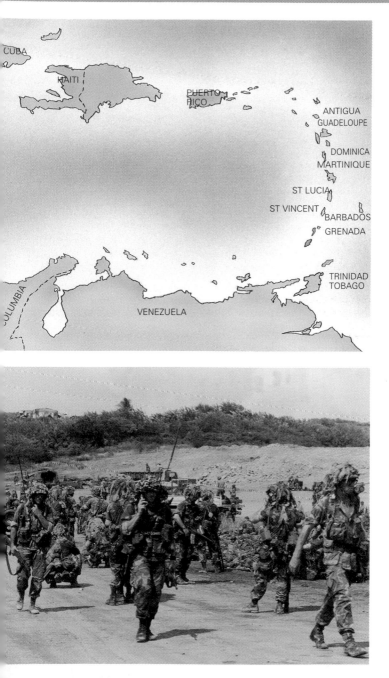

*ove: Paratroops of 82nd Airborne move out on patrol from Port
lines airfield following its seizure, October 25, 1993.*

▶ Cuban colony being readied as a major military bastion to export and undermir democracy." Of particular concern was the position of some 1,000 U.S. citizen especially the 600-odd young Americans at the True Blue Medical School ne the Port Salines airfield. The prospect of these youngsters being held hostag by the Marxist government was serious and would have provided a far wors crisis than even that of the Iranian embassy staff. For their part, the Easte Caribbean States saw the violence and disintegration of political institutions island as an unprecedented threat to peace and security in the region.

Information on the resisting troops and their disposition in Grenada wa fairly sparse, but the U.S. forces had three immediate objectives within th overall mission of capturing the island and restoring a democratic governmer These three tasks were the freeing of the 600 medical students, the release the governor (Sir Paul Scoones) and the defeat of the Cuban troops on th island.

U.S. Navy SEALs were responsible for capturing the governor's residenc and Marines for the Pearls Airport on the island's east coast. The crucial ta was, however, the taking of Port Salines airfield, which was being construct and guarded by Cubans. This task was given to the Rangers.

Execution

The assault by the 24th Marine Amphibious Unit on Pearls Airport began 0500 hours (local) on October 25, while H-hour for the Rangers was 0536. Th was the first major combat operation for the two participating Ranger units the Fort Stewart, Georgia-based Ist Ranger Battalion, and the Fort Lew Washington-based 2nd. The Rangers left the staging airfield on Barbados in t

Below: This MC-130E brought Rangers to the island of Grenada and no takes cargo on its return flight.

Above: Marine escorts one of 1,100 captured Cuban soldiers into an interrogation center for PW processing.

early hours aboard MC-130E Hercules aircraft of 8th Special Operations Squadron, lst Special Operations Wing, USAF, based at Hurlburt Field in Florida. (The lead planes carried members of the 1st Battalion, with the 2nd following closely behind.) These aircraft were accompanied by AC-130 Hercules gunships (the famous "Spectres" of the Vietnam War) of 16th Special Operations Squadron.

As they came in over Port Salines, searchlights were suddenly switched on, which quickly found the lumbering C-130s and enabled the anti-aircraft guns to open up on the aircraft and descending parachutists. The AC-130s were quickly called into action and silenced most of the Cuban guns. Among the lead elements in the assault was a 12-man team from the 317th Tactical Airlift Wing responsible for combat control of the drop, and these were quickly inside the air traffic control building.

On the ground, the Rangers, told to expect some 500 Cubans (350 "workers" and a "small" military advisory team) found themselves under attack from some 600 well armed professional soldiers. The Cubans were armed with mortars and machine guns, and had at least six armored personnel carriers. A brisk battle developed in which the Rangers quickly gained the upper hand, and by 0700 they were in complete control. The runway was cleared of obstacles (boulders, vehicles, pipes) and at 0715 the first C-130 of the second wave was able to land with reinforcements.

The Rangers then moved out, heading for the medical campus; brushing aside snipers and scattered resistance, they reached their ▶

▶ objective by 0830 hours and were greeted by some very relieved students. The campus was secured by 0850, although the other medical school at Grand Anse was not liberated until the following day.

Assessment
The liberation effort accomplished what it set out to do. The booty of the effort confirmed U.S. intelligence reports that the USSR and Cuba were turning Grenada into a military base in the Western hemisphere. The long-term implications of this were that the island could eventually have become a staging area for the subversion of nearby countries; it would also have considerable value as a transit point for troops and supplies moving from Cuba to Africa and from Europe and Libya to Central America.

Captured documents indicated that the USSR and North Korea, as well as Cuba, had made secret treaties with the Grenada Revolutionary Military Council, and had agreed to provide the leadership with more than $37.8 million in artillery, anti-aircraft weapons, armored personnel carriers, small arms, and ammunition. The Soviet Union had tried hard to keep these arrangements secret. In fact, it wasn't until 18 months after the arms shipments began that they established diplomatic ties with Grenada.

The convincing list of documents found in the aftermath of Grenada included a roster of Grenada's militia; a summary of Political Bureau meetings; a top-secret report from a Grenadian double agent who attempted to infiltrate the CIA operation in Barbados; rosters and correspondence concerning the training of Grenadian troops in the USSR, Cuba and Vietnam; and a training agreement between Grenada and Nicaragua. In all, there was more than enough documentary evidence to still the voices of those who criticized the operation from a political standpoint. From yet another standpoint, the military one, it was a success - and one in which U.S. special forces acquitted themselves well.

Above: Men of 82nd Airborne stand watch as they guard over the equipment of their comrades who have gone out on patrol.

Below: One justification of the operation was the safety of these young U.S. students at the True Blue Medical School.

Invasion of Panama (1989)

The aims of Operation Just Cause, the U.S. invasion of Panama in 1989-9[ ] were the capture of the dictator, Manuel Noriega, and the installation of democratic government. The United States sought to minimize casualties an[ ] destruction by using overwhelming force, and one of the components involve[ ] was the Joint Special Operations Task Force (JSOTF). Part of the JSOTF wa[ ] Task Unit Papa (TU Papa), whose mission was to deny use of the Paitilla Airfie[ ] and to hold it until relieved about five hours after H-hour, a crucial operatic[ ] since it was the base for Noriega's private jet and other aircraft which might b[ ] used to spirit the dictator out of United States' hands. TU Papa consisted of tw[ ] elements, one of which was the ground force comprising three SEAL platoor[ ] (Bravo, Delta and Golf platoons) and command, control, communications, an[ ] mortar elements, plus a small USAF liaison team to call in fire support from a[ ] AC-130H gunship which would be flying overhead; a total of 62 men. Th[ ] second element was the support team, which included surveillance forces, [ ] signals intelligence team, a psychological operations team, and boat crews; [ ] total of 26 men.

The operation started at 1930 19 December, when the ground forc[ ] launched from the Howard AFB beach in fifteen combat rubber raiding cra[ ] (CRRC), while two patrol boats left from Rodman Naval Station. All the CRR[ ] covered the eight miles to the objective by 2330 and two combat swimme[ ] swam ashore to reconnoitre the landing site and marked the beach with [ ]

*bove: Rangers celebrate neutralizing a Panamanian Army 0.5in
nachinegun above the entrance to Rio Hato airfield.*

strobe light. When all was clear, the main ground force landed near the end of Paitilla runway at 0045 20 December and were just preparing to advance inland when they heard firing and explosions from another attack and realized that surprise had been lost. The commander immediately ordered an advance along a trail and, having found a convenient hole in the security fence, the men were soon on the airfield near the southern end of the runway, where they formed into platoons. A report was then received that Noriega was about to arrive in a small plane, so Delta platoon set an ambush halfway up the runway for a few minutes, but then continued their advance toward the control tower, while the other two platoons, Golf and Bravo, moved up the grass apron on the west side of the runway.

Golf platoon arrived opposite the three northernmost hangars at 0105 and saw that men of the Panamanian Defense Force (PDF) were guarding the center hangar, which was known to house Noriega's jet, and another hangar to the ▶

Left: Having cleared Toijos/Tocumen airport, the 75th Rangers moved on to take and clear the Comandancia.

197

► north. The Americans and the Panamanian guards were shouting demands to each other when one of the SEALs saw a PDF man adopt a firing position, so he immediately opened fire. This resulted in a short but fierce firefight in the ►

Right: Speed of action characterized all SEAL operations during Operation Just Cause, including the use of these RIBs.

Below: Gunner aboard an AC-130H gunship loads a 105mm howitzer.

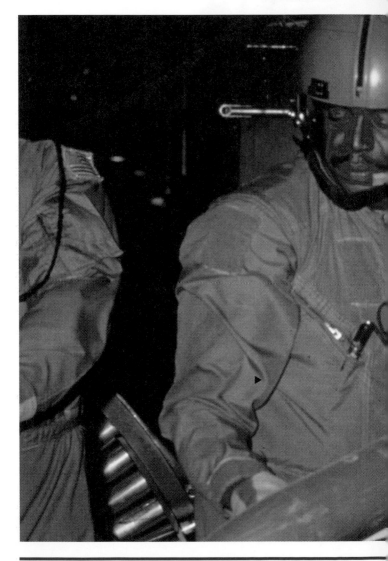

Above: SOF language skills were put to good use during the operations in Panama, helping to establish good relations.

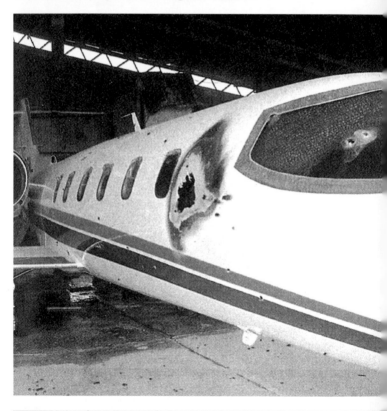

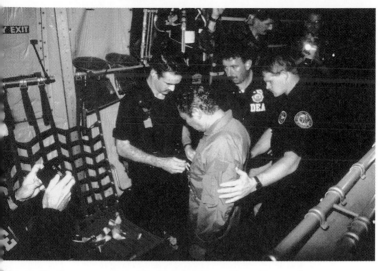

Above: Having surrendered to Special Operations Forces, former dictator, Noriega, is arrested by DEA agents.

►course of which eight SEALs were wounded, five seriously. Commander Golf Platoon used his radio to report casualties and request assistance, whereupon Commander TU Papa ordered the other platoons to reinforce Golf platoon, and in the course of this move forward another two SEALs were wounded. However, the combination of SEAL fire discipline and superior firepower soon took effect and the remaining PDF defenders withdrew at about 0117.

By 0146 TU Papa was able to report the airfield secure and a medevac helicopter arrived at 0205 to recover the wounded. By 0315 the SEALS had set up a more defendable perimeter on the southeast side of the airfield and further reinforcements in the shape of the reaction platoon from Rodman AFB arrived a few minutes later. Throughout all this, an AC-130H gunship had been circling overhead ready to give supporting fire, but was unable to do so as reliable communications with the ground force had not been established.

At dawn, patrols conducted a thorough reconnaissance of the airfield and hangars, while other SEALs dragged airplanes onto the runway to block its use. Noriega's jet was seriously damaged by machine gun fire to render it unusable. TU Papa should have been replaced some five hours after H-hour – ie, about 04400-0500 20 December – but in the event the relief force did not arrive until 1400 21 December when five CH-47 Chinook helicopters delivered a Ranger company and the SEALs left aboard the same helicopters. Thus, a planned five-hour operation had actually lasted thirty-seven hours, with the deaths of four SEALs and eight others wounded, but the mission had been achieved, the airfield was secure, and no Panamanian had been able to escape from it.

Left: Noriega's personal jet was deliberately damaged so that he would be unable to use it to flee his country.

201

Attack on Wireless Ridge (1982)

The battalion attack by the British 2nd Battalion, The Parachute Regiment (2 Para), on Wireless Ridge, on June 13-14 during the Falklands War in 1982, is an excellent example of an action by a highly trained, fit and experienced infantry unit. This action is of particular interest because 2 Para was the only battalion in the Falklands War to carry out two battalion attacks, and thus the only one to be able to put into practice the lessons learned, in their case at high cost, at Goose Green on May 28.

On June 11, 2 Para was moved by helicopter from Fitzroy on the south coast to a lying-up position west of Mount Kent. At 2300 hours the battalion set off on foot to an assembly area on a hill to the north of Mount Kent, ready to support either 3 Para in their attack on Mount Longdon or 45 Commando Royal Marines, whose mission was to take the position known as Two Sisters. Both attacks were successful, leaving 3 Para, 45 Commando and 42 Commando firmly established.

On June 12, 2 Para moved forward some 9 miles (15km), skirting Mount Longdon on its north-western side, to an assembly area in the lee of a steep escarpment which offered some cover from the sporadic artillery shelling. Orders were received in mid-afternoon for an attack on Wireless Ridge that night, but this was later postponed to the following night.

On June 13 Argentinian Skyhawk attack aircraft flew in low from the west. Intense fire from the ground prevented this attack from being pressed home, but a number of moves in preparation for the forthcoming British battalion action were delayed, especially the registration of targets by the artillery and mortars.

At Goose Green 2 Para had been very short of fire support. In this battle, however, they were to have two batteries of 105mm light guns in direct support, the mortars of both 2 and 3 Para, naval gunfire support from ships within range, as well as the battalion's own machine gun and MILAN anti-tank missile platoons. Last, but by no means least, a troop of Scimitar (1x30mm

Below: The Falkland Islands have been the subject of a dispute between Argentina and Britain for nearly 200 years.

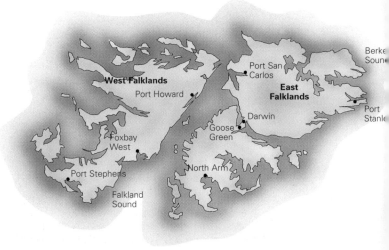

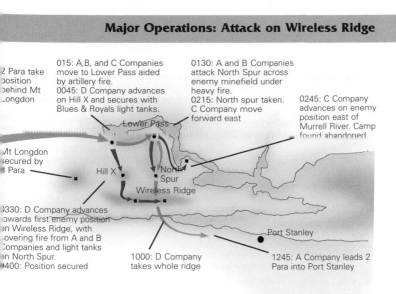

015: A,B, and C Companies move to Lower Pass aided by artillery fire.
0045: D Company advances on Hill X and secures with Blues & Royals light tanks.

0130: A and B Companies attack North Spur across enemy minefield under heavy fire.
0215: North spur taken. C Company move forward east

0245: C Company advances on enemy position east of Murrell River. Camp found abandoned

2 Para take position behind Mt Longdon

Lower Pass

Mt Longdon secured by 3 Para

Hill X

North Spur

Wireless Ridge

0330: D Company advances towards first enemy position on Wireless Ridge, with covering fire from A and B Companies and light tanks on North Spur.
0400: Position secured

1000: D Company takes whole ridge

Port Stanley

1245: A Company leads 2 Para into Port Stanley

Above: When the British attack on Wireless Ridge succeeded, the Argentine position in Port Stanley became untenable.

cannon) and two Scorpion (1x76mm gun) light tanks of The Blues and Royals were an integral part of 2 Para's battle plan.

The battalion moved out at last light (2030 hours local). As they moved to the forming-up places (where the troops shake out into battle formations), the sort of report a commanding officer dreads was received: Intelligence had just discovered a minefield in front of A and B Companies' objective. At this stage, however, there was no alternative but to go ahead. ▶

Below: A paratroop company is briefed prior to the assault on Wireless Ridge, using a quickly made ground model.

The artillery supporting fire started at 0015 hours on June 14 and C Company crossed the start-line at 0045 hours. D Company reached its firs objective with little trouble, finding that the enemy had withdrawn, leaving a few dead in their slit trenches. While D Company reorganized, enemy 155mm airburst fire began to fall on their position. Meanwhile, A and B Companies began their advance, B Company through the minefield.

Some sporadic fire came from a few trenches, but was quickly silenced and 17 Argentine prisoners were taken and a number killed in this phase of the battle – the remainder fled. Several radios (still switched on), telephones and a mass of cable suggested that the position had included a battalion headquarters. As A and B Companies started to dig in, accurate and fairly intense enemy artillery bombardment began, which was to continue for some nine hours.

Following the success of A and B Companies, D Company crossed its second start line at the west end of the main ridge, while the light tanks and the machine guns moved to a flank to give covering fire. The ridge itself was a long spine broken in the middle, with each section some 900 yards (300m) in length. The first feature was taken unopposed and there was then a short delay while the British artillery readjusted to its targets for the next phase. During this time the second feature was kept under heavy fire by the light tanks, the

machine guns and the MILAN missile being used in a direct-fire artillery role!

Just as the attack was about to start, the commanding officer received a new piece of intelligence, that instead of one enemy company at the other end of the ridge there were two! This was hardly likely to impress the Paras who by this stage of the campaign had established a considerable moral ascendency over the Argentines, but in the early minutes of this final phase of the battle D Company received some casualties as the enemy fought back with unexpected vigor, withdrawing one bunker at a time. As the Paras poured onto the position, however, the enemy suddenly broke and ran, being continuously harassed off the position by the machine guns of the British Scorpions and Scimitars, and chased by the exhilarated Paras.

As D Company began to reorganize they, too, came under artillery fire, as well as remarkably effective small arms fire from Tumbledown Mountain and Mount William to the south, which had not yet been captured by 5 Infantry Brigade. The enemy could be heard trying to regroup in the darkness below the ridge, and to the south in the area of Moody Brook.

At daybreak a rather brave, but somewhat pathetic enemy counterattack ▶

Below: Three wounded paras show the brutal reality of war; as this picture was taken the man on the left breathed his last.

developed from the area of Moody Brook, which seems to have been some sort of final gesture. It petered out under a hail of artillery, small arms and machine gun fire.

This seems to have been the signal to many Argentines that the game was up, and shortly afterwards ever-increasing numbers of disheartened and disillusioned Argentine soldiers were observed streaming off Mount William, Tumbledown and Sapper Hill to seek short-lived refuge in Port Stanley.

A and B Companies of 2 Para were now brought forward onto Wireless Ridge, and the battalion's night attack was successfully concluded. The Paras had lost three dead and 11 wounded. Lack of time and opportunity precluded counting the Argentine casualties, but it has been estimated that, of an original strength of some 500, up to 100 may have been killed, 17 were captured, and the remainder fled.

The taking of Wireless Ridge illustrates the standards achieved by a crack unit. In this night battle, it defeated a force of equal strength, which was well prepared and dug-in and occupied a dominant feature. No. 2 Para had learned the lessons of Goose Green well. They had also given the lie to the allegation that parachute units lack "staying power." It is, perhaps, unfortunate that the battle of Goose Green, deservedly famous, has overshadowed this later minor classic at Wireless Ridge.

Right: A confused and frightened young Argentine soldier, escorted by a hardened British paratrooper.

Below: A blindfolded Argentine prisoner is led away by British Royal Marines, his war over.

Below: The Falklands landscape is dominated by granite outcrops like this one, which is demonstrably in British hands.

Operation Desert Storm (1991)

Operation Desert Strike, the 1991 Coalition war against Iraq, saw the larges
concentration of international special forces in any combat. Australian and Nev
Zealand provided a combined ANZAC SAS Squadron (133 men), while th
French contingent included elements of the Foreign Legion and 6th Parachut
Division. The UK sent almost the entire SAS Regiment to Saudi Arabia: som
700 men of A, B, and D Squadrons, plus 15 reservist volunteers from
Squadron; indeed, the only element omitted was G Squadron, which wa

committed to other operations and on counter-terrorist stand-by in the UK. Also in the Gulf were a squadron of the Royal Marine SBS and RAF special operations aircrew.

By far the largest contribution came from the United States, under the ▶

Below: The sky above Tel Aviv as Scud missiles home in on the city, in a deliberate attempt to force Israel into the war.

► aegis of Special Operations Command (SOCOM) and collectively forming the Joint Special Operations Task Force (JSOTF). The naval element was commanded by Naval SPECWARGRU (Special War Group) ONE and included SEAL Teams 1, 2, 3, 4, 5, and 8; SDV (SEAL Delivery Vehicle) Teams 1 and 2; and SPECBOATU (Special Boat Units) 11, 12, 13, and 20. Largest in terms of numbers was the U.S. Army contribution which comprised: Delta, 1st Special Forces Group, 5th Special Forces Group, and 160th Special Operations Aviation Regiment (SOAR). There were also large elements from 82nd and 101st Airborne Divisions. The U.S. Air Force also deployed large special warfare elements to the Gulf, under the command of 1st Special Operations Wing (1 SOW), which comprised five "Special Operations Squadrons" (SOS): 8th SOS – MC-130E Combat Talon; 9th SOS – HC-130H Combat Shadow tankers; 16th SOS – AC-130H Spectre gunships; 20th SOS – MH-53J Pave Low helicopters

and 55th SOS – MH-60 Pave low helicopters. The U.S. Marine Corps provided reconnaissance specialists.

Land Missions

The first missions tentatively assigned to both the SAS and Delta were to rescue their national hostages, who had been grabbed by the Iraqis at the outbreak of conflict. The hostages were, however, released before any such operation could be mounted. Then, just before the ground war started, the British commander in the Gulf, General de la Billiére, obtained General Schwarzkopf's agreement to deploy special forces behind the Iraqi front line ▶

Below: An Iraqi Scud aboard its 8-wheeled launcher. A major SF effort was mounted to destroy these vehicles.

▶ with the aim of distracting the enemy's attention from the forthcomin. operations, and two squadrons of SAS duly deployed on January 20, 1991. O the 24th, however, their mission was abruptly changed to the anti-Scud role which it remained for the remainder of the war, and in which they were joine by the remainder of the SAS deployed to the Gulf.

Western intelligence staffs knew that Iraq had received some 820 Soviet F 17 missiles (NATO = "Scud-B") in the early 1980s, of which some 200 missile were launched against Iran in 1988. By 1990, Iraq had developed a modifie version, the al-Hussein, which had greater range, but at the expense of reduce payload. Some 400 of these missiles were built, which, in December 199 were located in 28 static sites and on some 36 Russian-built 8-wheeled mobil launchers.

Iraq had demonstrated a willingness to use poison gas in artillery shells against both the Iranians and the Kurds, and there was therefore a serious possibility that they had managed to develop chemical warheads for the al-Hussein. The situation became more acute in December 1990, when Saddam launched several demonstration missiles.

Despite this evidence, the threat they posed – particularly psychological – was still not fully appreciated until Iraqi Scuds actually started to impact on targets in Israel on January 18 1991. As a result, Coalition military commanders were suddenly forced to undertake a search-and-destroy battle against the ▶

Below: One of the largest bombs ever made, this BLU-82 was destined to avenge the loss of an AC-130H named "Spirit 03."

▶ Scud launch sites in order to prevent Israel entering the war in retaliation, whi
would almost certainly have resulted in most of the Arab contingents leavi
the Coalition. The only troops in a position to do this were the elite forces of t
British SAS and those of U.S. JSOTF, including Delta.

The energetic campaign waged by British and U.S. special forces drove t
mobile Scud launchers back out of range of Israel, although sporadic launch

Above: U.S. special forces gather in a wadi somewhere inside Iraqi territory during the Gulf War.

took place until the end of the war. Both the SAS and Delta carried out numerous direct attacks on Iraqi Scud sites, but their main task was to locate and report potential targets to Coalition air forces. Initially, the air-tasking

217

▶ system was too slow, with aircraft arriving long after the Scud launchers had departed, but rapid changes, including "cab-ranks" of airborne ground-attack aircraft ready for immediate response, quickly overcame this. In clear daylight the ground troops "talked" aircraft down onto their targets, while at night or against camouflaged targets they used laser target designators.

The SAS's operational area was around Iraq's H-2 airfield, and was designated the "southern Scud Box," although it was more popularly known as "Scud Alley." This was an area some 20 miles (32km) long by 17 miles (26km) wide (340sq miles/830sq km). Into this were placed three 8-man patrols on road watch, staking out the MSRs (Main Supply Routes) to watch for and report on movement by SCUD convoys. The U.S. JSOTF arrived in early February and comprised Delta Force, SEALs, and 160th Special Operations Aviation Regiment (SOAR), equipped with MH-60 Black Hawks and MH-47E Chinooks. The JSOTF operated around Al Qaim, in the "northern Scud box," nicknamed "Scud Boulevard."

A second target was the Iraqi fiberglass communications cable system which had recently been installed and which consisted of one or more cables buried up to 30ft (10m) below the surface. These were used because they provided greater security than microwave systems, since buried cables could not be located, intercepted or destroyed – or so the Iraqis thought. The weakness was that, for technical reasons, repeaters were required at frequent intervals, which were located at the bottom of manholes and it was these that were found and destroyed by SBS and SAS patrols.

Both Americans and British made use of specialized light vehicles. Delta used Fast Attack Vehicles (FAV) while the British deployed four mobile groups each consisting of eight Land Rover 110s, a Unimog truck carrying fuel, supplies, and spares, and several motor-cycles. Typical vehicle armament included Browning 0.5 cal machine guns, M19 40mm grenade launchers, and 7.62mm GPMGs, but each group also carried a number of 66mm LAW (light anti-tank weapon) and Milan ATGW (anti-tank guided weapon). Operating so many vehicles gave rise to a need for resupply and repair, so the SAS produced a resupply convoy of some 12 4-ton trucks which was installed in a wadi some 75 miles (120km) inside Iraqi territory, where it carried out maintenance and repairs over a 5-day period and then drove back to Coalition territory without incurring a single loss.

Air Missions

The majority of special operations air support was provided by the USA and the tasks included transporting and supporting SF teams deployed inside Iraqi territory. This was the task of MH-53Js, which were also able to use their night vision devices to look for Scuds. 1st SOW was also responsible for combat rescue and extracted several downed aircrew before the Iraqis could capture them.

One unusual mission was performed by the MC-130 Combat Talons, which dropped a number of BLU-82 "Daisy Cutter" fuel/air bombs. These devices, originally developed during the Vietnam War, contained 6.7 tons (15,000lb/6,804kg) of high explosive and were dropped from the tail ramp at a height of some 6,000ft (1,800m), achieving an accuracy of approximately 50ft (15m). The effect of the enormous explosion was dramatic: the noise was stupefying and the blast caused death up to 3 miles (5km) distant. Indeed, some observers were under the impression that tactical nuclear weapons were being used. British air support or special forces came from RAF Chinook, Army Lynx, and Navy Sea King helicopters.

Losses

Both American and British special forces incurred losses, some due to Iraqi action, others to the wild terrain and harsh weather. An 8-man SAS team, for example, was detected and pursued by Iraqi troops, during which four men died. The worst U.S. losses occurred on February 21, when an MH-60 helicopter hit a sand-dune in bad visibility, killing all seven occupants: four aircrew and three from Delta. In addition, a USAF AC-130 of 16th SOS was shot down by Iraqi ground fire during the battle to retake the town of Khafji; all 14 aboard were killed.

Assessment

The attacks on the Scud sites was an excellent example of the use of special forces being used in a strategic role. Had they failed and the Iraqi Scud campaign against Israel been more successful, the outcome of the Gulf War might have been quite different.

One of the problems facing the special forces in the Gulf was poor intelligence, at both strategic and tactical levels. At the higher level this included a serious underestimation of the Scud threat and some very misleading analyses of the Iraqi organization and capability. At the lower level the SF were told it would be warm, so they took thin clothing, only to find it was bitterly cold and they suffered accordingly until Arab coats were sent in to them.

Below: General Schwarzkopf thanks special forces, including Delta members, for their hazardous Scud-hunting missions.

Special Forces' Weapons

VIRTUALLY every country today has a special force unit, carefully selected and trained to a high degree of physical and mental fitness an then maintained at a high state of readiness to deal rapidly and effectivel with the unexpected. These units may be used for special operations in conventional war setting, for anti-terrorist operations (for example, to fre hostages in a kidnap), or for operations in support of the civil police agains increasingly sophisticated criminals, such as, for example, the use of U.S military units in the fight against drug smugglers or terrorists attempting t attack the United States' homeland.

This extraordinary breadth of possibilities means that special force unit must have at their disposal a very wide range of weapons and equipment ranging from standard military issue to special 'one-offs' developed for particular operational need. Further, such units need to train on almost an weapon in the world. Most units keep small stocks of a variety of foreig weapons, both those which are used by friendly forces and those used b potential enemies. Any weapon in any field is a likely candidate for use b special forces around the world; for the purposes of this book, however, w have carefully selected those which are typical in their field.

The first requirement in selecting a weapon is to establish precisel what must be accomplished in a particular mission. If the job is to clea hallways, for example, the weapon is likely to be a shotgun, a P7 pistol or sub-machine gun (SMG) rather than a 5.56mm or, worse, a 7.62mm servic rifle. If the situation involves terrorists with multiple hostages in adjacer rooms, the choice might even center on the most suitable type c ammunition. The required end effect must be gauged; is it required to k the target, to wound or to deter without actually hitting? Also, will a clea well-judged shot be possible, or will it be a snatched shot taking advantag of a fleeting glimpse? Will the engagement take place in daylight, poor c artificial light, or in the dark? Most of these questions cannot be answere in advance of the incident, so one of the primary requirements for a specia force is as good a selection of weapons, ammunition and sights as possible

One of the leading requirements for any weapon is a very high degre of reliability. Every weapon should work first time, every time; when a hi team dashes into a room containing hostages and terrorists there is n scope at all for an SMG to misfire or for a grenade to fail to detonate. I addition, the weapons have to be small, sometimes small enough to b hidden in an attaché case or under a raincoat.

Weapons need to be accurate and have predictable behavior. Moder conditions place troops and police in situations where they have to deal wit terrorists, agitators or just plain criminals who deliberately surroun themselves with innocent people. Weapons of the greatest precision an accuracy are needed, enabling marksmen to take out targets standin within inches of others who must not be harmed.

Special forces units look first to their national resources and to th standard issue weapons of their armies. However, these weapons are ofte too large, too heavy, too unwieldy, too inaccurate or otherwise unsuitabl and the next option is to seek nationally-produced special weapon designed to meet the unit's operational requirements. Today, howeve special forces are ready to purchase foreign weapons, even when their ow arms industry can produce something generally similar. Thus, for exampl many Western countries, even those with their own weapons industry, us the German Heckler & Koch MP5 SMG. However, apart from their specialis roles, special forces also take part in more conventional operations requirin conventional infantry weapons and here there is less scope for the esoteri specially in the heavier weapons – there are few alternatives where machine guns, anti-tank weapons and air-defense missiles are concerned.

The basic weapon of any special force remains the rifle and most armed forces have now converted to 5.56mm, resulting in small, handy weapons. But, there is increasing evidence that the next generation of weapons could be very different, using new types of ammunition, such as saboted caseless rounds, while the whole weapon may well look quite unlike the rifle as we know it today.

Special forces units, with their need for small, handy, close-range weapons have frequently in the past turned to the SMG in preference to the rifle. World War II commando units, for example, were characterized by the Thompson, Sten, U.S. M3 or Soviet PPS-43. Such weapons were certainly light and easy to use; they were also highly inaccurate (except at the closest possible quarters), frequently unreliable and dangerously unsafe. Also, because they almost invariably used blow-back systems, their rounds had short range and relatively poor stopping power.

There was a school of thought in the 1980s and '90s which postulated that the new generation of 5.56mm rifles would be so small, light and handy that they would render the SMG obsolete. Undoubtedly as the SMG has become more sophisticated there has been a degree of convergence between its characteristics and those of the rifle, but the two have yet to meet. Indeed, in many respects the modern 5.56mm rifle is simply too powerful for the very close-quarter role in which most special force units now specialize. Thus, there is a modern range of very effective and efficient SMGs, which are small, handy and have a high rate of fire; with few exceptions they fire the 9mm Parabellum round, although new calibers appear from time to time, such as Russian 5.45mm.

If there has been convergence between the rifle and SMG at one end of the small arms spectrum, there has been an even greater one at the other end, where some SMGs are now only a little larger than pistols. For example, the Heckler & Koch MP5K SMG is 12.8in (325mm) long and weighs 4.4lb (2kg) empty, while the archetypal pistol, the Browning, is 7.9in (200mm) long and weighs 1.8lb (0.8kg). Nevertheless, the pistol still retains its value for clandestine use, being easy to hide and fire, although – ospite what is depicted on TV – it is extremely difficult to use accurately over about 25yd (23m).

After a period when sniper rifles seemed to go out of fashion they are now very much back in business and apart from a few adaptations of existing service rifles there is an increasing number of specially designed weapons. Thus, the British-made Accuracy International L96A1 and the Soviet Dragunov SVD sniper rifles are each unique designs, bearing no relation to any other rifles in their national inventories.

Shotguns, once the province of the sportsman, are now firmly also in the military environment, the requirement being for a closequarter weapon firing a large number of pellets over short ranges, but military requirements have led to specially designed weapons rather than simply using sporting designs. The Italian Franchi SPAS, for example, is a rugged weapon which fires four rounds per second, enabling a trained shot to put 48 pellets a second onto a 3 x 3ft (1 X 1m) target at a range of 44yd (40m).

A new breed of weapon which has appeared in the past decade is the "anti-materiel" rifle, typically of 0.5in (12.7mm) caliber, which fires a very heavy round with a high degree of accuracy at ranges of some 1,000yd (915m). It can obviously be used against people, but its main value is against harder targets such as cars, truck and helicopters.

M9 (Model 92SB/92F) 9mm pistol

Country of origin: Italy.
Manufacturer: Beretta, Italy and Beretta USA.
Type: semi-automatic pistol/personal defense weapon.
Caliber: 9mm (approximately .355 inches).
Weight: 32.0oz (1.0kg).
Dimensions: length, gun 8.5in (217mm); barrel, 4.9in (125mm); width 1.5in (38mm); height 5.5in (140mm).
Magazine: 15-round box.
Muzzle velocity: ca 1,100ft/sec (335m/sec).
Rifling: 6 grooves, r/hand.

The M9 9mm pistol was the outcome of a direction from Congress for a no developmental program to standardize all United States forces with one pist which should also comply with the relevant NATO standards. This involved th

replacement of a variety of handguns including the venerable, but greatly respected and liked Colt M1911A1 .45-caliber pistol, which had served the U.S. armed forces for some eighty years, as well as a number of .38-caliber revolvers. The U.S. Army was designated the lead service and duly ran a competition for what was to be an "off-the-shelf" buy. Beretta modified their Model 92 to meet the new requirement and the resulting weapon, the Beretta 92SB, was the clear winner. Following some further changes to meet U.S. Army requirements, the new weapon entered service as the Pistol M9 in 1985. Initial orders were for som 500,000 weapons, but with the contract stipulating that production must b transferred from Italy to the United States after two years.

The M9 pistol fires the standard NATO 9mm round. It is entirely coated a Teflon-derived material and the barrel is chrome-plated. Its action uses th locked-wedge design pioneered in the Walther P-38. The weapon is loaded the orthodox manner by inserting the charged magazine into the butt, followin which the slide grip is used to pull the action to the rear, cocking the hamme and then released to chamber a round. On firing, gas pressure drives the barr and slide to the rear, locked together by a wedge, but, having traveled som 0.3in (8mm), the locking wedge pivots downwards, disengaging from the slid the barrel immediately stops but the slide continues rearwards to complete th reloading cycle. Unlike many automatic pistols, these Beretta models are of open slide design; ie, the greater part of the barrel is exposed and not covere by the slide. It has several safety features to help prevent accidental discharg can be fired in either single- or double-action modes, and can be unloaded wh the safety is in the "on" position without having to activate the trigger.

Above: Marksman fires the U.S. armed forces standard issue Beretta M9 pistol.

Left: Since being accepted by the U.S., the Beretta-designed pistol is now the standard in many countries.

bove: Unlike many other pistols, the M9 has an open slide, leaving the arrel exposed, which works extremely well.

The changes required by the U.S. Army were virtually all concerned with e grip and included an enlarged trigger guard to enable the firer to use a two-anded grip, an extension to the base of the magazine, and a slight curve to the ot of the front edge of the butt. The Beretta M9/92F is now the standard stol in the U.S. Special Operations Forces, as well as the rest of the U.S. med services. It is also used by the Italian and many other armed forces, as ell as para-military forces, such as the French *Gendarmerie Nationale*.

Steyr 9mm Special Purpose Pistol (SPP)

Country of origin: Austria.
Manufacturer: Steyr, Austria.
Type: semi-automatic pistol/personal defense weapon.
Caliber: 9 x 19mm Parabellum.
Weight (gun): 45oz (1,300g).
Dimensions: length, gun 12.7in (322mm); barrel, 5.1in (130mm).
Magazine: 15- or 30-round box.
Muzzle velocity: ca 1,214ft/sec (370m/sec).
Rifling: 6 grooves, r/hand.

The Steyr 9mm Special Purpose Pistol (SPP) is generally similar to the Steyr Tactical Machine Pistol (TMP), but whereas the latter, despite its name, is properly categorized as a submachine gun, the SPP is most definitely a pistol. The SPP's frame and top cover are made of a synthetic fiber material, and the weapon does not have the forward grip of the TMP, although there is a small extension of the fore-end of the body, which is intended to keep the firer's fingers away from the muzzle. The SPP fires the 9 x 19mm Parabellum round in the semi-automatic mode only. The cocking-handle is at the rear of the weapon and the weapon is recoil-operated, the breech being locked by a rotating barrel. The box magazine is housed in the pistol grip and there are two sizes: for fifteen and thirty rounds, respectively. The Steyr SPP is used by a small number of special operations forces.

Right: The Steyr SPP falls midway between a pistol and an SMG; it fires 9mm rounds in semi-automatic only.

SIG-Sauer 9mm P-228/.40 S&W P-229

Country of origin: Switzerland.
Manufacturer: SIG-Sauer (Switzerland/Germany).
Type: semi-automatic pistol/personal defense weapon.
Caliber: P-228 9mm; P-229 0.40in S&W/ 0.357in SIG.
Weight (gun): 29oz (830g).
Dimensions: length, gun 7.1in (180mm); barrel 3.9in (96mm).
Magazine: 12-round box.
Muzzle velocity: 1,115ft/sec (340m/sec).
Rifling: 6 grooves, r/hand.

These two pistols are virtually identical, except that the SIG-Sauer P-228 fires the 9mm Parabellum round, while the P-229 fires the 0.40 S&W or 0.357in SIG round. They are, in essence, a modified version of the earlier P-225 with a larger magazine and there is a substantial commonality of parts between the three weapons. The P-228 has been purchased by many United States' government agencies, including the U.S. Army (9mm Compact Pistol M11), the Federal Bureau of Investigation (FBI) and the Drug Enforcement Agency (DEA), and by the British Ministry of Defence. The P-229 is chambered for 0.40in S&W or 0.357in SIG rounds, all that is required to change from one to the other being a change of barrel. For both of these calibers the magazine holds 12 rounds. The firearm uses a machined stainless steel slide which is manufactured in the United States, with an aluminum alloy frame manufactured in Germany. There are three control levers all on the left side of the weapon. Nearest the muzzle is the release lever for stripping; the middle lever, just below the slide, is the decocking lever; the rearmost lever is the slide latch. Like all SIG pistols, the P-229 has an automatic firing-pin safety, operating without a traditional safety control lever, with the first shot when the hammer is at half-cock requiring a longer trigger pull. Both the P-228 and P-229 are fitted with high contrast Stavenhagen sights, but a tritium enhanced foresight and luminous rearsights can also be fitted.

Right: The SIG P-229 is used by numerous special forces, and is both rugged and dependable, as well as easy to use.

SIG-Sauer 9mm P-239 Pistol

Country of origin: Switzerland.
Manufacturer: SIG-Sauer (Switzerland/Germany).
Type: semi-automatic pistol/personal defense weapon.
Caliber: 9mm.
Weight: gun 23oz (780g).
Dimensions: length, gun 6.8in (172mm); barrel 3.6in (92mm).
Magazine: 7/8/10-round boxes (see text).
Muzzle velocity: 1,115ft/sec (340m/sec).
Rifling: 6 grooves, r/hand.

The SIG-Sauer P-239 was specifically designed with female users in mind, to meet the increasing requirement created by female shooters in armed forces, special forces, law enforcement agencies and para-military organizations. Company research established that because women's hands are smaller than men's, they need a pistol which packs the same performance, but in a physically smaller package., although the smaller size also makes the pistol easier to conceal, whether the shooters are women or men. This size reduction has been achieved by restricting the number of rounds in the magazine to eight in the 9mm version (seven in .40 S&W and .357SIG versions) in order to eliminate the double-stacking of rounds and thus produce a smaller butt. A ten-round magazine is, however, available as an optional extra. The P-239 is a mechanically locked, recoil-operated, auto-loading weapon. The sights are adjustable, the rear sight having six notches, while five different foresight posts are available. As with earlier SIG pistols, the P-239 has a machined, stainless steel slide with a light alloy frame and is black anodized. Three versions are available, firing NATO standard 9mm Parabellum, the American 0.40 Smith & Wesson, or SIG's own, newly developed .357in round which is more powerful and with a higher muzzle velocity than earlier rounds.

Right: The SIG P-239 was designed with female users in mind and is slightly smaller than other pistols.

Heckler & Koch .45in Mk 23 (SOCOM) Pistol

Country of origin: Germany.
Manufacturer: Heckler & Koch, Germany/USA.
Type: semi-automatic pistol/personal defense weapon.
Caliber: 0.45in ACP.
Weight: gun 42oz (1,200g).
Dimensions: length gun 9.7in (245mm); barrel 5.9in (150mm).
Magazine: 12-round box.
Muzzle velocity: 850ft/sec (260m/sec).
Rifling: Polygonal; r/hand.

In 1990 U.S. Special Operations Command (SOCOM) issued a new operational requirement for an Offensive Handgun Weapon System consisting of three elements: a handgun; a laser-aiming module (LAM); and a sound/flash suppressor. A number of very demanding criteria were announced publicly and any arms manufacturer in any country in the world was allowed to enter although, in the event, only two did so: Colt, with a Knight's suppressor; and Heckler & Koch with one of their own company's suppressors. Each of the two companies produced thirty Phase I prototypes, the eventual winners being the Heckler & Koch pistol, but with the Knight's suppressor, even though it was most unusual for a component from a losing entry to be selected. The LAM was

Right: Special forces trooper with the SOCOM pistol; 7,500 have been procured, plus suppressors.

Below: The H&K 0.45in Mk 23 Mod 0 pistol, usually known as the "SOCOM pistol", with Knight's suppressor attached.

made by Insight Technology of Londonderry, New Hampshire. The pistol was a development of Heckler & Koch's 0.45in version of an earlier model called the USP, but with a longer slide, a slight extension of the barrel for the screw attachment for the suppressor, and mountings for the LAM. It was accepted for U.S. service as the "Pistol, Caliber .45in, Mark 23 Mod 0" (but is usually known, simply, as the "SOCOM Pistol") and deliveries started in May 1996.

The LAM is attached to the underside of the pistol ahead of the trigger guard and projects a red spot onto the target, enabling the weapon to be sighted with great accuracy. The suppressor screws onto the muzzle and provides a substantial reduction in both flash and noise, the latter being aided by the fact that the bullet is just sub-sonic, thus avoiding the characteristic "crack" of a supersonic bullet.

Left: This pistol has the Laser-Aiming Module (LAM) mounted in front of the trigger-guard for very precise aiming.

Below: The bare weapon, showing three levers for (from front to rear): disassembly, safety and holding open. Note also the screw thread on the muzzle for attaching the suppressor.

MEU(SOC) Pistol

Country of origin: USA.
Manufacturer: specially trained armorers at MCB, Quantico, Virginia.
Type: modified .45 caliber pistol.
Caliber: .45 ACP.
Weight: gun with empty magazine 2.5lb (1.1kg); gun with loaded magazine 3.0lb (1.4kg).
Dimensions: length gun 8.6in (219mm); barrel 5.0in (128mm).
Magazine: 7-round box.
Muzzle velocity: 830ft/sec (252m/sec).
Rifling: 6 grooves; l-hand.

The M1911A1 was the principal handgun used by the U.S. military for many decades and the great majority have now been replaced by the Beretta M9 9mm pistol. However, a number of M1911A1s will undoubtedly remain in service for some years to come, including the Marine Corps' MEU(SOC) pistol.
    The original M1911A1 semi-automatic pistol was a recoil-operated magazine-fed semiautomatic weapon, firing a single round each time the trigger

was squeezed, which is referred to as "single action only." In such a mechanism, the thumb safety may be activated only once the pistol is cocked, whereupon the hammer remains in the fully cocked position until the safety has been deactivated. (This differs from more modern "double action" pistol designs, which allow the hammer to move forward to an uncocked position when the thumb safety is activated.) The M1911A1 was much liked by users, who set particular store by its reliability and lethality, but its "single action" mechanism required them to be thoroughly familiar with it, especially when carrying it in the "ready-to-fire" mode. As a result accidents did happen and orders were often given for M1911A1s to be carried without a round in the chamber, but even so unintentional discharges were frequent occurrences.

The MEU(SOC) pistol was the outcome of a requirement for a "backup weapon" for Marines armed with the Heckler & Koch 9mm MP5-N Close Quarters Battle weapon (submachine gun) and, since the new M9 9mm automatic pistol was judged unsuitable, selected M1911A1s have been modified for this role. The M1911A1 was chosen because of its inherent reliability and lethality, as well as its availability, while the modifications make the M1911A1 design more "user friendly" by resolving its shortcomings. The

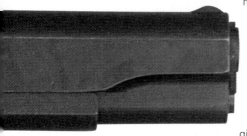

modifications included in the MEU(SOC) pistol include: a high quality barrel; more precise trigger; rubber coated grips; rounded hammer spur; new, easier to use combat sights, and an extra-wide grip safety, suitable for both right- and left-handed firers, which gives not only greater comfort and controllability, but also assists the firer in making a quick, follow-up, second shot. In addition, the old magazines are replaced by a new type, made of stainless steel and with rounded plastic follower and extended floor plate. Some 500 M1911A1s were converted, each being hand-built by specially trained armorers at the Rifle Team Equipment (RTE) shop, Quantico, Virginia.

Left: The MEU(SOC) pistol is an M1919A1 rebuilt by hand by Marine armorers at the workshops in Quantico, Virginia.

Browning Hi Power 9mm Mk3

Country of origin: Belgium.
Manufacturer: FN, Herstal, Belgium.
Type: automatic pistol.
Operation: short recoil Browning mechanism.
Caliber: 9 x 19mm NATO.
Weight: gun with empty magazine 2.0lb (0.93kg); gun with loaded magazine 2.3lb (1.1kg).
Dimensions: length pistol 7.9in (200mm); barrel 4.6in (118mm).
Magazine: 13-round box.
Muzzle velocity: 1,148ft/sec (350/sec).
Rifling: 6 grooves; right-hand.

This, the most widely used military handgun of all time, was designed in th
early 1920s by John Moses Browning and, following minor modifications
placed in production by FN Herstal. During the 1930s and 1940s it wa
produced in vast numbers in at least six countries and is still in production at FI
as the Hi Power HP Mk3. The Mk3 has retained the well-proven Brownin
mechanism, as well as all of the major parts and vital advantages of the earlie
models. The simple and sturdy mechanism also ensures long component lif
and simple maintenance. The Mk3 has also retained the Hi Power's prove
safety mechanisms, including: the mechanical safety lever; a visible hamme
which gives an instant indication of whether or not the weapon is cocked; hal
cock notch, which catches the hammer if it slips during cocking or de-cockin

*Above: One of the most modern versions, the Hi
Power Practical available in 9mm, 0.4S&W
calibers; note the wrap-around rubber grips,*

Right: The 9mm Browning has been used by the British Army's special forces for many years.

firing-pin spring which prevents inadvertent discharge if the weapon is dropped with a round chambered; and a magazine safety that disengages the trigger when the magazine is removed. Improvements incorporated into the Mk3 include new ergonomic grips to improve handling and contribute to the shooter's comfort; new sights to improve accuracy; and an ambidextrous safety for improved security when being used by left-handed shooters.

The Browning HP has been used by many special forces in the past thirty years but in many cases has been replaced by newer weapons such as the Glock 17 and the various SIG-Sauer models. Nevertheless, the Browning Mk3 is still used by a number of special forces.

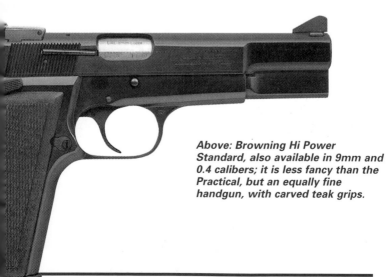

Above: Browning Hi Power Standard, also available in 9mm and 0.4 calibers; it is less fancy than the Practical, but an equally fine handgun, with carved teak grips.

Glock Model 17

Country of origin: Austria.
Manufacturer: Glock, Austria.
Type: semi-automatic pistol/personal defense weapon.
Caliber: 9 x 19mm Luger/Parabellum.
Weight: gun with empty magazine 1.4lb (0.63kg).
Dimensions: length gun 7.3in (186mm); barrel 4.5in (114mm).
Magazine: 17-round box.
Muzzle velocity: 1,263ft/sec (385m/sec).
Rifling: 6 grooves; r/hand.

Glock caused something of a surprise when it won a competition for a handgun for the Austrian Army with its Model 17. The company had never before produced a military pistol, even though this was the designer's seventeenth patent, but this very effective weapon has been adopted by numerous armies and special forces, including the Israeli *Unit Yamam*. The Glock Model 17 introduced the company's design with a steel slide mounted on a polymer frame with alloy inserts, which results in a very light overall weight. In addition the unique Glock "safe action" trigger is activated only by a proper pull from the operator's finger, eliminating the need for other manual safety devices, and resulting in a very safe weapon.

Variations include the Model 17L with longer barrel and slide, Model 18 which is a fully automatic version of the Model 17, and Model 19 which is slightly smaller and lighter. The weapon is also produced in a variety of calibers including 10mm Auto (Model 20), .45 ACP (Model 21), and .40 S&W (Model 22).

Manurhin Revolver 0.357 Magnum MR73

Country of origin: France.
Manufacturer: Manurhin, France.
Type: semi-automatic pistol/personal defense weapon.
Caliber: .357 Magnum Express or 9 x 19mm Luger/Parabellum.
Weight: gun unloaded 2.1lb (0.95kg).
Dimensions: length gun 9.2in (233mm); barrel 4.0in (102mm).
Magazine: 6-round cylinder.
Muzzle velocity: 1,312ft/sec (400m/sec).
Rifling: 6 grooves; r/hand.

The MR-73 was introduced in 1973 and has achieved great success. It has a conventional double action, with a side-opening, six-round, cylindrical magazine, and is available in various barrel lengths and calibers, including 9mm, .32 SW Long and .38 Special. All versions feature all-steel construction, with the barrel produced by the cold-hammering process. The weapons are hand-assembled and have very carefully

*bove: The Glock 17 has become the weapon-of-choice for several
pecial forces; it is accurate, handy and very safe.*

*bove: The French-manufactured Manurhin MR-73 is used by many
ench special forces, with whom it is very popular.*

djusted actions. The very high standards result in long life and extreme
ccuracy, albeit making them among the most expensive weapons in their
ass. Nevertheless, the MR-73 has become the standard handgun for special
rces such as RAID and GIGN, as well as the French Gendarmerie.

Heckler & Koch 9mm MP5

Country of origin: Germany.
Manufacturer: Heckler & Koch.
Type: special operations forces close-quarter battle submachine gun.
Operation: delayed blowback.
Caliber: 9 x 19mm Parabellum.
Weight: gun empty 5.6lb (2.6kg); gun with 30-round magazine 7.4lb (3.4kg).
Dimensions: length gun, stock extended 26in (660mm); length gun, stock folded 19.3in (490mm); barrel 8.9in (230mm).
Muzzle velocity: 1,312ft/sec (400m/sec).
Magazine: 15- or 30-round box.
Rate of fire: cyclic 800rpm.
Rifling: 6 grooves; r/hand.
Specifications are for MP5-N.

The Heckler and Koch MP5 is used by large numbers of the world's elite force and it is probably no exaggeration to say that its basic combination of compact size, low weight, accuracy, lethality and outstanding reliability make it the world's leading close quarter battle (CQB) weapon. In the U.S. armed forces is fielded, among others, by Marine Corps Force Reconnaissance Companies and Marine Security Force Battalions, and by numerous civilian agencies including the FBI's Hostage Rescue Team. In foreign countries it is the "weapon of choice" for such prestigious units as the German GSG 9, the British SAS and London's Metropolitan Police firearms unit.

The MP5 uses the same roller-delayed blowback operating principle as the Heckler & Koch's (H&K) G3 rifle to fire from a closed and locked bolt in both automatic and semi-automatic modes. It features good handling qualities coupled with interchangeability of most parts with other weapons in the H&K range. The MP5 can fire semi-automatic, fully automatic or in three-, four-, five-round bursts. In the latter mode the effect is achieved by a small ratchet counting mechanism which interacts with the sear. Each time the bolt cycles the rear the ratchet advances one notch until the third, fourth or fifth cyc

Below: The MP5 has an extending stock and the selector includes a 3-round option. It is seen here with a 15-round magazine.

Above: MP55D, with silencer and laser sight, enabling the marksman to know precisely where the round will hit.

Below: The working parts of the MP5 showing the roller-delayed blowback system.

▶ allows re-engagement of the sear. Firing also ceases the instant the trigger is released, regardless of how many rounds have been fired in the current burst. The actual number of rounds in each burst is pre-set in the factory, and cannot be altered by the firer.

The MP5 uses metal stampings and welded sub-group parts. The receiver is constructed of stamped sheet steel in nineteen operations (several combined) and is attached to the polygonal rifled barrel by a trunnion which is spot-welded to the receiver and pinned to the barrel. The trigger-housing, butt stock and fore-end are fabricated from high-impact plastic.

There is a variety of specialized versions. MP5K has a shorter barrel with a vertical foregrip underneath, and the butt is replaced by a simple cap. MP5SD is a series of silenced weapons: MP5SD1 has no stock; MP5SD2 has a fixed stock; and MP5SD3 has a retractable stock. The MP5-N, as fielded by the U.S. Marine Corps, has a retractable butt stock, a removable suppressor, and an illuminating flashlight integral to the forward handguard, which is operated by a pressure-switch custom-fitted to the pistol grip.

Below: Three SEALs armed with MP5s secure a "prisoner" during a demonstration of their skills.

Above: MP5K (K=kurz [short]) is very compact, only a little larger than a pistol, and small enough to fit in a briefcase.

Uzi, Mini-Uzi and Micro-Uzi

Country of origin: Israel.
Manufacturer: Israeli Military Industries (IMI), Ramat Ha Sharon, Israel.
Type: special operations forces close-quarter battle submachine gun.
Operation: blowback.
Caliber: 9mm Parabellum or .45in.
Weight: gun, empty 7.7lb (3.5kg).
Dimensions: length gun, stock extended 25.2in (640mm); barrel
Range: maximum effective 328ft (100m).
Muzzle velocity: 1,280ft/sec (390m/sec).
Magazine: 256/32/40-round box (9mm); 16-round box (.45in).
Rates of fire: cyclic 600rpm (9mm); 500rpm (.45in).
Rifling: 4 grooves, r/hand (9mm); 6 grooves, l/hand (.45in).

A young Israeli Army major named Uziel Gal, an arms expert, designed an
produced a new submachine gun, the Uzi, which was introduced in 195
and quickly became one of the most widely used SMGs in the Wester
world. Gal based his design on the Czechoslovakian post-war Models 2

nd 25 SMGs, which had been a major departure from pre-war and wartime esign practice. Early SMGs were not known for their accuracy, and to vercome this the Czech designers developed a concept wherein the bolt ctually closed over the rear end of the barrel, thus enclosing the cartridge. Major Gal kept this and another clever Czech design feature, in which the nagazine was inserted through the pistol grip.

The Uzi is a simple blow-back design in which the action is cocked by rawing the bolt to the rear, whereupon the sear rotates up to engage and old it open. The trigger mechanism is also simple. A coil spring is used to ension the sear; pulling the trigger to the rear allows the sear to move own and rotate out of engagement with the bolt. The bolt's own coil spring rives it forward, stripping a cartridge from the magazine, chambering it and ring it as the striker in the bolt face impacts the primer. The gas pressure enerated by the exploding cartridge then drives the bolt to the rear, ▶

elow: The Mini-Uzi; when the wire folding stock is retracted the veight is symmetrically disposed around the pistol grip.

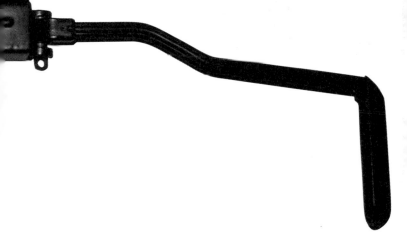

▶ extracting and ejecting the fired case as it goes, until it comes up again[st] the bolt stop, whereupon the spring drives it forward at the start of a ne[w] cycle.

In all the years that the 9mm Uzi has been in production, there hav[e] been only two significant changes. A grip safety, which blocks the trigg[er] unless depressed, was added to all models, and a special version was als[o] produced in small numbers to fire the .45in Automatic Colt Pistol (AC[P]) cartridge. Optional attachments include a short bayonet and a barr[el-] mounted searchlight. A grenade-launcher may be screwed to the front [of] the receiver in place of the barrel-locking nut.

In 1981 Israeli Military Industries (IMI) introduced a smaller versi[on] designated the "Mini-Uzi," which is identical in operation, but smaller a[nd]

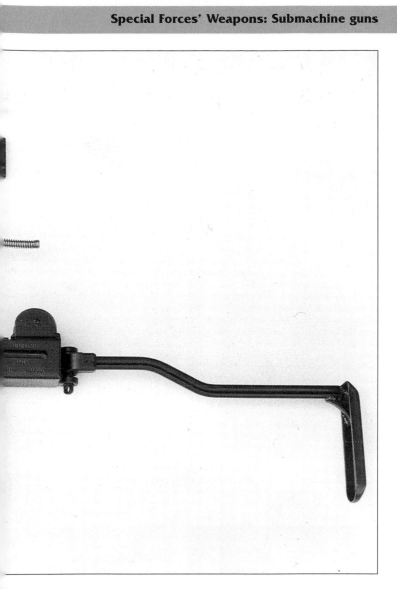

Above: Major components (from top) - slide cover; bolt; body; barrel-locking nut; and barrel. Magazine is in pistol grip.

ighter; it weighs only 5.9lb (2.7kg). It is chambered for 9mm only, and can take either the standard 25- or 32-round magazines or a new short 20-round magazine. This was followed in 1982 by the Micro-Uzi, which is less than 10in (254mm) long with the shoulder stock folded and has a firing rate of some 1,200rpm.

In addition to the Israeli forces, the Uzi is in use in Belgium, Germany, ran, the Netherlands, Thailand, Venezuela, and many other countries. It also continues to be used by many special forces, although it has been replaced n most by the Heckler & Koch MP5.

L34A1 Sterling silenced SMG

Country of origin: UK.
Manfacturer: Sterling, Dagenham, England.
Type: submachine gun.
Operation: blowback.
Caliber: 9mm Parabellum.
Weight: gun 8.0lb (3.6kg).
Dimensions: length gun, 34.6in (864mm); barrel, 7.9in (198mm)
Muzzle velocity: 1,020ft/sec (310m/sec).
Magazine: 34-round box.
Rate of fire: 550rpm.
Rifling: 6 grooves; r/hand.

The L34A1, which entered service in 1966 and is still in service with severa special forces, is the silenced version of the British L2A3 Sterling, with which i shares many components. The silenced weapon is, however, almost 2lb (1kg heavier and considerably longer, due to the large silencing device fitted arounc and beyond the barrel. Most silenced weapons require special rounds, but the L34A1 is unusual in firing standard 9mm Parabellum ammunition. The barre itself is the same length as on the unsilenced version, but has 72 radial holes drilled in its walls to allow the propellant gases to escape, thus reducing the muzzle velocity of the bullet. Beyond the end of the barrel there is a spira diffuser, which consists of a series of discs, each with a hole in the centre through which the bullet passes. Propellant gas follows the round but is deflected back by the end cap to mingle with the advancing gasses, thus ensuring that the gases leaving the barrel do so at a low velocity. The silencec Sterling is an effective weapon and has been used by the British and othe armies, principally by special forces, although some have also got into the hands of various terrorist groups.

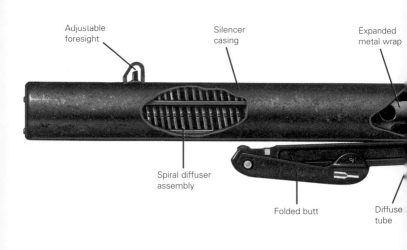

Adjustable foresight

Silencer casing

Expanded metal wrap

Spiral diffuser assembly

Folded butt

Diffuse tube

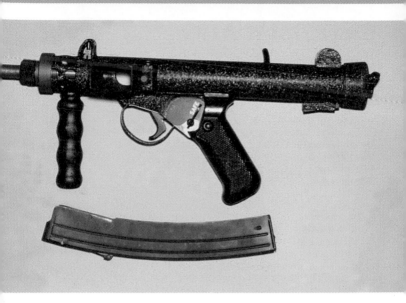

Above: Sterling Mk VIII, a very short barrel weapon mid-way between a pistol and a submachine gun.

Below: The L34A1 silenced Sterling is very quiet, but this reduces muzzle velocity making it a very close range weapon.

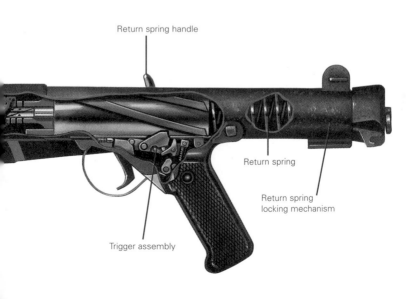

Return spring handle

Return spring

Return spring
locking mechanism

Trigger assembly

Steyr 9mm AUG

Country of origin: Austria.
Manufacturer: Steyr-Mannlicher, Steyr, Austria.
Type: submachine gun.
Operation: blowback.
Caliber: 9mm Parabellum.
Weight: gun 7.3lb (3.3kg).
Dimensions: length gun 26.2in (665mm); barrel 16.5in (420mm).
Muzzle velocity: 1,312ft/sec (400m/sec).
Magazine: 25- or 32-round box.
Rate of fire: cyclic 700rpm.
Rifling: 6 grooves; r/hand.

Steyr-Mannlicher produces the very successful AUG (*Armee Universal Gewerh*
= universal army rifle) assault rifle and the weapon shown here, introduced in
1986, is the submachine gun model in that range. Externally the two weapons
appear very similar and many elements are common to both, including the
bullpup layout, plastic casing, canted carrying handle with inbuilt x1.5 optical
sight, forward handgrip and pistol grip with handguard. But, although it bears an
outward resemblance to the assault rifle, the submachine gun has substantial

differences internally. It fires the 9 x 19mm Parabellum round rather than the rifle's 5.56mm and the barrel is shorter: 16.5in (420mm) compared to 20.0in (508mm). The method of operation is also different in that the submachine gun version has a new bolt and operates by blowback from a closed bolt position. The magazine housing is fitted with an adapter enabling it to accommodate the new magazine holding 9mm rounds. The submachine gun's barrel can be fitted with a screw-on silencer.

Below: The Steyr 9mm AUG is the submachine gun version of the very successful AUG assault rifle.

Steyr 9mm Tactical Machine Pistol (TMP)

Country of origin: Austria.
Manufacturer: Steyr-Mannlicher, Steyr, Austria.
Type: submachine gun.
Operation: locked breech.
Caliber: 9mm Parabellum.
Weight: gun 2.9lb (1.3kg).
Dimensions: length gun 11.1in (282mm); barrel 5.1in (130mm).
Muzzle velocity: 1,180ft/sec (360m/sec).
Magazine: 15- or 30-round box.
Rate of fire: 900rpm.
Rifling: 6 grooves; r/hand.

The TMP is one of those weapons which do not fit neatly into any one category, its small size and lack of a butt-stock suggesting a pistol, while its full automatic firing and forward handgrip are more akin to a submachine gun, and it is treated as such here. The receiver is made from a synthetic material and incorporates a rail along the top for an optical sight, if required. Internally, there is a guide-rail for the bolt, and the operating system consists of a locking breech and a rotating barrel. There is no butt stock, enabling the cocking handle to be mounted at the foot of the back-plate, the weapon being cocked by pulling it straight to the rear. The barrel is threaded to accommodate a cylindrical sound suppressor, which is longer than the weapon itself.

Below: Steyr TMP with its sound suppressor which is actually longer than the weapon itself.

Below: The small, stockless TMP is an elegant design, with a foregrip and a combined pistol-grip/magazine housing.

FN 5.7mm P-90

Country of origin: Belgium.
Manufacturer: Fabrique Nationale, Herstal, Belgium.
Type: submachine gun.
Operation: blowback, closed-bolt.
Caliber: 5.7mm.
Weight: gun 5.5lb (2.5kg).
Dimensions: length gun 19.7in (500mm); barrel 10.4in (263mm).
Muzzle velocity: 2,345ft/sec (715m/sec).
Magazine: 50-round box.
Rate of fire: 900rpm.
Rifling: 8 grooves; r/hand.

The futuristic-looking FN P-90 was designed as a self-defense weapon for us
by support and technical troops whose primary function is not direct comba
using rifles or machine guns. There are many such troops on a moder
battlefield, including: headquarters personnel; engineers; gunners; comm
unicators; army aviators; and logistics troops. The P-90 is a submachine gu

*Below: Among the many novel features of the P-90 is the ammunition
feed system, in which the rounds are stored transversely in a clear
plastic magazine which lies along the fop of the weapon.*

which has been designed from basic principles and incorporates a host of new and imaginative ideas. The shape of the weapon is based on extensive ergonomic research and care has been taken to ensure that the weapon can be used with equal ease by left- or right-handed firers, while its smooth contours ensure that it will not snag on the firer's clothing or equipment. The magazine, made of clear plastic, is positioned along the top of the receiver and contains fifty rounds which, in a unique arrangement, lie in two rows across the line of the weapon. These are pushed forward by a spring and as they arrive at the end of the magazine they are, first, fed into a single row and, secondly, rotated through 90 degrees, thus aligning them with the chamber, into which they are then fed. The carrying handle incorporates a tritium-illuminated sight, but there are also conventional iron sights on the top of the receiver. A totally new round was designed by FN for use in this weapon: the 5.7 x 28mm. This is lead-free and causes extensive wounds to humans, since it is designed not only to transfer the maximum energy to the target, but also to "tumble" inside the target. Two versions are also available for special forces, and these have a number of optional accessories, including a silencer.

SAF 9mm

Country of origin: Chile.
Manufacturer: FAMAE, Santiago, Chile.
Type: submachine gun.
Operation: blowback.
Caliber: 9mm Parabellum.
Weight: gun 5.9lb (2.7kg).
Dimensions: length gun 25.3in (640mm); barrel 7.9in (200mm).
Muzzle velocity: 1,280ft/sec (390m/sec).
Magazine: 30- or 20-round.
Rate of fire: 1,200rpm.
Rifling: 6 grooves; r/hand.

The Swiss SIG 540 assault rifle is manufactured under licence in Chile by Fabricas y Maestranzas del Ejercito (FAMAE) at Santiago, Chile, and that company has developed a new submachine gun, the SAF 9mm, which uses a large number of features from the SIG 540. The weapon works by blowback, both barrel and chamber are chrome-plated, and, unlike the SIG 540, it has a three-round burst capability. There are three basic models: standard, with fixed or folding stock; silenced, with fixed or folding stock; and the Mini-SAF, which is intended for concealed carriage. This Mini-SAF has the same basic mechanism as the larger weapon, but has a very short barrel (4.5in/115mm), a forward handgrip and no butt stock. It takes the standard 30-round, translucent magazine but there is also a 20-round version for maximum compactness. Both magazines have slots and studs to enable them to be connected back-to-back, thus effectively doubling the capacity. The Mini-SAF in service with the Chilean armed forces, special forces and police, but, as far as is known, has not been exported.

Right: Developed primarily for use by its own SF, the Chilean standard SAF model is a neat SMG design.

*ove: Intended for covert
ork the Mini-SAF features
short barrel and a forward
nd-grip.*

257

Glauberyt PM-84

Country of origin: Poland.
Manufacturer: Lucznik, Badom, Poland.
Type: submachine gun.
Operation: blowback.
Caliber: 9mm Makarov (see text).
Weight: gun 4.6lb (2.1kg).
Dimensions: length gun 22.6in (575mm); barrel 7.3in (185mm).
Muzzle velocity: 1,083ft/sec (330m/sec).
Magazine: 15- or 25-round box.
Rate of fire: 600rpm.
Rifling: 6 grooves; r/hand.

The first known Polish submachine gun was the *Blyskawicza*, which wa
manufactured clandestinely by the Polish resistance in 1943-44. Its design wa
based on the British Sten Mk2, but with minor changes to suit the local, an
very limited, production capabilities. The current series of submachine guns ar
manufactured by Zaklady Metalowe Lucznik, at Radom, Poland. The first o
these was the PM-63 (also designated Wz-63), fielded in 1963 and now phase

out of production in Poland, although it may still be in production in China. This weapon was notable for its unusual reciprocating receiver and was chambered for the Soviet 9 x 18mm Makarov, which was the standard Warsaw Pact round.

The PM-04 is an updated version of the PM-63, in which the major change is that the bolt and other moving elements are now housed inside the receiver, so that there are no external reciprocating parts. The butt strut is hinged just behind the pistol grip and folds down and forwards until it clips below the receiver, with the butt plate acting as the forward hand-grip. The pistol grip acts as the housing for 15- or 25-round box magazines. With the butt folded, the pistol grip is at the point-of-balance, enabling single rounds to be fired with one hand, although for automatic it would be usual to hold the forward hand-grip. Like the PM-63, the PM-84 *Glauberyt* is chambered for the 9 x 18mm Makarov round and this version is widely used in the Polish forces. A new version, PM-84P, appeared in 1985 for the export market, which is chambered for the 9mm Parabellum round, the weapon being slightly heavier at 4.75lb (2.2kg). The latest version is the PM-98, which is an updated version of the PM-84P and is slightly larger still, weighing 5.1lb (2.3kg).

Below: Latest in this range of Polish SMGs, the PM-98 has a folding stock, is chambered for the 9mm Parabellum round.

Mechem BXP 9mm

Country of origin: South Africa.
Manufacturer: Mechem, Silverton, South Africa.
Type: submachine gun.
Operation: blowback.
Caliber: 9mm.
Weight: gun 5.8lb (2.7kg).
Dimensions: length gun 23.9in (607mm); barrel 8.2in (208mm).
Muzzle velocity: 1,250ft/sec (380m/sec).
Magazine: 22- or 32-round box.
Rate of fire: 800rpm.
Rifling: 6 grooves; r/hand.

The BXP 9mm submachine gun, which entered service in 1984, is one of a number of weapons developed in South Africa during the period when tha

country was subjected to an international arms embargo, while concurrently involved in a series of conflicts in the southern part of the continent. The BXP has a short, box-shaped receiver and a very short barrel with a screw-on flash suppressor, which can be removed and replaced by a large, cylindrical noise suppressor. In its normal mode the barrel is fitted with a short, vented jacket. One very unusual feature for a submachine gun is that the BXP can be fitted with a grenade-launcher attachment for use in anti-riot situations to project CS and other types of grenade. The twin-strut butt folds down and forwards, with the butt plate swiveling to lie under the receiver and act as a fore-grip. The BXP is used by the South African armed forces, special foreces, and police, and has also been exported to a number of other countries.

Below: Mechem BXP with its sound suppressor fitted; to its right, normal barrel and alternative screw-on flash suppressors.

Bison 9mm

Country of origin: Russia.
Manufacturer: Izhmash OJSC, Izhevsk, Russia.
Type: submachine gun.
Operation: blowback.
Caliber: 9 x 18mm Makarov.
Weight: gun 4.6lb (2.1kg).
Dimensions: length gun 26.0in (660mm); barrel 10.0in (250mm).
Muzzle velocity: 1,115ft/sec (340m/sec).
Magazine: 64-round helical.
Cyclic rate: 650-700rpm.
Rifling: 4 groooves; r/hand.

The Bison submachine gun was designed by a team led by Viktor Kalashnikov
the son of the much respected weapons designer, Captain Mikhail Kalashnikov
who was responsible for weapons such as the AK-47 and AK-74. With such
heritage, it is not surprising that the Bison uses many well-proven Kalashniko

omponents to produce a weapon with many interesting features. It operates n the blowback principle, and the left-folding, twin-strut buttstock, trigger mechanism, receiver cover and magazine catch all come straight from other Kalashnikov designs.

The barrel protrudes a considerable distance from the front of the receiver nd is completely surrounded by a forestock, which has three horizontal cooling lots in each side. The most unusual feature is the totally new type of magazine, which is helical in shape and is secured under the forestock with its ear-end engaged in the magazine feed and held in place by a Kalashnikov magazine catch. The magazine holds 64 rounds and, while the prototype was made from pressed steel, production versions are made of translucent plastic. he first prototype (Bison 1) fires either 9 x 18mm Makarov pistol rounds or the ewer and more powerful 9 x 18mm "Special." Bison-2 fires the newer Special" round only as does the Bison-3, but the latter also has a different tyle folding butt. This very interesting weapon is now in production for the pecial forces in at least one country.

elow: "Designed by Kalashnikov" ensures an interesting and innovative esign, as in this Bison 9mm SMG.

MAT49

Country of origin: France.
Manufacturer: Manufacture d'Armes de Tulle (MAT), France.
Type: submachine gun.
Operation: blowback.
Caliber: 9mm.
Weight: gun 7.9lb (3.6kg).
Dimensions: length gun 28.8in (720mm); barrel 9.0in (228mm).
Muzzle velocity: 1,2870ft/sec (390m/sec).
Magazine: 20- or 32-round box.
Rate of fire: 600rpm.
Rifling: 4 grooves; r/hand.

The MAT49 submachine gun was designed and built at the Manufactur
d'Armes de Tulle (MAT) and had an excellent reputation among French troops
As the number indicates, it was first adopted by the French Army in 1949 an
subsequently saw considerable service in Indo-China, Algeria and most o
France's other small wars. The MAT49 has a conventional blowback design, bu
also incorporated a number of unusual, but useful features. One of these wa
that the magazine housing, complete with magazine, could be folded forwarc
and clipped out of the way under the barrel, and only had to be swung back an
down to be ready for instant use. This, combined with the telescopic ste
stock, makes the weapon particularly suitable for use by paratroops and speci
forces. Another feature is the safety, which is in the rear of the pistol grip ar
has to be squeezed to enable the weapon to fire; among other benefits, thi
prevents accidental discharge by dropping, always a potential problem wit
submachine guns. An ejection port cover is also fitted to help keep dirt out o
the internal mechanism of the gun. The 9mm MAT49 was used by the Frenc
Army and is still in use by the armies of many former French colonies. A larg
number of MAT49s were captured by the Viet Minh and Viet Cong during th
Indochina wars and were later converted to take the Soviet 7.76mm Type
round. These weapons can be recognized by the longer barrel and 35-roun
magazine, and they are also capable of a somewhat higher cyclic rate of fire o
900 rounds per minute.

Above: Three French soldiers armed with the MAT49. Note that center man has the magazine folded forward.

Below left: MAT49 with stock folded. The steeply canted pistol grip includes the large, built-in "safety".

Below right: MAT49 with stock extended. The most unusual feature was that the magazine housing could fold forwards.

Steyr AUG 5.56mm

Country of origin: Austria.
Manufacturer: Steyr, Austria.
Type: assault rifle.
Operation: gas.
Caliber: 5.56 x 45mm.
Weight: gun 7.9lb (3.6kg).
Dimensions: length gun 31.1in (790mm); barrel 20.0in (508mm).
Muzzle velocity: 3,182ft/sec (970m/sec).
Magazine: 30-round box.
Rate of fire: 650rpm.
Rifling: 6 grooves; r/hand.

The *Armee Universalgewehr* (AUG = universal army rifle) was designed in response to an Austrian Army requirement for a new assault rifle and it entered service in 1977, but even after more than twenty years' service its bullpup design and unusual shape still give it a futuristic appearance. The AUG has a solid, indestructible feel and all users report that it is very reliable and accurate. It is fitted with a Swarovski x1.5 scope mounted in the carrying-handle. Barrels can be changed rapidly, locking into a machined steel ring, which is contained within the cast aluminum breech housing; the bolthead locks into the same steel ring. The gun uses a rotating bolt that recoils along two substantial guide rods, the right one housing the operating rod. Both rods impinge on recoil springs contained with the buttstock. The use of polymers extends to the firing unit, most components of which were originally of plastic, although some of these were later replaced by metal parts. The AUG is rated as an excellent weapon, although its trigger pull of 10lb (4.5kg) is criticized by some as being unnecessarily heavy. The casing can be finished in black, sand or olive drab colours, while the magazine is translucent to enable the firer to see how many rounds remain unfired. Following entry into service with the Austrian Army in 1977 (where it is designated the StuG-77 [*Sturmgewehr* = assault rifle]), the AUG has been adopted by a number of other countries, including Australia, Djibouti, Ireland, Malaysia, Morocco, New Zealand, the Oman, and Tunisia, and is the weapon of choice with their special forces. According to some reports, the AUG is also used in small

Above: Paratrooper with AUG in the hip firing position, using the sling to steady the weapon.

Left: The futuristic shape of the AUG. It has sold well and is used by a number of special forces.

Above: From top, assault rifle, carbine and SMG; all are 5.56mm, the only major difference is in the barrel length.

Above right: AUG-P is a sub-machine gun version, but chambered for the 9mm Parabellum round.

Right: An Austrian Army NCO shows how light is the AUG. Note that the forward handgrip is folded forwards.

► numbers by the British SAS and U.S. SEALs. Small quantities have also found their way into terrorist hands, including the Colombian M-19 Marxists.

Variants can be easily assembled by changing a few components, including: carbine (16.0in/407mm barrel); submachine gun (13.8in/350mm barrel); and light support weapon (bipod, heavy 24in 621mm barrel, 40-round magazine). Some variants can be equipped with the M203 40mm grenade launcher. The latest version is the AUG A2, introduced in 1997, which features redesigned cocking handle and new sight rails that allow quick removal of the standard sight and installation of new mounts which comply with the appropriate STANAG (Standardized NATO Agreement).

CZ 2000 5.56mm

Country of origin: Czech Republic.
Manufacturer: Ceska Zbrojovka (CZ), Prague, Czech Republic.
Type: assault rifle.
Operation: gas.
Caliber: 5.56 x 45mm NATO.
Weight: gun empty 6.6lb (3.0kg).
Dimensions: length gun 33.5in (850mm); barrel 15.0in (382mm).
Muzzle velocity: 2,985ft/sec (910m/sec).
Magazine: 30-round box.
Rate of fire: 800rpm.
Rifling: 6 grooves; r/hand.

The Czech Republic's new range of infantry weapons was revealed in 1993 an it was said at that time to be under development in both 5.45mm and 5.56m versions; in the event, only the NATO 5.56 x 45mm version has bee developed, clearly in anticipation of Czech membership of NATO. At the time was unveiled, the family was known as the "Lada" system, but that name ha since been dropped in favour of "CZ 2000."

The CZ 2000 family is built around a core of standard components, whi differ only in the barrel sub-assemblies and accessory kits. The weapon is ga operated and uses a rotating bolt, derived from that used in the Russia Kalashnikov rifle, which locks into the barrel at the moment of firing and fire

full automatic, single rounds or three-round bursts. It has a pressed steel receiver with plastic furniture, and a twin-tubed, side-folding butt (there is no solid butt version). The 30-round magazine is made of clear plastic so that the firer can see how many rounds it contains, but the M16 magazine can also be used. The CZ 2000 Short Assault Rifle appeared in 1995 and is a lighter and shorter version; indeed, it is virtually a submachine gun. The receiver, butt, trigger group and pistol grip are the same, but the barrel is considerably shorter (7.3in/185mm compared to 15.0in/382mm), which has resulted in a shorter gas cylinder. In addition, the slotted flash suppressor has been replaced by a more conventional coned type. The CZ 2000 series also includes a light machine gun version.

Below: The Czech-designed CZ 2000 assault rifle; the built-in bipod is an increasingly common feature of such weapons.

FA MAS F-1 5.56mm

Country of origin: France.
Manufacturer: Manufacture d'Armes de St. Etienne, St. Etienne, France.
Type: assault rifle.
Operation: delayed blowback.
Caliber: 5.56 x 45mm French (see text).
Weight: gun empty 8.1lb (3.7kg).
Dimensions: length gun 29.8in (757mm); barrel 19.2in (488mm).
Muzzle velocity: 3,150ft/sec (960m/sec.)
Magazine: 25-round box.
Rate of fire: 950rpm.
Rifling: 4 grooves; r/hand.

The FAMAS (*Fusil Automatique, Manufacture d'Armes de St. Etienne*) was introduced into service in 1980 and has proved to be an effective and generally well-conceived weapon for general service and special forces' use. It fires the 5.56 x 45mm French round from the closed bolt position, using a delayed blowback mechanism that was derived from the French AA-52 general-purpose machine gun. A black plastic lower handguard, pinned to the barrel and receiver, extends to the magazine well and cannot be removed. Because it has a "bull-pup" configuration, the trigger mechanism and pistol grip have been mounted to the lower handguard, forward of the magazine housing. Among the features of the FA MAS are the prominent carrying handle (which also houses the sight), left- or right-side ejection, a three-round burst option, and a built-in bipod whose legs fold individually against the receiver when not in use. A slightly modified version, FA MAS G-2, is offered for export; this has a revised trigger guard and is chambered to fire the standard 5.56 x 45mm M193 or NATO rounds.

Above: The MAS; the prominent "bridge" serves as a carrying handle and houses the sighting system.

Below Left: The MAS stripped for field cleaning; note the sights on the body group, normally covered by the handle.

Below: The MAS's light weight and short length make it easy to carry and to handle.

5.45mm AK-74-SU

Country of origin: Russian Republic.
Manufacturer: Russian State Factories.
Type: assault rifle.
Operation: blowback
Caliber: 5.45 x 39.5mm Russian.
Weight: gun empty 5.9lb (2.7kg).
Dimensions: length gun 26.6in (675mm); barrel 8.1in (206mm).
Muzzle velocity: 2,411ft/sec (735m/sec).
Magazine: 30-round box.
Rate of fire: 700rpm.
Rifling: 4 grooves; r/hand.

The Kalashnikov-designed AK-74-SU is one of a series of outstanding weapons produced by the Soviet Union, and its small size and great hitting power make it ideal for special forces use. It is correctly designated an assault rifle, although in terms of size and weight it is as small as many SMGs. The barrel is only 8.1in (206mm) long and is fitted with a screw-on, cylindrical attachment at the front of which is a cone-shaped flash suppressor. The AK-74-SU fires standard, full-charge rifle ammunition, in this case, the Russian 5.45 x 39.5mm. Due to the shortness of the barrel, the gas is tapped off very close to the chamber which results in a very high pressure for such a small weapon, and the muzzle attachment is an expansion chamber, designed to reduce the pressure acting on the gas piston; it also serves as a flame damper. The weapon is fitted with basic iron sights, the rear sight being a basic flip-over device marked for 220yd (200m) and 440yd (400m), although the latter range seems somewhat optimistic for such a weapon. The internal mechanism is identical to that of the AK-74 except that the gas-piston, return-spring and its associated guide-rod are shorter. The weapon also has a very simple skeleton stock which folds forwards along the left side of the receiver.

The various versions of this very capable series of weapons are as follows. The AKM, introduced in 1959, was a modified version of the famous AK-47, incorporating various changes to simplify the manufacturing process. There were two variations: AKM-S with a two-strut folding stock, and AKM-SU, a shorter version for armored infantry. All these had been chambered for the 7.62 x 39mm Soviet round, but the AK-74, introduced in 1974, was chambered for the new 5.45 x 39.5mm round and was generally smaller and lighter. This, again, had two sub-types, AKS-74 with a folding stock, and the AK-74-SU described here.

Above: Russian paratrooper with a 5.45mm AKR submachine gun, a shortened lightened version of the AKS-74.

Below left: Standard version of the AK-74 with fixed stock; note removable cleaning rod below the barrel.

Bottom: AKS-74 carbine version for paratroops/SF, with stock which folds sideways to lie along the left side of the weapon.

M16A2 5.56mm semi-automatic rifle

Country of origin: United States.
Manufacturer: Colt Manufacturing, USA; Fabrique Nationale, Belgium.
Type: assault rifle.
Operation: gas, semi-automatic.
Caliber: 5.56 x 45mm NATO.
Weight: empty 6.4lb (2.9kg); with 30-round magazine 8.8lb (4.0kg).
Dimensions: length overall 39.6in (1,007mm); barrel 20.0in (510mm).
Muzzle velocity: 3,110ft/second (948m/sec).
Magazine: 30-round box.
Rates of fire: cyclic 800 rounds per minute; sustained 12-15 rounds per minute; semiautomatic 45 rounds per minute; burst 90 rounds per minute.
Rifling: 4 grooves; r/hand.
Specifications for M16A2.

The forerunner of this brilliant weapon was the 7.62mm AR-10, designed by Eugene Stoner, which first went into production in 1957. It was a very advanced weapon employing plastic and aluminum wherever possible, in contrast to the traditional wood, but the overall design proved too light to fire the powerful NATO cartridge for which it was designed. It was manufactured in small quantities between 1957 and 1962; it was purchased by the armies of Burma, Nicaragua, Portugal and the Sudan, and was tested by the Singapore Police

Below: M60 machine gun team – the nearest man is armed with the M16A2 rifle, the current production version.

Above: U.S. Army soldier armed with the M16A1 assault rifle; this was the original version, now replaced by the M16A2.

Below: The M16 5.56mm is simply one of the greatest and most influential rifles ever designed.

▶ Because of its shortcomings, a new design, the AR-15, was produced designed around the totally new 5.56mm high velocity round. This weapon firs appeared in 1957 and was put into production by the Colt company from Jul 1959 onwards. The AR-15 soon became popular, in particular as a jungle rifle not least because it was light and easy to handle by small men, and it soo found markets in various countries in the Far East. When U.S. troops firs became involved in Vietnam they were armed with the M14, firing the 7.62mn standard NATO round, which quickly proved itself to be most unsuitable, an the AR-15 was soon pressed into service as the M16.

Stoner's mechanism has no piston, the gases simply passing through tube and striking directly on to the bolt; this is simple and efficient, but mean that the weapon needs careful and regular cleaning to clear it of fouling. It ha been intended that the M16 should have the same effective range as the M1 it replaced, but it proved most effective at ranges of 215yd (200m) or less although this was quite adequate for the jungles of Indochina. When first issue to troops, the M16 encountered a number of widely publicized problems, man of them due to stoppages arising from a lack of care and cleaning, but bette training, preventive maintenance, and several design changes resulted in th weapon which quickly became the world standard, with some 3,690,000 havin been manufactured.

The M16A2 is a product-improved version of the M16A1, with man enhancements which result in an even better weapon. The most important c the changes are intended to improve accuracy and controllability. One of th most important of these is a heavier, stiffer barrel with a 1-in-7 twist, enablin it to fire the standard NATO M855 (SS-109) 5.56 x 45mm ammunition, whic increases effective range and penetration (M16A2 also fires the older M19 ammunition). A burst-control device is fitted so that when the weapon is i automatic mode only three rounds will be fired at a time, thus both increasin accuracy and reducing ammunition expenditure. In addition, a compensato situated on top of the muzzle reduces muzzle climb, improving the firer' control – and thus accuracy – in both burst and rapid semi-automatic fire. Finall

Below: Sentry stands guard duty armed with M16 rifle fitted with the M203 grenade launcher - a highly effective combination.

Above: Two Special Operations Capable Marines armed with M16A2s; note camouflage paint scheme on weapon on left.

Above: The M16A2 is light, handy and easy to carry, an ideal weapon for the modern infantryman.

concerning accuracy, there is an improved rear sight with easy adjustments for range and wind. Other changes include a modified upper receiver which deflects ejected cartridge cases in order to protect left-handed firers, redesigned handguard to give a better grip, and new and stronger buttstock and pistol grip, while the trigger guard can be removed to enable the weapon to be fired when the firer is wearing mittens. The M16A2 can fire 40mm grenades when equipped with the M203 Grenade Launcher.

Various versions of the M16 and M16A2 are used by special forces around the world, who admire its hitting power, lightness and reliability.

5.56mm Colt Commando

Country of origin: United States.
Manufacturer: Colt, USA.
Type: assault rifle.
Operation: semi/full auto, gas-operated, locking-bolt.
Caliber: 5.56 x 45mm M193.
Weight: gun empty 5.4lb (2.4kg); loaded 7.1lb (3.2kg).
Dimensions: length gun, stock extended 29.9in (760mm); length gun, stock compressed 26.8in (680mm); barrel 11.5in (290mm).
Muzzle velocity: 3,050ft/sec (924m/sec).
Magazine: 20- or 30-round box.
Rates of fire: cyclic 700-1,000rpm.
Rifling: 6 grooves; r/hand.

The Colt Commando (Colt Model RO933) is one of those weapons which do no fit neatly into any one particular category and is variously described as a assault rifle or carbine or submachine gun, but in this book it is being treated a an assault rifle. The weapon is, in fact, a shorter and handier version of the M1 and was originally intended for use in the Vietnam War as a close-quarte survival weapon. Mechanically, it is identical to the M16 but has a much shorte barrel, which reduces the muzzle velocity a little and makes it slightly les accurate at longer ranges. The short barrel also causes considerable muzzl flash which is overcome by a 4in (100mm) flash suppressor; this can b unscrewed, when required. The Colt Commando has a telescopic butt with four-position click-stop, enabling overall length to be adjusted between 26.8 30in (68-76.2cm).

The Commando features selective fire and a holding-open device, and actuated by the same direct gas action as the M16. In spite of the limitation on range, the weapon proved useful in Indochina and although it had bee designed as a survival weapon it fitted the submachine gun role so well that was later issued to the U.S. Special Operations Forces and has also been use in small numbers by the British SAS.

Soon after the weapon's introduction in the late 1980s, it was adopted b the Israelis and large numbers were imported by them as replacements for th M16 and Israeli Military Industries (IMI) Galil rifles used at the time. It is issue to almost all personnel in the civilian special forces units and is also used b most military special forces units, as well. In the late 1990s there was a mov to replace the Commando with the locally designed and produced IMI Magal,

*bove: The Colt Commando was originally developed for use in the
ietnam War as a close-quarter survival weapon.

46mm version of the Galil Micro Assault Rifle (MAR). Some 4,000 Magals
ere taken into service but suffered from such severe mechanical problems
at they were taken out of service again and the Commando reinstated. When
sed by Israeli Special Forces units, the Colt Commando is fitted with a Trijcon
ght and a tactical flashlight.

The Colt Commando is considered by Israeli users to be a reliable and
onvenient weapon especially when they have to deploy tactically from
ehicles. In addition, the short barrel is good for concealment during undercover
perations. Also, since special forces engagements, particularly in urban areas,
e almost always at short range, the Commando's limited maximum effective
nge of 330yd (300m) is of no importance.

*elow: The Commando is used in large numbers in Israel, by military
d paramilitary soldiers, and by civilian guards.*

Galil 5.56mm AR

Country of origin: United States.
Manufacturer: IMI, Israel.
Type: assault rifle.
Operation: gas-operated.
Caliber: 5.56 x 45mm NATO.
Weight: gun 9.6lb (4.4kg).
Dimensions: length gun 38.6in (979mm); barrel 18.1in (460mm).
Muzzle velocity: 3,116ft/sec (950m/sec)
Magazine: 35- or 50-round box.
Rate of fire: 700rpm.
Rifling: 6 grooves; r/hand.

Israel's Galil assault rifle, was first fielded, chambered for the 7.62mm NAT
round, in 1973. It had a rich, battle-tested heritage. The gas and rotating bo
system used was that of the Russian AK-47 Kalashnikov, while the firin
mechanism came from the U.S. M1 Garand, but credit for the weapon's over
design goes to an Israeli Army officer, Major Uziel Gal, who was als
responsible for the Uzi SMG. The weapon uses a rotating-bolt gas system an
with the exception of the stamped steel breech cover, is fully machined. Th
foregrip is wood, lined with Dural, and has ample clearance around the barr
for heat dissipation. When extended, the butt-stock has a positive latchin
system which prevents wobble by wedging the hinge end's tapered latchin
lugs into corresponding slots. The ambidextrous safety switch on the left sid
is a small lever, but its reciprocal right side member also acts as an ejection po
cover. There is a bipod, which folds and rotates into a slot in the underside
the foregrip. The Galil 7.62mm ARM was produced in three versions with on
minor differences between them: assault rifle/light machine gun; assault rifl
(basically the ARM, but minus the bipod); and the SAR (short assault rifle
which had a shorter barrel (15.8in/400mm) long.

Following the example of other countries, particularly the United States, th
IDF then moved to 5.56mm (.233 Remington) and a scaled-down version of th
Galil was produced (specifications above), which was some 4in (10cm) short
but only some 3oz (85g) lighter. Apart from size, the only noticeable differen
between the two weapons is that the 7.62mm weapon has a straight magazin
while in the 5.56mm the magazine is curved. Like the larger caliber weapon, th
5.56mm Galil has been produced in three versions: assault rifle/light machin
gun; assault rifle; and short assault rifle. There is also a sniper version of th
7.62mm rifle and a "micro" version of the 5.56mm version for special forces

Above: The Israeli soldier standing right carries the standard 5.56mm Galil; his comrade (center) carries an M16.

Below left: Assault rifle version of the 5.56mm Galil; note folded stock and curved magazine.

Below: Section machine gun version of the earlier 7.62mm Galil; note straight magazine and folded bipod.

IMI Galil Micro Automatic Rifle (MAR)

Country of origin: Israel.
Manufacturer: IMI, Israel.
Type: automatic rifle.
Operation: gas, rotating bolt, locking lugs.
Caliber: 5.56 x 45mm M855/SS109.
Weight: gun 6.6lb (2.98kg); gun with loaded magazine 8.2lb (3.7kg).
Dimensions: length gun 27.8in (707mm); length butt folded 16.0in (406mm); barrel 7.7in (195mm).
Muzzle velocity: 2,330ft/sec (710m/sec).
Magazine: 35-round box.
Rifling: 6 grooves; r/hand.

The latest version of the Galil family is the Galil 5.56 Micro Assault Rifle (MAR), usually known as the "Micro Galil'" which was designed particularly to meet the needs of Israeli Special Forces. The weapon is very short – shorter, in fact, than some SMGs – and on its early trials demonstrated all the known vices and virtues of the rest of the Galil family. On the plus side it is very small, making it highly suitable for covert operations, fires 5.56mm as opposed to 9mm ammunition, and it is both rugged and reliable, as is to be expected from an army with the combat experience of the IDF. But, on the negative side, its very short barrel means that it is not particularly accurate, and it gives its handlers the impression that it is heavy for its size. Also, as delivered, it does not have mounting rails for telescopic sights or night vision devices. Perhaps the most serious problem is that it has poor heat dissipation, resulting in overheating during either full automatic or more than two magazines of rapid single shots, particularly on the forward handguard. It was this, above all others, which led to the weapon being rejected (at least in its initial form) by some Israeli Special Forces units. However, a few examples were purchased for use as personal defense weapons by senior Army officers.

Above: The Israeli Galil MAR (Micro Automatic Rifle) with stock folded along the right-hand side of the receiver.

The MAR was then developed into the Magal which was purchased by the Israeli Police and is also on offer for export, although no known orders have been placed.

There has also been further development of the MAR. The new version has a new foreguard which solves the overheating problem and also provides a rail for mounting telescopic sights. A 100-round magazine is also available.

Below: Latest version has a new handguard, which is much better insulated from the barrel and thus does not overheat.

PSG-1 7.62mm

Country of origin: Germany.
Manufacturer: Heckler & Koch , Germany.
Type: sniper rifle.
Operation: semi-automatic.
Caliber: 7.62 x 52mm NATO.
Weight: gun 17.0lb (8.1kg).
Dimensions: length gun 47.5in (1,208mm); barrel 25.6in (650mm).
Muzzle velocity: 2,723ft/sec (830m/sec).
Magazine: 5- or 20-round box.
Rifling: 4 grooves; r/hand, polygonal.

Like many other modern sniper rifles, the *Präzisionsschutzengewehr-1* (PSG-
= precision marksman's rifle - 1) was developed in the early 1980s to meet th
renewed German military and police requirement for a long-range and ver
accurate weapon. The PSG-1 uses Heckler & Koch's roller-locked bolt syster
and fires in semi-automatic mode, single-shots only. Its design was based o
that of the G3 military assault rifle, but it is fitted with a polygonally bored
heavy, free-floating barrel. The trigger, fitted with an adjustable trigger shoe,
normally set to break at 3.3lb (1.5kg). A special, low-noise, bolt-closing devic
is fitted and the stock has an adjustable comb and butt-pad that allow fitting t
individual shooters. A bipod attaches directly to the stock. The PSG-1
normally fitted with the Hensoldt 6 x 42 scope with LED-enhanced manu
reticle. The scope-mounted activator produces a helpful red dot fc
approximately 30 seconds, plenty of time to get off a critical shot. Windage an
elevation adjustment are by moving base, with six settings from 110 to 655y
(100 to 600m) and there is a fine adjustment facility to compensate for ar
mounting offset angle.

Above: Trooper of Brazil's 10 Batalhao de Forces Especials with H&K .62mm PSG-12 semi-automatic sniper rifle.

This is the weapon-of-choice for snipers in several special forces and, articularly, for use in counter-terrorist and hostage-release operations.

Below: The PSG-1, based on the G-1 assault rifle, is a semi-automatic, ingle-shot weapon firing 7.61mm NATO rounds.

Dragunov 7.62mm SVD

Country of origin: Soviet Union (Russia).
Manufacturer: Russian State Armament Factories.
Type: sniper rifle.
Operation: semi-automatic.
Caliber: 7.62 x 54mm Russian.
Weight: gun 9.5lb (4.3kg).
Dimensions: length gun 48.2in (1,225mm); barrel 24.5in (622mm).
Muzzle velocity: 2,723ft/sec (830m/sec).
Magazine: 10-round box.
Rifling: 4 grooves; r/hand.

Development of the SVD began in 1963 and the weapon entered service with the (then) Soviet Army in 1967. It quickly became the standard sniper rifle for most Warsaw Pact armies, as well as those of allies, and it was built under licence in China, Iraq and Romania. The SVD was generally considered to be one of the best sniper rifles of its era and is still in service with special forces in various parts of the world. The SVD was normally issued on a scale of one to a motorized rifle platoon, and selected riflemen received regular, centralized sniper training. The SVD is long, but largely due to its open stock it is actually lighter than previous Russian sniper rifles.

Many Western sniper rifles retain a bolt mechanism, but the SVD is gas operated, using a system similar to that of the AKM assault rifle, but modified to take a short-stroke piston in order to avoid the shift of balance inherent in long-stroke systems, and which would upset a sniper's point-of-aim. The SVD has a combined flash suppressor/compensator and can mount the standard AKM bayonet. There is a cheek-pad atop the open butt-stock and it is fitted with a detachable, non-variable, 4x telescopic sight, with an extension tube to afford eye relief. Four magazines, a cleaning kit, and an extra battery and lamp for the telescopic sight are included with the weapon. It fires only in the semi-automatic mode.

Right: Hungarian paratrooper with a Russian Dragunov 7.62mm x 54 sniper rifle. The Dragunov is a well-respected, reliable and very accurate weapon, used by many armies.

Above: An Afghan tribesman showing off his Dragunov sniper rile, which is fitted with a telescopic sight.

L96A1 7.62mm

Country of origin: United Kingdom.
Manufacturer: Accuracy International, England.
Type: sniper rifle.
Operation: hand-operated bolt action.
Caliber: 7.62 x 51mm NATO.
Weight: gun 14.3lb (6.5kg).
Dimensions: length gun 47.0in (1,194mm); barrel 25.8in (655mm).
Muzzle velocity: 2,788ft/sec (850m/sec).
Magazine: 10-round box.
Rifling: 4 grooves; r/hand.

The 1960s and 1970s were the high period of the Cold War with a marked emphasis on highly mobile warfare, with the infantry mounted in armored personnel carriers. During this period sniper rifles went out of fashion. Starting in the early 1980s, however, there was a strong resurgence and many models are now available. One weapon designed from the start for sniping (as opposed to an adapted service rifle) was the Accuracy International Model PM, which was designed to meet challenging criteria. It had to have guaranteed first round accuracy; unchanging zero; a stock unaffected by environmental changes; bipod; stock and trigger adjustable to meet individual firer's requirements; telescopic sight; reliability; interoperability; and economy. The solution fixed upon by A.I. was to use a massive and very stiff integral chassis, which is impervious to environmental changes and is precisely reproducible. The barrel is made of stainless steel and has a normal accuracy life in excess of 5,000 rounds. It attaches to the action by a screw thread bedding against a locking ring, and can be changed in approximately five minutes without stripping the rifle. The sniper can carry out all but the most major repairs on his weapon himself, three Allen keys and a screwdriver being the only tools required. All accessories mate directly to the chassis, including the stock, butt, spacers, sling swivels, trigger unit, magazine and catch, handstop and bipod.

The weapon entered service with the British armed forces in 1985 as the L96A1, and also serves with a number of overseas armies, including the Swedish Army, which designates it the Psg-90. Accuracy International has recently started to market the .50in (12.7mm) AW, one of a growing number of large caliber sniping weapons now available.

Above: The Accuracy International L96A1 sniper rifle, fitted with a PM x42 telescopic sight and a bipod.

Above middle: A complete sniper kit in an attaché case. The suppressor is a "Thundertrap" gives 35dB noise reduction; ammunition is 0.308 Winchester.

Left: Sales of the AI L96A1 have steadily increased; it is now used by many armies and special forces.

M24 Sniper Weapon System

Country of origin: USA.
Manufacturer: Remington, USA.
Type: sniper rifle.
Operation: bolt action.
Caliber: 7.62 x 51mm NATO (.308 Winchester).
Weight: empty 8.7lb (4.0kg); with loaded magazine 12.1lb (5.5kg).
Dimensions: length 43in (1,090mm); barrel 24in (610mm).
Muzzle velocity: 2,800ft/sec (853m/sec).
Range: maximum effective 875yd (800m).
Magazine: 5/10-round, detachable internal magazine.
Rifling: 5 grooves; r/hand.

The M14 7.762mm semi-automatic rifle was introduced into U.S. Army service in the 1950s together with an associated sniper version, the M21, which was made more accurate and fitted with a Leatherwood telescopic sight, but otherwise little altered (and was still semi-automatic). Some 1,435 M14s were converted and fielded in time to see service in the Vietnam War, but by the mid-1980s these M21s were in a somewhat worn-out condition. In addition, as the prospect of a war in Western Europe receded, so did the possibility of campaigns in desert or barren countryside increase, where ranges, even for infantry work, would be much longer. As a result, the U.S. Army ran a competition for an up-to-date replacement sniper rifle, the operational requirement stating that the new weapon must have a maximum effective range of some 1,100yd (1,000m), a stainless steel barrel, and a Kevlar-graphite stock, and – a significant reversion – bolt-operated. The various competitors were whittled down to two – Steyr of Austria with their SSG rifle and Remington with the Model 700BDL – and, after final shoot-off, the latter was selected. This weapon was then standardized in 1987 as the Model 24 Sniper Weapons System (M24 SWS) chambered for the 7.62 x 51mm NATO (.308 Winchester) round. It has recently been upgraded to AT1-M24 Tactical Rifle standard, which is an all-round improvement to the original M24. All components in the sniper weapon are carefully machined to ensure smooth, reliable operation, even in the most severe operating conditions.

With the Leupold Ultra M3A 10x42 telescopic sight the M24 has a maximum

ffective range of some 875yd (800m), but also has detachable emergency
on sights. The M24 has a stainless steel barrel with 5-groove rifling,
naking one turn in 11.25in (286mm) in a right-rand twist; barrel life is
otimated at about 10,000 rounds. The stock is made of
evlar/graphite/fiberglass composite, with aluminum bedding-blocks, and
oth stock length and butt-plate are adjustable to suit the firer. The bipod is
:movable and a suppressor can be fitted, if required.

:elow: The second man holds an M24 Sniper Weapon System (SWS), a
olt-action rifle, using the Remington 700 action.

M40A3 7.62mm

Country of origin: USA.
Manufacturer: Marine Corps Marksmanship Training Unit, Quantico, Virginia.
Type: sniper rifle.
Operation: bolt-action; rotating bolt with two lugs.
Caliber: 7.62 x 51mm NATO (.308 Winchester).
Weight: weight, bare weapon 9lb (4.1kg); weight, including scope 14.5lb (6.6kg).
Dimensions: length overall 44in (1,117mm); length, barrel 24in (610mm).
Range: maximum effective 1,000yd (914m).
Muzzle velocity: 2,550ft (777m) per second.
Magazine: 5-round detachable box.

During the Vietnam War the Marine Corps decided to adopt a new sniper rif
and in April 1966 Remington suggested using a specially built version of its ve
successful Model 700, a highly successful weapon which traced its ancest
back to the British P14/U.S. M1917 rifle of World War I vintage. Designated th
Model 40XB by Remington, it was adopted by the Marines as the M40 an
some 995 were built by Remington for the Corps. They proved very successf
and in the mid-1970s the Marines decided to upgrade them, using the sam
Remington 700BDL action, but with different stocks and scopes. This modifie
weapon, the M40A1, entered service in the late-1970s. Each weapon

Above: This Marine Corps sniper is using his M40A1 aboard a helicopter, using a special mount.

individually built by trained and qualified armorers at the Marine Corps Marksmanship Training Unit, Quantico, Virginia, and must pass the most stringent tests before being released for service. Over the years the M40 has been undergone various modifications, the latest standard being M40A3.

The M40A3 fires the standard 7.62 x 51mm NATO round (0.308 Winchester) and is fitted with a commercially available, competition-grade, heavy barrel, a special fiberglass stock and butt pad, a modified Winchester floorplate and trigger guard, and a specially modified, light-pressure trigger. The weapon uses match-grade ammunition and is equipped with a special Unertl x10 sniper scope. With this scope, but without ammunition, it weighs approximately 14.5lb (6.6kg). It has a built-in five round mag-azine. The Remington Model 700 not only provides the basis of the Marines' M40A1, but is used in the Army's M24 Sniper Weapon System (qv), as well as being used as a sniper rifle by many police forces across the United states.

Left: Range practice for a U.S. Marine Corps sniper. His weapon is the M40A1, a Remington 700 rebuilt by Corps armorers at Quantico.

Royal Ordnance Arwen 37

Country of origin: United Kingdom.
Manufacturer: Royal Ordnance, England.
Type: anti-riot weapon.
Operation: gas-operated.
Caliber: 37mm.
Weight: weapon empty 6.8lb (3.1kg); weapon loaded 8.4lb (3.8kg).
Dimensions: length weapon 29.9-33.1in (750-840mm).
Magazine: 5 rounds, circular.
Rate of fire: 60rpm.

In the 1970s British soldiers were facing hostile crowds in Northern Ireland, and they were equipped with either rifles or the totally inadequate L67A1 38mm riot gun. The latter was an adaption of the Verey Pistol, which had been originally designed to launch illuminating flares, and had an extremely short defective range, which forced the firer to get extremely close to a crowd, and was single-round weapon which had to be broken to extract the used cartridge and replace it with a new one. In addition, the existing plastic round was unsatisfactory.

The resulting "Crowd Control System" appeared as a prototype in 1979 and after a lengthy development stage entered production in 1981. A number of versions have been developed including the Arwen 37 Multi-S, very close-range weapon which has no stock and a shorter 6.5in (165mm) barrel, while the Arwen 37 Multi-V is designed for use in a ball-mounting in a vehicle. An even lighter version is the Arwen Ace, a single-shot version, which weighs only 5.1lb (2.3kg).

The Arwen 37 and Arwen Ace are obviously very specialized weapons, for use in very specific tactical situations. There is a wide variety of rounds including kinetic energy, irritant smoke, frangible-nose, smoke screen, and unspecified "special rounds." A number of special forces include these weapons in their armories.

Above: The 5-shot Arwen 37 is a short-range weapon intended for close-range use against rioters or hostage takers.

Left: The Arwen ACE is one of a series of weapons firing specially-developed 37mm baton and smoke anti-riot rounds.

Ithaca 37

Country of origin: United States.
Manufacturer: Ithaca Gun Company, Ithaca, New York.
Type: shotgun.
Operation: manual pump-action.
Caliber: 12-gauge.
Weight: gun empty 7.0lb (3.1kg).
Dimensions: length gun 20.0in (508mm).
Magazine: 8-round tubular magazine

The Ithaca "Featherlight" Model 37 pump-action repeater is a weapon designe
to be free of stamped steel components, even to the trigger group. The solid stee
receiver does not have the usual ejection port on the right, because it ejects shell
straight out of the bottom. Its unique action is centered around a dual-duty she
carrier that lifts live shells up to feed straight into the chamber.

The type of barrel in Ithaca's "Deerslayer" model has been fitted to
combat shotgun to provide a weapon capable of firing rifle slugs with optimur

*Right: The Ithaca Model 37 Stakeout,
which is a standard Model 37 with the
stock removed, pistol grip added, and
shorter barrel. The magazine is also
shorter; as a result the weapon carries five
instead of eight rounds – four in the
magazine, and one in the chamber.*

ccuracy as well as being capable of firing the usual loadings. A number of short-barreled cylinder-bored configurations are in use with U.S. conventional military forces, Special Operations Forces and police forces. The Model 37 "Stakeout" is a standard model, but with the butt removed, pistol-grip added, and the barrel and magazine shortened, restricting capacity to five rounds (one chambered, four in the magazine). This version has an overall length of 18.8in (47.0cm) and weighs 6.5in (2.9kg).

Above: The Ithaca Model 37 pump-action shotgun is light and accurate, and is used by several special forces.

Mossberg 500 ATP

Country of origin: United States.
Manufacturer: Mossberg, USA.
Type: shotgun.
Operation: manual pump-action.
Caliber: 12-gauge.
Weight: gun empty 6.7lb (3.1kg)
Dimensions: length gun 40.3in (1,000mm); barrel 20.3in (470mm).
Magazine: 8-round tubular magazine.

Shotguns are of particular use to special forces, since they can be stowed easily inside vehicles and brought into action quickly, when their devastating effect is described as "reloadable Claymores." There are two main types of Mossberg in use with U.S. forces, one with a six-shot and the other with an eight-shot magazine, the latter being the more generally used. It is designed for maximum reliability and has an aluminum receiver for good balance and light weight.

The cylinder-bored barrel is proof-tested to full Magnum loads, provides optimum dispersion patterns and permits firing of a variety of ammunition. The shotgun has two extractors and the slide mechanism has twin guide bars which help prevent twisting or jamming during rapid operation. A late modification has been the creation of a muzzle brake by cutting slots in the upper surface, thus allowing gas to escape upwards and exerting downward force which prevents the muzzle from lifting during firing. The ATP-8 version has no butt-stock, and a pistol grip is added, resulting in an extremely compact weapon.

Right: The pump action shotgun has a devastating effect when used in close quarter engagements.

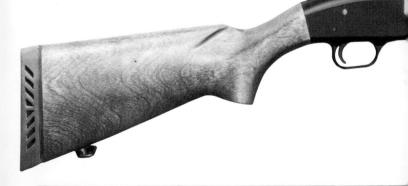

Above: The Mossberg 500 ATP8 is widely regarded as one of the most reliable pump-action shotguns of its generation.

Remington 870 Wingmaster

Country of origin: United States.
Manufacturer: Remington Arms Co., Bridgeport, Conn., USA.
Type: shotgun.
Operation: manual pump-action.
Caliber: 12-, 20-, 28- or 40-gauge (see text).
Weight: gun 7.5lb (3.4kg).
Dimensions: length gun 45.5in (1,156mm); barrel 25.0in (635mm) (see text).
Magazine: 5- or 8-round, tubular.

The Remington 870 was introduced in 1950, since when over four million have been produced in a wide variety of models, with barrel lengths varying from 18in (457mm) in the Police Model to 30in (762mm) for 3in (76mm) Magnum cartridges, and in four gauges: 12-, 20-, 28-, and 40-gauge. Normal magazine capacity is five rounds, but an extension giving eight-round capacity is also available. It has a strong and positive action, with double action bars, and all except the Police and Special-Purpose models are fitted with walnut stocks and fore ends. One shortcoming in earlier models occurred when cartridges not pushed fully into the magazine might slip and cause a stoppage, but this was rectified in later versions. Other later modifications included fitting the "Rem" internally threaded choke system, and recoil pads on the 12- and 20-gauge models.

This weapon is used by a number of Special Forces around the world, and is the shotgun of choice among Israeli special forces units.

Above: U.S. soldiers firing Remington 870s fitted with launchers for tear-gas grenades; range is about 80yd (73m).

Below: The Remington 870 is widely used by special forces, particularly in Israel, where it has proved invaluable.

Barrett 0.50in Model 82A1

Country of origin: USA.
Manufacturer: Barrett Firearms Mfg. Co., USA.
Type: anti-materiel/sniper rifle.
Operation: recoil-operated.
Caliber: 0.50in Browning (12.7 x 99mm).
Weight: gun 44lb (13.4kg).
Dimensions: length gun 61.0in (1,550mm); barrel 29.0in (737mm).
Muzzle velocity: 2,798(ft/sec (853m/sec).
Magazine: 11-round box.
Rifling: 8 grooves; r/hand.

Introduced in 1983, the Barrett "Light Fifty" fires the 12.7 x 99mm (0.50in Browning) round and was intended for use as a high-power, long-range sniper weapon. The "Light Fifty" operates on the short-recoil principle, with a substantial amount of energy being imparted by the cartridge to the bolt-face whereupon both barrel and bolt-carrier start to travel to the rear. Once the bolt-carrier disengages from the barrel, the latter is moved forward again by a spring, while the bolt-carrier extracts and ejects the spent cartridge case and then loads a new round. The M82A1 has both iron sights and a x10 optical sight. It is normally fired from the built-in bipod, but can also use the standard U.S. Army M60 tripod. Maximum effective range is 1,800m (1,970yd). In the early 1990s the Provisional IRA (PIRA) forces in Northern Ireland included a sniping team armed with one of these awesome rifles; at least one was captured by the British security forces.

The next version, the M82A2, which was introduced in 1992, involved some major redesign, although the basic mechanism remained unchanged, but the major components were moved around to change it into a bullpup configuration. This involved placing the shoulder rest beneath the butt immediately behind the magazine housing, allowing the rear end of the receiver to pass over the firer's shoulder in a manner similar to a recoilless rocket launcher. The pistol grip/trigger group was moved forward of the magazine housing, while a reversed pistol grip served as the forward handgrip. There was

Above: Sniper team with a Barrett "Light Fifty" which is not only very accurate but also has a devastating effect.

no built-in bipod, as in the M82A1 and the weapon could be fired without one. The overall result is a slightly smaller, lighter and simpler version of the M82A1: length, 55.5in (1,410mm); weight 29lb (12,2kg).

These weapons can be and are used against people, with devastating effect. However, their primary use is against materiel targets, such as vehicles, radar dishes, aircraft, and armored vehicles. They can also be used to detonate unexploded ordnance or sea mines from a safe distance. Barretts are known to be used by the U.S. Marine Corps and some Israeli Special Forces, and are doubtless included in the armories of other special forces.

Below: The length of the magazine indicates the size of the 12.7mm rounds fired by the Barrett Model 82A1.

Model 96 Falcon 12.7mm

Country of origin: Czech Republic.
Manufacturer: Zbrojovka Vsetin, Vsetin, Czech Republic.
Type: anti-materiel rifle.
Operation: bolt action.
Caliber: 12.7 x 108mm DshK.
Weight: gun, loaded 32.9lb (14.9kg).
Dimensions: length gun 54.3in (1,380mm); barrel 36.5in (927mm).
Muzzle velocity: 2,790ft/sec (850m/sec).
Magazine: 5-round box or manual.
Rifling: 8 grooves; r/hand.

The Model 96 Falcon is one of a gradually increasing number of heavy rifles firing 12.7mm rounds, a caliber which has previously been the province of the heavy machine gun. The Model 96 was originally designated the OPV 12.7mm and was fitted with a 140.4in (1,027mm) barrel, which was capable of firing either the 12.7 x 99mm (0.50in Browning) or the 12.7 x 108mm Russian DshK rounds. This presumably proved too ambitious, since the production weapons have two barrels: one is 36.5in (927mm) long for the 12.7 x 108mm round, the other 33.0in (838mm) long for the 12.7 x 99mm round. The weapon is manually operated, using bolt action, with the prominent bolt lever projecting from the right-hand side of the weapon. The considerable recoil from the 12.7mm round

is attenuated in part by a large, four-baffle muzzlebrake, the remainder by a buffer spring in the tubular, detachable butt. The barrel screws on to the receiver and is locked in position by a spring-actuated lever. There is a detachable five-round box magazine, but if the firer wishes to use manual feeding, he can insert a cover over the magazine well. Maximum effective range is claimed to be 2,000m (2,187yd) with the optical sight and 1,000m (1,094yd) at night. There is a carrying handle for moving the weapon into position, and the barrel and butt can be removed for transportation over longer distances. A 10 x 40 scope is supplied with the weapon, with a sight reticle which can be illuminated by internal batteries. Iron sights are also fitted.

Below: The Model 96 is a bolt-operated weapon and can be used to attack light armored vehicles.

Technika M2 Gepard 12.7mm

Country of origin: Hungary.
Manufacturer: Technika, Budapest, Hungary.
Type: anti-materiel rifle.
Operation: long-recoil, semi-automatic.
Caliber: 12.7 x 108mm DShK
Weight: gun loaded 26.5lb (12.0kg).
Dimensions: length gun 60.2in (1,530mm); barrel 43.4in (1,100mm).
Muzzle velocity: 2,756ft/sec (840m/sec).
Magazine: 5- or 10-round box.

The Hungarian firm, Technika, produced a series of heavy rifles in the 1980s
and 1990s, all with the type name Gepard. The first in the series, the
Gepard M1, was a bolt-action, single-shot weapon firing the Russian 12.7 x
108mm DshK round and was described as a sniper rifle, it being claimed
that any adequately trained shot could achieve a 12in (300mm) group at
660yd (600m) range. Firing an AP-T (armor-piercing - tracer) round, the
weapon could penetrate 15mm of homogenous armor at a range of 660yd
(600m), enabling it to pass through most cover in rural or urban
environments. The pistol grip doubles as the bolt handle. To reload, it is
rotated in an anti-clockwise direction and then pulled to the rear, ejecting
the spent cartridge; a new cartridge is then inserted, the bolt closed, the
hammer cocked (this requires a separate action), and the weapon aimed
and fired.

The Gepard M1A1 is essentially the same, but includes a frame, which car

be used either to carry the weapon or as a firing rest. The Gepard M2 was developed from the M1 and is intended for the anti-materiel role, but has an entirely different, semi-automatic action, using a positive locking, long-recoil system, which is fed from either a five- or ten-round box magazine. The M2 has a cylindrical receiver and a cylindrical cradle which extends almost to the muzzle, together with a built-in bipod and a short butt. The M2A1 is a shortened version intended for use by airborne troops, the barrel being only 32.7in (830mm) long.

The makers have said that both the M1/M1A1 and M2/M2A1 could easily be converted to take the 0.50in Browning (12.7 x 99mm) round, but, so far as is known, this has never been implemented. A Gepard M3, round has been developed which is chambered for the 14.5 x 114mm Russian round; this is similar in design to the Gepard M2, but, scarcely surprising in view of the forces involved, has a hydraulic recoil buffer.

Below left: The M1A1 Gepard uses a positive-action, long-recoil semi-automatic system.

Bottom: Like the M1, the M2 Gepard fired the Russian 12.7x 108mm round, but is more compact and lighter.

PGM 0.5in (12.7mm) Hecate

Country of origin: France.
Manufacturer: PGM, La Chambre, France.
Type: anti-materiel/sniper rifle.
Operation: bolt action.
Caliber: .50in Browning.
Weight: 30.4lb (13.8kg).
Dimensions: length gun 54.3in (1,380mm); barrel 27.6in (700mm).
Muzzle velocity: 2,788ft/s (830m/s).
Magazine: 7 round box.
Rifling: 8 grooves; r/hand.

PGM produces two sniper rifles: the Commando, chambered for 7.62 x 51mm NATO caliber, and the Hecate for 0.50in Browning. It is intended for interdiction shooting; long-range demolition, particularly of unexploded ordnance and sea mines; and for long-range counter-sniping. Maximum effective range depending upon the firer, is of the order of 1,650yd (1,500m). The Hecate is based on a high-grade aluminum-alloy chassis, with a steel receiver, to which are attached the barrel and stock. It has a fluted barrel, which both reduces weight and enhances cooling, and which has a large and very efficient muzzle brake, which considerably reduces the recoil into the firer's shoulder. There is a built-in bipod and a further leg (monopod) on the butt to help maintain the rifle in position during a long wait. For carrying, the stock can be removed and there is a handle at the point of balance of the remaining mass. The weapon will fire any type of .50in Browning ammunition, including armor-piercing, incendiary

Below: 7.62mm PGM Commando sniper rifle is an effective weapon, with folding stock and interchangeable barrels.

Above: The PGM also comes in a 0.5in version, designated the Hecate; note the unusual flash eliminator.

nd tracer, but the greatest accuracy is achieved with hand-loaded ball. Maximum effective range is a little over 1,640yd (1,500m). The Hecate was one f two finalists in the British Army's Long-Range-Large Caliber competition, and as narrowly beaten by the Accuracy International 338 Super Magnum.

M60E3 7.62mm

Country of origin: United States.
Manufacturer: various.
Type: general-purpose machine gun.
Operation: gas.
Caliber: 7.62 x 51mm NATO.
Weight: 18.9lb (8.6kg).
Dimensions: length 42.4in (1,080mm); barrel 25.5in (650mm).
Muzzle velocity: 2,800ft/sec (853m/sec).
Feed: metal-link belt.
Rates of fire: cyclic 550-600 rounds per minute; rapid 100 rounds per minute, sustained 100 rounds per minute (barrel changes required approximately every 100 rounds).
Rifling: 4 grooves; r/hand.

The U.S. Army based the design of its first post-war general-purpose machine gun (GPMG) on the best features of the German MG42 and its assault rifle version, the FG42. The resulting M60 entered service in 1950 and relies largely on metal stampings, rubber, and plastics. In a major innovation, it used the then newly agreed NATO standard 7.62 x 51mm round. It is gas-operated with fixed headspace and timing which permits rapid changing of barrels, which must be done regularly to prevent overheating. There is a built-in folding bipod, fitted with cooling fins, and the weapon can also be mounted on a tripod for use in the sustained fire role.

The latest version is the M60E3, which is lighter than the original M60 and has a number of differences from the original, virtually all of them intended to save weight, although there is also a simplified gas system, which does not require safety-wire to prevent loosening. But the new lightweight barrel is not safe for use in overhead fire and is not capable of sustaining a rapid rate of fire of 200 rounds per minute without catastrophic failure. Although the main purpose in the M60E3 is to assist the gunner by reducing the load he has to carry, the outcome is a weapon with some firing limitations and a loss of reliability that severely limits its use. This gun will be replaced by the M240G.

There are three main rounds for combat use – M61 Armor-piercing, M62 Tracer and M80 Ball – with the preferred combat mix being four M80s followed by one M62, which enables the gunner to observe the fall-of-shot and quickly bring his ▶

Right: U.S. paratrooper with the greatly improved M60E3, which overcame many shortcomings of the earlier versions.

► fire onto the target. M61 rounds are used against lightly armored targets and M80 against lighter targets and personnel. As usual there are also rounds for training on the weapon (M63 Dummy) and for field exercises (M82 Blank), which can only be used if a blank-firing attachment is installed over the muzzle. Maximum range is of the order of 4,000yd (3,658m)

although maximum effective range is somewhat less. The M60 continues to be used on helicopters including the UH-1, H-2, H-3, CH-47 and UH-60.

Below: Machine gun team with M60. Note the belt of cartridges below the firer's right hand.

Above: This M60 is fitted with a blank-firing attachment, necessary to enable the gun to fire on automatic in exercises.

M240G

Country of origin: Belgium.
Manufacturer: FN Mfg. Inc., Columbia, SC, USA.
Type: light machine gun.
Operation: gas-operated.
Caliber: 7.62 x 51mm NATO.
Weight: 24.2lb (11kg)
Dimensions: length overall 48.0in (1,220mm); barrel 24.,7in (630mm).
Muzzle velocity: 2,800ft/sec (854m/sec).
Feed: metal-link belt.
Rates of fire: cyclic 650-950 rounds per minute; rapid 200 rounds per minute;
sustained 100 rounds per minute.
Rifling: 4 grooves; r/hand.

The M240 was originally a ground-operated machine gun, developed b
Belgian arms company Fabrique Nationale (FN) and known by them as th
MAG (*Mitrailleuse d'Appui Générale* = general-purpose machine gun).
was then selected in 1976 by the U.S. Army for use in armored vehicles an
was produced under licence as the M240. It is now widely used by the U.S
armed forces in its M240, M240C and M240E1 versions as the coaxia
remotely operated MG in a turret and as a pintle-mounted MG with spad
grips. In these forms it is used in numerous vehicles, including the M
Abrams tank, M2/M3 Bradley Infantry/Cavalry Fighting Vehicles and Marin

*Right: Armored vehicle commander
with his pintle-mounted 7.62mm M240
machinegun. Note flash suppressor on
muzzle and ammunition box attached
to the left of the weapon.*

Corps LAVs (light armored vehicles).

The M240 was designed around the NATO standard 7.62 x 51mm cartridge. It is also used as the M240D in helicopters. After extensive operational and technical tests, it was subsequently selected in 1995 as the ground replacement for the M60; this required a bipod to be fitted and a tripod to be developed. In this form it was selected as a replacement for the M60, first by the Marine Corps and subsequently by the Army. The M240 has many similarities to the M60, but has far superior reliability and maintainability. The major changes for the ground role are the addition of a flash suppressor, front sight, carrying handle for the barrel, buttstock, infantry length pistol grip, bipod, and rear sight assembly. Maximum range is some 4,100yd (3,700m), but maximum effective using a tripod is 1,940yd (1,800m).

The M240D 7.62mm machine gun is the aircraft version, which is normally mounted on a pintle in the aircraft but can also be dismounted for ground use in an emergency. As configured for aircraft use, the gun is fitted with front and rear sights and spade grip and rear face trigger. In this form it weighs 25.6 lb. and is 42.3 inches long. When dismounted a buttstock assembly, buffer assembly, bipod, and a conventional trigger are fitted and it weighs 26.2lb (11.9kg) and is 49.0 inches long (1,245mm). In both versions the barrel assembly includes a three-position gas plug, with positions for firing at 750, 850 or 950 rounds-per-minute.

PK 7.62mm

Country of origin: Russia.
Manufacturer: Russian State factories.
Type: general-purpose machine gun.
Operation: gas.
Caliber: 7.62 x 54mm Russian.
Weight: gun on bipod 19.8lb (9.0kg); gun on tripod 36.3lb (16.5kg).
Dimensions: length 45.7in (1,173mm); barrel 25.9in (658mm).
Muzzle velocity: 2,930ft/sec (894m/sec).
Rate of fire: 500-550 rounds per minute
Rifling: 8 grooves; r/hand.

The Russian PK was introduced into service in 1960 and is a fully automatic gas-operated, general-purpose machine gun (GPMG) which was designed by taking the best elements of other Soviet weapons, including the Kalashnikov rotating bolt, Goryunov cartridge extractor and barrel-change, and Degtyarev feed system and trigger. There are four known variants in the basic PK series: PK – standard machine gun with bipod; PKB – machine gun without stock and with revised trigger for use in a pintle-mounting (eg, on the roof of a vehicle); PKS – machine gun on light tripod for sustained fire or AA; PKT – vehicle version, without sights or stock and with trigger group replaced by an electrical solenoid for remote control. Maximum effective range with tripod is 2,200yd (2,000m), while maximum range is some 7,500yd (6,800m).

The PKM is a later, lighter version of the PK with a bipod and hinged butt rest, and with weight reduced to 18.5lb (8.4kg). The PKMS is a PKM on a tripod, while another version, the PKB, does not have a stock.

The PK-series of weapons are very easy to handle, have little recoil, and do not tend to climb when fired on automatic. They are also lighter, more reliable and easier to maintain than the U.S. M60, although their maximum range is marginally less. They are likely to be found in any Russian or former Warsaw Pact Army or special forces unit, as well as in numerous foreign armies.

Above: A widely-used Russian machine gun, the RPK was a development of the 7.62mm AK-47 assault rifle.

Below: A PKMS 7.62mm GPMG mounted on its tripod. It is a highly regarded weapon; note the hollow stock.

Squad Automatic Weapon (SAW), M249

Country of origin: Belgium.
Manufacturer: FN Mfg. Inc., Columbia, SC, USA.
Type: bipod-mounted combat machine gun.
Operation: gas.
Caliber: 5.56 x 45mm NATO.
Weight: with bipod and tools 15.2lb (6.9kg); 200-round box magazine 6.9lb (3.2kg); 30-round magazine 1.1lb (0.5kg).
Dimensions: length overall 40.9in (1040mm); barrel 20.6in (523mm).
Muzzle velocity: 3,000ft/sec (915m/sec).
Feed: metal-link belt or 30-round box.
Rates of fire: cyclic 725 rounds per minute; sustained 85 rounds per minute.
Rifling: 6 grooves; r/hand.

The M249 Squad Automatic Weapon (SAW) is used to engage dismounted infantry, crew-served weapons, antitank guided-missile teams and thin-skinned vehicles. Fielded in the mid-1980s, the SAW filled the void created by the retirement of th

Above: Standard FN Minimi with ammunition.

Left:The SPW is a special forces version of M249. It has a new barrel, pistol grip, detachable bipod, new folding stock and rails for scopes, while the carrying handle and magazine well have been deleted. SPW is 4lb (1.9kg) lighter than the standard M249.

▶ Browning Automatic Rifle (BAR) during the 1950s, because interim automatic weapons (M14 Series/M16A1 Rifles) had failed as viable "base of fire" weapons. The weapon was developed from the Belgian Fabrique Nationale (FN) Minimi specifically to meet the requirements of the U.S. Army and Marine Corps. Original orders were met from the FN factory but a production line was subsequently established in the USA.

The U.S. Army's concept for a Squad Automatic Weapon was formulated in the 1960s as a weapon under the squad commander's control, which would have greater range than the M16 Armalite but would be lighter and easier to handle than the 7.62mm M60 LMG. The weapon selected to meet this requirement was the FN Minimi but with certain minor changes to meet U.S. military specifications and to suit U.S. manufacturing processes, the main external differences being in the shape of the butt and the handguard. The M249 is very smooth in operation and displays an exceptional degree of reliability. Fully combat ready, with a magazine of 200 rounds, bipod, sling and cleaning kit, the M249 weighs 22lb (9.97kg), which is still 1lb (0.4kg) less than an empty M60! It is normally fired using the built-in bipod, but a tripod is also available.

The M249 SAW is a lightweight, gas-operated, magazine or disintegrating metallic link-belt-fed, individually portable machine gun capable of delivering a large volume of effective fire. The gunner will normally fire at 750 rounds per minute, but this can be increased to 1,000 rpm on the squad leader's authority if circumstances require it; for example, if the rate-of-fire has been slowed due to adverse conditions. The M249 provides accurate fire approaching that of the rifle yet gives the heavy volume of fire common to a machine gun. The M249 replaces the two automatic M16A1 rifles in the rifle squad on a one-for-one basis in all infantry type units and in other units requiring high firepower.

There are six types of a ammunition available for the M249 SAW, of which two are combat rounds: M855 Ball (light materiel targets, personnel); M856 Tracer

Above: Standard FN Minimi with 200-round box magazine fitted and long barrel.

Below: Short barrel model with cranked carrying handle and other minor changes.

(observation of fire, incendiary effects, signaling). The usual combination of these is four M855 followed by a single M856, which enables the gunner to use the tracer-on-target (TOT) method of adjusting fire to achieve target kill. Other rounds are used for training: M193 Ball and M196 Tracer are for range work; M199 (inert round for weapon training); and M200 Blank (which can only be used if a blank-firing attachment is fitted to the weapon). The live rounds can be fed to the gun in two ways, the most usual being by a 200-round disintegrating belt, but it can also fire ammunition from a standard M16 magazine, which is inserted into a well in the bottom of the gun. When employed in the sustained fire role, the M249 is mounted on a tripod, to increase its stability, to make minute adjustments in the aim, and to enable it to fire bursts of more than three rounds without wandering off the target. The FN company also markets a "Para" model with a sliding stock and shorter barrel; it is a little lighter than the standard weapon but is shorter and easier to handle in confined spaces. This is the basis for the U.S. Army's Short Squad Automatic Weapon (SSAW), currently under development, in which the SAW is shortened by more than 10in (250mm) This developmental effort is intended to produce a weapon that is easier to maneuver when fighting in the urban environment and also to give improved Airborne/Air Assault jump ability. Maximum effective range against an area target is some 1,100yd (1,000m), but maximum range is of the order of 3,940yd (3,600m).

IMI 5.56mm Negev

Country of origin: Israel.
Manufacturer: IMI, Israel.
Type: general-purpose machine gun
Operation: gas.
Caliber: 5.56 x 45mm M193 or NATO.
Weight: gun 16.5lb (77.5kg).
Dimensions: length butt extended 40.2in (1,020mm); length butt folded 30.7in (780mm); barrel 18.1in (460mm).
Muzzle velocity: 3,280ft/sec (1,000m/sec).
Feed: 30- or 35-round box magazine, or belt.
Rate of fire: 850/950rpm.
Rifling: 6 grooves; r/hand.

The Israeli Army used the Galil (qv) family of small arms from the 1960s onwards, in which the light machine gun version (ARM) differed only minimally from the assault rifle. The Negev, however, which was announced in 1990, was designed from the start as a multi-purpose light machine gun and is not an adaptation of an assault rifle; somewhat perversely, however, and as described below, it can be adapted to serve as an assault rifle. The Negev is gas-operated, fires from an open bolt, and employs a rotating bolt that locks into a barrel extension. It is normally fed by magazines, but has an adapter that enables it to fire 200-round belts. A bipod with finned legs is fitted as standard. The Assault

Negev is an assault rifle version, which has the same internal mechanism, but has a shorter barrel; it has a forward handgrip, but there is no bipod. This reduces overall length with butt folded to 25.6in (650mm) while the total weight is reduced to 15.4lb (7.0kg). This enables the weapon to be used as an assault rifle, albeit a somewhat heavy one. All weapons in the Negev series can be used to launch grenades and all have a three-position gas regulator, which can be adjusted to launch grenades or to fire at either 850 or 950rpm. Maximum range is 7,437yd (6,800m), but maximum effective, firing from a tripod, is 2,200yd (2,000m).

Below: The IMI Negev light machine gun is fitted with a three-position gas regulator, for 850/950rpm or grenade launching.

M2HB 0.5in (12.7mm)

Country of origin: United States.
Manufacturer: Saco Defense (earlier versions by numerous contractors).
Type: heavy machine gun.
Operation: recoil.
Caliber: 0.50in (12.7mm) Browning.
Weight: gun 84lb (38kg); M3 tripod 44lb (19.9kg); total 128lb (58kg).
Dimensions: length overall 61.4in (1,560mm); barrel 45.0in (1,143mm).
Muzzle velocity: 2,930ft/sec (894m/sec).
Feed: 110-round, metal-link belt.
Rate of fire: 500-550 rounds per minute.
Rifling: 8 grooves; r/hand.

The M2 is employed by many armies to provide automatic suppressive fire in both offense and defense, and is used against personnel; soft-skinned and lightly-armored vehicles; low, slow flying aircraft, particularly helicopters; and small boats. It is a particular favorite of forces such as the U.S. SFOD-Delta and the British SAS for its capabilities as a vehicle-mounted weapon. John Browning's automatic, belt-fed, recoil-operated, air-cooled, crew-operated M2 machine gun first appeared in 1933. It was intended principally for use on multiple anti-aircraft mounts, but there was a second version for use as a tank turret gun and a third for use on a ground mount. The latter is crew transportable, although with a weapon weight of 84lb (38kg) and a further 44lb (19.9kg) for the tripod, this can only be for short distances.

The M2 has spade grips and a leaf-type rear sight. Ammunition is fed into the weapon by a disintegrating metallic link-belt, and by minor adjustments to the gun this can be fed from left or right. The weapon works on the usual Browning system of short recoil. When the cartridge is fired the barrel and breechblock, securely locked together, recoil for just under an inch, at which point the barrel is stopped by means of an oil buffer. At this stage the pressure has dropped sufficiently for the breechblock to unlock and continue to the rear under the initial impetus given to it by the barrel, extracting and ejecting the empty case and extracting the next live round from the belt. Once the rearward action has stopped the compressed return spring takes over to drive the working parts sharply forward, chambering the round, locking the breechblock,

Above: A single 0.5in M2HB mounted on a British Land Rover turns a simple field car into a lethal weapons system.

and firing the cartridge, after which the cycle recommences and continues for as long as the trigger is pressed and there are rounds in the belt. Most guns will fire automatic only, but those intended for ground use are equipped with bolt latches to enable single rounds to be fired if necessary.

When it first appeared the weapon functioned well enough mechanically, but showed an unfortunate tendency to overheat, so that after firing some 70-80 rounds in a continuous burst the firer had to make a considerable pause to allow the barrel to cool. Operationally, this was totally unacceptable, so a new heavy barrel version, the M2HB, was adopted, as a result of which the problem was completely solved. The M2HB was used by the United States and many other countries in the course of World War II and has continued in wide-scale use up to the present time.

In U.S. service, the gun is used either on the M3 tripod mount for ground use, on the M63 anti-aircraft mount for air defense, or various types of ship- ▶

Below: M2HB in its ground role mounted on a sturdy tripod enables very accurate fire to be laid down.

► board mounting for naval use. There are also a fixed mount and a soft mount for use in a wide variety of vehicles.

The M2HB uses a wide variety of ammunition and new types continue to be developed. One of the most recent is the M903 SLAP which was developed by the U.S. Marines in the 1980s and happened to be ready for use in the Gulf War in 1991. This is, in effect, a miniature version of the armor-piercing, discarding sabot (APDS) round used by in tank guns. This uses a 0.30in (7.6mm) penetrator made of tungsten as the penetrator, which is held in place in the barrel by a 0.50in (12.7mm) sabot, which disintegrates as it leaves the muzzle.

The result is a round that requires no modification to the weapon, provided the barrel has a stellite lining. The round is very fast, with a muzzle velocity of 3,98ft/sec (1,215m/sec) compared to 2,930ft/sec (894m/sec) for a normal round, and has a significantly flatter trajectory, resulting in increased accuracy. There is also a M962 SLAP-T (tracer) round to take advantage of this capability. The SLAP round is capable of penetrating two-to-three times the thickness of armor compared to other 0.5in (12.7mm) rounds. The maximum effective range for a tripod-mounted M2HB using normal ammunition is 2,200yd (2,000m); which reduces to 1,640yd (1,500m) for the SLAP round against 0.75in (20mm) "High Hard Armor" (HHA).

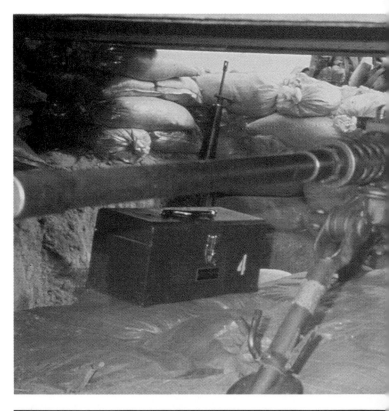

Above: A new version of the M2HB from Fabrique National with a quick-change barrel and other minor improvements.

Below: A U.S. Army M2HB machine gun post in the Arabian desert during Operation Desert Storm in 1991.

Grenades

Grenades are of great value to special forces, since they give the individual soldier a form of local artillery which ranges in effects from high-explosive, through fragmentation, stun and smoke, to illuminating and signaling. They are easily carried and are used by both terrorists and anti-terrorist forces. The distance which an average trained soldier can throw a grenade varies widely: in peacetime conditions and in the open, a distance of about 44-50yd (40-46m) can probably be achieved by most, but in operational conditions, where the soldier may be encumbered by other weapons and his equipment and may also be under hostile fire the distance is probably somewhat less. The range can be greatly extended by rifle-mounted launchers or by automatic grenade launchers, both of which fire specially designed grenades out to ranges far beyond a man's throwing capabilities.

Fragmentation Grenades

A typical modern version of the "traditional" offensive hand-grenade is the M67 Fragmentation Hand Grenade used by the U.S. Army, Marine Corps and Special Operations Forces. The basic components are a steel sphere, painted olive drab and with a yellow band, a handle, safety-pin, fuze, detonator and explosive, with a total weight of 14oz (400g). The body of the grenade is spherical in shape, 2.5in (6.4cm) in diameter and is constructed of steel; it is designed to fragment into hundreds of small pellets when the 6.5oz (184g) of Composition B explosive is detonated. The grenade can be thrown about 44yd (40m) by an average, trained soldier and the steel pellets produce casualties over an effective range of some 50ft (15m) although men may be wounded at considerably greater distances. It is, therefore, essential that the thrower should take cover immediately prior to the explosion.

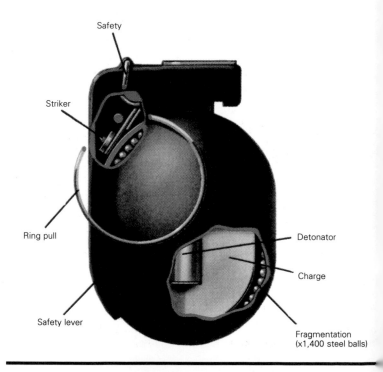

Safety

Striker

Ring pull

Safety lever

Detonator

Charge

Fragmentation
(x1,400 steel balls)

Above: Simulated exercise by elite force members preparing to assault with a Haley & Weller stun grenade. The noise and flash temporarily stun opponents such as hostage takers.

Left: The MISAR MU-50G controlled-effect grenade is either thrown by hand or launched from the Franchi Spas 12 shotgun.

M203 40mm Grenade Launcher

Country of origin: United States.
Manufacturer: Colt.
Weight: launcher, empty 3.0lb (1.4kg).
Bore diameter: 40mm (1.6in) .
Dimensions: length overall 15in (381mm); barrel 12in (310mm).

The M203 was developed by the AAI Corporation to meet a U.S. Army requirement for a lightweight, single-shot, breech-loading, pump-action, shoulder-fired grenade-launcher. The result was a very handy weapon which can be attached to lugs underneath the barrel of any version of the M16 rifle, with its own trigger and sighting system. The M203 can fire a wide variety of 40mm low-velocity grenades, including: high explosive; high-explosive air-burst; buckshot; anti-armor; smoke, illuminating; and riot control. The sighting system has two elements: the primary sight consists of an aperture and post system, while the secondary system is a folding, graduated lead sight, which is mounted on the forestock and uses the rifle's own foresight blade as a front aiming reference. The launcher weighs 3lb (1.4kg) had has a maximum effective range of 382yd (350m) against an area target and 164yd (150m) against a point target, and a minimum safe range in combat of 33yd (31m). The M203 is light, unobtrusive and does not, in any way, interfere with the normal functioning of the rifle. M203s are widely used by U.S. Special Operations Forces, including SEALs, Delta and Rangers, as well as by many foreign forces.

Right: The M203 40mm Grenade Launcher fits underneath the rifle adding greatly to the squad's firepower.

Mk 19 Mod 3 40mm Machine Gun, Mod 3

Country of origin: United States.
Manufacturer: Saco Defense Industries.
Type: automatic grenade launcher.
Operation: blowback.
Caliber: 40mm.
Weight: gun 72.5lb (32.9kg); cradle 21.0lb (9.5kg); tripod 44.0lb (20.0kg); tot
137.5lb (62.4kg).
Dimensions: length 43.1in (1095mm).
Range: maximum 2,400yd (2,200m); maximum effective 1,750yd (1,600m).
Rate of fire: cyclic 325-375rpm; rapid 60rpm; sustained 40rpm.
Muzzle velocity: 790ft/sec (241 m/s).

Grenades have long been valuable weapons in the infantryman's close-quarte
armory, providing significant explosive effects at ranges outside that of hand-to
hand combat, and with much more rapid response than mortars or artillery
They originated as hand-thrown weapons, but during World War II devices wer
developed which could be attached to the muzzle of a rifle; these had greate
range than hand-thrown weapons, but the rate-of-fire was slow. In the earl
1960s the Mark 18 rapid-fire grenade launcher was developed , which wa
hand-cranked and fired 40mm grenades held in a continuous cloth belt. Thes

vere used in some numbers during the Vietnam War, especially by the Navy's
verine patrol units. It was the latter requirement that led the Navy to develop
fully automatic grenade launcher, the Mk 19 Mod 0, which appeared in 1966,
ut this proved both unsafe and unreliable and although many of the problems
vere solved with the Mk 19 Mod 1 which appeared in 1972, the weapon only
eached maturity in the Mk 19 Mod 3, which was also adopted by the Army in
983.

Today's Mk 19 Mod 3 is an air-cooled, blowback-operated weapon, using
arious types of 40mm grenade, which are fed to the weapon in a disintegrating
netal-link belt. The weapon can be ground-mounted on a tripod, ship-mounted
n a variety of naval mounts, or mounted in a vehicle turret (eg, LVTP-7A1).
here are currently three types of operational ammunition: M383 high-explosive
IE) grenade, and the M430I and M430A1 high-explosive dual-purpose (HEDP)
renades. In addition, there are also the M385I/M918 training rounds and
I922/M922A1 dummy rounds. The M430I HEDP 40mm grenade will pierce
rmor up to 2in (51mm) thick, and will produce fragments to kill personnel
vithin 16ft (5m) and wound personnel within 50ft (15m) of the point of impact.

*elow: The Mk19 Machine Gun launches 40mm grenades at a sustained
ate of 60 rounds per minute.*

Irritant Grenades and Stun Grenades

Irritant Grenades

The term "irritant grenades" covers a variety of non-lethal, offensive weapon containing a gaseous payload (usually referred to euphemistically as "smoke" which will cause varying degrees of discomfort. These can be used to dispers rioters or to temporarily overcome terrorists in a variety of situations, such a hostage release. Friendly troops must don respirators before such grenades a thrown, and in the open air the extent of the effects is very much dependent upo the direction and strength of the wind.

The most commonly used content is "CS gas" (CS is the abbreviation for *orth chlorobenzylmalononitrile*), although this is something of a misnomer, since actually a white solid powder, which is usually dispersed into the air with an age such as methylene chloride to form a cloud.

The U.S. Army uses the M25A2 riot-control hand-grenade, which has a bod made of compressed fiber or plastic, which can be filled with a variety of agents, of which are mixed with silica aerogel to increase the dissemination efficiency. Th total weight of the grenade is 8oz (227g). The effective radius of the agent is abou 5.5yd (5m) from the point of detonation, although small fragments may be throw as far as 27yd (25m). The body is gray with red band and red markings. Anoth grenade, the M7A2 Hand-Grenade, contains only CS gas. In appearance it has a gr body with a red band and red markings.

The main advantages of CS gas are that in the open air its effects wear off only a few minutes, there are no known long-term effects, and there has nev been a case of a death due to exposure to CS, anywhere in the world. The ma primary effects of CS gas is to cause a severe burning sensation in the eye streaming tears (hence its common name of "tear gas"), coughing, and ove production of mucus from the nose. CS also acts as a skin irritant, causing a burnir sensation on any expose skin, and in extreme cases the victim may also suffer fro nausea and vomiting. These effects, coupled with the general situation in which the victim finds him/herself, then usually induces panic and a deep-rooted urge to leave the scene, which is precisely what the security forces are seeking to achieve.

Stun Grenades

The existence of stun grenades first became known during the Iranian Embassy siege in London in 1980. Traditional fragmentation grenades are designed to cause death and injuries, which makes them unsuitable for use where hostages or innocent bystanders are involved. To overcome this, the stun grenade is designed to cause an extremely loud explosion and emit a very bright flash of light, causing immediate disorientation, but without any physical injuries. These grenades have proved extremely useful and are now carried by almost all counter-terrorist special forces units.

A typical device is the British Haley & Weller E182 stun grenade which is 2.2in (50mm) in diameter, 4.1in (104mm) long and weighs 9oz (250g). The safety pin is on a ring which is pulled free and on being thrown the firing lever is released in the normal way, but, unusually, does not fly off. The grenade contains a small electric cell and the firing lever closes a circuit which, after 0.5 a half–second time delay, then initiates the main 0.4oz (12g) charge. This releases 16 sub-munitions, the first of which detonates after 2 seconds, followed by the others at 3-4 second intervals. Each sub-munition explodes with a very loud noise and emits a 22 million candela flash. U.S. forces use the M-84 stun grenade which weighs 8.3oz (235g).

A variation on this theme is the U.S. Army's Mk3A2 "concussion offensive hand grenade" (usually called simply the "concussion grenade") is designed to be used in close combat to produce enemy casualties while minimizing danger to friendly personnel.

Right: The British Haley & Waller E-182 multi-burst disorientating (stun) grenade.

Below: These grenades are intended to disable terrorists for a vital few seconds.

Al Mar Combat Smatchet

Country of origin: United States.
Manufacturer: Al Mar Knives Inc., Lake Oswego, Oregon, USA.
Type: fighting knife.
Blade shape: broad leaf shape, with serrated edges.
Dimensions: length overall 15.0in (381mm); length main blade 10.0in (257mm); width blade 3.0in (76mm).
Grip: black Lexan plastic with longitudinal grooves and lanyard hole.
Sheath: black leather with leg tie.

The "smatchet" is a unique shape, the blade being shaped like a broad leaf ar the overall appearance being somewhat reminiscent of a medieval Celtic sho sword. But this is, in fact, a modern design which has its origins in a weapor designed during World War II for use by British and United States command troops. The purpose was to kill enemies very quickly and with a minimum effort. The official handbook recommended that it be used for driving into a enemy's stomach, chopping his neck, wrist or arm to sever the main arterie or, if all else failed, the pommel could be rammed into the enemy's face. Or of the major features of the weapon is that it creates a deep, debilitating wour without great effort on the attacker's part. However, the size and the shape the smatchet also mean that it can be used as a general-purpose camp ar survival tool for cutting and trimming, and even as a digging tool. Its flat, larg surface can also be used as a paddle in a canoe.

The blade, which measures 10 x 3in (257 x 76mm), has serrated section on both edges for more effectively cutting difficult materials such as rope ar webbing. There is a single hole drilled through the blade near the guard, so th the owner can identify the edges, even in total darkness by feel. This allov him to use one side as a "working edge" and keep the other razor sharp f emergency use.

Above: The Combat Smatchet in its sheath. It is designed as a killing weapon, but can also be used around a camp-site.

Left: The Smatchet's shape is reminiscent of a medieval short-sword, but note serrated sections for cutting ropes and canvas.

BuckMaster

Country of origin: United States.
Manufacturer: Buck Knives, El Cajon, California, USA.
Type: combat/survival knife.
Blade shape: Bowie.
Dimensions: length overall 12.5in (318mm); length blade 7.5in (191mm).
Grip: bare metal with checkering and slots; no covering.
Sheath: plastic and Cordura sheath, including sharpening stone and clips for accessories.

The BuckMaster knife was produced in the 1980s and early 1990s and is no longer in production, but is still very widely used in both military and civilian circles. Its design was based on that of the U.S. Army's M9 bayonet, but with some very imaginative additions. It is very strongly made of tough but lightweight components, and the stainless steel blade has a plain convex main edge and a heavily serrated clip edge, while the spine has rear-facing saw teeth. The handle is hollow with a screw cap, which is removed to reveal a compartment containing two anchor pins which are then screwed into holes

each end of the guard, thus enabling the knife, in combination with a strong cord, to be used as either an anchor or a grapple. The hollow handle has sufficient space to accommodate other survival items, if required.

Despite its many advantages, the knife suffers some drawbacks. The handle is made of steel and while it is checkered and grooved to provide a good grip, it does not have any covering, which means that in very cold conditions, and if the handler is not wearing gloves, his skin could adhere to the handle. The screw-in anchor pins seem on the face of it to be a very good idea, but unfortunately they do not always provide an adequate and secure holdfast, with possibly dire consequences for the user. Finally, if used as a dagger to stab an enemy, the rearward facing saw teeth tend to snag on the flesh, making it difficult to withdraw the knife. The sheath is particularly well designed and includes a sharpening stone and a pouch for carrying small items such as a Silva compass.

Below: The Buckmaster's two anchor pins are carried in the hollow handle and screw into holes at either end of the guard.

Gerber Mark II

Country of origin: United States.
Manufacturer: Gerber Division, Fiskars Inc., Portland, Oregon, USA.
Type: fighting knife/dagger..
Blade shape: dagger, with serrated edge near hilt.
Dimensions: length overall 11.5in (292mm); length blade 6.5in (165mm).
Grip: cast aluminum, incorporating double guard, black epoxy-coated, with lanyard hole.
Sheath: black Cordura belt sheath with leg tie.

There are absolutely no pretences or equivocations about this knife – it is a fighting dagger intended for killing. It was developed by the Gerber company during the Vietnam War and incorporates the advice of military knife-fighting experts. It is a development of the Fairbairn-Sykes concept of a fighting dagger and is a no-frills design, with a 6.5in (165mm) blade made of 0.25in (64mm) 440A stainless steel, hardened to Rc 57-59 and blackened. The blade is a parallel-sided dagger type, with a strong spear point and serrations on each edge for extra cutting power. This blade is designed to be equally effective whether stabbing, slashing, ripping or cutting.

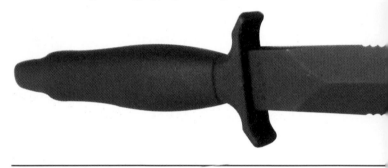

Gerber Patriot

Country of origin: United States.
Manufacturer: Gerber Division, Fiskars Inc., Portland, Oregon, USA.
Type: combat/survival knife.
Blade shape: Bowie-style, clip point.
Dimensions: length overall 10.6in (269mm); length blade 6.0in (152mm).
Grip: molded Zytel handle with checkering and lateral grooves, finger groove.
Sheath: rigid plastic with safety-catch.

This is a solid, well-made and straightforward combat/survival knife, which has been specifically designed for airborne and special forces, and is one of the very few knives to be "jump certified" for use in parachute jumps. The blade, which is made of stainless steel with a black finish, is Bowie-style and is angle ground with a long clip false edge. The simple but effective handle is made of molded Zytel with checkering and longitudinal grooves for

Right: The safety catch on the sheath prevents inadvertant release of the Patriot when taken on a parachute jump.

The handle is a single aluminum casting, which is contoured to fit the hand well, and incorporates a double guard with forward angled points. The handle has a truncated-cone pommel which, if all else has failed, may be used as a "skull-crusher." The knife comes with a simple black Cordura sheath with a lanyard for securing to the thigh.

For reasons no longer clear, the Gerber Mark I fighting knife was developed *after* the Mark II described here and, apart from the fact that both are fighting knives, there is virtually no resemblance between the two. With its simple, elegant lines, excellent proportions and classical shape this is an ideal weapon for the 21st century which would not have looked out of place amidst the Borgias in XIVth century Italy.

Below: The Gerber Mark II is a killing knife, pure and simple, and is designed to be equally effective whether cutting, slashing, stabbing or cutting.

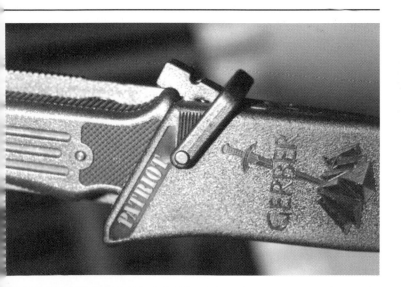

▶ extra grip and is contoured to provide a finger groove for the first finger. The full-length tang runs through the entire length of the handle and there is a cylindrical butt piece with a lanyard hole.

The safety features which result in its acceptance for use by airborne troops are in the sheath, which is made of rigid black plastic which is so strong that it is not possible for the blade to break through and injure the wearer, even if he falls on it while landing. In addition, there is a two-stage locking device, comprising a clip and a locking latch. When the knife is slid

into the sheath the clip catches the tip of the guard and clicks into place, thus holding the knife securely. To ensure absolute safety, however, the locking latch is then moved up by the thumb into the "locked" position, from which it cannot be released either by accident or in a heavy landing, since it requires positive action by the wearer to release.

Below: The Patriot is a supremely simple combat knife, the result of painstaking design by the maker, Gerber.

Wenger Swiss Army Knife "Super-Talent" Model

Country of origin: Switzerland.
Manufacturer: Wenger, Switzerland.
Type: multi-purpose military/civilian knife.
Tools: 21 blades/implements.
Dimensions: length overall 3.5in (89mm); length main blade 2.8in (71mm).
Grip: red plastic scales with Swiss flag logo.

It is generally assumed that there is just one "Swiss Army Knife" but in fact not only is there a whole series of designs, but there are actually several different companies making them. The great bulk of the production is split roughly 50:50 between the firms of Victorinox, which is located in the German-speaking canton of Schwyz, and Wenger, in the French-speaking Jura region. There are

also some much smaller cutlers, but Wenger and Victorinox are the only two entitled to use the legally protected symbol of the federal cross on the numerous civilian versions, which certifies their Swiss authenticity. By a gentleman's agreement Wenger uses the red cross with a circle around it and proclaims its products to be the "Genuine Swiss Army Knife" while Victorinox uses the red cross without a border and advertises that its products are the "Original Swiss Army Knife."

There are now many models, the one shown here being the Wenger "Super-Talent," which has a truly bewildering array of implements and gadgets, including various types of knife and saw blades, scissors, ruler, compass, pliers, corkscrew, Philips screwdriver, bottle-opener and magnifying glass. Some of these devices, such as the screwdriver, are fitted with a patented locking

device which engages as soon as pressure is applied to the tip, thus ensuring that it does not suddenly "fold." The great majority of soldiers in most armies carry one of these invaluable implements – they cannot be used to actually kill the enemy, but there seems to be an implement for almost any other task!

Left: One of many models of the "Swiss Army Knife", a ubiquitous device which has achieved legendary status among soldiers and special forces in many armies.

M18 Claymore

Country of origin: United States.
Type: directional, free-standing anti-personnel mine.
Weight: total 3.5lb (1.6kg); explosive 1.5lb (0.7kg).
Dimensions: length 8.5in (216mm); width 1.4in (35mm); height (mine body) 3.3in (84mm).
Warhead: directional fragmentation; 1.5lb (0.7kg) layer of composition C-4 explosive, plus 700 steel spheres (each 10.5 grains).
Arming: Manual.
Fuzing: Command.

The M18A1 Claymore mine has proved its value time and again for both conventional troops and special forces. The mine is a small rectangular device which sits on four metal legs and can be placed underneath bushes or in grass in places where it is very difficult to see. The mine body is slightly curved so

Right: The Claymore mine has proved a significant advance in infantry tactics with its ability to provided accurate and focussed fire-power.

that, when activated, it fires its warhead of 700 small steel balls in a fan-shaped pattern, covering a 60-degree horizontal arc, at a maximum vertical height of some 6.5ft (2m) (ie, the height of a man) with a maximum effective range of 100yd (00m), although the optimum effect is at about 50yd (45m). The danger area for friendly forces is 250yd (229m) in front and 18yd (16m) to the sides and rear of the mine, although those within 100yd (90m) should be in a covered position for protection against secondary missiles.

There are two very significant military features of the Claymore. The first is that it provides firepower to the infantry between the maximum range of hand grenades and the minimum safe distance from own artillery shells and mortar bombs. Secondly, unlike normal mines, it can be aimed so that it covers a specific approach, an alleyway, corridor or a track known to be used by the enemy. The Claymore can be detonated by a trip-wire or by direct command from an observer.

RPG-7V

Country of origin: USSR/Russian Federation.
Manufacturer: Basalt State Munitions Company, Russia.
Type: anti-armor/anti-personnel rocket launcher.
Caliber: launch tube 1.57in (40mm); rocket 3.35in (85mm).
Weight: launcher 15lb (7kg); grenade 4.95lb (2.25kg).
Dimensions: length rocket launcher 38.5in (990mm).
Warhead: high-explosive anti-tank (HEAT).
Muzzle velocity: 984ft/sec (300m/sec).
Effective range: moving target 328yd (300m); stationary target 550yd (500m).

Even though the RPG-7 has been the standard anti-tank grenade launcher in the Soviet/Russian Army for some forty years, it is still of relevance today, since it is available around the world in vast numbers and is still very effective against light armored vehicles and buildings. Indeed, it has been developed to keep pace with modern technology and remains a front-line weapon with some fifty armies, serving both conventional and special forces units.

The original RPG-7, which entered service in 1962, replaced an earlier weapon which had been developed from the German World War

Above: At one time issues to Soviet special forces, the RPG-7 is now more likely to be used by terrorists and guerrillas.

Left: Chinese soldier with the Type 56 copy of the RPG-7; despite its age, it remains a devastating weapon.

Panzerfaust; an improved version, the RPG-7V, came into service in 1968. The projectile is ejected from the launch-tube by a small charge which carries it forward about 20ft (6.1m) where the main rocket fires, thus protecting the firer from the rocket exhaust. The HEAT warhead will penetrate some 12.6in (32cm) of armor and there is an alternative HE warhead for use against personnel. The PGO-7 and PGO-7V optical sights are frequently supplemented by the NSP-2 infra-red night-sight. There is also a special folding version of the weapon, designated RPG-7D, for use by paratroops. A new anti-tank grenade, the PG-7BR, was introduced in the 1980s for use against tanks fitted with the new types of ceramic armor, which has two charges in tandem: the first defeats the outer layer of armor, thus clearing the way for the second charge to penetrate the inner layer.

Even in the hands of unskilled and illiterate troops this weapon has proved to be highly effective against bunkers and buildings, troops, vehicles of all types, and even helicopters if properly used. Like many other Soviet weapons, the RPG-7V was widely distributed and a few even appeared in Ulster in the hands of the Provisional IRA.

Shoulder-launched Multiple-purpose Assault Weapon (SMAW)

Country of origin: United States.
Type: man-portable, anti-armor rocket launcher.
Weight: to carry 16.6lb (7.5kg); ready-to-fire (HEDP) 29.5lb (13.4kg); ready-to-fire (HEAA) 30.5lb (13.9kg).
Dimensions: bore diameter 3.3in (83mm); length, carry-mode 29.9in (759mm); ready-to-fire-mode 54in (1,372mm).
Propulsion: rocket motor.
Performance: maximum effective range 574yd (500m).
Warhead: shaped charge.
Crew: two.

SMAW was fielded in 1984 and was formed by combining the Israeli B-300 rocket launcher with a British-designed 9mm spotting rifle. The launcher consists of a fiberglass launch tube with the 9mm spotting rifle built into its right side, and a combination of open battle sights and a mount for optical or night sights. The system can launch three types of 3.3in (83mm) diameter rockets. The original weapon was the High Explosive, Dual Purpose (HEDP) rocket, which is intended for use against bunkers, brickwork and concrete walls, as well as against light armor. The second weapon, which was developed and issued later, is the High Explosive Anti-Armor (HEAA) rocket, which is effective against most current tanks, although not those fitted with spaced or explosive/reactive armor (ERA). The third round is the Follow Through Grenade (FTG), in which the shaped-charge front warhead has a full-caliber, follow-through grenade for use against concrete and brick walls.The rounds for the 9mm spotting rifle are ballistically matched to the rockets and increase the probability of a first-round hit. SMAW was a U.S. Marine Corps-designed weapons system and is being replaced by Predator in USMC service.

A new version for the Marine Corps is SMAW-CS (CS = confined space) which has a propulsion system specially desgined to enable the missile to be launched from within houses during fighting in urban areas. This new propulsion system enables SMAW -CS to be fired without the backblast and noise associated with the earlier version, but without any reduction in range or airspeed.

During the Gulf War the U.S. Army borrowed 150 launchers and 5,000 rockets and this led to the development by the Army of SMAW-D, which was, in effect, an adapted version of the Marine Corps' SMAW but with a disposable launcher. This was put into small-scal production (6,000 missiles). SMAW-D fires the same HE warhead as the Marines' SMAW but weighs only 15l (6.8kg); it can breach earth and timber defences, masonry walls and defeat lightly skinned armored vehicles at effective ranges of 16-550yd (15-500m). The Army then turned to the XM-141 Bunker Defeat Munition (BDM); see Predator entry.

Top Right: SMAW launches three types of 83mm rocket, designed to attack either armored or concrete targets.

Right: SMAW was created by combining the Israeli B-300 rocket-launcher with a British 9mm spotting rifle.

Predator

Country of origin: United States.
Manufacturer: Lockheed Martin.
Type: shoulder-launched anti-armor/anti-personnel weapon.
Weight: 20lb (9.1kg).
Dimensions: length 35in (890mm).
Engine: two-stage (soft launch) rocket.
Performance: range 19-656yd (17-600m).
Warhead: explosively formed penetrator/follow through fragmentation grenade.
Crew: one.

In the early 1990s the U.S. Marine Corps and the Army discovered that they were both developing an individual, shoulder-launched, short-range rocket system. The Marines were working on the Short-Range Anti-Armor Weapon (SRAW), whose primary purpose was as an anti-tank weapon, while the Army was developing the Multi-Purpose Individual Munition (MPIM), which could be used against both tanks and defensive positions, such as bunkers. On examination it transpired that there were many similarities, so it was decided to bring the two programs together to produce a weapon which would deal effectively with hostile armored vehicles, as well as personnel hidden behind walls, or inside earthen or wooden reinforced bunkers. This new joint weapon would then replace LAW, AT-4, and other light shoulder-fired weapons, and will complement, rather than replace, Javelin. The Marine Corps has since named its version "Predator," while the Army has retained the designation MPIM, at least for the time being.

It was decided that the bunker-busting and wall-penetrating requirements could be met by a missile which combined the SRAW propulsion system with the MPIM's warhead, while the anti-armor requirement could be met by the SRAW propulsion system and SRAW warhead. The SRAW launcher was also adopted. In other words, the solution was the SRAW missile system with two alternative warheads.

Below: Predator, short-range, fire-and-forget missile is launched on a desert firing range.

Above: Predator uses a soft-launch technique and, as shown here, the main motor does not fire until well clear of the firer.

Predator is a short-range "fire-and-forget" assault missile, using a "soft" launch technique; ie, on pressing the trigger, a low-thrust rocket propels the missile until it is well clear of the launch tube, whereupon the second, higher-thrust stage kicks in and accelerates the missile towards the target; this both protects the firer and also enables the missile to be launched from within a confined space. Predator has an inertially-guided autopilot, which determines range and lead prior to missile launch,.thus increasing accuracy against moving targets. The launcher is fitted with a x2.5 telescopic sight, which is compatible with current and future night vision devices.

In its anti-armor role, the missile has a similar "fly-over, shoot-down" attack profile to that of the TOW-IIB, with the warhead using an explosively-formed penetrator which is lethal against all current main battle tanks including those equipped with explosive reactive armor. The complete system weighs some 20lb (9.1kg) and the carrier/launcher is thrown away following launch. This Marine Corps anti-armor version will enter service in 2002-03 and a total of 18,190 are currently on order. It is capable of destroying all modern main battle tanks, including those fitted with explosive reactive armor.

The Army is still working on its BDM version which will employ an Army-developed a "double-whammy" warhead, in which an explosively formed penetrator punches a hole through the target, allowing a follow-through anti-personnel fragmentation grenade to enter the enclosure beyond and explode.

FIM-92A Stinger Weapons System

Country of origin: United States.
Manufacturer: Hughes (prime); Raytheon (missile).
Type: close-in air defense, two-stage missile system.
Weight: system 34.5lb (15.7kg); missile 22lb (10.0kg); warhead 2.2lb (1.0kg).
Dimensions: length 5.0ft (1.5m); diameter 3.0in (76mm); wingspan 3.6in (91mm).
Powerplant: Atlantic Research Mk 27 dual-thrust, solid-fuel rocket motor.
Performance: speed 2,300ft/sec (1,500mph/2,414kmh)); maximum effective altitude FIM-92A 11,480ft (3,500m), FIM-92B/C 12,470ft (3,800m); maximum effective range FIM-92A 4,400yd (4,000m+); FIM-92B/C 5,250yd (4,800m); minimum effective range 220yd (200m).
Guidance: FIM-92A passive IR homing; FIM-92B/C passive IR/UV homing.
Warhead: 2.2lb (1.0kg) HE blast smooth-case fragmentation with time-delay contact fuze.
Crew: two.

Stinger's small-size and great effectiveness have made it a favorite among special forces for two decades. Development of the FIM-92A Stinger began in the mid-1960s, but the system suffered a long and troubled development period, although once its problems had been resolved it has settled down to become an extremely effective weapons which will remain in front-line service to the 2020s and beyond. Stinger as a battlefield system which will attack low-altitude, jet or propeller-driven aircraft and helicopters. It is a "fire-and-forget" weapon, based on a passive infrared seeker, a proportional navigation system, all-aspect engagement capability, and IFF (Identification-Friend-or-Foe), while recent upgrades have improved the missile's range and maneuverability, and enhanced its resistance to countermeasures. In addition, what started as a Man-Portable Air Defense System (MANPADS), is now fielded aboard a number

Below: Stinger's small size and proven effectiveness have made it a great favorite with special forces for over 20 years.

Right: Stinger is known to have destroyed at least 270 fixed- and rotary-winged aircraft in a wide variety of conflicts around the world.

of platforms, including the Bradley IFV (Bradley-Linebacker), HMMWV (Avenger), Light Armored Vehicle (LAV), and various helicopters. It is in service with the U.S. Navy, Marine Corps, Army and Air Force, and with many foreign armed forces.

In the MANPADS version the firer has a grip-stock which contains the electronics, sight, and trigger assembly, and all that is required to prepare for launch is to attach a missile tube to the reusable launch unit. The missile is tested and loaded into this tube in the factory and no further testing or maintenance is required.

Of the 15,669 FIM-92A Basic Stingers produced, most of those remaining in service are with foreign forces. FIM-92B Singer-POST (= Passive Optical Seeker Technique) had a a microprocessor-controlled homing head, using dual infrared (IR) and ultraviolet (UV) image-scanning guidance to enhance target detection capabilities; some 600 were produced in 1983-87. FIM-92C Stinger-RMP (Reprogrammable Micro-Processor) is intended to correct known operational deficiencies and exists in Block I and Block II versions. Stinger-RMP Block I has software and hardware changes, including a new roll-frequency sensor, a new lithium battery, improved computer processor and memory, and a ring-laser gyro which eliminates the need to super elevate prior to firing. The Army is acquiring some 10,000 Stinger-RMP Block I missiles, which will remain in the inventory until at least 2014. FIM-92D Stinger-RMP Block II, with yet further enhancements, was under development when it was "zero-funded" in the Army's FY 2001 budget request and is, therefore, effectively dead. Air-to Air Stinger [ATAS] is an adaption of the man portable Stinger RMP for use in helicopters and includes a full night capability to give helicopters an anti-helicopter capability.

Stinger is known to have destroyed at least 270 fixed-wing aircraft and helicopters, including one Argentine Pucara shot down in the Falklands War and one Indian aircraft shot down by Pakistani forces during the 1999 Kashmir conflict. By far the largest number of successes were achieved by the Mujahideen in the Afghan war when they were supplied with Basic Stinger and, despite minimal training, achieved an 80percent success rate against Soviet aircraft and, in particular, helicopters. Stinger systems were widely deployed during the 1991 Gulf War, but there were no known engagements, principally because knowledge of their very presence was sufficient to force the Iraqis to keep their helicopters well out of range.

AGM-114K Hellfire II/ Longbow Hellfire

Country of origin: United States.
Manufacturer: Martin Marietta.
Type: helicopter-launched anti-tank missile.
Weight: basic 100lb (45.4kg); Longbow 108lb (49.0kg)
Dimensions: length basic 64in (1.6m), Longbow 69.2in (1.8m); diameter all 7in (17.8cm); wingspan all 1.0ft (0.3m).
Propulsion: single-stage, single-thrust, solid-propellant rocket motor.
Performance: speed approx 825kt (950mph/1,530km/h); range > 3.1 miles (5km).
Warhead: shaped charge 14.8lb (6.7kg).

The AGM-114 Hellfire Air-to-Ground Missile System (AGMS) provides anti armor capability for attack helicopters and, in a recent development, also fo some Unmanned Aerial Vehicles (UAVs). The missile entered service in 198: and has undergone many updates, the most recent involving the addition of a radar-frequency seeker to the existing laser seeker. Hellfire II and Longbow Hellfire are the latest production versions, the combination of Hellfire II's precision guidance and Longbow Hellfire's fire-and-forget capability providing the battlefield commander with flexibility across a wide range of mission scenarios, permitting fast battlefield response and a degree of mobility no afforded by other anti-armor weapons.

AGM-114A Basic Hellfire, the original Army version, is no longer in service and stocks are being expended in live-fire training. The AGM-114B was the naval and marine version, from which it differed in having an additiona

Below: U.S. Army technician checks the loading of an early model AGM- 114 Hellfire missile aboard an AH-64.

Above: British-built Westland Longbow Apache displays its weaponry, including 16 Hellfire II missiles.

electronic arm/safety device required for shipboard use. The AGM-114C/D/E were experimental versions, none of which entered production. Next came AGM-114F Interim Hellfire missile with a tandem warhead designed to defeat explosive-reactive armor (ERA); a number were ordered by the Army, but none by the Navy; production ended in 1994.

The current version, AGM-114K Hellfire II, has been in production since 1993, and features tandem warheads for defeating ERA, electro-optical counter-countermeasures, semiactive laser seeker, and a programmable autopilot for course selection. The weapon can also be employed against concrete bunkers and similar fortifications. The missile is powered by a single-stage, single-thrust, solid-propellant motor, with arming taking place some 164-328yd (150-300m) from the launcher. Maximum velocity is about 950mph (1,530km/h).

There are two engagement methods: autonomous and remote. In an autonomous engagement requires the launch aircraft conducts the entire operation from target location, through identification, firing, guiding until it is destroyed. In contrast, in a remote engagement the aircraft simply acts as a launcher, despatching the missile to the general location of the target, where another aircraft or a ground observer, designating with a laser, guides the missile to its intended target. This remote engagement requires coordination, but has the advantage that the launch aircraft can remain masked behind terrain, greatly reducing its visible launch signature, thereby increasing aircraft survivability. Remote engagements, however, and planning between the "shooter" and the "observer."

The Longbow Hellfire missile is an adverse weather, fire-and-forget, anti-armor "fire-and-forget" version of the Hellfire missile. The Longbow fire-control radar system will locates, classifies, and prioritizes targets for the Longbow Hellfire missile and is being integrated into the Army's entire AH-64D Apache attack helicopters and into one-third of its RAH-66 Comanche armed reconnaissance helicopters. ▶

The main advantages of the Longbow missile include: weather capabilit (rain, snow, fog, smoke, and battlefield obscurants); millimeter wave countermeasures survivability; fire-and-forget guidance, which allows the Apache Longbow to launch and then remask, thus minimizing exposure to enemy fire; an advanced warhead capable of defeating reactive armo

configurations projected into the 21st century; and reprogrammability to adapt to changing threats and mission requirements.

Below: Hellfire provides AH-64s with a "fire-and-forget" capability, attacking targets in rain, snow, fog or smoke.

Israeli Air Industries (IAI) Nimrod

Country of origin: Israel.
Manufacturer: Israeli Air Industries (IAI).
Type: vehicle/helicopter-launched anti-tank/bunker busting missile.
Weight: n/a.
Dimensions: length 9.4ft (2,850mm); diameter 8.3in (250mm); wingspa
19.7in (500mm).
Propulsion: single-stage, single-thrust, solid-propellant rocket motor.
Performance: speed Mach1+; range ground-launched 28,400yd (26km), ai
launched 21,870yd (20km).
Warhead: shaped charge.
Guidance: laser homing.
Platforms: Land Rover Defender; CH-53 helicopter.

The IAI Nimrod is a laser-homing missile system, which can be used t

attack tanks, ships or semi-hard ground targets such as buildings or bunkers. In the ground role it is normally mounted on a Land Rover Defender, but it has recently been installed on Isaraeli Air Force CH-53 helicopters to give them an anti-tank capability when deployed on special forces' long-range penetration missions. In this installation, there are two pods, each containing four missiles, which are mounted low on the forward fuselage on the mounts normally taken by the long-range fuel tanks, thus reducing the range. While the original range of the Nimrod ground-to-ground version is 26km, in its CH53 airborne version the Nimrod has only a 20km range.In the IDF ground role Nimrod is used primarily by *Sayeret Maglan* as a vehicle-mounted installation.

Below: Israeli Air Force CH-53 launches a trials model of the IAI Nimrod missile from its four-cell missile pod.

MAPATS (Man-Portable Anti-Tank System)

Country of origin: Israel
Manufacturer: Israel Military Industries (IMI), Israel.
Type: man-portable anti-tank missile system.
Weight: missile 40.8lb (18.5kg); missile in container 65lb (29.5kg); tripod an
battery 32lb (14.5kg); traversing unit 55lb (25kg); guidance unit 46.2lb (21kg,
launch tube 12.1lb (5.5kg); night vision system 14.3lb (6.5kg,).
Caliber: 5.8in (148mm).
Dimensions: length missile 5.1ft (156mm).
Propulsion: single-stage, single-thrust, solid-propellant rocket motor.
Performance: launch 230ft/sec (70m/sec), maximum velocity 1,000ft/se
(305m/sec); time of flight to 4,375yd (4,000m 19.5 seconds; maximum rang
>5,470yd (5,000m); armour penetration >31in (800mm).
Firing angles: traverse 360º, elevation -20º to +30º
Warhead: shaped charge 7.9lb (3.6kg).

Codenamed *Hutra* by the IDF this system is essentially a laser-guided adaptation of the U.S. Army's TOW system, but is now being marketed world-wide by IMI and known sales include a number to the Chilean Army. The *Hutra* is used for close-to-medium range engagements normally mounted on a jeep. Alternatively it can be backpacked by a three-man team, one to carry the missile in its container, the second the launcher and the third the tripod, with the ancilliaries shared between them, although even very fit men would be unable to carry the system over a long distance. On firing, the missile is propelled out of the launch tube by the ejector motor which then falls away as the main motor cuts in. The missile rides down the laser beam reflected from the target and the system is immune to jamming and entirely autonomous. A variety of warheads is available for different targets.

Below: MAPATS is a laser-guided version of TOW.

Body Protection

Bullet-resistant garments were developed from the 1920s onwards, but these were both bulky and heavy, as well as very expensive and were not widely used. More practicable protective vests were developed In World War II; these were made of ballistic nylon and were a little lighter and somewhat easier to wear, but while they were effective against shrapnel and artillery fragments (hence the name "flak jacket") they would not stop a high velocity rifle or pistol bullet. Then, in the 1960s, three factors came together. First, the number of fatalities among U.S. law enforcement officers began to increase dramatically; second, various national and international terrorist movements began to cause increasing deaths among police and military trying to deal with them; and, third, new materials began to become available.

Initially, even this body armor was bulky and while the wearer could move with relative ease it was still fairly obvious that he/she was wearing it. Today, however, new materials mean that body armor is not only very much more effective in stopping bullets and, in some cases, attacks with pointed weapons such as daggers, but it is also much less obtrusive and can be worn as a matter of routine, rather than something to be donned only for special occasions. Conventional textile-based ballistic vests are designed to stop soft-nosed bullets which flatten on impact, but offer little or no protection against the knives, which are increasingly being used, and which simply cut through the textile layers. New knife resistant armors are specifically designed to overcome this threat and many of them use layers of metal plates, chain-mail or metallic wires. In addition to dealing with projectiles and knives, special forces in counter-terrorist situations are often also threatened by fire and many units now wear coveralls made of flame-resistant materials such as Nomex.

The other item of uniform is the helmet, now no longer made of steel and heavy, but of man-made fiber, which is both lighter and much more ballistically efficient. Increasingly the helmet is also being used as a mount for spotlights, laser projectors, visors and individual radio sets. All such military helmets have a characteristic shape and the Israelis now use a large, floppy camouflage covering to

Below: U.S. special forces show that modern body armor is much less bulky than that of even just ten years ago.

Above: This Force Recon Marine is wearing body armor to protect his torso, goggles to protect his eyes.

break up this outline, known as the *mit'snefet* (= clown's hat); made of cloth, it is reversible, with woodland pattern on one side, desert-pattern on the other. Helmets are also made to differing standards of ballistic effectiveness. In the Israeli Army, for example, the majority of helmets provide protection only against fragments whereas elite counter-terrorist units have bullet-proof helmets made of ceramic armor, although their weight means that they can only be worn for relatively short periods.

If modern body armor is a throwback to earlier times, so, too, is the latest concept of the overall appearance of the soldier. In the 18th Century, for example, soldiers wore high hats to make them look taller and shoulder-boards to make them look wider, which, in combination with an elaborate uniform, was intended to make the man look more imposing to the enemy. So, today, the all-black appearance of combat uniforms such as those of the British SAS, coupled with either a respirator or a Balaclava helmet to guarantee anonymity, all combine to present a terrorist with a thoroughly frightening and awe-inspiring enemy.

Respirators

At the beginning of the 21st century, the threat from biological and chemical weapons (BCW) is greater than ever, while the threat of the use of nuclear devices is not as remote as it was 10-20 years ago, with the relevant technologies becoming increasingly available, not only to governments, but also to terrorists. As a result, protection against such attacks has become an urgent requirement for special forces, both military and police, the basic requirement being a full-face respirator, covering the mouth, nose and eyes, with a clear face mask or eye-pieces to enable the wearer to see.

There are three types available, the first being the air-purifying respirator, in which the mask is fitted with one or more filters and the purified air is pulled in by the wearer's lungs. Such masks are the least-expensive and least-complicated option, but any leak in the mask, either due to a poor fit or to puncture makes them ineffective. Second is the supplied-air respirator, which uses the same type of filter cartridge as the air-purifying respirator, but in this case the filter is attached to a battery-operated canister, in which a fan forces air through the filter, and the purified air then runs up to the mask. This system produces filtered air at a small positive pressure, which ensures that if there is a leak the external contaminated air is kept out. However, the filter life is somewhat shorter, but more importantly it depends upon a supply of charged batteries and, expressed in absolutely fundamental terms, if the battery dies, so, too, does the wearer.

The third option is the self-contained breathing apparatus (SCBA) system, in which the operator wears a full-face mask supplied with high-pressure purified air from tanks. This is undoubtedly the best system, but while tanks giving just a few minutes supply are reasonably small, tanks with an endurance of 30 minutes or more (the practicable maximum is about 60 minutes) are both heavy and bulky. In addition, recharging requires special equipment, and the overall system costs are much greater. However, where a large fire is involved, there will be a great deal of smoke containing an unknown mix of poisonous gases, while the fire itself will consume most or all of the oxygen in the air SCBA systems are ideal for firefighters as the fire appliance can carry replacement tanks or refilling equipment, and, in any event, a firefighter spends a limited time in the burning building. For soldiers on the battlefield or on a counter-terrorist operation the weight and limited air time pose major obstacles, although there may be some occasions where it is essential.

Modern combat respirators must be strong, leak-proof and well-fitting, and need to protect the wearer against all known chemical and biological agents in aerosol, liquid and vapour form, all this while enabling the wearer to carry on with his mission, and able to see, breathe and communicate. Possible threats include: nerve-, tear- and blood-agents; chemical agents such as chlorine phosgene, choloropicrin and diphenylchloroarsine; and radioactive particulates resulting from a nuclear explosion (ie, fall-out). In some anti-terrorist operations such as hostage retrieval, it may be necessary for the security forces to use explosive devices that result in fires or dense smoke in a confined space. In such situations the atmosphere can become oxygen deficient very rapidly and the NBC, or smaller anti-riot filters normally used with the respirator, will not sustain life. In such cases, it is necessary for the standard respirator to be quickly converted into an SCBA.

In addition to the filtration system, the respirator requires protective-coated eyepieces with a wide field of vision and good anti-misting characteristics coupled with the ability to accept internally-mounted corrective inserts for spectacle wearers as well as externally-mounted lens filters. As the respirators may be worn for a long periods they also need some arrangement to enable the wearer to drink in safety. Finally, because wearers need to be able to communicate, the respirator also needs to enable the wearer to communicate clearly both with those around him and by radio and/or telephone.

Avon NBC SF10 Special Forces Respirator

One example of a modern respirator is the SF10, which was developed from the Avon S10, which had been designed to meet a British/NATO requirement for a ▶

Right: The latest Avon SF10 respirator is specifically designed to meet the needs of special forces in anti-terrorist operations.

Below: Twenty years ago respirators were bulky and hard to wear for lengthy periods; modern types are greatly improved.

▶ respirator for standard issue to all members of the armed forces. It entered service in 1986 and has proved very successful; it has since been adopted by the armed forces of of Australia, Kuwait, Malaysia and New Zealand. This design was then refined to meet the needs of special forces, resulting in the Avon SF10 model, which is particularly intended to cope with the conditions met in anti-terrorist assaults and hostage rescue operations.

The SF10 provides protection against high levels of CS CR and other types of irritant gases, aerosols and smokes. It is fitted with two cheek-mounted screw-in access mounts; one will always be fitted with a filter, while the other can be fitted with either a second filter or a blanking-plug. Alternatively, the second canister mount can be fitted with a demand valve and a small compressed-air cylinder, thus converting it to an SCBA system and giving the wearer a few minutes in which to escape in conditions of oxygen depletion. The SF10 has two eyepieces with enhanced impact resistance, but there are external screw-threads for additional tinted lenses, which can be added or removed by hand, even when wearing protective gloves. There is also a high-quality microphone, enabling the wearer to communicate either to others in the vicinity or using a radio transmitter. The SF10, complete with its filter, weighs less than 28oz (800gm).

Filters

Filters remove poisonous chemicals and deadly bacteria from the air using one (or more) of three different techniques. The first is particle filtration, which works on the same principle as a handkerchief placed over the mouth to keep dust out. Respirators designed to guard against biological threats use a very fine particulate filter, most of which will remove particles as small as 0.3 microns. Since the particles come to rest in side the filter, it eventually becomes clogged and has to be replaced.

Organic chemical threats generally take the form of mists or vapours which cannot be stopped by particulate filtration and these are dealt with by activated charcoal filters, using charcoal which has been been treated with oxygen to open up millions of tiny pores between the carbon atoms, giving surface areas of the order of 300-2,000m2/gm. This material adsorbs most chemical agents (ie, it

attaches to them by chemical attraction) and the huge surface area gives countless bonding sites. Activated charcoal is good at trapping carbon-based impurities and chlorine but has no effect at all on others, such as sodium and nitrates, which will simply pass through. As with the previous case, the filters eventually become clogged and have to be replaced.

The third type of filter involves the use of chemicals which react with the agent to neutralize its effect. Thus, for example, in World War I sodium thiosulfate was used to remove chlorine, and hexamethyltetramine to remove phosgene.

Avon NBC AFM12 Filter Canister

The Avon AFM12 filter canister is cylindrical in shape and is designed to be screwed on to a NATO standard (STANAG 4155) thread on an appropriate respirator. The canister has a diameter of 4.5in (115mm) and a depth of 2.4in (61mm), and weighs 8.5oz (270gm). It is made of glass-filled Noryl and contains both charcoal and particulate filters. The extruded, pelletised charcoal is impregnated with metallic salts (copper and chromium) and triethylenediamine (TEDA). The particulate filter is filled with high-efficiency glass-fiber/vinyon copolymer, which is co-pleated with a polypropylene netting.

Below: Respirators are made to meet specific needs, such as this model for members of explosive ordnance disposal teams.

M998 Truck High Mobility Multipurpose Wheeled Vehicle (HMMWV)

Country of origin: United States.
Manufacturer: AM General.
Type: multi-purpose truck.
Weight: 5,200lb (2,359kg).
Dimensions: length 15.0ft (4.6m); width 7.1ft (2.2m); height 6.0ft (1.8m) reducible to 4.5ft (1.4m).
Engine: V8, 6.2 litre displacement, fuel injected diesel, liquid cooled, compression ignition; 150hp at 3,600rpm.
Performance: maximum road speed 55mph (89kmh); road range 350 miles (563.2km); fording without preparation 2.5ft (762mm), with deep water fording kit 5ft (1.5m); maximum grade 60%; side slope 40deg.
Armor: none.
Armament: various (see text).
Crew: two (depends on role).

The High Mobility Multi-purpose Wheeled Vehicle (HMMWV/"Humm-Vee") is a lightweight, four-wheel drive, air-transportable, air-droppable family of vehicles which includes versions for utility/cargo, carrying shelters, weapons carriers, ambulances, TOW launcher carriers and scout-reconnaissance, to name but a few. Payload varies according to the body style, ranging from 1,920lb (871kg) on the M997 four-litter ambulance to 5,300lb (2,404kg) on the Expanded Capacity variant, but is generally in the 1¼ ton (1,270kg) range.

The HMMWV was produced as the replacement for the M151 series of jeeps. It is powered by a high performance diesel engine, and has automatic transmission

Below: The HMMWV can be adapted for almost any purpose; this one is armed with the TOW missile system.

Above: HMMWV armed with two four-cell launchers for the Avenger missile system.

and four-wheel drive. All HMMWVs are designed for use over all types of roads, in all weather conditions and are extremely effective in the most difficult terrain. The HMMWV's high power-to-weight ratio, four-wheeled drive and high ground clearance combine to give it outstanding cross-country mobility.

The M988 Cargo/Troop Carrier Without Winch is the basic item from which all other versions are derived. In many cases there are two vehicles for the same role, differing only because one has a self-recovery winch and the other does not; for example, the "M1038 cargo/troop carrier with winch" is identical to the M988 mentioned above except for the addition of the winch, and both vehicles are used to transport equipment, materials, and/or personnel. In the cargo carrier configuration, the vehicle is capable of transporting a payload, including the two-man crew, of 2,500lb (1,134kg). A troop seat kit is required to convert it into a troop carrier in which configuration it can carry ten people, normally two crew and eight passengers. Alternatively, the vehicle can be configured for a four-man crew. The vehicle can, when fully loaded, climb 60 percent slopes, traverse a side slope of up to 40percent , and ford hard-bottom water crossings up to 30in (760mm) deep without a water fording kit and up to 60in (1520mm) deep with the kit. The M1038 is identical to the M998 except that it is fitted with a self-recovery winch. This winch is capable of up to 6,000lb (2,720kg) 1:1 ratio line pull capacity and can support payloads from 2,500 - 4,400lb (1,134-1,996kg) depending on the model. In both cases, the M998A1 and M1038A1 are the models with the latest modifications.

The M1097 is a higher payload capacity version, which is capable of transporting a payload (including crew) of 4,575lb (2,075kg) in the cargo role, or a two-man crew and eight passengers in the troop-carrier role. It has a troop seat kit for personnel transport operations, a 200amp umbilical power cable to power shelter equipment, and stowage racks for ammunition and equipment. To accommodate the higher payload capacity, the vehicle has a reinforced ▶

▶ frame, crossmembers, lifting shackles, heavy duty rear springs, shock absorbers, reinforced control arms, heavy duty tires, and a transfer case and differential with modified gear ratio. The M1097A1 is equipped with the self recovery winch which can also be used to recover like systems and has the latest modifications applied to the vehicle.

The HMMWV is particularly popular with special forces, for whom it provides a highly versatile vehicle, especially as a weapons carrier.

Below: Humm-Vee armed with a Mk19 40mm grenade launcher; new uses are always being found, for this excellent vehicle.

Desert Patrol/Light Strike Vehicle

Country of origin: United States.
Manufacturer: Chenowyth Racing.
Type: high-speed, special forces patrol vehicle.
Weight: gross vehicle weight 2,700lb (1,225kg).
Dimensions: length 13.4ft (4.1m); height 6.6ft (2.0m); width 7.9ft (2.4m).
Engine: Volkswagen gasolene engine; 200hp.
Performance: maximum road speed >60mph (97kmh); acceleration 0-30mph (0-49kmh) in 4sec; range >200 miles (322km); maximum slope 75 percent; maximum side slope 50 percent; ground clearance 16in (41cm); payload 1,500lb (680kg).
Armor: none.
Armament: see text.
Crew: three.

The Desert Patrol Vehicle (DPV), a joint program between the Marine Corps and United States Special Operations Command (USSOCOM), is a modified version of the off-road, three-man, 2 x 4 racing vehicle designed and built by Chenowyth Racing of El Cajon, California. The DPV was designed to provide greater mobility than that of the HMMWV and to operate anywhere a four

Right: The DPV provides low profile, highly mobility firepower and reconnaissance for special forces, particularly in desert conditions.

wheel drive vehicle can, but with greater speed and increased maneuverability. The DPV is air transportable in all but the smallest fixed-wing transport aircraft, the C-130, for example, can carry four, while the CV-22 Osprey, CH-53 Super Stallion and the MH-47D Chinook can each carry two. This high performance vehicle can perform numerous combat roles including: special operations delivery vehicle, rescue downed aircrew, command and control vehicle, weapons platform, rear area combat operation vehicle, reconnaissance vehicle, forward observation/ lasing team, military police vehicle, artillery forward observer vehicle and many more.

The vehicle has three weapons stations , which can accommodate any three from: Mk 19 40mm automatic grenade launcher, 0.50in (12.7mm) M2HB machinegun, M60 7.62 machine gun, AT-4 anti-tank missile, low-recoil 30mm cannon, and TOW missile launcher. Hand-held missile launchers such as Dragon and Stinger can also be carried.

The vehicle is currently operated only by SEAL Team 3, which covers the Middle East theater of operations, and normally deploys them in pairs for mutual support. It will in future be operated more widely, the new vehicles being due to enter service in 2004-05; USSOCOM plans to procure 44, although this may be increased to 50.

BMD-3 Airborne Infantry Fighting Vehicle (AIFV)

Country of origin: Russia.
Manufacturer: State vehicle factories.
Type: airborne infantry fighting vehicle (AIFV).
Weight: gross vehicle weight 12.7tons (12,900kg).
Dimensions: length 19.7ft (6.0m); height 7.4ft (2.25m); width 10.26ft (3.13m).
Engine: diesel; 450bhp.
Performance: maximum road speed 43mph (70kmh); maximum water speed 7mph (10kmh); cruising speed 28mph (45kmh); road range 310 miles (500km); ground pressure, wide track 4.6psi (0.32kg/cm2), standard track 6.8psi (0.48kg/cm2).
Armament: 1 x 30mm AP 2A42 gun; 1 xc 9M111 Konkurs anti-tank guided missile; 1 x 7.62mm MG coaxial; 1 x 5.45mm RPKS-74 MG bow; 1 x 30mm AG-17 grenade launcher.
Crew: two (driver, commander/gunner); six troops.

Two requirements for a parachute-landed force are the ability to move rapidly around the battlefield and to provide their own integral defense against armored counter-attacks. Western armies meet this requirement by converting standard military vehicles (eg, HMMWV) but the Soviet Army developed a series of vehicles specifically for the airborne role. One of the most outstanding of these was the *boevaya mashina desantnya* (BMD), of which the first version, BMD-1,

Below: Soviet-era designers were able to produce many AFVs, such as this BMD-1, which were widely admired in the West.

Above: Russian paratroops exit over the sides of their BMD-1, which was delivered to the training area by parachute.

was seen by Western observers in the 1973 Red Square parade.

This vehicle has subsequently been developed into a variety of versions, the latest of which is the BMD-3, which entered service in 1990 and introduced a host of new features. The most dramatic innovation was that it can be dropped with the full crew inside the vehicle using the PBS-950 parachuting system. This is claimed to be highly reliable, while the fact that the crew is already together cuts out the assembly time when they parachute down individually.

BMD-3 has a very heavy weapons fit, comprising a turret-mounted 30mm 2A42 automatic gun with twin belt feed and a 9P135M Konkurs anti-tank guided missile launcher, with four missiles. In the glacis plate at the front are a 30mm AG-17 grenade launcher (on the driver's left) and a 5.45mm RPKS-74 light machinegun (driver's right), both mounted in ball joints. The BMD-3 has a hull of all-welded aluminum construction and all seats are suspended from the roof (ass opposed to being mounted on the floor) to give the crew protection against mine injuries. The inside is much roomier than earlier versions and the vehicle has full NBC protection using a filter-ventilation unit to overpressurize the combat compartment.

The BMD-3 uses a new power-train, with a new diesel engine giving a considerable improvement in performance over BMD-1 and -2, driving through a new hydromechanical transmission. In addition, there is a new type of hydropneumatic suspension which enable the driver to alter the vehicle's ground clearance between 5in (130mm) and 21in (530mm).

Land Rover Defender/Perentie

Country of origin: United Kingdom.
Manufacturer: Land Rover, Solihull, England.
Type: multi-purpose light combat vehicle.
Weight: Defender 110 6,723lb (3,050kg); Perentie 6x6 LRP 10,670lb (4,840kg)
Dimensions: Defender 110 length 14.4ft (4.4m), width 5.9ft (1.8m), height 6.6ft (2.0m); Perentie length 19.7ft (6.0m); width 7.2ft (2.2m); height 6.0ft (2.0m).
Engine: various, including 2,500cc petrol (4 in-line); 3,500cc petrol (V-8) 2,500cc diesel (4 in-line); Isuzu 3,900c BD1 diesel (4 in-line).
Performance: maximum road speed 55mph (89kmh); road range 350 miles (563.2km).
Armament: various (see text).
Crew: two (depends on role).

Defender 4 x 4

Land Rover multi-purpose light cargo vehicles have been in production since the early 12950s, with military versions being produced in large numbers for many armed forces. The current military model, the Defender, is produced in three

Right: Armored version of the Land Rover Defender in use with the United Nations in former Yugoslavia.

basic versions, designated Defender 90, 100 and 130, respectively. The latest product-improved versions are the Defender 90XD and Defender 110XD (XD = eXtra Duty).

Various Defender models are produced for special forces, the most widely used being the Defender Special Operations vehicles (SOV), which employs a Defender 110 chassis, but with a cut-down superstructure. It can be fitted with a host of small-arms mounts, including those for 30mm cannon, 51mm mortar, LAW80, general purpose machineguns (12.7mm, 7.62mm or 5.56mm) and 40mm grenade launchers. Crew is up to six, including the driver and commander.

The XD range looks from the outside like standard Defenders (the only external differences are wing-mounted air louvers and the rear-lamp clusters), but underneath it is virtually a new vehicle, with redesigned body, suspension, bushes, mountings, chassis and axles, while Goodyear produced a totally new 7.50 x 16 tire. Innovations include longitudinal girders with built-in seat-belt anchorage and beefed-up overhead bars which provide a roll-over cage rather than simply supporting the canopy.

One version, the Defender CAV-100 Armored Patrol Vehicle looks like an ▶

▶ innocuous cargo truck – which is precisely what is intended. In many tactical situations, particularly special forces operations in a non-wartime environment, the media and agitators are quick to see the arrival of tracked or heavy wheeled armored personnel carriers to escalate the situation. The defended APV overcomes this since, although it appears to be non-aggressive, it is, in fact, protected by a new Courtauld-made armor, which uses high-performance glass reinforced composites to give better protection than the equivalent steel armor, but with 20 percent less weight. The windscreen and sidescreens are made of multi-laminate glass with a polycarbonate inner liner.

Perentie 6 X 6

A modified version of the Land Rover 4 x 4, named the Perentie, was developed in Australia. It was generally similar to the British design but with modifications to suit Australian conditions, including a new 4-speed transmission and the Isuzu 3.9 liter, 4-cylinder diesel engine. A further development is the Perentie 6 x 6, which is a unique and somewhat larger and heavier Australian design, with the same Isuzu engine, but this time supercharged. Front suspension is by live axle and coil springs, while the rear bogie employs two leaf springs and a load sharing rocker on each side. Tires are 750R16LT 10-ply on 6Fx16 rims. The long-range patrol/special forces vehicle is open and without doors, and is lighter than the normal Perentie. It is fitted for radio (FFR) and standard fittings include a winch, machinegun mounting and mounts on the rear bulkhead upon which a 250cc motor-cycle can be mounted. Two spare wheels are recessed into the bodywork.

Below: The Special Operations Vehicle, delivered by air-landing or by parachute, carries a wide variety of weapons.

Above: An Australian adaptation for the SASR, the Perentie has 6 x 6 drive, very low profile and heavy armament.

Bell AH-1F HueyCobra, AH-1W SuperCobra, and AH-1Z

Country of origin: United States.
Manufacturer: Bell Helicopter Textron.
Weight: 12,200lb (5,534kg); maximum gross 16,800lb (7,620kg).
Dimensions: length 45.6ft (13.9m); height 13.1ft (4.0m); rotor diameter 48.0ft (14.6m).
Powerplant: 2 General Electric T700-GE-401 rated at 1,725shp (1,286kW).
Performance: maximum airspeed, 190kt (219mph/ 352kmh); maximum range (20 minutes reserve fuel) 350nm (530 miles/854km); endurance 3 hours 3 minutes.
Weapons: maximum weapon load 3,914lb (1,775kg) (see text).
Crew: two (pilot/commander; gunner/co-pilot).
Specifications for AH-1W.

The prototype AH-1 HueyCobra (Bell Model 209) first flew in 1965 as the company-funded HueyCobra. At that time the U.S. Army had just identified an urgent need for an armed helicopter in Vietnam and had set in train a development project that would culminate in the large, complicated and very expensive Lockheed AH-64 Cheyenne. However, since the HueyCobra was immediately available, an order for 110 was placed in April 1966. The Cheyenne

was cancelled in 1972 and because the AH-1 was still the only suitable aircraft available but a very good one it was ordered in ever larger numbers by the Army (1,075 AH-1G), while the Marine Corps developed the twin-engined AH-1T SeaCobra. From this was developed the much more powerful AH-1W SuperCobra, with deliveries starting in 1986. It now serves in large numbers with the Marines, and is also in service with many overseas armed forces.

The original AH-1G retained most of the dynamic components of the UH-1B/C Huey transport, but introduced a new narrow fuselage with stub wings to carry weapons and to help offload the rotor in cruising flight. All models of the attack helicopter had the pilot seated above and behind the co-pilot/gunner who manages the nose sight system and fires the chin turret. The pilot normally fires the wing stores and can also fire the chin turret when it is in its stowed (fore/aft) position, which it reverts to as soon as the gunner releases the slewing switch. The gunner can also fly the aircraft and fire the wing stores in an emergency.

The SuperCobra can carry a wide variety of weapons, the actual mix depending upon the mission, and the oad depending upon fuel carried, range required and ambient conditions. The aircraft carries both TOW and Hellfire anti-armor missiles and is being qualified to carry the Maverick missile. The SuperCobra was the first attack helicopter to qualify to carry and launch both the Sidewinder air-to-air missile and the Sidearm anti-radiation missile, both of which use the same LAU-7 rail launcher. The SuperCobra can also fire a range of rockets, for example 70mm rockets armed with submunition warheads or the larger 127mm Uni rocket bombs. The aircraft carries a three-barrel 20mm Gatling gun with 750 rounds of ammunition for close range (up to 2km) engagements. The Night Targeting System (NT), jointly produced by Tamam Division of Israel Aircraft Industries Ltd. and Kollsman, integrates a Forward Looking Infrared (FLIR) which provides automatic target tracking with a laser designator/rangefinder and video recorder.

The aircraft is powered by twin General Electric T700-GE-401 turboshaft engines providing a total of or 3,380shp (2,410kW). In standard conditions and with an air-to-air missile load the SuperCobra can take off and climb out at more than 13.5ft/sec (4.1m/sec) on only one engine. It can also hover Out-of-Ground ▶

Below: The Bell HueyCobra was developed from the UH-1 Huey as an "interim" gunship in the 1960s; it is still in service.

▶ Effect (OGE) at 3,000ft (914m) with a load of four TOW and four Hellfir missiles, full turret ammunition and rockets.

The "H-1 Program" for the AH-1W is currently in the development phase which, if successful, will lead to a new and even more capable version, the AH-1Z. This will involve the remanufacture of the Marine Corps' entire fleet of AH-1W SuperCobra and UH-1N utility helicopters, one of the most notable features being the replacement of the famous twin-bladed, semi-rigid, teetering rotor by a new and very advanced four bladed, hingeless, bearingless rotor system. First flight of the AH-1Z took place in December 2000 and the flight test program should be completed by summer 2003, following which deliveries to the USMC will begin in 2004. The improvement in flight characteristics provided by the four bladed configuration will lead to significant increases in the flight envelope, maximum speed, vertical rate-of-climb and payload, coupled with dramatic reductions in the rotor vibration level.

In addition to this work, Lockheed Martin is developing a longer range Target Sight System (TSS) for the AH-1Z, which includes a FLIR based on a 3-micron staring array, CCD TV and eyesafe laser rangefinder/designator. Longbow International (a joint venture of Lockheed Martin and Northrop Grumman) is also developing the Cobra Radar System for the AH-1Z, which is based on the Longbow millimetre wave radar on the AH-64D Apache. This will be housed in a pod, which can be mounted on a wingtip or in a stores position and will automatically search, detect, classify and prioritize multiple moving and stationary targets.

The H-1 Program also includes provision of a whole range of new electronic warfare systems. Among these will be new radar warning, missile warning, and laser warning systems. Other enhancements will include a new infrared countermeasures system, and a chaff and infrared flare dispenser.

The story of the AH-1 is very similar to that of two other U.S. stalwarts, the

Below: U.S. Marine Corps AH-1W SuperCobra is powered by two GE turbojets giving a top speed of 219mph (352km/h).

Above: U.S. Army AH-1S is similar to AH-1W but with one engine and a plate-glass (as opposed to molded) canopy.

B-52 bomber and the Minuteman missile, in that it was designed in the 1950s but has proved so adaptable that it can be redesigned and improved at regular intervals, enabling it to remain at the forefront of military technology and operational effectiveness for more than half a century. Also like those other two systems, the AH-1 has been criticized from time-to-time for complexity and expense, but it has, in fact, proved to be exceptionally cost-effective and remains in front-line service long after many of its competitors have been forgotten and its critics have fallen silent.

Boeing AH-6J, MH-6J, A/MH-6 "Little Bird"

Manufacturer: Boeing (formerly McDonnell-Douglas; formerly Hughes).
Dimensions: rotors turning, length 30.8ft (9.4m), fuselage 24.9ft (7.6m); height 8.5ft (2.6m); fuselage width6.2ft (1.9m); rotor diameter 26.3ft (8m).
Weight: maximum gross 3,000lb (1,361 kg); normal takeoff 2,403lb(1,090kg); empty 1,875lb (896kg).
Powerplant: Rolls-Royce/Allison 250-C30 turboshaft, 425shp.
Performance: maximum level speed, 150mph (241kmh); range with normal load 300 miles (485km); hover out-of-ground effect 6,000ft (1,830m); endurance 2h 30m; vertical climb rate 27ft/sec (8.4m/s)
Payload: external load 1,216lb (550 kg); 2/3 troops internally, or 6 on external platforms in lieu of weapons.
Weapons: see text below.
Crew: two (pilot/commander; observer/co-pilot).
Specifications for AH-6J Light Attack Helicopter.

A highly modified version of the McDonnell Douglas 530 series commercial helicopter, the AH-6J is a gas-turbine engined, dual-control, light attack helicopter, which is primarily employed in close air support of ground troops and special forces, target-destruction raids, and armed escort of other aircraft. The AH-6J is usually (but not always) flown by two pilots on most overland flights, but the two pilots become mandatory for overwater operations.

The AH-6J is capable of mounting a variety of weapons systems, including: the M134 7.62mm Minigun (a six-barrel, air-cooled, Gatling-type weapon), M261 seven-round and M260 19-round rocket launchers for 2.75in FFAR rockets; AGM-114 Hellfire anti-tank missiles (maximum of four); and the .5in (12.7mm) machine gun. However, the normal aircraft configuration consists of two 7.62mm Miniguns with 1,500 to 2,000 rounds per ▶

Right: The MH-6 is unusual in carrying its passengers sitting outside the aircraft.

▶ gun, and two seven-round 2.75in (70mm) rocket pods.

The MH-6J is basically identical to the AH-6J, but is modified to transport up to eight people, the two crew plus six combat troops sitting on the sills facing outwards with their feet on the skids. In this configuration it is capable of conducting overt and covert infiltrations, exfiltrations, and combat assaults over a wide variety of terrain and environmental conditions. It is also used for command-and-control and reconnaissance missions. The aircraft can be rapidly configured for fast-rope and STABO operations, while special racks can be fitted to enable two motorcycles to be carried. Some aircraft are equipped with Forward Looking Infrared Radar (FLIR), a passive system that provides an infrared image of terrain features and ground or airborne objects of interest. Each aircraft is equipped with the AN/APR-39 Radar Warning Receiver (RWR) system, which detects and identifies hostile search/acquisition and fire control radars, and provides audio and video alerts to the flight crew.

One particular advantage of the AH-60/MH-60's very small size, is that it can easily be deployed by any U.S. Air Force transport aircraft. A C-141 is capable of transporting up to six MH-6s and a C-130 is able to transport up to three MH-6s, with a rapid upload/offload capability. On arrival at the destination MH-6s can be offloaded, restored to flight configuration, fueled and take-off within 15 minutes. Self-deployment is unlimited, provided refueling facilities are available at a maximum of 270nm (410 miles/660km) intervals.

The A/MH-6 MELB (Mission Enhancement Little Bird) is a variant of the AH-6J optimized for support of short-range operations in hostile areas. Among its roles are fire support and personnel recovery missions and it includes the necessary equipment for shipboard operations. Production began in FY 2000, and a total of 40 MELBs have been built. It has an upgraded six-bladed main and four-bladed tail rotor system;

Right: The passengers on this MH-6 Little Bird appear to be very casual and relaxed.

Boeing CH-47D Chinook

Manufacturer: Boeing Vertol.
Type: medium-lift transport helicopter.
Weight: empty 22,379lb (10,151kg); normally take-off 46,000lb (20,866kg); maximum take-off 50,000lb (22,679kg).
Dimensions: length, fuselage 51.0ft (15.4m), rotors turning 98.9ft (30.1m) rotor diameter (each) 60.0ft (18.3m); height 18.9ft (5.8m).
Powerplant: two Textron Lycoming T-55-L- 712, each 3,750shp (2,796kW) for take-off, 3,000shp (2,237kW) continuous.
Performance: maximum speed at sea-level 161kt (186mph/298kmh); cruising speed at optimum altitude 138kt (159mph/256kmh); maximum operational radius 100miles (115km); ferry range 1,093nm (1,259 miles/ 2,028km).
Payload: 55 troops, or 24 litters, or 22,798lb (10,341kg) externally, or 13,907lb (6,308kg) internally.
Crew: three (pilot, copilot, loadmaster).

The CH-47 Chinook is another of those great designs which seem to get everything just about right first time and is then capable of being continuously developed and refined over a long period of service in this case 40 years, with another 20, at the very least, to go. The design was an enlarged and improved version of the Vertol CH-46, and the prototype CH-47A (then designated YHC-1B) flew in September 1961. Since then well over a thousand have been built and in 2002 most of those are still in frontline service with many armies and air forces, both in the United States and abroad. The most significant feature of the design was to base it on a long unobstructed cabin with a large ramp at the after end, making it ideal for use by troops, vehicles, light guns and cargo. This was achieved by mounting both rotors and engines above the fuselage, and by fitting sponsons outside the cabin to carry the undercarriage, fuel tanks and other services. The twin rotors are connected by a transfer shaft, so that if one engine has problems the other can power both rotors for a safe landing.

The CH-47 has served in the U.S. armed forces in two main versions, mainly as a medium-lift transport. The Army bought 354 CH-47As, followed by 108 CH-47Bs, which had more powerful engines and increased diameter rotor blades. The CH-47C had even more powerful engines, but also included a number of other significant improvements such as increased fuel tankage; 270 were delivered to the Army, most of which were later refitted with composite rotor blades. Meanwhile, large numbers were being sold to foreign customers and some of the enhancements they had requested were fed back into the U.S. program, resulting in the CH-47D, which entered service with the Army in May 1982. The Army's CH-47D fleet is a mix of upgraded earlier models plus some new-build. The enhancements include engines with better battle survivability, night-vision compatible flightdeck, triple (instead of single) cargo hooks and a pressurized system, for faster and safer refueling.

The MH-47D and E are heavy assault helicopters based on the CH-47 airframe, but optimized for special operations see following entry.

The CH-47 has been constantly in combat in virtually every campaign undertaken by the Army starting with deployment to Vietnam in the mid-1960s. As just one example, one air assault by the 101st Airborne Division's 2nd Infantry Brigade, involved 5,000 soldiers, 126 UH-60 Blackhawks and 60 CH-47D Chinooks, and during the first day alone the latter lifted 131,000 gallons (c. 500,000 liters) of fuel together with large quantities of ammunition. In the Bosnia peacekeeping operations in the 1990s, over a six month period, a CH-47D aviation company with 16 aircraft flew 2,222 hours, carried 3,348 passengers, and transported over 3,200,000lb (1,452,000kg) of cargo.

The Improved Cargo Helicopter (ICH) program is intended to extend the life of the present CH-47D airframes to 2025-2030, giving them the extraordinary service life of 60 years. This will involve the total remanufacture of the aircraft, one major aim being to reduce vibration, which is a major cause of reliability problems and thus of maintenance costs. There will also be a new cockpit and new digital command and communications systems. The ICH will be capable of carrying 16,000lb (4,900kg) of either external or internal cargo. The first ICH is due to be fielded in 2003-04, with a total of 300 being achieved by 2015. The remaining 131 CH-47Ds will not be modernized. A separate program involves upgrading the engine to the more powerful T-55-714 standard, which offers improvements in hot/high conditions. The ICH and the enhanced engine are intended to keep the Army's CH-47 fleet fully serviceable and up-to-date until the Joint Transport Rotorcraft (JTR) begins to enter service in the 2020-2030 timeframe.

Below: In its transport role, the CH-47 has proved capable of shifting large and awkward loads over long distances.

MH-47D/E Chinook

Manufacturer: Boeing.
Type: special operations medium-lift helicopter.
Weight: maximum take-off 54,000lb (24,490kg).
Dimensions: length rotors turning, 99ft (30m); width blades folded 12.4ft (3.8m); maximum height 18.9ft (5.76m).
Powerplant: two AlliedSignal T55-L741s turboshafts, each 4,867shp max.
Performance: maximum speed, 145knots (168mph/270kmh); service ceiling, 10,150ft (3,094m); self-deployment range 1,260nm (1,456miles/2,342km).
Payload: 33 to 55 troops or 24 litters and 2 attendants.
Armament: 2-4 machine guns (see text).
Crew: two pilots plus provision for combat commander,

The MH-47 is a twin engine, tandem rotor, heavy assault helicopter based on the CH-47 airframe, and conducts overt and covert infiltrations, exfiltrations, air assault, resupply, and sling operations over a wide range of environmental conditions. The aircraft can perform a variety of other missions including shipboard operations, platform operations, urban operations, water operations, parachute operations, FARP operations, mass casualty, and combat search and rescue operations. The MH-47 is capable of operating at night during marginal weather conditions. With the use of special mission equipment and night vision devices, the air crew can operate in hostile mission environments over all types of terrain at low altitudes during periods of low visibility and low ambient lighting conditions with pinpoint navigation accuracy of plus/minus 30 seconds on target. MH-47s can be transported in C-5 and C-17 transport aircraft (two in each), or can self-deploy over extended distances using ground or aerial refuel. The 160th SOAR(A) currently operates two models: the MH-47D Adverse Weather Cockpit (AWC), operated by 3/160; and the MH-47E, by 2/160.

The MH-47D Adverse Weather Cockpit (AWC) is a specifically modified for long range flights. It is equipped with weather avoidance/search radar; an aerial refueling probe for in flight refueling; a personnel locator system (PLS) used in conjunction with the PRC-112 for finding downed aircrews; FLIR; a navigation system consisting of a mission computer utilizing GPS/INS/Doppler navigation sources; secure voice communications, including FM, UHF with Have Quick II, VHF, HF, Saber and SATCOM radios; a Fast-Rope Insertion/Extraction System (FRIES) for insertion of

Below: U.S. Army Rangers drive off the ramp of an MH-47.

Right: Army MH-47Es are modified CH-47Ds with enhanced range, special avionics and in-flight refuelling capability.

personnel/equipment and extraction of personnel; a defensive armament system consisting of two M-134 machine guns (left forward cabin window, right cabin door) and one M-60D machine gun located on the ramp; and an internal rescue hoist with a 600lb capacity.

The MH-47E has been specifically designed and built for the special operations aviation mission. It has a totally integrated avionics subsystem which combines a redundant avionics architecture with dual mission processors, remote terminal units, multifunction displays and display generators, to improve combat survivability and mission reliability; an aerial refueling (A/R) probe for inflight refueling; external rescue hoist; and two L714 turbine engines with Full Authority Digital Electronic Control (FADEC) which provides more power during hot/high environmental conditions. Two integral aircraft fuel tanks replace the internal auxiliary fuel tanks commonly carried on the MH-47D AWC, providing 2,068 gallons of fuel with no reduction in cargo capacity.

MH-47D/E standard mission equipment includes:

- Aircraft communications equipment consisting of FM, UHF (with HAVE QUICK II capability), VHF, HF, SATCOM, and the Motorola Saber. The MH-47E is equipped with SINCGARS VHF-FM single channel ground and airborne radio system.
- Automatic Target Hand-off System (ATHS) providing the capability of data bursting pre-selected/ formatted information to other equipped aircraft or ground stations.
- A navigation system consisting of a mission computer utilizing GPS/INS/Doppler navigation sources for pinpoint navigation.
- Weapons systems, in three weapons stations: left forward window, right cabin door, and at the ramp. The forward stations mount a 7.62mm minigun and the ramp station mounts an M60D 7.62mm machine gun. A crew member at each station manually operates the weapon. The weapons are used primarily for self-defense and enemy suppression.

MH-47D/E mission-flexible equipment includes:

- FLIR: AN/AAQ-16.
- Map display generator (MDG) (MH-47E only): when used with the data transfer module (DTM) it displays aeronautical charts, photos, or digitized maps in the Plan and 3D modes of operation.
- Cargo compartment expanded range fuel system (CCERFS), consisting of one and up to three ballistic-tolerant, self-sealing tanks. Each tank holds 780 gallons of fuel. They are refillable during aerial refuel operations.
- Forward area refueling equipment, (FARE), consisting of fueling pumps, hoses, nozzles, and additional refueling equipment to set up a two-point refueling site. Amount of fuel dispensed is dependent upon range of operation required of the tanker aircraft.

Twenty-five MH-47Es are fielded by Army SOF, and planned upgrades include aircraft systems modifications, avionics system upgrades, and aircraft survivability enhancements.

Boeing (McDonnell Douglas) AH-64 Apache and Longbow

Country of origin: United States.
Type: attack helicopter.
Manufacturer: Boeing (McDonnell Douglas).
Weight: weight empty 11,015lb (4,996kg); primary mission gross weight 14,694lb(6,665kg); maximum take-off 17,650lb (8,006kg).
Dimensions: length 48.1ft (14.7m); height 16.8ft (5.1m); rotor diameter 48.0ft (14.6m).
Powerplant: two General Electric T700-GE-701 turboshafts, each 1,696shp (1,265kW).
Performance: maximum airspeed, 197kt (365kmh); cruising158kt (293kmh); hover ceiling (IGE) 13,400ft (4,084m), (OGE) 10,200ft (3,109m); maximum range (internal fuel) 428nm (689km); g limits +3.5 to -0.5.
Weapons: (see text).
Crew: two crew: pilot and copilot/gunner
Specifications for U.S. Army AH-64D.

Helicopters entered military service in the mid-1940s but were initially employed in the transport and casualty evacuation roles and it was not until the mid-1950s that the need for an armed helicopter was fully recognized. The U.S

Above: The latest AH-64D Apache Longbow is now in service with the U.S., British and Dutch armies.

Below: The "pancake" radome atop the rotor mast is the major recognition feature of the Longbow Apache.

Army's first attempt to develop such an aircraft – the Lockheed AH-56 Cheyenne – turned into a very expensive failure, partly because it was large and extremely complicated, but also because it was far ahead of its time and stretched the technology of the day way beyond its limits. As a result, the Army turned to the AH-1 Hueycobra, a modified version of the UH-1 transport helicopter, as an interim measure, but the requirement remained for a specialized attack helicopter which could fly all types of front-line missions, by day or night and in all weathers. So, a new project was started in 1972 with Bell and Hughes submitting designs, and the latter company's was declared the winner in December 1976, although production was not authorized until 1982. Hughes was subsequently taken over by McDonnell Douglas and that company has, in its turn, been bought by Boeing. Today, the U.S. Army has more than 800 Apaches in service and over 1,000 have been exported to many countries around the world. The Apache was first used in combat in 1989 in the U.S. military action in Panama and later in the Gulf War. It has also supported low-intensity and peacekeeping operations world-wide, including in northern Iraq, Bosnia and Kosovo.

The U.S. Army version of the AH-64 is powered by two General Electric T700-GE-701C gas-turbine engines, rated at 1,890shp each, enabling the aircraft to cruise at a speed of ▶

▶ 145mph (233kmh), with a flight endurance in excess of three hours. Combat radius is approximately 93 statute miles (150km), but the addition of a single external 230gal (870) fuel tank enables this to be extended to some 186 miles (300km), although this is dependent upon a number of factors, including weather, temperature, and payload. Ferry range on internal fuel is 430 miles (690km), but this can be considerably extended by the addition of up to four 230gal (870) external tanks. The AH-64 is air transportable in the C-5, C-141 and C-17.

The AH-64D Longbow Apache is equipped with the Northrop Grumman millimeter-wave Longbow radar, which incorporates an integrated radar frequency interferometer for passive location and identification of radar emitting threats. This operates in the millimeter band which ensures not only that it is unaffected by poor visibility or ground clutter, but also, because of its very narrow beamwidth, that it is also resistant to countermeasures. The AH-64D's primary weapon system is the Lockheed Martin/Boeing AGM-114D Longbow Hellfire air-to-surface missile which has a millimeter-wave seeker to allow the missile to perform in full fire-and-forget mode. Range is 5-7.5miles (8

Above: Two early versions of the AH-64 Apache, clearly showing the chin-mounted gun.

Left: Also an early model AH-64 Apache, showing the weaponry carried on the stub wings.

12km). The Apache can also be armed with air-to-air missiles (Stinger, Sidewinder, Mistral and Sidearm) and 2.75in rockets. The Longbow Apache carries the combination of armaments necessary for the particular mission and in the close support role a typical loadout would be sixteen Hellfire missiles on four 4-rail launchers and four air-to-air missiles. A 30mm automatic Boeing M230 Chain Gun is located under the fuselage. It provides a rate of fire of 625 rounds per minute and the helicopter can carry up to 1,200 rounds of ammunition.

The Longbow Apache can effect an attack in thirty seconds. The radar dome is unmasked for a single radar scan and then remasked. The processors determine the location, speed and direction of travel of a maximum of 256 targets. The Target Acquisition Designation Sight, TADS (AN/ASQ-170) and the Pilot Night Vision Sensor, PNVS (AN/AAQ-11) were developed by Lockheed Martin. The turret-mounted TADS provides direct view optics, television and three fields of view forward looking infra-red (FLIR) to carry out search, detection and recognition and Litton laser rangefinder/designator. PNVS consists of a FLIR in a rotating turret located on the nose above the TADS. The image from the PNVS is displayed in the monocular eyepiece of the Honeywell integrated Helmet And Display Sighting System, HADDS, worn by the pilot and copilot/gunner.

The Apache is equipped with an electronic warfare suite consisting of:
- AN/APR-39A(V) radar warning receiver from Litton and Lockheed Martin;
- AN/ALQ-144 infra-red countermeasures set from BAE Systems (formerly Sanders, a Lockheed Martin company); AN/AVR-2 laser warning receiver from Raytheon (formerly Hughes Danbury Optical Systems); AN/ALQ-136(V) radar jammer developed by ITT; and chaff dispensers.

Eurocopter AS.532 Cougar

Country of origin: France.
Manufacturer: Eurocopter.
Type: medium-lift transport helicopter.
Weight: empty 9.546lb (4,330kg); normal take-off with maximum internal load 19,841lb (9,000kg); maximum take-off with external load 20,615lb (9,350kg).
Dimensions: length, fuselage including tail rotor 51.0ft (15.5m), length rotors turning 61.3ft (18.7m) rotor diameter (each) 60.0ft (18.3m); height 16.1ft (4.9m); rotor diameter 51.2ft (15.6m).
Powerplant: two Turbomeca Makila 1A1 each rated at 1,877shp (1,400kW).
Performance: maximum level speed at sea-level 150kt (173mph/278kmh); cruising speed at sea level 141kt (163mph/262kmh); range 334nm (384miles/618km); endurance 3hours 20 minutes.
Crew: crew two (pilot, copilot); troops 21.
Specifications for AS.532UC.

The Eurocopter AS.532 Cougar is a development of the SA.330 Puma which entered service in the early 1960s. The French Army was one of the first to use troop-carrying helicopters as an integral part of an attack force, a technique that had been developed in the war in the Algeria (1956-63), using mainly Sikorsky S-55 and S-58 helicopters. As a result, the Army produced a requirement which more closely reflected their needs, leading to the Sud Aviation SA.330 Puma being placed in production in both France and the UK. This was a successful design which was sold to many countries and many examples are still flying.

Sud Aviation was then absorbed into a new company, Aerospatiale, and in the early 1970s a developed version of this helicopter appeared, designated the AS.332 Super Puma. A dozen versions of the type are now available, with some 100 of the civil version in service, while some 200 military variants, (re-designated Cougar in 1990), are operational with 37 armies and air forces, many of which use them for special forces operations. The military versions now in service are the AS.332 Cougar Mk1 and AS.532 Cougar Mk2, and most of these are produced as either transports (prefix "U") or armed versions "prefix "A").

AS.532 Cougar UC/AC
The Cougar UC carries 21 troops and can be fitted with various items of additional equipment such as radar/missile detectors and decoy-launchers, while crashworthy passenger seats are also an option. The Cougar AC is the armed version which is fitted with side-mounted machine-guns and external armament pods containing either 20mm guns or 68mm rocket-launchers. Both versions can carry an underslung load of 4.5 tonnes.

AS.532 Cougar UL/AL
The Cougar UL/AL is virtually identical to

the UC/AC version but with a longer fuselage which increases carrying capacity to 25 troops or 6 stretchers and 10 "walking wounded." A specialist version of this model is the AS.532 UL HORIZON, of which six are in service with the French Army; this is the platform for the Horizon (*Hélicoptère d'Observation Radar et d'Investigation sur ZONe*) battlefield ground surveillance system. As withe AC, the AL is an armed version of the UL, with side-mounted machine guns and external armament pods containing either 20mm guns or 68mm rocket-launchers. Both versions can carry an underslung load of 4.5 tonnes.

AS.532 Cougar Mk2 U2/A2
This is the latest Mk 2 version of the Cougar with more powerful Makila M1A2 engines and a lengthened fuselage, which increases carrying capacity to 29 troops or 12 stretchers. Many of the systems have also been simplified with the aim of maintaining efficiency but reducing costs; this, the undercarriage is now fixed (reducing cruising speed by some 8kt) and the fuel system has been greatly improved. Again, an armed version is available.

Other versions
Other versions include the AS.532 Cougar UE, which is the basic version with long fuselage of the military Cougar MK1 range, and the Cougar AS.532 SC, which is the navalized version for shipboard use.

Below: Cougars of the French Army, which has used these helicopters on many special forces' operations.

Mil Mi-24

Country of origin: Russia.
Manufacturer: Mil, Russia.
Type: attack helicopter.
Weight: empty 18,740lb (8,500kg); normal take-off with maximum internal load 24,470lb (11,100kg); maximum take-off 27,557lb (12,500kg).
Dimensions: length, fuselage 57.4ft (17.5m), length overall, rotors turning 70/9ft (21.6m); wingspan 21.3ft (6.5m); rotor diameter 60.0ft (18.3m); height 13.9ft (4.2m); rotor diameter 56.8ft (17.3m).
Powerplant: 2 Klimov (Isotov) TV3-117 turbines, each 2,200shp (1,640kW).
Performance: maximum level speed, clean, at optimum altitude 168kt (192mph/310km/h); cruising speed at optimum altitude 140kt (162mph/260kmh); range, normal 405nm (466 miles/759km); combat radius, normal fuel 86nm (99 miles/160km), with auxiliary fuel tanks 135nm (155 miles/250km); service ceiling 14,763ft (4,500m); hover out-of-ground-effect (OGE) 4,921ft (1,500m), inside-ground-effect (IGE) 7,218ft (2,200m); vertical climb rate 50ft/sec (15m/sec).
Payload: internal load 8 combat troops or 4 litters; external weapons 3,307lb (1,500kg); external (no weapons) 5,511lb (2,500kg).
Armament: 1 x 4-barrel 12.7mm Gatling-type machine gun (turret-mounted); 57mm rockets; AT-2C (Swatter) ATGMs.
Crew: crew two (pilot/commander, gunner/observer/copilot).
Specifications for Mil Mi-24D.

The original Mil Mi-24 (NATO = Hind-A, -B, -C) helicopters were developed by the Soviet Air Force as flying armored personnel carriers and were created essentially by adding a new two-man cockpit to the engines, dynamic components and eight-man troop-carrying cabin of the very successful Mil Mi-8 (Hip), with the addition of stub wings which carried rocket and guided missile

Below: Civilian markings disguise a Russian Interior Ministry Mi-24PS used to deploy SWAT teams in assault operations.

Above: A recent version is the Mil Mi-24P, in which the chin 12.7mm MG is replaced by a single twin-barrel 30mm cannon.

launchers. The prototype flew in 1970 and it was produced in some numbers in three closely related versions. The growing importance of the anti-tank role, however, led to a major redesign, resulting in the Mil-24D (Hind-D), which rapidly became one of the most influential battlefield aircraft of the 1980s and 1990s. It was deployed throughout the Warsaw Pact and also became the most notorious aircraft of the Afghanistan War. It has many of the characteristics of its contemporary, the AH-64 Apache, but with the added capability of being able to transport eight troops, if required.

The Hind-D has tandem bubble canopies for the pilot and gunner, with a 12.7mm YaKB machine gun in a chin-mounted turret and six hardpoints, three under each wing. A considerable variety of stores can be carried, but a typical load would be eight AT-6 ATGMs, and two 57mm rocket pods. Extra ammunition can be carried in the cargo compartment. There is considerable emphasis on survivability: all aircraft have an over-pressurization system for NBC operations, and both the armored cockpits and rotor head are constructed of titanium and are intended to withstand 20mm cannon hits.

The stub wings provide some 25 percent the total lift in forward flight, although there is a problem in that in a low-speed, steeply banked turn, the inner wing can lose its lift, but not the outer wing, which leads to excessive roll. This has to be countered by increasing airspeed, and this, coupled with the Hind's size and weight, reduce its maneuverability, which results in them normally being operated in pairs, for mutual protection.

Virtually all of the earlier Hind-A, -B and -C variants have been scrapped, or upgraded/modified to the Hind-D (export = Mi-25) or -E (export = Hind-35) standards. The other major service version is the Mi-24P (Hind-F) which has an increased all-up weight of 26,455lb (12,000kg); export version of this model is designated Mi-35P. Two versions in service in small numbers are the Mi-24RCh (Hind G-1), which carries out NBC sampling and Mi-24K (Hind G-2) for photo-reconnaissance and artillery spotting.

Sikorsky CH-53E Super Stallion

Country of origin: United States.
Manufacturer: Sikorsky Aircraft Division of United Technologies Corp.
Type: heavy transport helicopter.
Weight: empty 33,338lb ((15,072kg); maximum takeoff 69,750lb (31,640kg).
Dimensions: length fuselage 67.5ft (20.3m); length, rotors turning 88.3ft (26.5m); height 24.9ft (7.2m); main rotor diameter 72.3ft (21.7m).
Powerplant: three General Electric T64-GE-416 turboshafts, each 4,300shp (3,266kW).
Performance: speed 160kt (184mph/294kmh); ceiling 12,450ft (3,795m); range 578nm (665 miles/1,064km); ferry range 886nm (1,338 miles/2,153km).
Payload: 37 troops, or 24 litter patients plus four attendants, or 8,000lb (3,600kg) cargo.
Crew: three (two pilots, one aircrewman).
Specifications for CH-53E.

The CH-53D Sea Stallion, which entered service with the U.S. Marine Corps in the mid-1960s, is a heavy-lift helicopter, powered by two General Electric T64 turboshafts. It is capable of lifting 7 tons (6.4 metric tonnes), or 37 passengers in its normal configuration and 55 passengers with centerline seats installed. There are currently 54 in active units and 18 with reserve units, and the fleet has been regularly upgraded , recent improvements including an elastomeric rotor head, external fuel tanks, crashworthy fuel cells, new radios, and defensive electronic countermeasure (ECM) equipment.

By the mid-1970s the Marine Corps required much greater lifting power, but from an aircraft that was still able to operate from its amphibious platforms. Rather than produce a new design, Sikorsky devised the much simpler solution of fitting a third engine to the existing airframe, which solved the problem very satisfactorily, resulting the CH-53E Super Stallion. The CH-53E entered service in 1981 and since then has been the Corps' heavy lift helicopter, operating from LHAs (Landing-ship, Helicopter, Assault), LPHs (Landing Platform, Helicopter) and now LHDs (Landing-ship, Helicopter, Dock). The helicopter lifts 16 tons (14.5 metric tons) at sea level, transporting the load 50 nautical miles (57.5 miles) and returning. Among the heavier loads routinely carried are Light

Armored Vehicles (LAVs) which weigh 26,000lb (11,804kg). The aircraft has an endurance of 4 hours 30 minutes, but is equipped with a refueling probe enabling it to refuel in flight. There are 160 in service.

In just one example of its capabilities, during Operation Eastern Exit in January 1990, two CH-53Es flew from their ship standing offshore to Mogadishu, capital of Somalia, where they landed at the American Embassy to rescue American and foreign diplomats. Each leg, outward and return, was some 460nm (532 miles/856km) long. The entire operation took place under cover of darkness and involved two air-to-air refueling for each aircraft. It was entirely successful.

There are various ongoing programs to increase service life, enhance reliability and reduce maintenance, and thus cut the operating costs until the CH-53E is replaced, which is currently intended to start in 2015. Such a Service Life Extension Program (SLEP) could be applied to both CH-53Es and CH-53Ds.

Below: Marines emplane aboard a Marine Corps CH-53, a type which has served the Corps well for some 40 years.

Sikorsky MH-53J/M Pave Low

Country of origin: United States.
Manufacturer: Sikorsky Aircraft Division of United Technologies Corp.
Type: long-range Special Operations Forces helicopter.
Weight: empty 23,569lb (10,691kg); maximum take-off 42,000lb (19,050kg); war emergency 50,000lb (22,680kg).
Dimensions: length fuselage 67.5ft (20.3m); length, rotors turning 88.3ft (26.5m); height 24.9ft (7.2m); main rotor diameter 72.3ft (21.7m).
Powerplant: two General Electric T64-GE-100 turboshafts, each 3,936shp (2,935kW).
Performance: maximum speed, clean, sea-level 170kt (196mph/315kmh); cruising speed at optimum attitude 150kt (173mph/278kmh); service ceiling 20,400ft (6,220m); hover ceiling IGE 11,700ft (3,565m); range on internal fuel 468nm (540 miles/868km).
Armament: maximum of three 7.62mm miniguns or 0.5in machine guns.

Payload: 38 troops or 14 litters; external 20,000lb (9,000kg) cargo hook.
Crew: six (pilot/captain, copilot, two flight engineers, two gunners).

The most powerful helicopters flown by the U.S. Air Force in the Vietnam War were the CH-53 heavy transports and HH-53 combat rescue helicopters, the latter being universally known by their radio callsign as "Jolly Greens." In 1969 an HH-53B was fitted with a low-light TV system to give it some night-flying capability; designated Pave Low I, this was followed by the more ambitious Pave Low II, which led into the definitive Pave Low III. After trial installations in two aircraft, a total of nine CH-53Cs were converted into HH-53H Pave Low III aircraft. But then a special forces commitment was added together with yet ▶

Below: SEALs embark aboard Air Force MH-53 Pave Low on a warship flightdeck; note refuelling probe and nose radar.

▶ more new equipment, as a result of which the nine MH-53Hs and 32 other HH- and CH53s were modified and designated MH-53J. The modifications include improved Pave Low avionics, satellite communications and structural improvements and all were also adapted for shipboard operations, with automatic folding for the main rotor blades and tail rotor pylon. The MH-53J is also equipped with armor plating and has three gun positions, all of which can mount either 7.62mm miniguns or .50in machineguns.

The MH-53M Pave Low IV is a modified MH-53J that has been fitted with the Interactive Defensive Avionics System/Multi-Mission Advanced Tactical Terminal (IDAS/MATT), which enhances the aircraft's defensive capabilities, providing instant access to the total battlefield situation, through near real-time Electronic Order of Battle updates. It also provides improved threat avoidance and the ability FLIR airborne route re-planning, where necessary.

The primary mission of the MH-53J/M is to conduct covert, low-level, long-range undetected penetration into denied areas, by day or night, in adverse weather. The tasks include infiltration, exfiltration, or resupply of Special

Operations Forces, such missions being conducted by airdrop, airlanding, or using the heavy-lift sling. Six of the older MH-53Js are being de-modified to TH-53Bs exclusively for use in training.

MH-53Js have flown in a host of U.S. military operations over the past twenty years, including Operation Just Cause (Panama, 1989), Desert Storm (Gulf, 1990), Provide Comfort and Southern Watch (Gulf, 1992) and Provide Promise and Dony Flight (Balkans, 1992 onwards). In 1997 MH-53Js airlifted Americans out of Zaire and Albania, and in 1998 they returned to Saudi Arabia in support of the buildup to convince Iraq to comply with U.N. weapons inspections.

The current Air Force inventory comprises thirteen MH-53Js and twenty-five MH-53Ms, all in the active force. There are none of either type in either the Air National Guard or the Air Force Reserve.

Below: MH-53 under guard during Operation Sustain Hope, which brought relief to thousands of Kosovar refugees.

Sikorsky UH-60/S-70 family

Country of origin: United States.
Manufacturer: Sikorsky Aircraft Corporation.
Type: multi-role combat utility helicopter.
Weight: empty 13,648lb (6,191kg); ASW mission takeoff 20,244lb (9,182kg); maximum take-off (utility role) 21,88lb (9,926kg).
Dimensions: length: 64.8ft (19.6m); height 11.9ft (3.6m); rotor diameter 53.7ft (16.4 m).
Powerplant: two General Electric T700-GE-700 or T700-GE-701C engines 1,690shp (1,260kW).
Performance: maximum speed at 5,000ft (1,525m) 126kt (145mph/234kmh); operational radius 50nm (57.5miles/92.5km) for 3 hour loiter, or 150nm (173 miles/ 278km) for 1 hour loiter.
Ordnance: three Mk46 or Mk 50 torpedoes, plus .50-caliber machine guns in doorways.
Crew: four.

The Sikorsky S-70 was developed to meet an U.S. Army-Navy requirement fo a medium-lift helicopter for missions such as utility transport and ship-based ASW. It has since been produced in large numbers and in an ever-increasing variety of sub-types to meet new or changing requirements. This extremely versatile aircraft is now used by the U.S. Navy, Army, Air Force and Coast Guard (and also by many foreign armed forces) for a wide variety of duties, including anti-submarine warfare, search-and-rescue, drug interdiction, anti-ship warfare troop transport, Presidential transport, cargo lift, and special operations.

The original version for the U.S. Army was the transport/utility UH-60A Black Hawk, which was followed in production by the UH-60L, with an uprated powertrain; 1,463 of both types were ordered. The SH-60B Sea Hawk was the Navy's version, which shared some 83 percent of the parts of the UH-60A, intended for ASW duties aboard destroyers and frigates, 260 were ordered. The EH-60C was a specialized electronic warfare aircraft for the Army; 66 built. The Air Force entered the program with the proposed HH-60D Night Hawk, an extremely well-equipped version for combat rescue and special operations forces, particularly at night and in bad weather; one UH-60A was converted, but the project proceeded no further. Air Force attention then switched to a much less sophisticated version, the HH-60E, but this, too, was abandoned and the Air Force finally procured 98 HH/MH-60G Pave Hawk (see next entry) Meanwhile, the Navy developed another version, the SH-60F Ocean Hawk intended to provide inner zone ASW protection for carriers. Next in the series were the HH-60H Rescue Hawk and the very similar HH-60JJayhawk, which were for the Navy and Coast Guard, respectively; both were for combat rescue and covert operations, and both designs were closely based on that of the SH-60F. The MH-60K is a special operations forces version for the Army, and the UH-60L, which has already been referred to, is an uprated UH-60A. The UH-60M was cancelled and the UH-60N is a special model for the Marine Corps' Presidential Flight; nine were built. The latest model is the SH-60R for the Navy, which is a common standard for upgraded and modernized SH-60Bs and SH-60Fs.

The Navy's SH-60B Seahawk was developed as an airborne platform to be based aboard cruisers, destroyers, and frigates, which would deploy sonobouys to detect submarines and then launch

Above: Troops emplane aboard UH-60s, a type which has proved a great success with many users around the world.

torpedoes to destroy them. Another ASW version, the SH-60F Ocean Hawk, was developed to operate from carriers to provide inner zone ASW protection, but also to serve as "plane guard" and general utility transport for the carrier.

This difference between the SH-60B, SH-60F and HH-60H has proved something of a limitation in deployment and the survivors of all three types are now being upgraded to a new common standard, designated SH-60R. The package, formally known as the "SH-60(R) Multi-Mission Helicopter Upgrade" will extend all the helicopters, lives to 20,000 flight hours and will thus give the Navy a multi-mission platform for both anti-submarine and anti-surface warfare for the coming twenty-five years. The SH-60R's systems will cope with high numbers of contacts, both air and sea, in confined and shallow waters. It will be capable of operating with either a carrier group, or a surface action group, for which it will be equipped with a new multimode radar, FLIR sensor, ESM system and a retrievable, active, low-frequency sonar with significantly greater processing power. Two further stores stations will be added, but the MAD equipment will be deleted. The only other helicopter in the Navy's inventory will be the CH-60, a transport version of the SH-60. Thus, there will be just two sub types of one main type of helicopter in Naval service, achieving the goal of rationalization which the Navy set itself some years ago.

Below: Air Force HH-60G (top right) joins an MH-53 (bottom right) in refuelling from a HC-130 Combat Talon.

MH-60 Blackhawk

Country of origin: United States.
Manufacturer: Sikorsky Aircraft Corporation.
Type: special forces helicopter.
Weight: maximum takeoff with external load 23,500lb (10,660kg).
Dimensions: length rotors turning, 64.8ft (19.8m); width fuselage 7.75ft (2.36m); rotor diameter 53.8ft (16.4m); height, 16.9ft (5.2m).
Powerplant: Two GE T700-GE-701C turboshafts, each 1,870shp max.
Performance: maximum speed, 195kt (225mph/362kmh); service ceiling, 19,150ft (5,840m); self-deployment range, 1,150nm (1,330 miles/2,140km).
Crew: two flight crew plus up to fourteen fully equipped passengers.

The primary mission of the U.S. Army Special Operations Forces' MH-60 is to conduct overt or covert infiltration, exfiltration, and resupply of SOF across a wide range of environmental conditions. An armed version, the Direct Action Penetrator (DAP), has the primary mission of armed escort and fire support. Secondary missions of the MH-60 include external load, CSAR and MEDEVAC operations. The MH-60 is capable of operating from fixed base facilities, remote sites, or ocean-going vessels.

The 160th SOAR(A) operates three models of the Blackhawk:
- The MH-60K (Blackhawk) is a highly modified twin-engine utility helicopter based on the basic UH-60 airframe but developed specifically for the special operations mission. Improvements include aerial refueling capability, an advanced suite of aircraft survivability equipment, and improved navigation systems, including multi-mode radar to further improve pinpoint navigation in all environments and under the harshest conditions. Twenty-three MH-60Ks have been delivered to Army SOF, and upgrades of aircraft survivability and avionics are under way.
- The MH-60L is a highly modified version of the standard U.S. Army Blackhawk, configured for special operations use.
- The MH-60L Direct Action Penetrator (DAP) is an MH-60L modified to mount a variety of offensive weapons systems. Its mission is to conduct attack helicopter operations utilizing area fire or precision guided munitions and armed infiltration or exfiltration of small units. It is capable of conducting direct action missions as an attack helicopter or has the capability to reconfigure for troop assault operations. In the direct action role, it would not normally be used as a primary transport for troops or supplies because of high gross weights. The DAP is capable of conducting all missions during day, night, or adverse weather conditions. It can provide armed escort for employment against threats to a helicopter formation. Using team tactics, the DAP is capable of providing suppression or close air support (CAS) for formations and teams on the ground.

The following are standard systems always on board during tactical missions:
- Communications: the MH-60 avionics package consists of FM, UHF (HAVE QUICK II capable), VHF, HF, Motorola Saber, and SATCOM. MH-60K includes SINCGARS. All are secure capable. FLIR.

- Door guns: six-barrel 7.62mm miniguns, one each mounted outside both the left and right gunners' windows. They are normally operated by the crew chiefs. Sighting is by open steel sights, aimpoint, or AIM-1 laser.
- Ballistic armor subsystem: fabric-covered steel plating providing increased ballistic protection in the cockpit and cabin.
- Guardian auxiliary fuel tanks: two 172-gallon tanks providing range extension of approximately two hours (mains plus two auxiliary tanks: four hours total). Normal operational time without the Guardian tanks is approximately two hours ten minutes. Fast-rope Insertion/Extraction System (FRIES) bar, capable of supporting 1,500lb per side.

MH-60 mission-flexible systems are systems that can be mounted on the MH-60L to support a primary mission or enhance the capabilities of aircraft performing assault or DAP missions:

- AN/AAQ-16D AESOP FLIR. The AESOP is a FLIR with a laser range finder/designator (LRF/D). The Q-16D allows the DAP to detect, acquire, identify, and engage targets at extended ranges with laser guided munitions.
- Cargo hook. Mounted in the belly of the aircraft below the main rotor, the hook is capable of supporting external loads up to 9,000lb (4,082kg).
- External rescue hoist system. Eastern-Breeze hydraulic hoist capable of lifting 600lb (272kg) with 200ft (61m) of usable cable. Primary control is by the crew chief/hoist operator using a hand-held pendant.
- Internal auxiliary fuel system (IAFS). The MH-60 has wiring provisions for four additional 150gall (6821) on fuel cells which may be mounted in the cargo area, each of which provides approximately 50 minutes flight endurance. The maximum number of additional fuel cells may be limited due to ambient conditions and weight limitations. Use of all four IAFS tanks with the Guardian tanks reduces usable cargo area space to near zero. ▶

Below: The Army's 160th Special Operations Aviation Regiment flies MH-60L -60L DAP and -60K variants.

▶ • External extended range fuel system (ERFS) (MH-60L only). This consists of either two 230gal (1,0461) on, two 230gal and two 450gal (2,0461), or four 230gal jettisonable fuel tanks that can be mounted on the external stores support system for long-range deployment of the aircraft. Use of the ERFS restricts usage of the M-134 miniguns and specific configuration may be limited by center-of-gravity or maximum gross weight limitations, and/or ambient conditions.
- External tank system (ETS) (MH-60K only): two 230gal jettisonable fuel tanks can be mounted on the external tank system for long range deployment of the aircraft. Restrictions are as for ERFS. The ETS is capable of fuel replenishment by air refueling.
- Air refueling: the MH-60K is equipped with an air refueling probe that allows extended range and endurance by refueling from MC/KC-130 tanker aircraft.
- Personnel locator system (PLS), AN/ARS-6(V). This locates personnel

equipped with the AN/PRC-112(V) or equivalent survival radio.
• Command and control console. This provides four operator positions with
access to the four AN/ARC-182(V) multi-band transcievers and FLIR display.

The MH-60 DAP has integrated fire control systems and a pilot's heads-up
display (HUD) that combine to make the DAP a highly accurate and effective
weapons delivery platform both day and night. The DAP is capable of mounting
two M-134 7.62mm miniguns, two 30mm chain-guns, two 19-round 2.75in
(70mm) rocket pods, and Hellfire and Stinger missiles in a variety of
combinations. The standard configuration of the DAP is one rocket pod, one
30mm cannon, and two miniguns. The 7.62 miniguns remain with the aircraft
regardless of the mission.

*Below: Six-barrel Minigun is emplaced in an Army MH-60, a type which
has proved an excellent platform for SOF missions.*

Bell-Boeing V-22 Osprey

Country of origin: United States.
Manufacturer: Bell-Boeing.
Type: vertical takeoff and landing (VTOL) aircraft.
Weight: maximum for normal vertical takeoff, 47,500lb (21,550kg); STO takeoff 55,000lb (24,950kg); self-deployment 60,500lb (27,443kg).
Dimensions: fuselage length 57.3ft (17.5m); stowed, wing fore and aft 62.6ft (19.1m); width, proprotors turning 84.6ft (25.8m); width, blades folded, 18.4ft (5.6m); maximum height 22.6ft (6.9m).
Powerplant: two Rolls-Royce/Allison T406-AD-400 turboshafts, each 6,150shp.
Performance: maximum speed 377kt; cruise speed 240kt; service ceiling 26,000ft (7,925m); range, amphibious assault 515nm (780 miles/1,256km); self-deployment range, 2,100nm (3,184 miles/5,123km).
Ordnance: provision for two .50 caliber cabin machine guns.
Crew: two flight crew (pilot/co-pilot), 24 troops or 12 litters plus attendants, depending on role.
Specifications for MV-22A.

Below: The CV-22 has had a troubled history but promises to transform AFSOC operations when it enters service.

Above: CV-22 comes in for a vertical landing aboard a U.S. warship; the U.S. Marines and Navy has a variety of uses planned for the type.

The V-22 is a revolutionary aircraft using a novel tilt-rotor system that combines the vertical lift advantages of a helicopter with the fast forward speed of a fixed-wing aircraft. The joint U.S. Navy/Marines/Air Force program is led by the Marine Corps, with currently planned procurement of 446: Marines 348; Air Force 50; Navy 48. The version for the Marines, the MV-22A, is primarily intended as a replacement for aging CH-46 and CH-53 helicopters and is an assault transport for carrying troops, equipment and supplies, and which is required to operate from either ships or expeditionary airfields ashore. The Navy model, the HV-22A is required to provide combat search and rescue (CSAR), combat transport for special operations troops, and fleet logistic support transport. The Air Force CV-22A is required to support SOCOM missions, conducting long-range special operations missions; it will replace the MH-53J and MH-60J.

The V-22 is a tilt-rotor aircraft with a 6,500shp turboshaft engine/transmission nacelle and a 38ft (11.6m) rotor system mounted at each wing tip. The two proprotors are connected to each other by driveshafts, both for synchronization and to provide single engine power to both engines in the ▶

419

▶ event of one engine failing. The aircraft operates as a helicopter for vertical takeoff and landing, but once airborne the nacelles are rotated forward through 90 degrees for horizontal flight, thus converting it into a high-speed, fuel-efficient turboprop. For stowage aboard ship the rotor-blades fold and the wing rotates for maximum compactness.

The first flight occurred in March 1989 and since then a number of prototypes and pre-production models have been completed. The program has been dogged by controversy, which has been heightened by three well-

publicized crashes. The first occurred in 1991, with no casualties, the second in 1992 in which seven men died, but the third, in April 2000, was by far the worst, resulting in the deaths of 19 Marines. There are those who oppose the program, but the greatest need for the V-22 lies with the Marine Corps whose need to replace the small and elderly CH-46 is very urgent.

Below: U.S. Marines in a HA-LO drop from a CV-22, which will be especially useful in long-range, adverse weather operations.

Transall C.160/C.160NG

Country of origin: France/Germany.
Manufacturer: Transport Allianz (Transall).
Type: twin-engined medium transport aircraft.
Weight: empty equipped 63,400lb (28,758kg); normal take-off 97,433lb (44,200kg); maximum take-off 108,245lb (49,100kg).
Dimensions: length 106.3ft (32.4m); wing span 131.2ft (40m); height 38.4ft (11.7m); wing area 1,722sq ft (160.0m²).
Powerplant: 2 x Rolls-Royce Tyne RTy.20 Mk 22 each 6,100shp (4,550kW).
Performance: maximum speed at 14,765ft (4,500m) 289kt (333mph/536kmh); maximum cruising speed at 18,045ft (5,500m) 284kt (319mph/513kmh); range 2,428nm (2,796 miles/4,500km).
Payload: maximum 93 troops or 35,273lb (16,000kg).
Armament: none.
Crew: five.
Specifications for original production C.160.

This aircraft was the outcome of one of the first successful international projects and was conducted by a joint company known as Transport Allianz (Transall), a consortium comprising Nord Aviation (France), HFB (Germany), and VFW (Germany). The original missions for which the aircraft was designed were to transport men and stores, to drop paratroops, and medical evacuation, with electronic surveillance and communications relay added later. In the original production run, which ended in 1972, some 169 aircraft were built, of which 160 were delivered to the French *Armée de l'Air* and the German *Luftwaffe*, and the remaining nine to the South African Air Force. Subsequently, 20 of the

German aircraft were transferred to Turkey. France later reopened its production line and took delivery of 25 C-160NG (*nouvelle generation*), which had various minor improvements including air-to-air refueling. In addition to the transport role, eight French aircraft have been converted to the communications relay role (C-160H Astarte), and four as ELINT aircraft (C-160G Gabrielle).

The repeated reorganizations of the European aircraft industry resulted in transfers of responsibility: in 1976 to Aerospatiale (France) and MBB (Germany), but both are now part of EADS (European Aeronautics Defence and Space). All surviving French and German transport aircraft underwent modification and updating in the 1990s but in separate programs.

The Transall's main cabin can be configured to seat either 93 troops, 68 fully equipped paratroops, or 62 stretchers. In the cargo role, the aircraft can carry a maximum payload of 35,273lb (16,000kg), which can include armored vehicles, light tanks, or general cargo, either palletized or unpalletized. If required, the undercarriage can be raised to lower the fuselage for loading and unloading. In the parachute role, loads of up to 3,630lb (8,000kg) can be air-dropped.

The aircraft is powered by two Rolls-Royce Tyne turboprops, each driving a four-bladed, reversible-pitch, constant-speed propeller. Transall C.160NG are equipped with an in-flight refueling probe, which is mounted above the flight deck.

Below: Not as well known as the C-130 Hercules, the C.160 Transall is nevertheless a very capable tactical transport.

Lockheed C-130 Hercules (transport versions)

Country of origin: United States.
Manufacturer: Lockheed.
Type: intratheater airlift aircraft.
Weight: empty 69,300lb (31,434kg); maximum takeoff 135,000lb (61,236kg).
Dimensions: length 97.8ft (29.3m); height 38.3ft (11.4m); wingspan 132.6ft (39.7m).
Powerplant: four Rolls-Royce Allison T56-A-15 turboprops; each 4,300shp (3,080kW).
Performance: maximum cruising speed 321kt (370mph/595kmh) at 30,000ft (9,144m); range 4,210nm (4,848 miles/7,802km) with maximum fuel or 1,910nm (2,199 miles/3,539km) with maximum payload.
Payload: maximum passenger loads 92 troops or 64 paratroops or 74 litter **patients;** maximum allowable cabin load 36,000lb.
Crew: five (two pilots, navigator, flight engineer, loadmaster).

The C-130's versatility, combining long range and large capacity with an excellent short-field capability, have made it a favorite for use by special forces, most famously in the Entebbe rescue, but also in many hundreds of less well publicized operations.

The study for a new transport was initiated in 1951, with the first prototype C-130A flying in 1954, followed by the first production delivery to the USAF in December 1956. A total of 219 C-130As were delivered, powered by four Allison T56-A-1A turboprops with three-bladed propellers, followed by 134 C-130Bs with the uprated Allison T56-A-7 turboprops, four-bladed propellers,

additional fuel in the wings, strengthened landing gear and other improvements, most of which were later retrofitted to the C-130As. A U.S. Navy transport version of the C-130B was originally designated GV-1U, later C-130F, while several -A models were modified as C-140Ds, with wheel-ski landing gear for service in the Arctic and for resupply missions to radar stations along the Distant Early Warning line.

The next major transport version was the C-130E with two underwing fuel tanks, and increased range and endurance capabilities; 369 were delivered. A wing modification to correct fatigue and corrosion on the USAF's C-130Es has extended the life of the aircraft well into the 21st century, while ongoing modifications include a Self-Contained Navigation System (SCNS) to enhance navigation capabilities, especially in low-level environments, and a state-of-the-art autopilot, incorporating a Ground Collision Avoidance System. Next came the C-130H with uprated T56-A-T5 turboprops, a redesigned outer wing, updated avionics, and other minor improvements. Both C-130E and C-130H carry 6,700 gallons (25,363l)of fuel in six integral wing tanks, with a pylon under each wing for a 1,300 gallon (4,921l) fuel tank. Delivery of some 350 C-130H to the USAF started in 1975 and ended some years later, but was restarted with an order for eight to make up for losses in the Gulf War being funded in FY96.

USAF units are now equipped with the C-130H, which continues to be upgraded. Most C-130Hs have been fitted with the Night Vision Instrumentation System since 1993. Some aircraft with the ANG and Air Reserve are fitted for fire-fighting missions, others are fitted for aerial spraying, typically to suppress mosquito-spread epidemics and another seven,

designated LC-130Hs, are modified with wheel-ski gear for use in support of Arctic and Antarctic operations. Another upgrade is the C-130 Avionics Modernization Program (C-130X AMP) which will modify approximately 525 in-service aircraft of approximately thirteen different sub-types, to establish a common, supportable, cost effective baseline configuration for all C-130 aircraft, with a new avionics suite.

The current production model, C-130J, has a two-crew flight system, four Rolls-Royce-Allison AE-21-00D3 engines, all-composite Dowty propellers, digital avionics and mission computers, enhanced performance, and improved reliability and maintainability. These result in an all-round improvement in performance and availability. Another new version is the C-130J-30 which is 15ft longer, significantly increasing carrying capacity and range, enabling it to work as a strategic, as well as tactical, transport.

Left: The C-130 transport has made an incalculable contribution to special forces missions over the past 45 years and will serve on for many years to come.

AC-130H/U Spectre Gunship

Country of origin: United States.
Manufacturer: Lockheed.
Type: gunship for special forces operations.
Weight: empty 72,892lb (33,063kg); maximum gross 155,000lb (70,308kg).
Dimensions: length 97.8ft (29.3 meters); height 38.3ft (11.4m); wingspan 132.6ft (39.7m)
Powerplant: four Rolls-Royce Allison T56-A-15 turboprops; each 4,300shp (3,080kW).
Performance: maximum speed 330kt (380mph/612kmh) at 30,000ft (9,145m); cruising speed 320kt (368mph/592kmh); ceiling 33,000ft (10,060m), with 100,000lb payload; range 4,210nm (4,848 miles/7,802km) with maximum fuel or 1,910nm (2,199 miles/3,540km) with maximum payload; unrefueled combat radius (1 hour loiter), 500nm.
Crew: minimum tactical crew AC-130H 14, AC-130U 13; maximum 21.

The AC-130 Gunship is a basic C-130 transport, which has been modified as a heavily armed gunship to provide sustained and surgically precise firepower in a variety of scenarios. The AC-130 is a large aircraft and must operate at low altitude, so it can operate only within a permissive environments (ie, without a serious air defense threat), but within those limitations it is highly effective in the following roles: close air support (CAS); interdiction; armed reconnaissance; point defense; escort (convoy, naval, train, rotary wing); surveillance; combat search and rescue (CSAR); and landing/drop zone (LZ/DZ) support. It can also provide limited airborne

Below: An AC-130U gunship fires a spectacular array of counter-measures flares designed to thwart potential attack.

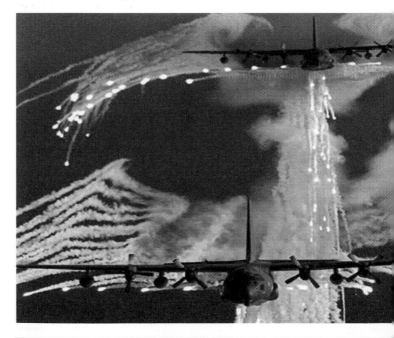

Above: AC-130 gunship; note the radar and electronics arrays and the barrel of the 105mm gun protruding under the engine.

command and control facilities, if required.

These heavily armed aircraft incorporate side-firing weapons integrated with sophisticated sensor, navigation and fire control systems to provide surgical firepower during extended loiter periods, at night and in adverse weather. The side-firing gunship delivers its firepower while in a pylon turn around the target. Targets are visible and can be attacked throughout the entire orbit and attack run-in headings are usually not desired. The Gunship is particularly effective at providing fire support for troops in contact (TIC).

Firing altitude depends on terrain, threat environment, and weather. Gun selection depends on target type and damage desired. To limit collateral damage, a live-fire area may be required to boresight weapons prior to employment. The Gunship weapons do not have a hard-kill capability against heavy armor or bunkers, but the 105mm ammunition has Superquick fuzes with both point detonation and 0.05 sec delay, concrete penetrators, and proximity fuzes for airburst. All 20mm, 25mm, and 40mm ammunition have point detonate fuzes. Although the AC-130H and AC-130U use very dissimilar avionics and other systems, fire support to the ground party is generally comparable.

Mission success is largely determined by the threat. The AC-l30 operates best during cover of darkness. It is extremely vulnerable during daylight operations and is most suited for operations in a low threat environment. By operating over an overcast, the AC-130U can degrade daylight threats, but must rely on the radar as its only sensor. Mission execution and desired objectives are seriously degraded by radar-guided antiaircraft artillery, surface-to-air missiles, and some IR MANPAD systems.

If radar threats are known or suspected, preemptive jamming or SEAD (suppression of enemy air defenses) is required. SEAD is preferable. Certain threats may dictate higher employment altitudes. However, sensor resolution decreases ▶

▶ with altitude: as range increases fire control accuracy degrades slightly, reducing the Gunship's ability to hit point targets. The threat environment limits the use of laser illuminators (the "BURN"), as it illuminates both the aircraft and the ground party to anyone properly equipped.

Thirteen AC-130Us were delivered for full operational capability by FY 2001. Extensive modernization is being carried out to AC-130H/U flight decks, and development is under way to equip the aircraft with more effective ammunition that will enable the aircraft to fire from beyond the range of antiaircraft weapons.

Spectre has an impressive combat history. During Vietnam, gunships destroyed more than 10,000 trucks and were credited with many life-saving

close air support missions. AC-130s suppressed enemy air defense systems and attacked ground forces during Operation Urgent Fury in Grenada. This enabled the successful assault of Point Salines airfield via airdrop and airland of friendly forces. Gunships had a starring role during Operation Just Cause in Panama by destroying Panamanian Defense Force Headquarters and numerous command and control facilities by very precise employment of ordnance in an urban environment. As the only close air support platform in the theater, Spectre was credited with saving many friendly lives.

Below: An AC-130U Spooky II gunship serving with AFSOC, which is tasked to deliver special operations combat airpower.

MC-130E/H Combat Talon I and II

Country of origin: United States.
Manufacturer: Lockheed.
Type: support aircraft for special forces operations.
Weight: empty 72,892lb (33,063kg); maximum take-off 155,000lb ((70,310kg).
Dimensions: length 97.8ft (29.3 meters); height 38.3ft (11.4m); wingspan 132.6ft (39.7m)
Powerplant: four Rolls-Royce Allison T56-A-15 turboprops; each 4,300shp (3,080kW).
Performance: maximum cruising speed 321kt (370mph/595kmh) at 30,000ft (9,144m); range 4,210nm (4,848 miles/7,802km) with maximum fuel or 1,910nm (2,199 miles/3,539km) with maximum payload.
Payload: maximum passenger loads 92 troops or 64 paratroops or 74 litter patients; maximum allowable cabin load 36,000lb.
Crew: five (two pilots, navigator, flight engineer, loadmaster).

The mission of the MC-130E Combat Talon I and MC-130H Combat Talon II is to provide global, day, night, and adverse weather capability to airdrop and airland personnel and equipment in support of U.S. and allied Special Operations Forces. The MC-130 conducts infiltration, exfiltration, resupply, psychological operations, and aerial reconnaissance into hostile or denied

Below: The MC-130H is instantly recognizable by its unique "boat-shaped" radome; note FLIR turret underneath.

Above: AFSOC operates 14 MC-130E Combat Talon aircraft, each capable of carrying 52 SOF troops.

territory using airland and/or airdrop. Both Combat Talons are capable of inflight refueling, giving them an extended range limited only by crew endurance and availability of tanker support. The MC-130E Combat Talon I is capable of air refueling helicopters in support of extended helicopter operations. MC-130 missions may be accomplished either single-ship or in concert with other special operations assets in varying multi-aircraft scenarios. Combat Talons are able to airland/airdrop personnel/equipment on austere, marked and unmarked LZ/DZs, day or night.

MC-130 missions, which may require overt, clandestine or low visibility operations, are normally flown at night using a high-low-high altitude profile. The high altitude portion is generally flown prior to penetrating and after exiting the target area. This portion of the flight will be flown at an average ground speed of 260 knots and at an altitude which minimizes fuel consumption and enemy detection. The aircraft will descend to low-level, terrain-following altitudes to penetrate hostile territory. Mission success may require the flight to be conducted at the lowest possible altitude consistent with flying safety, and at a ground speed between 220 and 260 knots. Night vision goggles (NVGs) may be used for night operations.

MC-130E/H aircraft are equipped with terrain-following, terrain-avoidance radar, an inertial and GPS navigation system, and a high-speed aerial delivery system. Some MC-130Es are also equipped with the surface-to-air Fulton recovery and helicopter air refueling systems. The special navigation and aerial delivery systems are used to locate small drop zones and deliver people or equipment with greater accuracy and at higher airspeeds than possible with a standard C-130E/H aircraft.

Fourteen MC-130Es and twenty-four MC-130Hs have been delivered. Special-to-role equipment includes: APQ-170 radar in an enlarged nose radome, with a FLIR turret underneath; low-level extraction system; defensive systems. Modernization plans include improved terrain following capability and enhanced situational awareness on MC-130H.

EC-130 Commando Solo

Country of origin: United States.
Manufacturer: Lockheed.
Type: airborne electronic broadcasting system.
Weight: empty 72,892lb (33,063kg); maximum take-off 155,000lb ((70,310kg).
Dimensions: length 97.8ft (29.3m); height 38.3ft (11.4m); wingspan 132.6ft (39.7m).
Powerplant: four Rolls-Royce Allison T56-A-15 turboprops; each 4,300shp (3,080kW).
Performance: maximum cruising speed 321kt (370mph/595kmh) at 30,000ft (9,144m); range 4,210nm (4,848 miles/7,802km) with maximum fuel or 1,910nm (2,199 miles/3,539km) with maximum payload.
Crew: five (two pilots, navigator, flight engineer, loadmaster), plus mission crew.

Commando Solo is an airborne electronic broadcasting system utilizing four EC-130E Rivet Rider (RR) aircraft operated by the SAF's 193rd Special Operations Group, Pennsylvania Air National Guard. Commando Solo conducts psychological operations and civil affairs broadcast missions in the standard AM, FM, HF, TV and military communications bands. Missions are flown at maximum altitudes possible to ensure optimum propagation patterns. This system may also be used to: support disaster assistance efforts by broadcasting public information and instruction for evacuation operations; provide temporary replacement for existing transmitters or expanding their areas of coverage; other requirements, which involve radio and television broadcasting in its frequency, range.

Below: EC-130E Volant Solo epitomizes the development of special equipment to meet unique SOF aviation requirements.

Above: EC-130E Commando Solo is used for PSYOPS broadcasts and also for jamming hostile communications.

The EC-130 flies during either day or night scenarios and is air-refuelable. A typical mission consists of a single-ship orbit, which is offset from the desired target audience. The targets may be either military or civilian personnel. Secondary missions include command and control communications countermeasures (C3CM) and limited intelligence gathering. Six aircraft have been modified to EC-130E specifications.

The EC-130 was deployed to both Saudi Arabia and Turkey in support of Desert Shield and Desert Storm. Their missions included broadcasts of "Voice of the Gulf," and other programs intended to convince Iraqi soldiers to surrender. More recently, in 1994, Commando Solo was utilized to broadcast radio and television messages to the citizens and leaders of Haiti during Operation Uphold Democracy. The EC-130s deployed early in the operation, highlighting the importance of PSYOP in avoiding military and civilian casualties. President Aristide was featured on the broadcasts which contributed significantly to the orderly transition from military rule to democracy.

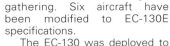

MC-130P Combat Shadow

Country of origin: United States.
Manufacturer: Lockheed.
Type: support aircraft for special forces operations.
Weight: empty 72,892lb (33,063kg); maximum take-off 155,000lb (70,310kg).
Dimensions: length 97.8ft (29.3m); height 38.3ft (11.4m); wingspan 132.6ft (39.7m).
Powerplant: four Rolls-Royce Allison T56-A-15 turboprops; each 4,300shp (3,080kW).
Performance: maximum cruising speed 321kt (370mph/595kmh) at 30,000ft (9,144m); range 4,210nm (4,848 miles/7,802km) with maximum fuel or 1,910nm (2,199 miles/3,539km) with maximum payload.
Crew: eight (two pilots, navigator, flight engineer, plus systems operators).

The mission of the MC-130P Combat Shadow is clandestine formation/single-ship intrusion of hostile territory to provide aerial refueling of special operations helicopters and the infiltration, exfiltration, and resupply of U.S. Special Operations Forces by airdrop or airland operations. To perform these missions, the primary emphasis is on night vision goggle (NVG) operations, but they can be accomplished during the day.

The MC-130P primarily flies missions at night to reduce probability of visual acquisition and intercept by airborne threats. Secondary mission capabilities may include airdrop of small special operations teams, small bundles, and combat rubber raiding craft; as well as NVG takeoff and landing procedures, tactical airborne radar approaches, and inflight refueling as a receiver.

Some aircraft have been modified with the Universal Air Refueling Receptacle Slipway Installation (UARRSI) system for inflight refueling as a receiver and all aircraft are modified with the self-contained navigation systems (SCNS) and Global Positioning System (GPS). The Special Operations Forces Improvement (SOFI) modification gives the aircraft an NVG HUD, a new modified radar, and an Infrared Detection System (IDS), greatly increasing the range and navigational accuracy.

The aircraft normally carries eight crew members. Depending on mission profile and duration, additional crew members are carried. All crew members are qualified in NVG/formation and helicopter air refueling. Special qualifications include high altitude low opening (HALO) airdrop, NVG airland, formation lead, inflight refueling (IFR), and Rigging Alternate Method Zodiac (RAMZ).

The MC-130P employs night terrain

contour (NTC) procedures using NVGs. The profile is flown at 500 feet above ground level using terrain masking. If necessary, the mission can be flown with visual and electronic-controlled emissions. The range of the mission depends on several factors: length of time on the low-level route, en route weather, winds, and the air refueling offload requirements. Portions of the profile may be flown at high altitude to minimize fuel consumption. NTC procedures will be used to avoid enemy detection in a non-permissive environment to get the aircraft to the objective area.

Air refueling is the primary mission of the MC-130P. The MC-130P normally flies in a formation of aircraft to provide the capability of multiple simultaneous refueling of large helicopter formations. An airborne spare tanker is also a part of the formation.

AFSOC MC-130P (referred to as the HC-130 prior to 1996) were deployed to Saudi Arabia and Turkey in support of Desert Storm. They operated from main bases and remote locations. Their missions included air refueling of Special Operations Forces helicopters over friendly and hostile territory, psychological operations, and leaflet drops.

Below: MC-130P Combat Shadow refuels an MH-53M Pave Low IV during humanitarian mission in Mozambique, 2000.

IAI/TRW Hunter UAV

Country of origin: Israel.
Manufacturer: IAI/TRW.
Type: multi-role, short-range, tactical UAV.
Weight: empty 1,300lb (590kg); maximum takeoff 1,600lb (725kg).
Dimensions: length 22.9ft (7m); height 5.6ft (1.7m); wingspan 29.1ft (8.9m).
Powerplant: 2 x Moto Guzzi 750cc pusher/puller.
Performance: maximum 109kt (125mph/200kh); cruise 70kt 78mph (126km/h); ceiling 15,000ft (4,750m); endurance 8-10 hours.
Launch: RATO booster or runway takeoff.
Recovery: Conventional landing with hook.
Armament: none.
Payload: Payload 200lb (90.7kg).

This battlefield system, originally known as the Short-Range UAV but subsequently renamed Hunter, was designed by Israeli Aviation Industries (IAI) at a time when the IDF's reputation for use of UAVs was high. Thus, the type was selected for development and production by the U.S. Army, a number were bought by Belgium, and a single system was trialled by the French Army. The U.S. program began in 1988 with the intention of procuring fifty systems, with a total of 400 aircraft, plus the associated ground and electronic equipment, for a cost of $US1.2 billion. The development history was troubled, including no fewer than twenty crashes, production was extremely slow, and by the time the project was cancelled in 1996 total program costs were expected to be of the order of $US2 billion.

Each system comprised four Hunter UAVs, plus their associated Modular Mission Payloads, but these were supported by a considerable array of ground equipment. This included: two ground control shelters, one mission planning shelter, one launch and recovery shelter, two ground data terminals, four remote video terminals, four air data relays, plus launch and recovery equipment and ground support equipment.

The Hunter system was developed to provide ground day and night reconnaissance, intelligence, surveillance, and target acquisition for army divisional and corps commanders, as well as naval task groups at sea. It was planned to give coverage of an area of 125 miles (200km) radius, provided that there was a line-of-sight between the UAV and the ground control station. If there was intervening terrain or to extend the range, it was planned to use a second Hunter as an airborne relay.

The theory was sound but, as happened with many of these second-generation UAV systems, the Hunter hit a number of problems. First, the overall system failed to meet army standards of reliability and second it could not respond in a sufficiently timely manner to the requirements of the artillery. Third, the method of relaying video images via a second Hunter rarely worked properly. Fourth, the complete system, including the aircraft ground equipment and people could not fit in the specified number and type of transport aircraft.

Despite these problems, limited production of seven systems was authorized in 1993 for the U.S. Army, followed by a similar authorization for eighteen systems for the Navy. Delivery began in 1994, but then even more problems were discovered and in January 1996 further production was halted after five complete systems had been delivered.

Curiously, despite their problems and the cancellation, those Hunter systems that did go into service proved valuable. They were used in trials programs for future UAVs and in Spring 1999 eight of the surviving Hunters took part in NATO's Operation Allied Force against the Serbians in Kosovo. They were based in Macedonia and flew 281 missions, and providing useful real-time video. One particular advantage was that they were able to operate at much lower altitude than manned aircraft which were restricted to higher altitudes for safety reasons. Five Hunters were lost, apparently shot down, one crashed, and two were damaged and returned to the USA for repair, while six replacements were sent to make good the losses. Despite these successes, however, the Hunter was still not acceptable as an operational system. The project was allowed to die and the Army turned to a new project named Outrider.

Below: The Hunter UAV was based on an Israeli design and although never declared operational has seen much service.

RQ-2 Pioneer

Country of origin: Israel/United States.
Manufacturer: Pioneer UAV Inc.
Type: reconnaissance, surveillance, targeting acquisition (RSTA) UAV.
Weight: maximum takeoff 416lb (188.7kg).
Dimensions: length 14.0ft (4.3m); height 3.3ft (1m); wingspan 16.9ft (5.2m).
Powerplant: 2-stroke, 2-cylinder 26hp gasoline engine
Performance: speed 100kt (115mph/185kmh); cruise 65kt (75mph/120kmh); ceiling: 15,000ft (4,572m); range <100nm (115 miles/185km); endurance <3.4 to 4 hours.
Launch: runway, wheeled (with or without rocket assistance) or pneumatic catapult.
Recovery: runway with hook, or net.
Armament: none.
Payload: 100lb (45kg).

The U.S. Navy was impressed with reports of the successful use of UAVs in the early 1980s and ran a competition for an interim system to provide imagery intelligence (IMINT) for spotters for naval gunfire support from its battleships, as well as to provide a UAV capability for the Marine Corps. Winner of the competition was a partnership of Mazlat (Israel) and AAI (USA) with an improved version of the Scout, an existing Israeli UAV. Deliveries began in 1986. This first generation U.S. UAV, named Pioneer, had a twin boom configuration,

Below: An RQ-2 is wheeled out prior to launch. The two men show the large size, which is seldom evident in aerial pictures.

Above: RQ-2 lifts off from a carrier flight-deck. It has proved very difficult to find a replacement and many remain in service.

with a pusher propeller driven by a 26hp two-stroke twin-cylinder piston engine, and a fixed tricycle landing gear. The sensors were mounted in a turret underneath the fuselage.

A total of nine systems, each with eight aircraft and the associated ground equipment, were procured by the Navy and the Marines. First deployment was aboard the battleship USS *Iowa* (BB-61), with three more systems being delivered to the Marine Corps in 1987. The Army joined the program in 1990, with one system on loan from the Navy.

Pioneers have been used in combat since the late 1980s, including the Persian Gulf tanker crisis in the late 1980s and the Desert Storm/Desert Strike when over 300 combat reconnaissance missions were flown. More recently it has flown in operations over Bosnia, Haiti and Somalia.

It had been intended that Pioneer would be replaced in the late 1990s by newer systems, but this has not yet occurred, so nine systems (each of eight aircraft) remained active in 2002: Navy 5; Marines 3; training 1. Some 30 of these aircraft were the result of an additional procurement order in the mid-1990s to Option 2+ standard with slight increases in aircraft weight and fuel capacity. A new more capable and more reliable sensor payload was approved in 1998. Thus, as so frequently happens with "interim"systems, the Pioneer has soldiered on for far longer than was ever intended and has outlasted many systems which were supposed to replace it.

AAV Shadow 200 Tactical UAV (TUAV)

Country of origin: United States.
Manufacturer: AAI.
Type: tactical UAV (TUAV).
Weight: maximum 328lb (149kg).
Dimensions: length 11.2ft (3.4m); wingspan 12.8ft (3.9m).
Powerplant: UEL AR741 208cc piston engine; 38hp.
Performance: maximum speed 115kt (129mph/207kmh); cruise speed 65-85 knots (73-95mph/105-137kmh); endurance 6-8 hours; radius 43nm (49 miles/78km); ceiling 15,000ft (4,570m).
Launch: runway, wheels, or hydraulic rail launcher.
Recovery: runway, wheeled, net or parachute.
Armament: none.
Payload: 60lb (27.2kg).

The Shadow 200 is the latest in the U.S. Army's search for a viable UAV-based tactical, day or night reconnaissance, surveillance and target acquisition system. The aircraft is a high-wing design with twin tailbooms and a fixed tricycle undercarriage. It is powered by a small 38hp gasoline engine driving a pusher propeller and is launched either by a conventional wheeled takeoff from a runway, or from a trailer-mounted rail launcher, with a hydraulic catapult. The aircraft can either make a conventional wheeled landing on flat ground about the length of a soccer field, or can be recovered using a deployable arresting hook on the aircraft and ground-based cables.

Each Shadow 200 tactical UAV system comprises three UAVs plus ground support, all of which is mounted in vehicles and trailers. There are two Ground Control Stations (GCS), which use ruggedized hardware and well-proven software to reduce development risk; each GCS is mounted in a shelter on the back of a standard military truck. There are also two Portable Ground Control Stations (PGCS), which are packaged in ruggedized transit cases to enable easy transport and rapid set-up and tear-down in the field. The PGCS, in conjunction with the Portable Ground Data Terminal, has full functionality to launch and recover the air vehicle, operate the payload, and receive and display payload data. The Remote Video Terminal provides forward battle commanders with a capability to view the area of operation using a flat panel display in near-real time. The system requires minimal operator training.The Ground Data Terminal has transceivers and an antenna system designed for lightness, mobility, and ease of shipment. No tools are needed for setting it up.

The system incorporates a number of technical improvements arising from lessons learned during UAV deployments, particularly during Operation Allied Force in Kosovo. The Army plans to buy forty-four Shadow 200 systems, but a firm production order had not been announced by mid-2002.

Below: The concept of an RPV seems simple, but development of workable platforms has proved very difficult.

Teledyne/Ryan Tier II Plus UAV (Global hawk)

Country of origin: United States.
Manufacturer: Teledyne/Ryan
Type: high-altitude, long-endurance UAV.
Weight: maximum take-off 25,600lb (11,612kg).
Dimensions: length 44.3ft (13.5); height 15.1ft (4.6m); wingspan 116.1ft (35.4m).
Powerplant: Rolls-Royce-Allison turbofan.
Performance: maximum cruising speed 340kt (391mph/630kmh); ceiling 65,000ft (19,812m); ferry range 13,500nm (15,525 miles/25,000km); endurance 36 hours.
Launch: runway; wheeled.
Recovery: runway, wheeled.
Armament: none.
Payload: 2,000lb (907kg).

The RQ-4A Global Hawk is a high-altitude, long-endurance UAV which provides field commanders with high resolution, near-real-time imagery of large geographic areas and can image an area the size of Illinois (40,000 nautical square miles) in just 24 hours. To achieve this it carries cloud-penetrating, Synthetic Aperture Radar/Ground Moving Target Indicator, electro-optical and infrared sensors and through the use of satellite and ground systems, can relay the imagery in near-real-time to battlefield commanders.

The RQ-4A has been under development since 1994. It is a large aircraft, 44ft (13.5ft) long and with a wingspan of 116ft (35.4m) and a mission ready weight of 25,600lb (11,612). A typical mission would be to fly 1,200 miles (1,931km) to the operational area, where it would remain on patrol for 24 hours before the flight home again. The entire flight from taxi out to taxi back, and including routes, heights and sensor activity, is programmed into the computer before take-off. The ground-based operators monitor the aircraft's activities and can change navigation and sensor plans during flight, where necessary.

Global Hawk currently is undergoing flight-testing at the U.S. Air Force Flight Test Center at Edwards Air Force Base, California, with 1,255.5 hours flown during 103 successful sorties. On 20 April, 2000, Global

Hawk Air Vehicle No. 4 deployed to Elgin AFB, Florida, to participate in two exercises that included its first trans-oceanic flight to Europe, and first mission flown in one theater of operations while being controlled from another. In April 2001 a prototype Global Hawk flew non-stop to Australia, a distance of 7,500 miles. It remained in the area for six weeks during which it carried out eleven sorties before returning to the USA, again in a non-stop flight.

The system is capable of both direct line of sight communications with the ground station by a common data link or beyond line-of-sight through a satcom link. In the future users detached from the ground station could directly receive imagery data from the Global Hawk.

In March, 1999, one of the Global Hawks lost control and crashed, which caused some two months delay in the testing program. However, since September 2001 at least one aircraft has been deployed to Afghanistan where it has proved a considerable success.

Below: The elegant shape of the Teledyne/Ryan RQ-4A Global Hawk; this type has successfully flown from the Continenatal United States to Australia, a dsitance of some 7,500 miles.

La Fayette-class frigate

Country of origin: France.
Builder: DCN, Lorient, France.
Type: surveillance frigate (*Fregate de Surveillance*).
Displacement: 3,100 tons standard; 3,600 tons full load.
Dimensions: length 410.1ft (125.0 m); beam 50.9 ft (15.5m); draught 13.45ft (4.1m).
Propulsion: 4 SEMT-Pielstick diesels; 2 shafts; 21,000bhp.
Performance: maximum speed 25kt; range 9,000nm at 12kt.
Armament: 8 x MM40 Exocet SSM; 1 x Crotale SAM system; 1 x 100mm Model 1968 CADAM gun; 2 x 0.5in (12.7mm) machine guns.
Aircraft: 1 helicopter.
Complement: 86.
Special forces: 24.

The great majority of surface warships have sufficient spare accommodation and deck-space to carry special forces to and from their missions, when required to do so. The French La Fayette-class frigates, however, are unique in having such facilities designed in from the start. In the mid-1980s French naval analysis indicated a requirement for a ship which could undertake national or international naval operations, including shadowing, deterrence and, if necessary, attack on hostile ships; intelligence collection; rescue of threatened French citizens; landing and recovery of special forces; support of amphibious operations; humanitarian missions; and, finally, search and rescue. The result was the La Fayette-class and ten were originally planned for the French Navy, although with the end of the Cold War this was later reduced to five, all of which are now in service. The design criteria were: stealth, reduced vulnerability to hits; good seakeeping; flexibility; a high degree of automation; and moderate costs. The outcome was a ship with a unique appearance in which the radar cross-section has been reduced by streamlining the hull, superstructure and masts; all openings are covered by hatches or curtains, and the foredeck and stern are completely enclosed. All external surfaces are inclined at 10 degrees and the opening for the ship's boats is covered by a large roller blind. Radiation absorbing material and paint are used wherever needed and all

reflecting equipment, such as capstans, bollards and fairleads are under cover.

The ships have separate accommodation for 24 special forces troops or commandos and the entire stern gallery beneath the helicopter flightdeck is made over to storage space for their equipment and boats. Finally, there is a large door in the transom through which the boats can launched and recovered. The door opens upwards and the underside includes a rail along which a small travelling crane can launch and recover the boats; this operation can be carried out clandestinely, even in a foreign port.

Six of these ships were built for Taiwan (Kang Ting-class), being delivered between 1996 and 1998, and a further three are under construction for the Royal Saudi Navy (Arriyad-class) for delivery between 2002 and 2005. However, neither of these classes has the special forces facilities and it must be presumed that the stern flat is used for other purposes.

Below: The French Navy's Lafayette-class frigates have built in accommodation and operational facilities for SOF.

Cyclone-class Patrol Coastal (PC) ships

Country of origin: United States.
Builder: Bollinger, Lockport, Louisiana, USA.
Type: coastal patrol combatants.
Displacement: full load 341 tons.
Dimensions: length 170ft (51.8m); beam 25ft (7.6m); draft 7.8ft (2.4m).
Propulsion: main four Paxman Valenta 16V RO-200 diesels, each 3,350bhp; generators two Caterpillar 306 diesels, each 155kW; fuel capacity 12,000 gallons (41,636l).
Performance: maximum speed 35kt; cruising speed 25kt; maximum range >3,000nm; endurance 10 days.

Armament: one Stinger launcher (6 missiles); 1 x Mk 38 Bushmaster 25mm rapid fire gun. Plus four pintles supporting any combination of: .50in M2HB machine guns; 7.62mm M60 machine guns; Mk 19 grenade launchers. Mk 52 Mod 0 chaff decoy launching system.
Complement: 4 officers, 24 enlisted.
Special forces: berthing for nine special forces troopers.

▶

Below: USS **Tempest** *(PC-2), one of 14 Cyclone-class Patrol Coastal (PC) craft, is assigned to Special Boat Squadron Two.*

► U.S. Naval Special Warfare Command (NSW) operates thirteen Patrol Coastal (PC) ships. Thirteen were delivered between 1993 and 1996, followed by the last one (PC-14), which was built at the insistence of the U.S. Congress, in 2000. The PC class has a primary mission of coastal patrol and interdiction, with a secondary mission of support to Naval Special Warfare, with specific tasks including forward presence, monitoring and detection operations, escort operations, non-combatant evacuation, and foreign internal defense.

The PC class operates in low intensity environments. Naval Special Warfare operational missions will include long range SEAL insertion/extractions, tactical swimmer operations, intelligence collection, operational deception, and coastal/riverine support. The Patrol Coastal ships, used successfully by joint operational commanders during both wartime and peacetime operations, have proved particularly effective in counter drug-smuggling operations. Indeed, *Thunderbolt* (PC-12) was lent to the U.S. Coast Guard from March to July 1998 to see whether the type was suitable for full-time transfer; the trial was successful, leading to a proposal that seven boats would by transferred to the USCG in the year 2000, but this has not taken place.

The last to be built, *Tornado* (PC-14), was completed with a hull lengthened by 9.0ft (2.74m) to enable it to accommodate the Combat Craft Retrieval System (CCRS) in the stern, by which it launches and recovers either a 36ft (11m) Rigid Inflatable Boat (RIB) or a SEAL Delivery Vehicle. Following the success of this installation, three in-service vessels, *Tempest* (PC-2), *Zephyr* (PC-8) and *Shamal* (PC-13), have also been converted. This upgrade significantly increases NSW's ability to support surveillance and interdiction missions. PCs normally operate as a two-boat detachment, which allows enhanced support and facilitates the assignment of one Mobile Support Team (MST) with each such detachment.

First-of-class, USS *Cyclone* (PC-1), has been stricken, but thirteen remain in U.S. Navy service, with nine operating from Naval Amphibious Base, Little Creek, Virginia, and four from Naval Amphibious Base Coronado, California.

Below: First-of-class USS Cyclone *(PC-1), designed for long-range, high-speed patrol/interdiction and to support SEALs.*

Pegasus-class Mk V Special Operations Craft

Country of origin: United States.
Manufacturer: Trinity-Halter Marine, Gulfport, Mississippi, USA.
Type: high-speed special forces insertion/extraction craft.
Displacement: standard 57 tons; full load 68 tons.
Dimensions: length 81.2ft (24.7m); beam 17.5ft (5.3m); draft 5.0ft (1.5m).
Propulsion: two MTU 16V396 diesels, each 2,285hp; two KaMeWa waterjets; total 4,506bhp; fuel capacity 2,600 gallons (11,820l).
Performance: maximum speed 45-48kt for 250nm in Sea State 2; cruising speed 25-40kt in Sea State 3; maximum range two engines at 45kt >600nm.
Armament: one Stinger launcher; five pintles supporting any combination of: .50in M2HB machine guns; 7.62mm M60 machine guns; Mk 19 grenade launchers. Mounting stations planned for GAU-17 minigun, Mk95 twin .50 cal machine gun, Mk 38 chaingun.
Complement: 1 officer, 5 enlisted.
Special forces: 16 special forces combat-loaded operators with 4 CRRCs.

The Mk V Special Operations Craft (SOC) is the newest vessel in the U.S.

Above: Pegasus-class Mark V Special Operations Craft, with RIB in foreground, was designed specifically for use by SF.

Navy's Special Warfare inventory, with ten detachments, each of two craft (20 boats) being delivered by March 1999. The Mk V SOC's primary mission is medium-range insertion and extraction for special forces in low- to medium-threat environments. The secondary mission is limited coastal patrol and interdiction (CP&I), specifically limited duration patrols, and low- to medium-threat coastal interdiction. Mk V SOCs normally operate away from base in two-craft detachments, with each detachment accompanied by a Mobile Support Team (MST). Each craft is road mobile on a special transport trailer, and one craft, mounted on its trailer and with its prime mover, can be air-transported in a single USAF C-5A Galaxy, with a total of two aircraft for the complete detachment. Once in location, typical employment pattern for the Mk V SOC is a 12-hour mission followed by a 24-hour turnaround, during which the MST will provide technical assistance and maintenance support, but the detachments are not responsible for providing their own ▶

Left: A Pegasus-class boat is loaded into a C-5 Galaxy, a valuable capability.

▶ security, messing, or accommodation while forward deployed.

The hull is designed for minimum radar and infrared signature and has a ramp at the stern for launching and recovering four inflated RIBs. Propulsion is provided by two MTU diesels, each driving a single KaMeWa waterjet for a top speed in excess of 50kt and a range in excess of 600nm at 45kt. Current

assignment is 12 at Special Boat Unit-1 (SBU-1) at Coronado, California, and eight to SBU-2 at Little Creek, Virginia.

Below: A Pegasus-class boat demonstrates its high-speed maneuverability; maximum speed is some 50 knots.

Naval Special Warfare (NSW) Rigid Inflatable Boat (RIB)

Country of origin: United States.
Type: high-speed raiding craft.
Weight: 14,700lb (6,668kg).
Dimensions: length 30ft (9.14m); beam 11.0ft (3.35m); draft 2ft (0.61m).
Propulsion: two Puckett-Caterpillar 3126 turbocharged diesels, each 470bhp; two KaMeWa RR280 waterjets; total 940bhp.
Performance: maximum speed >45kt; range 200nm at 33kt.
Armament: 7.62mm M-60 or 0.50in M2HB machine guns, or Mk 19 grenade launchers.
Complement: 3.
Special forces: 8.

The Rigid Inflatable Boat (RIB) is a high speed, high buoyancy, extreme weather craft with the primary missions of insertion/extraction of SEAL tactical elements to and from enemy occupied beaches, and coastal surveillance. The RIB is constructed of glass-reinforced plastic with an inflatable-tube gunwale made of a new hypalon neoprene/nylon reinforced fabric. There are two types of RIBs currently in the inventory; one is 24 feet (7.3m) long, the other 30 feet (9.1m). The RIB has demonstrated the ability to operate in light-loaded condition in Sea State Six and winds of 45 knots. For other than heavy weather coxswain

training, operations are limited to Sea State Five and winds of 34 knots or less. The 24-foot RIB carries a crew of three and a SEAL element.

The latest NSW RIB is deployed on USN amphibious ships. It has a 36ft (10.9m) Kevlar deep-vee hull with inflatable sponsons. It is powered by two 470hp Caterpillar diesels and two KaMeWa FF280 waterjets. At full load maximum speed is 45 knots, cruise is 33 knots, and range well over 200nm.

Thirty-six NSW RIBs were delivered to Special Boat Units (SBUs) in San Diego and Norfolk in October 1999; followed by a further 40 more in 2000. Each NSW RIB detachment consists of two NSW RIBs, detachment deployment packages, and prime movers (Ford F800 4x4 trucks, if land based), all of which are transportable on standard C-130 or larger military aircraft. In early 2000, Naval Special Warfare validated the Maritime Craft Air Delivery System (MCADS), which allows the RIB to be air-dropped. MCADS uses a 2,700lb (1,225kg) platform measuring 21ft (6.4m) long and 9ft (2.7m) wide to deliver the craft to the water drop zone. Once the platform and the RIB exit the aircraft, they are rigged to separate and descend under their own parachutes.

Below: RIBs, with their high speed and adverse weather capabilities, provide invaluable support for special forces.

Combat Rubber Raiding Craft (CRRC)

Country of origin: United States.
Type: outboard-powered inflatable boat.
Weight: 265lb (120kg) without motor or fuel.
Dimensions: length 15.4ft (4.7m); beam 6.3ft (1.9m); draft 2.0ft (0.6m).
Propulsion: 1 x 35-55hp Johnson or Evinrude outboard engine.
Performance: maximum speed no load 18kt; range dependent on fuel carried.
Complement: crew 1; passengers 7.

The quintessential outboard-powered inflatable Combat Rubber Raiding Craft

(CRRC) is used for clandestine surface insertion and extraction of lightly armed special operations forces and is capable of surf passages. It may be launched by air (airdrop/helo-cast), or by craft (LCU, LCM, PC). It may also be deck-launched or locked-out from submarines. It has a low visual electronic signature, and can be cached by its crew once ashore.

Below: The military use of inflatable raiding craft started in World War Two, since when their design has changed little.

Arctic 22 Rigid Inflatable Boat (RIB)

Country of origin: United Kingdom.
Builder: Halmatic, Havant, UK.
Type: high-speed raiding craft.
Weight: light 3,136lb (1,422kg).
Length: 23.6ft (7.2m).
Propulsion: two OMC or Suzuki DT140 outboards; 2 x 140shp.
Performance: maximum speed >40kt; range 30nm at 40kt.
Armament: none.
Complement: 1.
Payload: maximum 1.12 tons (1,138kg).
Special forces: 15.

As with other special forces, Britain's Royal Marines make extensive use of Rigid Inflatable Boats (RIB). Largest in current service are eight Halmatic Arctic 22 but there are also a large number of Halmatic Pacific 22s, which are 22ft (6.8m) long and are powered by a Ford diesel. With their deep-V bottoms and light weight, these RIBs are capable of speeds in excess of 40kt and provide seating for all their passengers, which is very necessary in view of successive had knocks as the boat skims across the water. They are also highly maneuverable, with their inflated sponsons preventing capsizes, no matter how violent the turn.

The Royal Marines also use a large number of Rigid Raiders which have a flatter, dory-like hull and without the inflatable sides. Typical is the Rigid Raider Mk3, which is 25.3ft (7.7m) long and with a beam of 9.2ft (2.8m). Powered by a single 220bhp Yamaha outboard it will travel at speeds of up to 36kt with a full load of eight special forces.

Below: British Arctic 22 RIBs, one of several types used by the Royal Marines and other special forces units.

Fast Intercept Class 145

Country of origin: United Kingdom.
Builder: Halmatic, Havant, UK.
Type: high-speed special forces boat.
Displacement: light 21,00lb (9,500kg).
Dimensions: length 48.0ft (14.58m); beam 9.3ft (2.85m); draft stationary 4.0ft (1.2m), draft at speed 2.7ft (0.8m).
Propulsion: three SeaTek T.D. each 720bhp, with Trimax surface drives; fuel capacity 440gall (2,000l).
Performance: maximum speed 74kt; range > 300nm at 33kt.
Armament: none.
Complement: 2.
Special forces: maximum 12.

The British Royal Marines' Special Boat Service (SBS) operates two remarkable very high speed fast interceptor craft (FIC) which were built by Halmatic in the UK to a design prepared by the Italian Fabio Buzzi (FB) design bureau which has achieved many successes in modern racing championships. Designated the MIL 50' design, the design pedigree of these boats is flawless. Fabio Buzzi established his own boat design and construction company when in his early twenties and started to build and test his designs on the international offshore racing circuit from 1978 onwards. Since then he has had numerous successes, established the world speed record for diesel-engined boats of 191.58kmh in 1979. Then in 1986 he established his own diesel engine design and construction company, SeaTek, to produce his own engine designs with which he again won many races. His designs have won 29 world championships and he himself has been the world champion six times.

The FB46' design, upon which the FIC 145 was based, was the Class 1 World Champion in 1988 and 1989, as well as the winner of the Venice-Monte Carlo event in 1991, 1992, and 1993. The FIC145 is designed to undertake a number of missions, including: intrusion; interdiction; commando operations; and offshore interception. These boats are designed to operate at high speed in sea conditions at up to force 5 on the Beaufort scale and their maximum speed of 74kt and cruising speed of 55kt (in sea states 4-5) are probably better

Above: Also used by the British Royal Marines is the Mark III VSV (Very Slender Vessel) with a very high top speed.

than those achieved by any other special forces boats.

The balsa-cored sandwich hull is laminated in Kevlar 49 and moulded in vinylester resin and the hull and deck form a very strong integral structure with the characteristic Fabio Buzzi twin steps to reduce water friction, while the boat is still able to operate in depths as shallow as 2.7ft (0.80m). The deck has a non-skid surface and a rail to ensure crew safety and the wheelhouse/cabin can accommodate up to a maximum of 15 people.

The boat is powered by three Fabio Buzzi-designed SeaTek 10-litre, 6-cylinder "Navy" engines, each providing 620bhp at 3150rpm and driving Rolla propellers. There are three rubber fuel tanks filled with aviation type open-cell synthetic sponge, which can hold a maximum of 440gall (2,000l).

Below: *Based in an Italian design, the FIC 145 has a maximum speed well in excess of 70 knots.*

Stridsbåt 90H-class

Country of origin: Sweden.
Builder: Dockstavarvet, Docksta; Gotlandsvarvet, Sweden.
Type: fast personnel landing craft.
Displacement: light 13.2 tons; full load 18 tons.
Dimensions: length 52.2ft (15.9m); beam 12.5ft (3.8m); draught 2.6ft (0.8m).
Propulsion: 2 x Saab-Scania 8V DSI-14 diesels; 2 x FF Jet FF-450 waterjets; 1,256bhp.
Performance: maximum speed 40kt (35kt fully loaded); range 160nm at 40kt, 240nm at 20kt.
Armament: 3 x 12.7mm machine guns (see text); fitted for but not with RBS-17 Hellfire SSM; 1 x 81mm mortar; 4 mines or 6 depth-charges.
Complement: 4.
Special forces: 21.

This is a remarkable design which was introduced in order to provide rapid transport for Sweden's coastal artillery special forces moving around the islands of the archipelago; several hundred are being produced for Sweden and others have been ordered by foreign armed forces. The design was prepared in the late 1980s and the first production boat was delivered in 1991. The boat is made entirely of all-welded aluminum with considerable

strengthening forward to enable the boats to be run up on to beaches at some speed, thus considerably reducing the time taken for the passengers to disembark. The boat has a troop-carrying capacity of 21 men, who sit on benches in a 151sq ft (14m²) cabin, and on the boat beaching they disembark forward through a passageway under the bridge and then down a ramp which is lowered from a door in the bow. Power is provided by twin Saab-Scania DSI 14S diesels driving FF waterjets, which give a maximum speed carrying a full load of some 35-37 knots. The boats have a V-hull form with reverse sheer, which gives a combination of high speed, shallow draft and a low profile for effective seagoing and shoreline camouflage.

The boats have been ordered in a series of batches from Swedish yards – *Dockstavarvet* in Docksta and *Gotlandsvarvet* in Farosund – and at least six of the boats built at *Dockstavarvet* are fitted out as command boats. All boats of the initial order for 125 were delivered by 2001 and an option for another 129 boats is now being exercised.

Norway has taken delivery of 36 of a version designated CB-90N, which are employed to deploy coastal artillery personnel armed with mobile versions of the RBS-17 (Hellfire) surface-to-air missile. There are four boats in each mobile battery, three serving as missile launchers and one for command. The Norwegian boats have more powerful engines and greater fuel capacity than the Swedish boats.

Left: These Swedish all-aluminum fast landing craft have proved very successful in service and are in large-scale use by both Swedish and Norwegian armed forces.

Klepper Two-man Military Kayak

Country of origin: Germany.
Manufacturer: Klepper, Rosenheim, Germany.
Type: two-man collapsible canoe.
Weight: total approx 81.5lb (37.0kg).
Dimensions: canoe length 17.0ft (5.2m); beam 34in (86cm).
Assembly time: <10 minutes.
Payload: 716lb (325kg).
Crew: 2.

Some special forces, such as the U.S. Navy's SEALs and the British SBS, have a primary maritime mission, while others are more land-based, but most of them include a seagoing and riverine capability. All such units use canoes, most of them of the two-man folding type, and the Klepper kayaks, used by the SBS, are among the world leaders. The most widely used model is the military version of the Quattro XT, which is 17ft (5.2m) long with a frame made of mountain ash, which clips together using 32 Duraloy connectors of a patented "slide-and-snap" design. The wood for the frame is air-dried for some three years and then given three coats of marine varnish, while the hull cover is made of Hypalon (natural rubber) bonded to an industrial-strength Trevira polyester core, which together have a life-expectancy of some 25-30 years. The upper deck is made from Egyptian cotton which will not permit water to penetrate but allows the inside of the hull to breathe, thus preventing a build-up of condensation.

A kayak of this nature is inherently vulnerable and various measures are taken to prevent damage. The bow and stern are reinforced with thick, contour-molded caps for protection when beaching or setting sail, while the keel is reinforced with additional Hypalon/Trevira layers to protect against damage from coral, rock, or man-made hazards. There are also four, internally mounted, full-length air sponsons, each containing some 150 liters of air, which give excellent buoyancy and stability, and prevent inadvertent capsizes.

Below: The Klepper Military Kayak is a militarized version of the company's successful 17ft (5.2m) Quattro XT.

SEAL Delivery Vehicle (SDV) Mk VIII Mod 1

Country of origin: United States.
Dimensions: length 22.0ft (6.7m).
Propulsion: rechargeable silver-zinc batteries.
Crew: 1 operator plus 3.

The SDV Mk VIII Mod 1 is similar in concept to a "human torpedo" in that it carries combat swimmers in their wet suits and sustained by their individual Self-Contained Underwater Breathing Apparatus (SCUBA). It differs, however, in that the swimmers sit inside a superstructure whereas the others sit astride the torpedo body. The SDV is carried inside the Dry Docking Shelters (DDS) carried by some U.S. Navy SSNs (see entry). The SDV has an electric propulsion system, powered by silver-zinc batteries, which can be recharged only by the parent submarine, thus setting a very strict limit on the endurance. The SDV is controlled by an operator using a control stick, who also has a computerized Doppler navigation sonar which displays speed, distance, heading, depth, and other piloting functions. The SDV carries a maximum of four swimmers, together with stores, weapons and mines.

Fourteen SDV Mark VIII Mod 0 were originally built, of which three were sold to the British Royal Marines in 1999. One of the U.S. Navy's remaining eleven was scrapped, while the remaining 10 underwent a major rebuild and modernization (SLEP = service life extension program) from 1995 onwards, following which they are designated SDV Mark VIII Mod 1. The rebuild included more powerful batteries, giving better speed and range, and modernized instrumentation.

Below: SEALs prepare to laumch their SDV from a dry deck shelter aboard USS Silversides (SSN-679).

Above: An all-electric Mark VIII SEAL Delivery Vehicle (SDV) is piloted by members of SEAL Team Two.

Dry Deck Shelter (DDS)

Country of origin: United States.
Builder: Electric Boat Co, Groton, Connecticut, USA.
Weight: 65,000lb (29.484kg).
Dimensions: length 38ft (11.6m); diameter 8.9ft (2.7m).
Capacity: one SDV, or 20 SEALs plus four CRRC.

The U.S. Navy's Dry Deck Shelter (DDS) allows for the launch and recovery of an SDV or combat rubber raiding craft (CRRC) together with their SEAL combat divers from a submerged submarine. Six DDS were built and each consists of three modules constructed as one integral unit. The first module is a hangar in which an SDV or CRRC is stowed. The second module is a transfer trunk to allow passage between the modules and the submarine. The third module is a hyperbaric recompression chamber. The DDS provides a dry working environment for mission preparations. In a typical operation the DDS hangar module will be flooded, pressurized to the surrounding sea pressure, and a large door is opened to allow for launch and recovery of the vehicle. A DDS can be transported by USAF C-5/C-17 aircraft, railroad, truck, or sealift, and installation takes between one and three days.

The ability to carry a DDS requires extensive modification to both the exterior and interior of the host submarine. Converted submarines capable of carrying one DDS and currently in service are: USS *L. Mendel Rivers* (SSN-686); *Los Angeles* (SSN-688); *Philadelphia* (SSN-689); *Dallas* (SSN-700); *La Jolla* (SSN-701); and *Buffalo* (SSN-715). The converted ex- ballistic missile submarine. USS *Kamehameha* (SSN-642) can carry two DDS.

Above: SEALs at work outside the Dry Deck Shelter (DDS), shown at top, aboard a submerged nuclear submarine.

Left: USS Kamehameha (SSN-642), a converted ballistic missile submarine enters harbor with two DDS mounted on her afterdeck.

Advanced SEAL Delivery System (ASDS)

Country of origin: United States.
Type: combat swimmer submarine.
Displacement: surfaced 55 tons; submerged 60 tons.
Dimensions: length 65.0ft (19.81m); beam 8ft (2.44m); internal height 8.3ft (2.5m).
Propulsion: electric drive; battery (14 silver-zinc cells); one electric motor; 67shp; one propeller, eight thrusters (see text).
Performance: speed submerged 8kt; range submerged 125nm at 8kt.
Armament: none.
Crew: 2.
Special forces combat swimmers: 8.

Whereas the SDV carries personnel in "wet" conditions, the ASDS is a submarine in its own right, carrying its crew and passengers in dry conditions within a pressure hull. The vessel is 65ft (19.8m) long, with a beam of 6.8ft (2.1m) and a height of 8.3ft (2.5m), and has a submerged displacement of 60 tons. It is propelled by a single 67hp electric motor which is powered by 14 silver-zinc cells, which are recharged from the parent submarine, giving it a submerged range of 125nm at 8kt. There are also eight retractable electric thrusters for precise maneuvering, which are arranged in two groups of four,

Right: The first ASDS, a vessel which took far longer, and proved far more expensive, to construct than originally planned. The men in front of the ASDS give an indication of its large size; note the shrouded propeller and absence of any form of conning tower.

one forward the other aft, in an X-configuration. The ASDS has a crew of two. The ASDS has a lock-out chamber that is controlled by operators for lock-out from an anchored position, which will usually be between 2-190ft (0.6-58m) from the sea-bed.

Unlike virtually every other submarine, the ASDS does not have a sail, but it does have a single electro-optical periscope which does not penetrate the hull. There is a ballast tank at each end of the ASDS's pressure hull. The lock-out chamber is amidships, with hatches at the top and bottom. The divers can exit/enter either hatch, but the ASDS mates with its mother ship using the bottom hatch only.

The ASDS is designed to mate with suitably modified SSNs of the Los Angeles (SSN-688)-class, of which six have been completed (see below). USS *Jimmy Carter* (SSN-23) and the first six boats of the West Virginia-class are being built with the necessary fittings already installed.

The first ASDS was delivered in 2000, some three years late and at a cost of $230million very considerably over budget. It is planned to procure six of these ASDS, but at a relatively slow rate, with the second being ordered in 2003 and the third in 2005, the current budget price for these being $US59million each.

Sang-O-class

Country of origin: North Korea.
Builder: Bong Dao Bo shipyard, Singpo, North Korea.
Type: special forces delivery submarine.
Displacement: surfaced 275 tons; submerged 360 tons.
Dimensions: length 111.5ft (34.0m); beam 12.5ft (3.8m); draught 10.5ft (3.2m).
Propulsion: 1 x diesel generator set, 300bhp (est); electric motor, 200shp (est); one shaft.
Performance: surfaced 7.2kt; submerged 4kt; range surfaced 1,500nm; range schnorkel 2,700nm/8kt; maximum operating depth 492ft (150m).
Weapons: 4 x 21in (533mm) torpedo tubes (bow); 4 x torpedoes.
Complement: 14.
Specifications for torpedo-armed version; see text for SF version.

The North Korean Navy obtained a number of diesel-electric patrol submarines from fellow-Communist countries. First were four Whiskey-class from the Soviet Union in the 1960s and these were followed by a number of Chinese-built Whiskeys and Romeos in the 1970s. This encouraged the North Koreans to establish several large submarine-building facilities at Mayang-do, where some eighteen copies of the Chinese Romeo (itself a copy of a Soviet design) were completed between 1976 and 1996.

North Korea has two enemies – South Korea and the United States and has long pursued a policy of infiltrating special forces into its southern neighbor's territory. The land border between the two countries is the most heavily defended international frontier in the world, although, even so, infiltrators have occasionally managed to cross. This has made the use of submarines a viable alterative, and a number of M100-D minisubs (also known as the Una-class) were bought from Yugoslavia in the 1980s. The North Koreans developed this design into a rather more effective vessel, known in the West as the "Yugo-class," some forty of which were built at one of their own shipyards. These displace 90 tons submerged and accommodate seven special forces troops.

The next stage was to design a completely new type, based on experience gained with the Romeo- and Yugo-classes, which has been given the U.S. Intelligence nickname of the Sang-O (= shark) class. A total of 22 is believed to have been built, in two versions. One is a conventional, if small, torpedo- armed patrol submarine, with four bow-mounted 21in (533mm) tubes and no reloads. The other type, however, is a dedicated swimmer delivery vehicle with a lock-out chamber and accommodation for up to fifteen special forces in the torpedo space. This special forces version cannot carry torpedoes, but can carry sixteen mines.

In a spectacular failure, one of these boats ran aground on the South Korean coast on 17 September 1996. On this occasion there were twenty-six men aboard and all appear to have got ashore, but the South Koreans quickly captured one and found the bodies of eleven men who had committed suicide, but it took them over six weeks to deal with the remainder, killing thirteen of them just one man escaped. The North Koreans insisted that it had been a training mission and that the boat had suffered an engine fault which resulted in it drifting on to the southern shore, a story which nobody believed.

Right: Sang-O-class mini-submarine, was designed solely to take infiltrators into South Korean waters on sabotage missions.

India-class (Project 940)

Country of origin: Soviet Union.
Builder: Soviet Naval Yard, Komsomolsk-na-Amur, USSR.
Type: rescue/special forces submarine.
Displacement: surfaced 3,900 tons; submerged 4,800 tons.
Dimensions: length 348ft (106m); beam 33ft (10m).
Propulsion: diesel-electric drive on two shafts; two diesel generators, two electric motors; 5,000shp for 15kt submerged.
Performance: speed submerged approx 10kt; diving depth (240m); endurance 45-50 days.
Armament: none.
Payload: two submersibles (see text).
Complement: 90-100.
Special forces: berthing for unknown number of *Spetznaz*.

[Author's note: Although none of the boats described here remains operational they are included as evidence of the capability and resources of the Soviet *Spetznaz*, which, given appropriate financial commitment, could easily be recreated elsewhere.]

From the early 1970s onwards a number of Western European countries, particularly Sweden and Italy, complained of Soviet espionage using submarines to reconnoitre coastal places such as harbor entrances, river mouths and, in the Swedish case, ship shelters. The Swedes produced photographic evidence showing parallel marks on the seabed which appeared to show the passage of a tracked vehicle, and their case was strengthened when a Whiskey-class diesel-electric submarine ran aground well inside national territorial waters in October 1982 and lay there for several days in full view of the world's press. Although much that was secret in the Cold War has since been made public, some mysteries remain, among them the activities and equipment of these submarine incursors, believed to be either KGB or *Spetznaz*.

Two submarines were constructed in the late 1970s at Komsomolsk in the Soviet Far East, designated Project 940 by the Soviet Navy and "India-class" by NATO. These were diesel-electric boats with a large casing ("turtleback") abaft the fin into which were set two wells. The announced mission of the India-class was the rescue of crews from sunken submarines, for which they carried two Deep-Sea Rescue Vehicles (DSRVs), which were carried to the scene of the accident in the wells in the India's casing. On arrival, the DSRVs would shuttle between the India and the sunken submarine, mating with both using a large circular hatch in its bottom.

Another unusual external feature was that the forward hydroplanes were mounted on the fin rather than in the bows, which was very unusual in Soviet diesel-electric submarines, and was probably intended to keep the boat very steady when launching or recovering the DSRVs whilst submerged. One India-class served in the Pacific and the other in the Northern Fleet; both were placed in reserve in about 1990 and scrapped in 1995-96.

The DSRVs, known as the Poseidon-class to the Soviet Navy, were short, stubby craft, some 37-40ft (11.3 12.2m) long and painted with bright orange and yellow stripes. Their maximum operating depth was believed to be about 3,000ft (1,000m); they were operated by a three-man crew and could take up to 24 survivors at a time from the sunken submarine. Despite their overt rescue mission, however, there was evidence that the India-class boats were also used as intelligence gatherers, employing either the DSRVs or some other type of submersible to infiltrate foreign waters.

Another Soviet submarine was the Project 865 involving two boats built in the 1980s for service in the Baltic. These were minisubs 92ft (28m) long and with a submerged displacement of 220 tons; ie, somewhat larger than the U.S. Navy's Advanced SEAL Delivery System (ASDS) see separate entry above. They carried a very small crew and three combat divers who entered and left via a lock-out chamber. They had a submerged speed of some 6kt, a range of some 540nm and an endurance of 10 days. The development was seriously flawed, both technically and financially, and its existence was revealed by a "whistle-blower." At the time (early 1990s), a Soviet Navy spokesman made a carefully worded statement that the Navy had never operated any spy submarines, but did not exclude the possibility of such submarines being operated by the KGB or *Spetznaz*.

Another submarine for "special" tasks was the Project 910 (Uniform), two deep-diving boats with a submerged displacement of some 2,000 tons. These were the smallest nuclear-powered boats built for the Soviet Navy and are believed to have operated under *Spetznaz* control in order to locate and gain access to the NATO and U.S. underwater cable linking SOSUS sensors to their land-based control centers.

Below: The India-class was supposedly a rescue submarine; in fact, it carried two tracked mini-subs on spy missions.

Los Angeles-class (DDS-modified)

Country of origin: United States.
Type: SSN, modified for special forces role.
Total converted: 5.
Displacement: surfaced 6,080 tons; submerged 6,927 tons.
Dimensions: length 360.0ft (109.7m); beam 33.0ft (10.1m); draught 32.0ft (9.8m).
Propulsion: 1 x S6G pressurized-water nuclear reactor; ca. 30,000shp; one shaft.
Performance: submerged maximum ca. 32kt (see text); maximum operating depth 1,480ft (450m); endurance 90 days.
Weapons: four 21in (533mm) torpedo tubes; 22 torpedoes.
Payload: one DDS (see text).
Complement: 141.
Special Forces: maximum 20 SEALs.

The Los Angeles (SSN-688)-class SSNs constitute one of the most expensive defense programs undertaken during the Cold War, and, with sixty-two units, it remains by far the largest class of SSNs ever built. Hull numbers ran continuously from SSN-688, completed in November 1976, to SSN-773, completed in September 1996, except for a gap in the numerical sequence from #726 to #749 which were allocated to Ohio-class SSBNs. This 20-year production run was unprecedented in submarine history.

Naturally, in a program involving so many boats produced over such a long period there have been changes, but the class can be divided into three broad groups, of which the first consisted of thirty-two boats (SSN-688 to SSN-718) which, apart from the changes of detail, were identical. When the Tomahawk SLCM was introduced, the weapons were stored in the torpedo room and launched from the torpedo tubes. All five boats modified to take the DDS are from this group, so the second and third groups will not be discussed further.

All Los Angeles-class were built for a thirty-year life, although experience suggests that with proper refits, recores of the reactor and modernization, they could actually be expected to last for up to fifty years. However, a mixture of factors, including the end of the Cold War, the resulting requirement to reduce operating costs and manning requirements, and a desire to avoid the costs of recoring during refits, are resulting in a steady reduction in the fleet. The U.S. Navy started to retire Los-Angeles class SSNs in the mid-1990s, the past retirements and future forecast

Below: The DDS is 38ft (11.6m) long, 8.9ft (2.7m) in diameter and provides outstanding facilities for covert operations.

Above: Most DDS are carried aboard Los Angeles-class SSNs, which have proved ideal mother ships for SEAL operations.

up to 2008 being: 1995 2; 1996 1; 1997 3; 1998 3; 1999 2; 2000 1; 2001 3; 2005 1; 2006 1; 2007 1; 2008 1. Thus, by 2008 some nineteen will have been retired.

Of those being retained, five have been converted to carry one Dry Deck Shelter (DDS) plus a detachment of SEALs. These are *Los Angeles* SSN-688, *Philadelphia* (SSN-690), *Dallas* (SSN-700), *La Jolla* (SSN-701) and *Buffalo* (SSN-715), each of which can mount one DDS on special fittings immediately abaft the fin. The closed end of the DDS is forward and the large circular door, hinged to port, faces aft. Each of these SSNs has had a special hatch installed to enable the SEALs to move between the DDS and the pressure hull, and there are also accommodation and administrative facilities for the SEALs inside the boat. As far as is known, these modifications do not affect the normal operational capabilities of the SSNs, but when traveling underwater with the DDS installed the additional hydrodynamic drag will reduced the maximum speed by some 3-5kt.

USS Jimmy Carter (SSN-23)

Country of origin: United States.
Type: SSN, equipped for special forces role.
Total built: 1.
Displacement: surfaced 7,467 tons; submerged 9,137 tons
Dimensions: length 380.0ft 0in (115.8m); beam 42ft 0in (12.8m); draught 36ft 0in (11.0m)
Propulsion: 1 x S6W pressurized-water nuclear reactor, 200mW; one pump-jet propulsor, 45,500shp.
Performance: submerged ca. 34kt; maximum operating depth 1,970ft (600m).
Weapons: 8 x 26.5in (673mm) TT (amidships); ca. 50 Mk 48ADCAP torpedoes or Tomahawk SLCM, or mines.
Payload: one DDS (see text).
Complement: 133.
Special Forces: maximum 50 SEALs.

USS *Jimmy Carter* (SSN-23) is one of the three-strong Seawolf-class, which has been equipped while under construction to give it a significant special forces capability. The Seawolf-class are the most advanced submarines currently at sea, but had a troubled inception. Work on a successor to the Los Angeles-class started in the 1980s but there was constant discussion about the precise nature of the requirement and the ever-increasing costs, and then, when these had been resolved, there was then a serious dispute over which yard Newport News or Electric Boat should build it. Then, during construction of the first-of-class, there were delays due to welding difficulties and these were followed by problems with the covers for the flank sonar arrays. At a less important level, traditionalists were upset by the numbers allocated SSN-21, -22, -23 which is totally out of sequence in the U.S. Navy's excellent and well-established hull-numbering system, and appears to have arisen out of the project title "SSN for the 21st Century" which was abbreviated to "SSN-21." The name of the third boat, *Jimmy Carter* (SSN-23), was also considered inappropriate by many, even though the ex-president is a former nuclear-qualified officer in the submarine service.

The Seawolf -class hull is of generally the same shape as that of the Los Angeles-class and is entirely covered in anechoic tiles. The sail is specially strengthened for under-ice operations and incorporates a large fillet at the forward end, designed to improve the waterflow over the structure. A shrouded propulsor replaces the customary propeller, and there are six fins: the customary cruciform, plus one

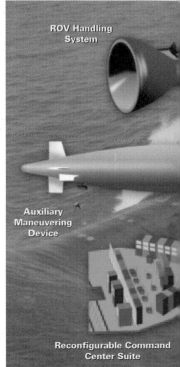

ROV Handling System

Auxiliary Maneuvering Device

Reconfigurable Command Center Suite

at 135 degrees and another at 225 degrees to the vertical.

The first two boats of the Seawolf-class are 7ft 0in (2.13m) shorter than the Los Angeles-class, but have a greater diameter to give a considerable increase in internal volume. Nevertheless, even this proved insufficient and the third boat, USS *Jimmy Carter* (SSN-23), has a 27ft (8.2m) plug abaft the sail to enable her to carry a fifty-strong special operations forces detachment and their equipment. There will not, however, be a DDS mounted on the upper casing, since the hangar for the SEALs boats and other equipment will be in the top level of the plug. A 5ft (1.5m) diameter airlock will provide access to the outside of the submarine. There will also be facilities for operating and controlling a variety of remotely operated vehicle (ROVs). This boat will not now be delivered until June 2004, some 2 years 3 months behind the original schedule and will result in a cost, for this one boat, of $US3.2billion.

The Seawolf-class is armed with eight 26in (660mm) torpedo tubes and carries a total of approximately fifty weapons, the actual mix of Tomahawk cruise missiles, Harpoon anti-ship missiles and Mk48ADCAP torpedoes, depending upon the operational situation, although the normal load-out of Tomahawks is 12. Mines can also be carried on a basis of two mines replacing each torpedo.

*Below: USS **Jimmy Carter** (SSN-23) will have unique facilities for special forces, as summarized in this diagram.*

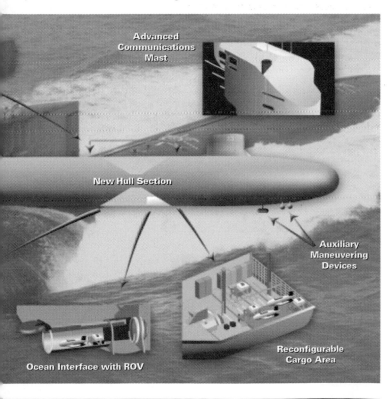

COSMOS SX.756

Country of origin: Italy.
Type: small submarine for special forces role.
Total built: not known (see text).
Displacement: submerged 118 tons.
Dimensions: length 91.2ft (27.8m); beam 18.4ft (5.6m).
Propulsion: diesel-electric.
Performance: submerged ca. 7kt; range surfaced 1,200nm, submerged 60nm; endurance 20 days.
Weapons: 2 x 21in (533mm) torpedo tubes; 2 x torpedoes; 8 x Mk414 limpet mines.
Payload: two COSMOS FX.60 swimmer vehicles; up to 2 tons explosive devices.
Complement: 6
Special forces: maximum 8 combat swimmers.

During World Wars I and II, Italy established a fine tradition of naval special forces, consisting of a mix of frogmen, human torpedoes and minisubs. That tradition has been kept alive by the firm of COSMOS s.p.a. in Livorno, Italy since the 1960s. The company is very secretive and since its products are intended for clandestine missions neither the company nor its customers advertise its products, but as it is still in business it must be assumed that it is continuing to find markets for its products. The boats vary in size, but all are diesel-electric powered, have a small crew and carry a number of special forces frogmen who enter and leave via a lock-out chamber.

The SX. 756 (details above) is operated by Pakistan (6) and South Korea (7). It should be noted that this is somewhat larger than the U.S. Navy's ASDS, and being diesel-electric it is autonomous and does not depend upon a mother ship for recharging. All the Pakistani boats were built in Pakistan under the direction of COSMOS engineers, while the first of the Korean order was built in Livorno and the remainder by Korea-Tacoma at Masan, Korea.

The SX.404 is smaller, displacing 40 tons and with an overall length of 52.4ft (17m). Taiwan operated a number in the 1960s which were employed for landing agents on the mainland but have since been scrapped. Pakistan has six which were delivered in the early 1970s; one was lost at sea and replaced.

The SX.506 displaces 58 tons, is 75ft (23m) long and has a crew of five and carriers eight swimmers. Colombia bought four in early 1970s of which two remain in service.

Considerable mystery surrounds how many submarines from this company's designs are actually in service. There were rumors in the late 1980s/early 1990s that the U.S. Navy had bought and was operating several, but these stories have never been confirmed from any independent source, and have always been strenuously denied by official spokesmen. Even the largest COSMOS design would certainly appear to be much less expensive than the U.S. Navy's Advance Swimmer Delivery System (ASDS) (see pages 470-471) and while possibly less sophisticated it is based on many decades of practical experience.

With the advent of new requirements for clandestine reconnaissance and of large naval forces operating in relatively shallow littoral waters, the day of the COSMOS type of small submarine may well have arrived, and when the COSMOS veil is lifted it may well be found that there are many more users than have ever been admitted.